Points of Controversy
Or
Subjects of Discourse

MLBD

SACRED BOOKS OF THE BUDDHISTS SERIES

Reprinted Under License from **Pali Text Society**

- **A Buddhist Manual of Psychological Ethics** : Translation of the First Book in Abhidhamma Piṭaka entitled Dhammasaṅgaṇī—With Introductory Essay and Notes by *C.A.F. Rhys Davids.*
- **The Book of the Gradual Sayings** : Translation of Anguttara Nikāya, the Fourth Collection of Sutta Piṭaka **(5 Vols.)**—Tr. by *F.L. Woodward* and *E.M. Hare.*
- **The Book of the Kindred Sayings** : Translation of Saṁyutta-Nikāya **(5 Vols.)**—Tr. ,Ed. & Introduction by *C.A.F. Rhys Davids,* Tr. by *F.L. Woodward.*
- **The Collection of the Middle Length Sayings** : Translation of Majjhima Nikāya, the Second Collection of the Sutta Piṭaka containing 152 suttas. **(3 Vols.)**—Tr. from the Pali by *I.B. Horner.*
- **Compendium of Philosophy** : Translation of Abhidhammattha-Saṅgaha)—With Tr., Introductory Essay and Notes by *Shwe Zan-Aung,* Rev. & Ed. by *C.A.F. Rhys Davids.*
- **Culavaṁśa** : Translation from German Translation by Wilhelm Geiger. A Continuation of *Great Chronicle of Ceylon* (Mahāvaṃśa) : **(2 Pts. in One)**—by *C. Mabel Rickmers.*
- **Dialogues of the Buddha** : Dīgha Nikāya, the First Collection of Sutta Piṭaka **(3 Vols.)**—Translation from the Pali by *T.W. Rhys Davids* and *C.A.F. Rhys Davids.*
- **Dictionary of Pali Proper Names (2 Vols.)**—*G.P. Malalasekera.*
- **English-Pali Dictionary** —*Venerable A.P. Buddhadata.*
- **The Expositor** : Translation of Atthaśālinī, Buddhaghoṣa's Commentary on Dhammasaṅgaṇī, the First Book of Abhidhamma Piṭaka—Tr. by *Pe Maung Tin,* Rev. & Ed. by *C.A.F. Rhys Davids.*
- **Conditional Relations [Paṭṭhāna] (2 Pts.)** Part I : Guide, Part II : Translation of Caṭṭasaṅgāyana Text of the Seventh Book of Abhidhamma Piṭaka—Tr. by *U. Narada Mula Patt Thana Sayadow,* Assisted by *U. Thein Nyun.*
- **The Jātaka or Stories of the Buddha's Former Births (6 Vols. in 3 Pts.)**: Translation from the Tenth Book of Khuddaka Nikāya of Sutta Piṭaka—Ed. by *E.B. Cowell,* Tr. by *Robert Chalmers, W.H.D. Rouse, H.T. Francis* and *R.A. Neil.*
- **Pali-English Dictionary**—*T.W. Rhys Davids* and *William Stede.*
- **Pali Metre** : A Contribution to the History of Indian Literature—*A.K. Warder.*
- **Points of Controversy** (Subjects of Discourse) : A Translation of the Kathāvathu from the Fifth Book of Abhidhamma Piṭaka—Tr. by *S.Z. Aung* and *C.A.F. Rhys Davids.*
- **The Sutra of Golden Light** : Translation of Suvarnabhasottamasūtra—*R.E. Emmerick.*

Pali Text Society
Translation Series No. 5

POINTS OF CONTROVERSY

Or

Subjects of Discourse

A Translation of the *Kathāvatthu*
from the *Abhidhamma-Piṭaka*

by

SHWE ZAN AUNG

MRS RHYS DAVIDS

Special Lecturer in Philosophy at Manchester University

"And he said, Open the window eastward. And he opened it."
Book of the Kings, II. xiii.17

MOTILAL BANARSIDASS PUBLISHERS
PRIVATE LIMITED • DELHI

*First Indian Edition: Delhi, **2016***
Fifth Reprint: Wiltshire, 2010
First Published: Wiltshire (UK) 1915

ISBN : 978-81-208-4064-5

Also available at
MOTILAL BANARSIDASS
41 U.A. Bungalow Road, Jawahar Nagar, Delhi 110 007
8 Mahalaxmi Chamber, 22 Bhulabhai Desai Road, Mumbai 400 026
203 Royapettah High Road, Mylapore, Chennai 600 004
236, 9th Main III Block, Jayanagar, Bengaluru 560 011
8 Camac Street, Kolkata 700 017
Ashok Rajpath, Patna 800 004
Chowk, Varanasi 221 001

MLBD Cataloging-in-Publication Data
Points of Controversy
or Subjects of Discourse
Translated by SHWE ZAN AUNG
and MRS RHYS DAVIDS
in *MLBD Sacred Books of the Buddhists Series*
ISBN : 978-81-208-4064-5
Includes *Kathāvatthu* from *Abhidhamma Piṭaka*
I. Buddhism II. Abhidhamma Piṭaka
III. Kathāvatthu IV. Aung, Shwe zan
V. Mrs. Davids, Rhys

Published by

Motilal Banarsidass Publishers Private Limited
www.mlbd.com • mlbd@mlbd.com
Printed by Replika Press Pvt. Ltd.

TO

ARNOLD CHARLES TAYLOR

EDITOR OF THE FIRST EUROPEAN EDITION OF THE *KATHĀ-VATTHU*

IN GRATEFUL APPRECIATION OF THE SERVICES THUS RENDERED TO PALI STUDIES

CONTENTS

THE POINTS OF CONTROVERSY ACCORDING TO THE CANONICAL ORDER

BOOK I

BOOK II

BOOK III

BOOK IV

BOOK V

BOOK VI

BOOK VII

BOOK VIII

BOOK IX

BOOK X

BOOK XV

BOOK XVI

BOOK XVII

BOOK XVIII

BOOK XIX

BOOK XX

BOOK XXI

BOOK XXII

BOOK XXIII

THE POINTS OF CONTROVERSY GROUPED ACCORDING TO THE SUBJECT OF DISCOURSE

I. *Of the Buddha :*

1. His Every-Day Usage, II. 10.
2. His Powers, III. 1, 2.
3. Enlightened through Enlightenment ? IV. 6.
4. His Marks, IV. 7.
5. Gifts to Him brought Blessing, XVII. 10.
6. Did he visit earth by proxy only ? XVIII. 1.
7. Did he teach by proxy only ? XVIII. 2.
8. Did he feel pity ? XVIII. 3.
9. Was everything of him fragrant ? XVIII. 4.
10. Could he work wonders against nature ? XXI. 4.
11. How do Buddhas mutually differ ? XXI. 5.
12. Do they pervade the firmament ? XXI. 6.
13. Do Bodhisats decree their own sufferings ? XXIII. 3.
14. Are Bodhisats assured prior to their last birth ? IV. 8; XIII. 4.

II. *Of Other Ariyans :*

A. The Arahant:

1. Can he fall away ? I. 2.
2. Can Māras defile him ? II. 2.
3. His knowledge; its limits, II. 2; IV. 10; XXII. 1.
4. Can he doubt ? II. 3.
5. Can others excel him ? II. 4.
6. Arahant and Layman, IV. 1.
7. Can he inherit Arahantship ? IV. 2; XXII. 5.
8. His Common Humanity, IV. 3.
9. Indifference to Sensations, IV. 5.
10. His Attainment as a Final Step, IV. 10.
11. As Adept, V. 2.
12. Does Karma affect him ? VIII. 11.
13. No more Accumulating Merit, XVII. 1.
14. No Untimely Dying, XVII. 2.
15. His Consciousness at Death, XXII. 2, 3.
16. Bogus Arahants, XXIII. 2.
17. Is his Emancipation complete ? XXI. 3; XXII. 1.

THE POINTS OF CONTROVERSY GROUPED ACCORDING TO THE DISSENTIENT SCHOOLS

I

THE VAJJIPUTT-AKAS (-IYAS) HELD

With the Sammitiyas :

1. That there is a persisting personal entity, I. 1.

With the Sammitiyas, Sabbatthivādins, Mahāsanghikas :

2. That an Arahant may fall away, I. 2.

II

THE SAMMITIYAS HELD THAT

1. There is no higher life practised among Devas, I. 3.
2. The convert gives up the corruptions piecemeal, I. 4.
3. The average man renounces passions and hate, I. 5.

With the Vajjiputtakas :

4. That there is a persisting personal entity, I. 1.

With the Mahāsanghikas :

5. That acts of intimation are moral acts, X. 10.
6. That latent bias is unmoral, XI. 1.

With the Andhakas generally :

7. That physical sight and hearing may be 'celestial,' III. 7.
8. That six senses obtain in Rūpa-heavens, VIII. 7.
9. That there is lust in Rūpa-heavens, XIV. 7.
10. That Karma and its accumulation are distinct things, XV. 11.
11. That material qualities are results of Karma, XVI. 8.

With some Andhakas :

12. That Jhāna has five, not four, stages, XVIII. 7.

With the Pubbaseliyas :

13. That vital power is psychical only, VIII. 10.
14. That previous Karma may cause an Arahant to fall, VIII. 11.
15. That there is an intermittent state, VIII. 2.

With the Rājagirikas and Siddhattikas :

16. That merit increases with utility, VII. 5.

With the Mahiŋsāsakas :

17. That acts of intimation are morally effective, VIII. 9.
18. That material qualities are morally effective, XVI. 7.

With Mahiŋsāsakas and Mahāsanghikas :

19. That three factors of the Eightfold Path are material, not mental states, X. 2.

With Vajjiputtiyas (MSS. sic), *Sabbatthivādins, and some Mahāsanghikas :*

20. That an Arahant can fall away, I. 2.

III

THE SABBATTHIVĀDINS HELD THAT

1. *Everything is, exists, is continually existing,* because it is, was, or will be matter and mind, and these continually exist, I. 6, 7.
2. *Penetration of truth is won bit by bit,* the past gains persisting, II. 9.

With the Uttarāpathakas :

3. That conscious flux may amount to *samādhi* (Jhāna, XI. 6).

With the Vajjiputtiyas (sic), *Sammitiyas and some Mahāsanghikas :*

4. That an Arahant may fall away, I. 2.

IIIa

OF THE SABBATTHIVĀDINS, THE KASSAPIKAS HELD THAT

4. Some only of the past and of the future exists, I. 8.

IV

THE MAHĀSANGHIKAS HELD

1. Confused notions as to sense, XVIII. 9, and ideation, X. 5; action and Karma, XII. 2; sense and Karma, XII. 3, 4, and Ariyan insight, XI. 2.
2. Confused notions as to the Path and sense, X. 3; and the Path and morals, X. 6.
3. That one can act by or with the mind of another, XVI. 1, 2.
4. That mind and morals are distinct, X. 7, 8, and moral growth is mechanical, X. 9.
5. That acts which are not moral must be immoral, X. 11.
6. That *iddhi* can confer longevity, XI. 5.
7. That self-restraint, as act (not as volition) is morally effective (Karma, XII. 1).

8. That moral and immoral motives can be immediately consecutive, XIV. 1.
9. That things were mutually related within fixed limits only, XV. 1, and not reciprocally (or symmetrically, XV. 2).
10. That Buddhas can persistently pervade any part of the firmament, XXI. 6, and that by *iddhi* they can suspend any natural law, XXI. 4.
11. That the decay and death of Arahants is not that of average humanity, XV. 6, but that a residual fetter of ignorance they do not cast off, XXI. 3.
12. *Some* held that the Arahant could fall away, I. 2.

With the Sammitiyas :

13. That acts of intimation are moral, X. 10.
14. That latent bias is unmoral, XI. 1.

With the Sammitiyas and Mahiṃsāsakas :

15. That three of the Eightfold Path factors are statements about material qualities, not about character, X. 2.

Some of the Mahāsanghikas held, with the Vajjiputtiyas (MSS. sic), *Sammitiyas and Sabbatthivādins :*

16. That an Arahant may fall away, I. 2.

V

The Andhakas in general:—(i.) Pubbaseliyas, (ii.) Aparaseliyas, (iii.) Rājagirikas, (iv.) Siddhatthikas—held

1. Confused views on object and subject (in the Satipatthānas), I. 9; on Modes of Existence, I. 10; on the sequences of conscious units, X. 1; on spiritual liberty, V. 1, IV. 10; on consciousness of 'the void,' XIX. 2; and on the 'goodness' of Nibbāna, XIX. 6.
2. That a unit of consciousness lasted a day, II. 7.
3. That utterance of a Shibboleth can induce insight, XI. 4, cf. Pubbaseliyas, 2.
4. That spiritual liberty supervenes while one is lustful, III. 3, and comes gradually, III. 4, as its blessings become foreseen, IX. 1.
5. That one may be conscious in the Unconscious sphere, III. 11, but not conscious in the 'Neither-conscious-nor-unconscious' Jhāna, III. 12.
6. That space is visible, VI. 7, also the elements of matter, senses, and action, (Karma, VI. 8).
7. That the present instant, and the future can be known, V. 8, 9.

8. That the past and future persist as possessions, IX. 12; thus in the Fourth Path, the Fruits of the earlier Paths persist as possessions, IV. 9.
9. That to bring about Jhāna, sense gets perverted V. 3.
10. That all knowledge is analytic, V. 5; when popular, truth is its object no less than when it is philosophical, V. 6.
11. That thought-reading is of bare consciousness only, V. 7.
12. That Arahantship is the realizing of a tenfold release, IV. 10; but the Arahant dies not wholly freed, XXII. 1.
13. That Karma produces land, VII. 7; also old age and death, VII. 8.
14. That resultant states themselves entail results, VII. 10; but Ariyan states are negations only, VII. 9.
15. That Assurance is unconditioned, VI. 1; so too is trance, VI. 5.
16. That the essential element in the sphere called Rūpa is the presence of matter, VIII. 5, but there is matter in the sphere called Immaterial *A-rūpa*, VIII. 8, as in the Rūpa-sphere also, XVI. 9, and lust in both, XVI. 10.
17. That a certain utterance may induce insight, XI. 4.
18. That X in the Path can discern Y's spiritual victories, V. 10.
19. That each Nidāna is predetermined, also impermanence itself, XI. 7, 8.
20. That Jhāna may be enjoyed as an end, XIII. 7.
21. That latent bias differs in kind from open vice, XIV. 5, and that the latter happens involuntarily, XIV. 6.
22. That there may be counterfeit consciousness, XXIII. 4.
23. That the Arahant accumulates merit, XVII. 1, and dies with meritorious consciousness, XXII. 2.
24. That there are no guards in Purgatory, and that animals are reborn in Heaven, XX. 3, 4.
25. That Buddhas differ mutually in many ways, XXI. 5, and choose the woes they undergo as Bodhisats, XXIII. 3; that all their powers are Ariyan, III. 2, and are common to their disciples, III. 1, and both can work wonders against nature, XXI. 4.
26. That a Buddha's daily habits, notably speech, are supramundane, II. 10.
27. That one in the First Path has not the five spiritual controlling powers, III. 6.

With the Sammitiyas :

28. That physical sight and hearing can be 'celestial' organs when conveying ideas, III. 7, 8.
29. That on entering the First Path, there is First Fruition, III 5.
30. That six senses and sensuous desires obtain in Rūpa-heavens, VIII. 7; XIV. 7.

8. The Unincluded may include erroneous views, XIV. 9.
9. The Arahant's knowledge may be defective, II. 2; (*probably the next two numbers also*).
10. Desire for ideas is not a source of Ill, XIII. 10.
11. Sound views are compatible with murderous hate, XII. 7.
12. The act of acquiring and the fruit of religious life are both unconditioned, XIX. 4, 3.
13. Knowledge of the Nidānas belongs to the Ariyan Paths and Fruits, XX. 6.
14. The Four Truths are unconditioned, VI. 3.
15. The objects of sense are desires, not the subjective experience, VIII. 4.
16. The Ambrosial as idea is a Fetter, IX. 2.

With the Sammitiyas :

17. That vital power is psychical only, VIII. 10.
18. That there is an intermittent state of existence, VIII. 2.
19. That Karma may cause an Arahant to fall, VIII. 11.

With the Mahiṃsāsakas :

20. That the Nidānas were unconditioned, VI. 2.

Vb

THE (i.) PUBBASELIYAS AND (ii.) APARASELIYAS HELD THAT

1. Everything has only momentary being, XXII. 8.
2. The embryo does not develop organs in sequence, XIV. 2.
3. All may be attended to at once, XVI. 4.
4. Arahants may be defiled by devils, II. 1.
5. Bodhisats are, when prophesied about, already in the Path, XIII. 4.

Vc

(iii.) THE RĀJAGIRIKAS HELD

1. That purgatorial retribution must last a whole '*k a p p a*,' XIII. 1.
2. That one in Jhāna-trance may die, XV. 9.

Vd

THE (iii.) RĀJAGIRIKAS AND (iv.) SIDDHATTHIKAS HELD THAT

1. The classification and association of ideas was a fiction, VII. 1, 2, and so too was the theory of 'mentals' (*cetasikā*) as adjuncts or properties of consciousness, VII. 3.
2. Giving (in so far as it is ethically meritorious) is a mental act only, VII. 4; things given here sustain life elsewhere, VII. 6.
3. Death cannot come untimely for an Arahant, XVII. 2.
4. All happens through Karma, XVII. 3.
5. The Karma of heinous crime brings a whole *k a p p a* of retribution, XIII. 1.

4. Initial application is a constant in all consciousness, IX. 8.
5. Material qualities are moral conditions (*hetū*), and have a mental object, IX. 3.
6. Dream-consciousness is unmoral, XXII. 6.
7. In heinous crimes want of intention does not exculpate, XX. 1.
8. Any abettor is capable of entering on Assurance of salvation, XIII. 3.
9. One in age-long purgatory cannot have 'good' consciousness, XIII. 2.
10. All is uncaused save Ill, XXIII. 5.
11. Sound views eliminate evil tendencies, XII. 8.
12. Emancipation is realized while one is hindered, XIII. 5; fettered, XIII. 6.
13. The worldly man can have the insight of Assurance, V. 4; XIX. 7.
14. The learner can discern the mind of the adept, V. 2.
15. He-of-seven-rebirths can only get assurance after the seven, XII. 5, 6.
16. Fruitions are retained as persisting possessions, IV. 4, cf. 9.
17. An embryo, a dreamer may penetrate truth, XXII. 4, 5.
18. Corruptions past and present may be got rid of, XIX. 1.
19. A layman may be Arahant, IV. 1; so may babes, IV. 2; embryos, dreamers, XXII. 5.
20. Distinctively Ariyan qualities may be moral, XIV. 4.
21. Everything in an Arahant is non-Āsava, IV. 3.
22. An Arahant dies like a Buddha, XXII. 3.
23. There may be bogus-Arahants, XXIII. 2.
24. A Buddha is one only in virtue of Bodhi, IV. 6.
25. A Marks-owner must be a Bodhisat, IV. 7.
26. A Bodhisat chooses his own sufferings, XXIII. 3.
27. The Buddha feels no pity, XVIII. 3.
28. The Sāsana has been, may be re-formed, XXI. 1.
29. Only the giver can bless the gift, XVII. 11.
30. Habitual repetition is no true relation, XXII. 7.
31. The doctrine of 'thusness,' XIX. 5.

Some Uttarāpathakas held that :

32. The Arahant dies in imperturbable absorption, XXII. 2.

With the Andhakas :

33. That Asura-rebirth constitutes a sixth sphere, VIII. 1.
34. That the six senses obtain in Rūpa-heavens, VIII. 7.
35. That trance-consciousness is unconditioned, VI. 5.
36. That views as such are un-moral, XIV. 8.
37. That natural kinds are immutable, XXI. 7; so too are Karma-processes, XXI. 8.
38. That there is but one Path, not four, XVIII. 5.
39. That everything of the Buddha was fragrant, XVIII. 4.
40. That he entered the Path in a previous birth, IV. 8.
41. That fruitions persist as possessions, IV. 9, cf. 4.

3. That there is self-restraint among devas, III. 10.
4. That the Arahant can exercise simultaneously six kinds of indifference, IV. 5.
5. That the sphere of Infinite Space is unconditioned, VI. 4.
6. That the Arūpa-sphere is simply cognition of immaterial things, VIII. 6, (? Andhakas).
7. That sensations are moral phenomena, X. 4.
8. That for a 'Seven-Rebirths-man,' in the Seventh rebirth, there is no evil destiny, XII. 9.
9. That duration, any stroke of time, is predetermined, XV. 3, 4.
10. That trance is (*contra* Hetuvādins) mundane, XV. 8.
11. That matter has moral concomitants, XVI. 6.
12. That the worldly man can experience the consciousness of three spheres at once, XXI. 2.
13. That the Arahant may feel doubt, and be excelled, II. 3, 4; probably a Pubbaseliyan view.

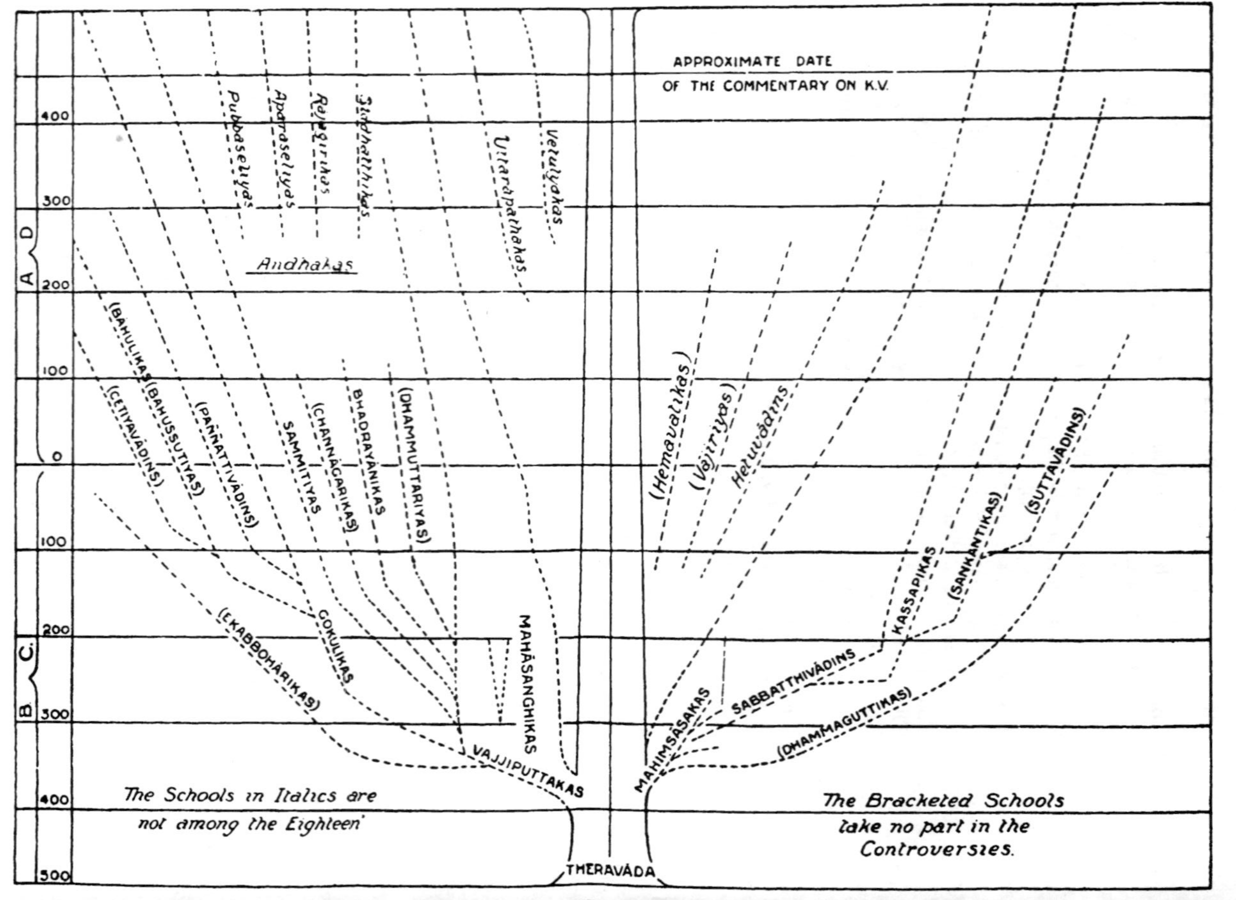

APPROXIMATE DATE
OF THE COMMENTARY ON K.V.
400
300
A D
200
100
0
100
200
B. C.
300
400
500
Pubbaseliyas
Aparaseliyas
Rajagirikas
Siddhatthikas
Andhakas
Uttarāpathakas
Vetulyakas
(Hemavatikas)
(Vājiriyas)
Hetuvādins
(BAHULIKAS)
(BAHUSSUTIYAS)
(CETIYAVĀDINS)
(PAÑÑATTIVĀDINS)
SAMMITIYAS
(CHANNĀGARIKAS)
BHADRAYĀNIKAS
(DHAMMUTTARIYAS)
GOKULIKAS
(EKABBOHĀRIKAS)
MAHĀSANGHIKAS
VAJJIPUTTAKAS
MAHIMSĀSAKAS
SABBATTHIVĀDINS
KASSAPIKAS
(SANKANTIKAS)
(SUTTAVĀDINS)
(DHAMMAGUTTIKAS)
THERAVĀDA
The Schools in Italics are not among the Eighteen
The Bracketed Schools take no part in the Controversies.

PREFATORY NOTES

THE original of this work—the Kathā-vatthu—is the fifth among the seven books, making up the third, or Abhidhamma Piṭaka of the Buddhist Canon. Its numerical order has been traditional from Buddhaghosa's days till the present time.[1] The Mahābodhivaṃsa ranks it third, but was that in order to make such clumsy verse-materials as book-titles scan?[2] Dr. Winternitz ranks it as 'the seventh book,' in good German prose, and thus without poetic excuse.[3] According to Ledi Sadaw Mahāthera, it holds a nearly midway position in its Piṭaka in virtue of the nature of its contents. Such, at least, is his explanation of the position of the next or sixth book—the Yamaka. The task of this work was to clear up difficulties left by the Kathā-vatthu. There would seem, then, to be nothing of chronological significance in the position of the latter. It is true that it refers apparently to passages in the first two Abhidhamma books:—the Dhammasaṅgaṇi and Vibhanga. But then it does not quote from the third and fourth books,[4] and it *does* refer to subjects belonging peculiarly to the matters treated of in the seventh book

[1] *Atthasālinī* (PTS ed.), p. 8; *K. V. Comy.*, p. 1; Ledi Sadaw' *Yamaka* (PTS ed.), ii. 220; *JPTS*, 1914, p. 116.

[2] P. 94 (PTS ed.):
'*Dhammasaṅgaṇi-Vibhangañ ca Kathāvatthuñ ca Puggalaṃ . . . Dhātu-Yamaka-Paṭṭhānam Abhidhammo ti vuccati.*'

[3] *Gesch. d. Indischen Litteratur*, ii, I. 137.

[4] *Dhātu-Kathā, Puggala-Paññatti.*

(Paṭṭhāna).[1] We are, therefore, entitled to conclude, as to its date relative to its own Piṭaka, only thus much: that the Kathā-vatthu was compiled when the *contents* of at least parts of the first, second and last books of the Abhidhamma Piṭaka were already established as orthodox doctrine in the Sāsana. Whether those works were, in Asoka's time, the completed compilations we now know as Dhamma-sangani, Vibhanga, Paṭṭhāna, is a further question.

But as to the other two Piṭakas—Vinaya, Sutta—there can be no question as to our volume being a much younger compilation. Other canonical books, notably the Niddesa's, the Paṭisambhidāmagga, the Thera-therīgāthā, and even the Saŋyutta-Nikāya, all of them in the Sutta-Piṭaka, quote, from other works in that same Piṭaka, passages given as authoritative doctrine, and hence belonging to a canonical stock of records. But the Kathā-vatthu quotes from a greater number of Sutta books than any of them, and from the Vinaya. It does not trouble to specify the sources it draws from. All, even the Vinaya, are for its compiler[s], 'Suttanta,' just as we would say, not Leviticus, or Luke, or King John, but 'the Bible,' 'Shakspeare.'[2] So that, if we accept the tradition followed by Buddhaghosa, the putative author of our Commentary, and assign Asoka's Council of Patna as the date when the Kathā-vatthu was completed, we can not only place this work in time—rare luxury for Indologists!—but assign a considerable, if indefinite priority in time to those literary sources (so accurately quoted),[3] which it invests with such constraining authority for all Sāsana disputants.

[1] See below, pp. 182, 294, 362. It does not refer to the sixth book, *Yamaka*, but it uses vokāra for khandha, which occurs, in the Piṭakas, perhaps only in these two works—very frequently in the *Yamaka*.

[2] The *Vibhanga* also refers to 'Suttanta' only.

[3] It is worthy of note that, while the citations from the 'Suttanta' are in almost perfect verbal agreement with the originals, as they are shown in the modern MSS.—I cannot of course vouch for the agree-

Finally, as to the book's own inner chronology, I have used above the term 'completed,' namely, at and for the Council of Patna, held approximately B.C. 246.[1] The orthodox tradition (see below, 1 p. f.) maintains that the outlines or heads of the discourses, 216, more or less, were drawn up by the far-seeing Founder himself, in anticipation of the warring opinions that would arise eventually within the Sangha or Sāsana, and threaten its disruption. The truth underlying, for me, this legend is the slow growth, by accretions, of the work itself. No work put together for a special occasion, or to meet an entirely new need,[2] could conceivably have assumed the 'patchwork-quilt' appearance of the Kathā-vatthu. I am not assuming that such a work would have grouped its discourses or Kathā's on the plan I have adopted in the 'Table of Contents grouped according to the Subjects of Discourse.' Many other ways of arranging might be selected. But that there would have been *some* plan is almost certain. The most plausible design would, perhaps, have been that of dealing with the views of each of the dissenting 'schools.'[3] This would have involved some overlapping and repetition, but repetition never had terrors for a Piṭaka-compiler! And this plan, according to the Commentary, *was* followed here and there to a limited extent. Thus we get a little series of debates on views ascribed to the Andhakas and others. But these series are never exhaustive of such views. Not even the late irrupting names of Hetuvādins and Vetulyakas got dealt with in uninterrupted sequence. On the other hand, we have such great subjects as Buddha, Arahant, insight (ñāṇa), emancipation, sense, consciousness, 'assurance,' the unconditioned, showing, in the geological phrase, an outcrop that re-appears erratically in now this, now that, Vagga, or

---

ment in the untraced quotations—there is here and there a discrepancy. See, *e.g.*, that on p. 206 (vii. 7).

[1] See C. M. Duff's (Mrs. W. R. Rickmers') *Chronology of India.*

[2] I am not dealing with the cheap, unhistorical hypothesis of 'faked' books.

[3] See Table of Contents grouped according to the schools.

division, none of which Vaggas has a title. Now, if we imagine that (1) each Kathā (or, at times, each two or more Kathā's) was framed by, or by order of, the heads of the Sangha at the time when each seceding school newly systematized and taught this and that heresy, or gave it occasional and special prominence, and that (2) such a new Kathā, or sub-group of them, was added, by memorial or scriptural registration, to the existing stock of Kathā's, then the puzzle of the Kathā-vatthu's asymmetry resolves itself into a relatively simple matter. It would not be easy to *insert* each new Kathā under a subject-heading. For memory and manuscript, new editions are even more inconvenient than in the case of printed books. Established sequences in the association of ideas are living growths, as hard to alter as the contents of palm-leaf MSS. Let anyone try to graft on memory, *e.g.*, by an interpolated clause in the Lord's Prayer. And just as the full Anglican 'morning service' of my young days had its four Lord's Prayers, and its three prayers for the Queen and family, because the ritual was an old accretion of 'offices,' so, in the Kathā-vatthu, we get a five-fold outcrop of Buddha-questions, and a six-fold outcrop about the Arahant, etc., scattered broadcast about the book, and including, now and then, even duplicated arguments. Even had the inclination to systematize been ready to overcome the inconvenience of re-arrangement, we may be very sure that ecclesiastical conservatism would have vetoed it.

To leave the Kathā's for the sects or groups—I prefer to call them 'Schools'—on whom the opinions debated about are fathered by the Commentary :—our translation includes no positive addition to existing research on that perplexing subject. It can, at best, claim to facilitate in some measure such additions in the future. It may prove helpful to the baffled historical inquirer to place on one side (if not faraway) the separate, and often grotesquely mispunctuated PTS edition of the Commentary,[1] and, in these pages, to

[1] The great service rendered by Minayeff's edition is not hurt by captious remarks.

read first the Comment, giving the little Ākhyāna, or occasion of the debate, followed at once by the debate itself, as if he were supping off Jātakas. This is, after all, the way in which the Pali tradition was taught from generation to generation: a kernel of doctrine enshrined in narrative and exegesis. The method of all Abhidhamma compilations involves elimination of everything particular, contingent, *ad-hominem*, and retention only of the more general, abstract, schematic *urbi-et-orbi* statements.[1] Hence the silence, in the Kathā-vatthu itself, as to the opinions or movements which, in the Commentary, are shown to have led to so many essays in controversy. And hence the dish of relatively dry and indigestible fare presented by the Kathā-vatthu, when we try to cope with it apart from its Commentary.

It is true, alas! that the commentator lacks either the will, or the power to enlighten us much regarding the schools he names. It may be that his superficial references partake of the characteristic negligence of the orthodox with respect to the non-conformist. It may be that his interest is chiefly engaged, not by the history of external movements, but rather by the varieties and evolution of ideas. Certainly the distinctions he draws among terms and their import are often interesting and valuable. Or it may be that, for him, most of the schools he names were *mere names* and no more. To which of these three possible causes, if to any of them, is the threadbare quality of his information due?

As I read him, it is the ideas that he finds living and interesting, not the human secessions. Only by one word does he here and there infuse life into his dissentient dummies:—the word etarahi, 'at the present day, now.' Of some of the contested points he writes, 'held now (or at present) by' M. or N. This expression occurs frequently up to the end of the fourth book (vagga); it then disappears till Books XVII., XVIII., when it re-appears concerning the Vetulyakas only. The following is a complete table of reference:—

[1] Cf. Ledi Sadaw, *JPTS*, 1914, pp. 116, 124.

'Held at the present day by the'—

Sammitiyas, I., 4, 5; II., 9.

Sabbatthivādins, I., 6; II., 9.

Andhakas, I., 9, 10; II., 1-7,[1] 9; III., 1-3, 5-7, 11-12; IV., 8, 9.

Gokulikas, II., 8.

Bhadrayānikas, II., 9.

Uttarāpathakas,[1] IV., 1-4, 6-8.

Vetulyakas,[2] XVII., 6; XVIII., 1.

It is true that the phrase icchanti, rendered on p. 64 by 'incline to [the belief]'—'will have it that' or 'accept' had been less literal—is in the present tense. And where it occurs (in a few early kathā's only), it applies to other schools also:—Vajjiputtiyas, Mahāsanghikas. Again, maññanti, 'imagine,' 'deem,' applied to the Kassapikas, in one passage only, is in the present. But then the 'historical present' is too common a feature in Pali idiom to lend reliable significance to the Commentator's usage here. Since, nevertheless, both the earlier and the later Chinese pilgrim chroniclers, Fa-Hian and Yuan-Chwang, testify to the existence of Mahāsanghika groups, the use of the present tense may after all be no mere rhetoric.

Those same pilgrims allude also to the survival in their day of another school, the Mahiŋsāsakas. Adding these two with the Kassapikas and the Vajjiputtakas, to those of the original seventeen seceders named in the foregoing list, we get *only eight out of the seventeen* who, by the verbal testimony of the Commentary and the pilgrims, were, or were possibly actually surviving when this work was written:—

Sammitiyas, Sabbatthivādins, Gokulikas, Bhadrayānikas,

[1] Held by the Pubbaseliya Andhakas only. By a regrettable oversight, for which my colleague is not responsible, *etarahi* has not been translated in our excerpts from the Comy. in II. 1, 5, 7; III. 5; IV. 1, 2, 7, 9. I hope that readers will correct the omissions for themselves.

[2] This body is twice mentioned in the *Mahāvaŋsa* as specially needing and receiving drastic repression at the hands of two kings in Ceylon, but at dates not later than the third and fourth centuries A.D. See Geiger's translation (PTS.), cf. pp. 259, 264 with xxxviii.

as 'at present holding,' etc.; Kassapikas, as 'imagining' such and such a view; Vajjiputtakas and Mahāsanghikas, as 'insisting on' such and such a view; and the last named, with the Mahiŋsāsakas, as met with by the Chinese pilgrims, the former in North India (Kashmir, Patna), the latter in Ceylon.[1]

Hence it may possibly be that, for our practical and unhistorical Commentator, the names of the *nine non-surviving* schools were simply convenient labels for certain ideas, which were useful only as additional exercises in doctrine and dialectic. And as to the names of the eight survivors, it may have seemed as unnecessary to give an account of them as it would seem to a modern exegesist to say anything about Lutherans or Independents as such.

I have indicated in the accompanying genealogical tree of the Sāsana (according to the Pali authorities) the relative surviving power discussed above. I have not attempted to make use of the Dīpavaŋsa simile of a banyan tree (nigrōdha).[2] Excellent in its context, it would have proved, graphically, too complicated. And in the figure 'kaṇṭaka,' used for the 'sects,' which is usually translated 'thorns,' it is not clear whether the offshoots of the banyan are meant, or other obnoxious growth. It is just conceivable that the author's botanical knowledge as to banyans was not strong. If on the other hand the 'runners' put forth by banyans, so beautifully illustrated in the seal of the Royal Asiatic Society, with its approximately true rune, *Quot rami tot arbores*, were properly covered by the term kaṇṭaka, then it is our lexicographists who are at fault.

To aid, it is hoped, further inquiry into the complicated problem of the Sāsana's history, I have drawn up two other diagrams illustrating the varying accounts of the

[1] The pilgrims testify also to the existence of Sammitiyas and Sabbatthivādins. On the whole subject cf. Rhys Davids, *JRAS*, 'The Sects of the Buddhists,' 1891, p. 409 ff. He points out that only three of the 'eighteen' schools are named in inscriptions of the second and third centuries A.D.

[2] See p. 5.

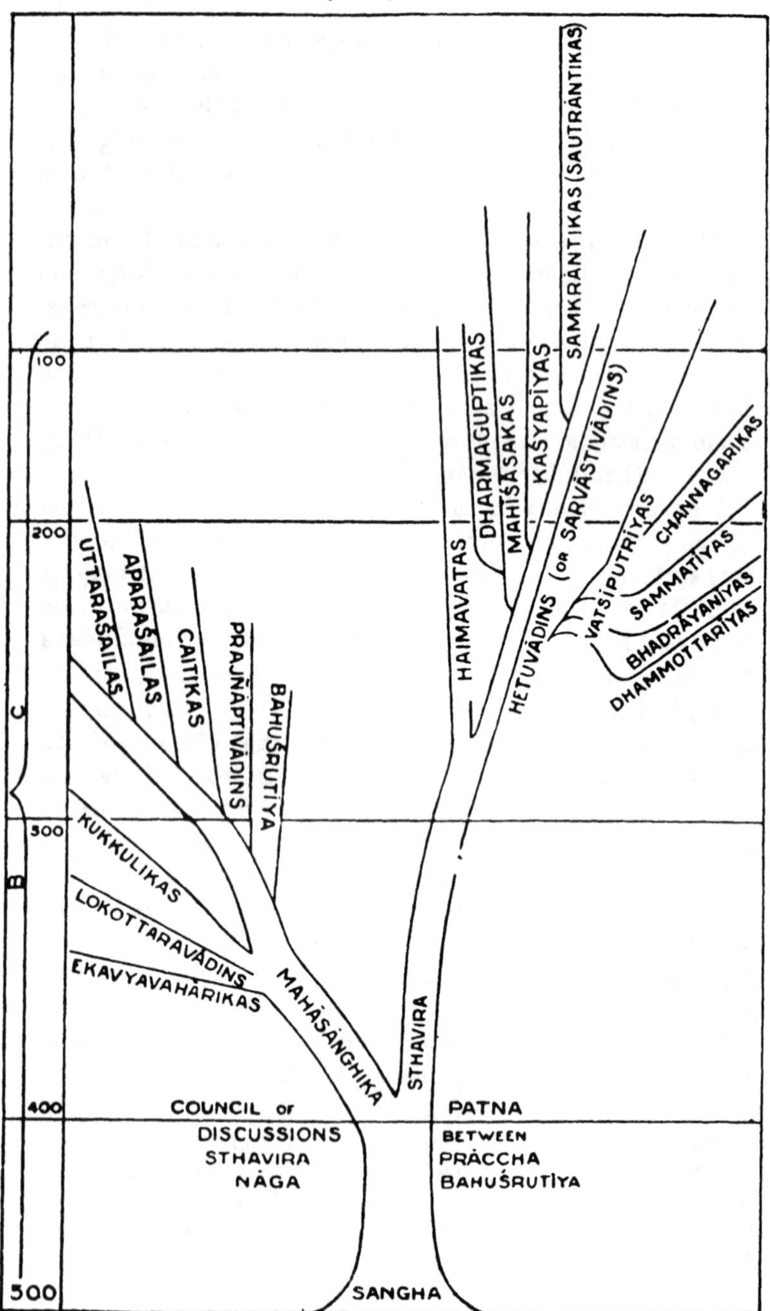

THE SECESSIONS ACCORDING TO VASUMITRA.

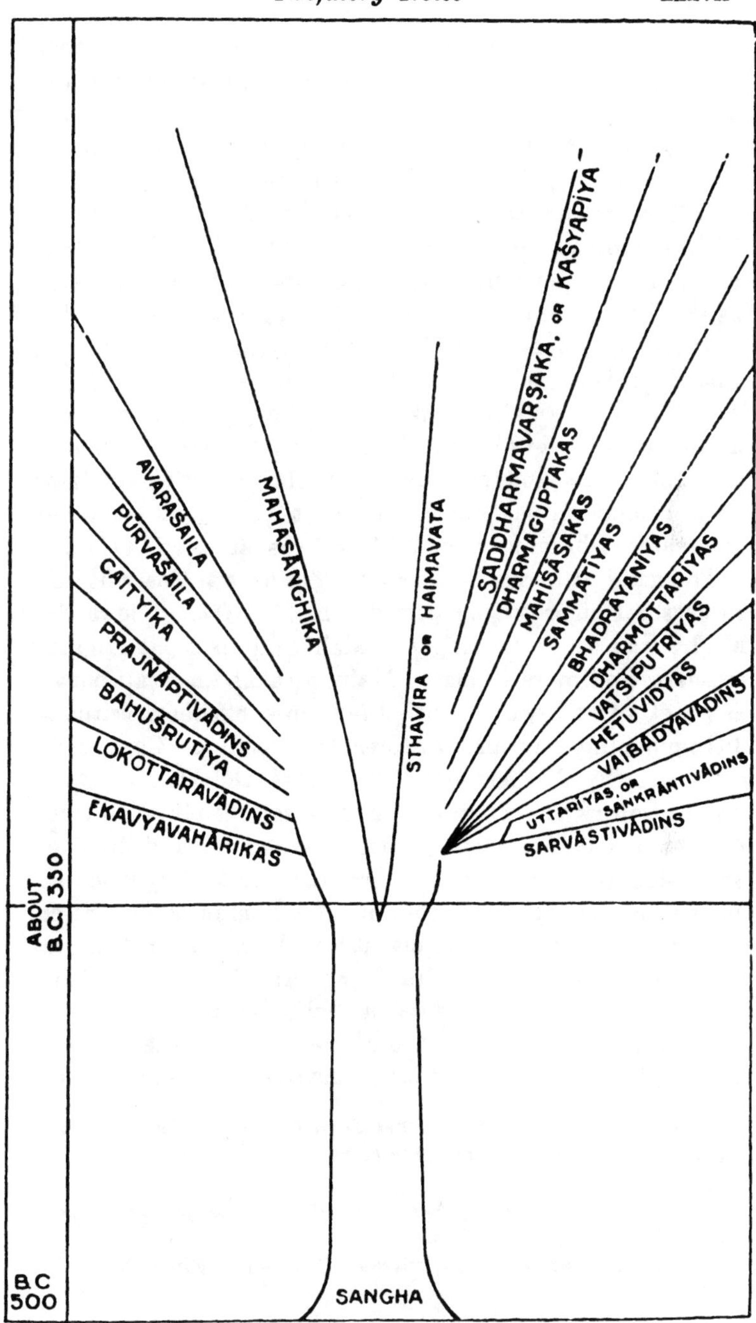

THE SECESSIONS ACCORDING TO BHAVYA.

secessions to be found in the sister epic of the Mahāvaṃsa, and in the Sanskrit works assigned to Vasumitra and Bhavya.

In that of the Mahāvaṃsa, agreeing in most respects with the Dīpavaṃsa, we note these differences:—The first secedents are not the Vajjiputtakas broadening out into the Mahāsanghikas, but are the latter only. The former are given as independently seceding, and the Mahiṃsāsakas as the third original seceders. The epic then states that 'thence there were born' Dhammuttariyas, Bhadrayānikas, Chandāgārikas (*sic*),[1] Sammiti's (*sic*), and Vajjiputtiyas. And 'from the Mahiṃsāsakas arose Sabbatthivādins, etc.,' as in the Dīpavaṃsa. Further we read that whereas the Theravāda and seventeen schools, with the six later ones, Hemavat[ik]as, etc.,[2] were located in India, two other secessions, Dhammarucīs and Sāgaliyas, arose in Ceylon.

The account in the Mahābodhivaṃsa,[3] ascribed by Professor Geiger to the period A.D. 975-1000, follows the Mahāvaṃsa in making the Mahāsanghikas the original seceders, and merely classes Mahiṃsāsakas and Vajjiputtakas (not -puttiyas)[4] with their nine offshoots, without distinguishing. It also restores the spelling: Channagārikā—the Six-Towners—and elaborates the Dīpavaṃsa similes, calling the Theravāda a Bo-tree, a sandalwood tree, and the offshoots parasitic, poisonous clusters and the like. And it identifies the terms Theravāda and Vibhajjavāda as the spoken doctrine collected by the Theras at the First Council:—'Theravāda' because it was the collective doctrine of the Theras; 'sambandha-vacanattā'; 'Vibhajjavāda' because the Lord of Sages was a 'Vibhajjavādin.'

Much more striking are the discrepancies in the account contained in Vasumitra's works surviving in Chinese and

[1] The *Dīpavaṃsa* MSS. read either Chandagārikā or Channagarikā. Our text (p. 4) has not got this quite correctly.

[2] See below, p. 5.

[3] P.95. Edited for PTS by A. Strong, 1891. W. Geiger, *Dīpavaṃsa and Mahāvaṃsa*, Colombo, 1908.

[4] Our Commentary has Vajjiputtiyas (MSS. *sic*) only in I. 2.

modern Tibetan translations.[1] Here we see no Mother-Theravāda-tree afflicted by 'parasites' or 'runners,' but a Sangha splitting in two through disputes led by four groups, three of whom are recognizable:—Theras (Sthavira), Nāgas, Bahussutiyas (one of the sects in the Pali account) and Prācchyas:—(?) the Eastern or Pācīnaka bhikkhus of the Second Council disputes.[2] Thus the orthodox Theravāda is reduced to one of two mutually dissentient halves. The Third or Patna Council is confused with the second. And in the offshoots we see variants of interest. The Lokottara (or Lokuttara) school appears. Gokulikas are Kukkulikas (or Kukkuṭikas). The Cetiyas become complex. The Hemavatas (the Himâlayan folk), otiose in our Commentary (p. 5), now stand as the conservative Sthavira or Thera school. The Hetuvādins, irruptive in the K a t h ā-v a t t h u, are identified with the Sabbatthivādins:—'They maintained that everything exists,' Vasumitra is made to say. The Suttavādins (Suttanta-, or Sauttrāntika-vādins) are considered to be not different from the Sankantikas. Four schools which, in our Commentary, split off from the Mahāsanghikas, are here made offshoots from the Sabbatthivādins. And whereas there is no mention of V a j j i p u t t a k a s as either the first seceders, or seceding with the Mahāsanghikas, we here find a school of Vatsīputrīyas among those that split off from the Sabbatthivādins.

Finally we have the account given by Bhavya in a work on the Schools, also known to us from a Tibetan source.[3] This is in substantial agreement with Vasumitra's, but Bhavya is less concerned to locate the secessions in successive centuries. He simply starts with one great schism in 'Dharmâśoka's reign,' '160 years after the Parinibbāna,' and states that, after that, all the remaining sixteen secessions took place 'gradually.' Among these,

[1] Wassiljew, *Buddhismus*, 244 f. Bunyiu Nanjio's *Catalogue*, App. I., No. 33.

[2] *Vinaya Texts*, iii. 401 (Cullav., xii. 2, 2).

[3] I take this from W. W. Rockhill's *The Life of the Buddha* (from Tibetan works), London, 1884, p. 181 f.

the Kukkulikas are dropped from the Mahāsanghika offspring, and the Channāgarikas from that of the Sthaviras. The number (eighteen) is made up by re-introducing the Mahīsāsakas, and by insertion of a Sanskritized form of the word Vibhajjavādins. The Hetuvādins, not derived from the Sabbatthivādins, appear as Hetu-vidyas, or as Muruntakas (or Muduntakas).

Bhavya further quotes a few discrepant opinions concerning one or more of the secessions current in his own day, but I cannot here dwell upon these. Nor am I out to maintain that versions of the movement among these dim old Dissenters, surviving only in relatively modern translations from Tibet and China, are quite so approximately trustworthy as those in the oldest Buddhist records. Seeing, however, that as the latter are slightly discrepant *inter se*, a *comparative* view in the growth of discrepancy, obtained from other than orthodox sources, becomes of considerable interest.

Beyond the having given such a view, I wish only to make one or two passing comments on these different records.

First (to work backwards), with regard to the curious emergence of a Vibhajjavādin school 'gradually' seceding from the Theravādins:—The reader will see, in the Commentator's opening narrative (p. 7),[1] that the Sangha-Centre had taken as their shibboleth or password a certain prevailing tendency in their Founder's teaching. To be an utterer-in-detail (v i b h a j j a v ā d i) was, according to the Nikāyas,[2] one of the four rational ways of answering enquiries:—Your reply was (1) a universal proposition, or (2) a number of particular propositions replying in detail, or (3) a counter-question,[3] or (4) a waiving aside an unintelligible or irrelevant question. Each kind of answer was, when apposite, equally commendable. Nevertheless, it is easy to discern that, whether established generaliza-

[1] The narrative in the *Mahāvaṃsa* gives a similar testimony. See also Oldenberg's *Vinaya*, Introduction, p. xli f.

[2] *Anguttara-Nikāya*, i. 197; repeated in *Milinda*, p. 145.

[3] Cf. that of Christ, *Mark* xi. 29.

tions were being arraigned by criticism, or whether, as in the Asokan age, errors springing from uncritical interpretations of doctrine were to be expunged, the 'Visuddhimagga'—'the path to purity'—of views, and the hall-mark of sagacious exposition lay chiefly in the '*Distinguo*' of the second mode of reply. And so we find Gotama Buddha, on one or two occasions in the Suttas, expressly repudiating the reply in universal terms, awaited by the interlocutor, and declaring, 'Herein am I a particularizer; I am no generalizer.'[1] Many, too, of the views debated in the Kathā-vatthu, are declared, in the Commentary, to arise through a lack of distinction in meanings.

We see, however, that even after a week's priming in doctrine by Tissa, the king was unacquainted with the term as an equivalent for the new 'State Church.' On hearing it, he turned to his preceptor for confirmation as to the Buddha having been a Vibhajjavādin. (The Mahāvaŋsa naïvely adds that the king was pleased, perhaps at the convenience of having a distinctive label for the special objects of his patronage.) Moreover, the Commentary, in assigning the speakers in the discourses, never calls the orthodox or Theravāda speaker Vibhajjavādin, but simply Sakavādin, 'own-adherent,' 'one of ours.' Hence the name may have remained throughout an occasional appellation only, like 'Methodists' for Wesleyans, till some local revival of it, past or current, misled Bhavya, or his informants. Why precisely the intellectual tendency, indicated by the name Vibhajjavādin, should have come to distinguish the orthodox from such standpoints as 'Eternalism,' 'Annihilationism and the rest, instead of such terms as Aniccavādin, Anattavādin, we do not know, nor ever shall. But a faked chronicle would almost certainly have chosen one of these.

[1] *E.g.*, *M.* ii. (Subha-Sutta). This is nearer the Buddhist distinction than to define Vibhajjavāda as 'religion of logic or reason,' as Childers (*Dict.*) does. He makes amends by an excellent explanation. A universal predication is not as such less 'logical' than a particular judgment.

The case of the Vajjiputtakas, Vajjiputtiyas, Vatsīputrīyas[1] may possibly be somewhat analogous. The 'Vajjiputtaka bhikkhus,' as we know from the Vinaya of the Canon itself, are said to have been the arch-disturbers of Sangha-concord a century after the Founder's death. On account of them the second or Vesālī Council was called together. According to our Commentary they amalgamated, after that, with the stronger growth of dissentients called Mahāsanghikas (*Dīpavaŋsa*: Mahāsangītikā). Yet, judging by the introduction to the second debate, they were *still considered as a distinct group*, siding with the Mahāsanghikas and two other schools in holding a certain view. There is no difference of meaning in the affixes -a k a, -i y a. They are like our 'New Zeal*ander*' and 'Eton*ian*.' The Mahāvaŋsa account juxtaposes both forms with an ambiguous result that is noticeable in Professor Geiger's translation (p. 26). This ambiguity may have misled Asiatic chroniclers. In the Sanskrit accounts,[2] as translated, the original move by Vajjiputtakas has been lost sight of, and, as with the term Vibhajjavādin, Vatsīputrīyas figure as an offshoot only. As such, nothing whatever is recorded of them in other documents.

The Gokulikas in the debates play the single rôle of pessimists. 'All the world,' they said, is, not a stage, but a fiery mass of misery—a k u k k u ḷ a.

On fire is all the world, is wrapt in smoke!
Ablaze is all the world, the heav'ns do quake . . .[3]

And the question suggests itself, as my friend Mr. B. M. Barua pointed out to me, whether one of the two Sanskrit versions of their name—Kukkulika—is not very likely the original, derived from their favourite text, and not from any

[1] On this last name see De la Vallée Poussin, 'Councils (Buddhist),' *Ency. Religion and Ethics*, 184, *n.* 1.

[2] Vatsīputrīyas is merely a Sanskritized form of the Pali.

[3] *Pss. of the Sisters* (from the *Saŋyutta* and *Therīgāthā*), pp. 101; 187. The simile is applied to the five khandhas, *Saŋyutta*, iii. 117; cf. i. 209.

teacher's or other family name. No Pali record that I have seen, however, departs from the 'Gokulika' reading.

Concerning the Cetiyavādins (pron: Chay'tiya), or School of the Shrine, there are interesting, if somewhat legendary, materials for the historian to sift. These are collected in Professor de la Vallée Poussin's able discussion on 'The Five Points of Mahādeva,' *JRAS.*, April, 1910, p. 413 ff. Sanskrit and late Tibetan writers there quoted have something to tell about one Mahādeva, who founded the School of the Caitika (= Cetiya), and put forward five heretical points, concerning which a council was held. There is possibly a confusion here with the Second Council, that of Vesāli, convened to decide concerning the ten indulgences[1] claimed by the Vajjiputtakas (*Vin. Texts*, iii. 401 f.). Mahādeva's points were purely speculative. As M. de la Vallée Poussin points out, they approximate to (though they do not coincide with) the points controverted below in II. 1-5 and 6. These points are all alleged to have been held by that leading sub-sect of the Andhaka school, called Pubbaseliyas, or East-Cliffmen. The Opposite Cliffmen (Aparaseliyas) share in one, 'others' in another of the points.

Now for our Commentary, these Cliff schools are of the Andhakas. And the Andhakas have been located about Kāñchipura and Amarāvati on the South-East Coast. Yuan-chwang travelled to that district, 'An-te-lo,' far south from Kosala. And I understand that the two opposite cliffs, with the deep gully between and the terraced caves above, have been practically identified.[2] But *no connection* between Andhakas and Cetiyavādins is made out in the Commentary.

On the other hand, if we consult the Vasumitra and Bhavya plans, we see in the one, Cetiyas, Uttaracetiyas and Aparacetiyas (North and South Shrinemen) ranged as parallel offshoots of the Mahāsanghikas, and Caityikas, Pūr-

[1] See below, p. 2: 'bases' or 'subjects,' *vatthūni*, as in *Kathāvatthu*. 'The Sects of the Buddhists,' *JRAS*, July, 1891, p. 411, *n*.

[2] Cf. Watters's *On Yuan Chwang*, London, 1905, ii. 209 f., 214 f.; Rhys Davids.

vaśailas and Avaraśailas (= Pubbaseliyas, Aparaseliyas) ranged in a similar relation in the other.

The presumption is, I think, fairly sound, first that there *was* a historical connection between the Cetiyavādins and the two Andhakas schools of the Commentary, secondly that, in the range of the Commentator's knowledge, both Cetiyavādin and the Andhaka schools were merely names, remote, provincial, standing for certain doctrines. Of Mahādeva he had apparently not heard. Anyway it is his method, however much or little he knew, to assign opinions exclusively to *groups*. But Vasumitra and Bhavya traced several schools to an individual teacher :—Bahussutiyas to Bahussutiya (the learned [doctor]); similarly the Dhammuttariyas (the 'Extraordinary or Super-normal'), the Bhadrayānikas ('Lucky Vehicle'), the Sammitiyas (Sammata, the complete), the Dhammaguttikas (Norm-guard), the Kassapikas (Kassapa, a common *gens* name). By the Commentary all this, whether history or word-myth, was severely let alone. Nevertheless the Pali word we have rendered by school is ā c a r i y a - k u l a, 'teacher-clan,'[1] which may refer to one or several teachers. And teachers there will unquestionably have been.

Places figured largely as the putative origin of group-names, presumably where the school was small, or at least unilocal only. It will ever probably remain a mystery how the conservative stock of Theravādins came to be connected with the Himâlaya (Hemavata) regions. No one knows after which six towns the Channāgarikas were called. And who shall reveal which divergent group or groups were covered by the intrusive name Uttarāpathakas :—'Northern-districters'? Equally mysterious are the intrusive Vetulyakas belonging to a group called the Great-Voiders—M a h ā - s u ñ ñ a v ā - d i n s.[2]

Here we come to the bodies not confined to one locality and named by some variety of *credo* :—Mahiŋsāsakas, the 'Earth-propagand-ers,'[3] Hetuvādin, Sabbatthivādin, etc. If

[1] See p. 8, *n.*

[2] Great Merit-ites (-p u ñ ñ a v ā d ā) is another reading.

[3] According to Wassiljew (*op. cit.*, p. 254, *n.* 5), of missionary origin.

I do not attach much weight to Vasumitra's identification of these last two with each other, it is partly because the latter were surviving when the Commentary was written, and partly because the heretical doctrines ascribed to each have nothing in common. It is true that neither have the controversies with the Hetuvādins anything to do with condition or cause or motive (hetu). But it is not essential that bodies named after some doctrinal emphasis should on just that point think heretically. The Hetuvādins may have been especially sound on hetu as against 'fortuitous origination,' or moral indeterminism.

Before leaving the schools of the Commentary to discuss the method of the Kathāvatthu itself, a word is in place to meet the inquiry that the general reader will naturally raise: Where among all these schools does the rise of Mahāyānism come in? The Chinese pilgrims speak of Mahāyānists and Hīnayānists, of Mahāsanghikas, Mahiŋsāsakas, Sabbatthivādins, and Sammitiyas, of Sthaviras, Lokottaravādins and of the Pubbasela and Aparasela Vihāras.[1] The date assigned to Fa-Hian is from about A.D. 400. The Commentary, as we have it, written either by Buddhaghosa, or, possibly, by 'one of his school' (as one says of a picture), is probably half a century later. Why are these well-known divisions in the Buddhist world omitted by the latter writer?

One thing seems fairly clear in this yet unsolved problem, namely, that Fa-Hian and Yuan-Chwang, whose Chronicles brought the dual distinction into prominence, will have given the Chinese versions of the names 'Mahā' and 'Hīna Yāna' to institutions which *they* recognized as such, either by firsthand observation or by hearsay—institutions which, in *Buddhaghosa's school*, were known under quite different titles. Of other theories put forward, it has been suggested that the Vaipulya Sūtras of the Mahāyāna

[1] See the lists in Rhys Davids's 'Sects of the Buddhists.'

Sūtras refer to the Vetulyakas of our Commentary.[1] That the title of 'amplitude,' 'abundance,' bestowed on certain Sūtras, is convertible into, or from Vetulya, can scarcely be seriously maintained. Nevertheless, it is possible that the 'Great Emptiness' school, to whom the Vetulyakas are said to belong, may refer to a group which the vague term Mahāyānist served to cover. S u ñ ñ a, empty, to wit, of s v a b h ā v a, essence or soul, came to serve, in Mahāyānist concepts, as tantamount to a n i c c a. Again, the Vetulyakas appear in the controversies as Docetists, and Mahāyānism strongly tends that way.[1] The vague, fluid term, Uttarāpathakas, must certainly have included groups that confessed Mahāyānist views, since among those debated is the peculiarly Mahāyānist hypothesis of t a t h a t ā:—'thusness' or 'suchness.'[2] And to the Mahāsanghikas a midway position between Mahā- and Hīna-Yāna has been assigned.[3] Certainly, their view of Buddhas persisting in or pervading any part of the firmament[4] is Mahāyānist in tendency.

But the extension of the name Mahāyānist was and is of a vague and fluid kind. Those to whom it was applied formed no close corporation. And this holds true of most of the so-called 'sects.' They frequently overlapped in their heretical views, as the grouped table of these will show. Rhys Davids[5] compares the relation of Mahāyāna to Hīnayāna schools with that of the various Roman and Greek Catholic schools to those of the early Christians; and the separateness between the '18' schools to that between Low, Broad, and High Churchmen in the Anglican Church. And it must be always borne in mind that all those who were implicated in the controversies here set forth were within the Sāsana. All, as we should say, were

[1] See *SBE*, xlix, part ii., p. 188 f.; Geiger, *Mahāvaṃsa* transl., p. 259, and references there given. Vai- is Sanskritized ve-.

[2] See Professor Anesaki's 'Docetism (Buddhist),' *Ency. Religion and Ethics*.

[3] XIX. 5.

[4] Professor Anesaki, *op. et loc. cit.*

[5] XXI. 6.

[6] 'Hīnayāna,' *Ency. Religion and Ethics*.

Buddhists. They may not, on certain matters, have been 'of us,' sakavādins, but they were certainly not 'hence outside,' ito bahiddhā, the term bestowed on teachers of other creeds. These are only once included together with Vajjiputtakas and Sammitiyas, and that is when the almost universally accepted dogma of a persisting personal or spiritual substrate is attacked (p. 18). 'And many other teachers not belonging to the Sāsana,'[1] is the phrase.

Had these been throughout the interlocutors, the debates could not have continued on the method adopted. Their premisses differed too much from those to which members of the Sāsana were bound. In this common stock of prescribed premisses lay the dialectical advantage of the Theravādin or Sakavādin. In your thesis, he is always saying or implying, you imply other theses, which commit you to a rejection of this or that orthodox doctrine. Hereby you virtually confess to sakkāya-diṭṭhi, to sassata-diṭṭhi, uccheda-diṭṭhi,[2] and so on. Now one of the Sāsana would be anxious to repudiate any such imputation.[3]

I here resist the temptation to be drawn aside by discussing the evolution of earlier attavāda, 'self-, or soul-theory,' into puggalavāda. It bristles with interest, but so also do the divided opinions as to infallibility or perfectibility of the Arahant, as to the humanity or divinity of the Buddha, or Buddhas, as to the real nature of spiritual growth or progress, the meaning and scope of the term 'Ariyan,' and many other points on which my

[1] Sāsana . . . bahiddhā ca bahū aññatitthiyā. According to Wassiljew, Mahādeva, the heterodox bhikkhu, is called a 'tirthika' (titthiya); according to Rockhill, he was a 'paribbājaka.' As either, he would be ito bahiddhā, a pāsaṇḍa-bhedako.

[2] Soul-theory, Eternal(-soul)-theory, Annihilation(of soul)-theory. See, *e.g.*, I. 138 f. (p. 19). The Pali-ist should note the usual substitution, in our Comy., of laddhi for the earlier (Piṭakan) diṭṭhi.

[3] *Cf.* Rhys Davids on the Milinda apologetics contrasted with the internecine debates of the *K.V.* *Milinda* (*SBE.*), ii., p. xxvi.

colleague has not sent me material for Appendix Notes. In short—M. de la Vallée Poussin has the *mot juste*—'there are so many "points" in the Kathā-vatthu.'[1] And better acquaintance with them will scarcely fail to stimulate further discussion. More in place here will be Mr. S. Z. Aung's remarks on the logical method of the dialectic on which I touched just now.

In reply (he wrote, in August, 1914) to your request, I think the best way is to present the logic of the Kathā-vatthu by a symbolical representation, *e.g.* in I. 1. § 1:

Adherent.—Is A B? (ṭhapanā)
Opponent.—Yes.
Adh.—Is C D? pāpanā)
Opp.—No.

Adh.—But if A be B, then [you should have said] C is D.
That B can be affirmed of A, but not D of C, is false.
Hence your first answer is refuted.
} (ropanā)

Or according to European logic:—

If A is B, then C is D.
[But C is not D.]
Therefore A is not B.

In this conditional argument, the minor premiss (bracketed) is suppressed.

The *antecedent* of the hypothetical major premiss is termed ṭhapanā, because the opponent's proposition, A is B, is conditionally 'established' for the purpose of refutation. The *consequent* of the hypothetical major premiss is termed pāpanā, because it is 'gotten' from the antecedent. And the *conclusion* is termed ropanā[2] because the refutation is placed on the opponent. Next:—

If D be denied of C,
then B should have been denied of A.
[But you *affirmed* B of A.]

[1] *Op. cit.*, p. 423.

[2] The three Pali words mean 'positing,' 'gaining,' 'lifting.'

[Therefore] that B can be affirmed of A, but not D of C, is wrong.

Or according to European logic :—

If C is not D, then A is not B
[But A is B.]
Therefore C is D.

This is the Paṭiloma, inverse or indirect method, as contrasted with the former or direct method, Anuloma. In both methods the consequent is denied. But if we reverse the hypothetic major in the latter method we get—

If A is B, C is D,
But A is B,
Therefore C is D.

By this indirect method the opponent's second answer is re-established. Next :—

(§ 3) *Opponent.*—If A is not B, then C is not D.

But you said A is not B, but C is D.

But if B can be denied of A, D should be denied of C.

(§) 4 Again (*Opp.*).—Is this bad refutation? Compare it with yours (§ 1). There we affirmed B of A. You claimed to refute us. But we were ill refuted, for see our reply in § 2, § 5. Not that way are we to be refuted. You, dear sir,[1] refuted badly, we refuted you well (in § 3). Hence our conclusion is sound.

These five sections (§§) constitute the First Refutation in Anuloma-Paccanīka-pakkha. The next five constitute the Second Refutation in Paccanīkânuloma-pakkha. Thus there are two Refutations under each of the four following *aspects* of this question of the person or soul :—

(1) Taken by itself, absolutely.
(2) ,, with reference to space.
(3) ,, ,, ,, ,, time.
(4) ,, ,, ,, ,, things.

[1] The courteous mode of address on both sides, and the absence of any polemical asperities, is a pleasant feature in the dialogues. The opponent, moreover, is sometimes allowed to have the last word.

Hence we get the so-called 'eight-faced view' (aṭṭha-mukha-vāda).[1]

Under 'Vacana-sōdhanaŋ'—the 'purging of terms,' the Commentator[2] develops the principles of Identity, Contradiction and Excluded Middle.

In the question, puggalo upalabbhati?—'is the person known [to exist]?' we have two terms A, B. A is either B or not B. If A = B, they both mean one and the same thing. But if A be not B, A is one thing, B another.

Adh.—If [all] A is B, will you admit that, in the former view, all B is A?

Opp.—No, but some B is A.

Hence it is clear that in and before Asoka's time, Buddhist logic was conversant with the 'distribution of terms,' and the 'process of conversion.'[3]

But I hold it highly probable that logic was regularly taught in ancient Taxila (Pali: Takka-silā, 'Logic-Cliff') before Aristotle's day. Reasons for this I have given elsewhere.

In categorical syllogism our books have the following technical terms, of the antiquity of which we have no sure record:—

(1) The udāharaṇa:—Yo yo aggimā so so dhūmavā—'Whatever is fiery, is smoky.'

(2) The upanayana:—Ayaŋ pabbato dhūmavā—'This hill is smoky.'

(3) The niggama[4]:—Tasmā tam aggimā—'Therefore it is fiery.'

'Smoky' in (1) and (2) is the hetu (condition). And as a fifth feature, an upamā (metaphor) may be introduced:—'Smoky like a hearth.'

S. Z. A.[5]

[1] Intended to be developed, when required, in every one of the kathās.

[2] Mr. Aung accepts the tradition that he was Buddhaghosa.

[3] The Yamaka is entirely an exercise in these processes. See vol. i., preface to PTS edition.

[4] The three terms mean: (1) Instance, example, 'adducing'; (2) 'leading up to,' subsuming; (3) departure or issue, cf. deduction (ni[r]) = de; gama, going.

[5] S. Z. A. has not had the opportunity of revising this letter in print.

Since writing this, my collaborator has discussed in a note printed in the Appendix the logical doctrine denoted by the term paṭisambhidā. Besides this, a four-fold logical doctrine of definition is constantly used in Buddhaghosa's Commentaries, and it may be seen, *in the making*, in the Nettipakaraṇa. But it does not appear, so far as I have seen, in the Abhidhamma-piṭaka.[1] Many of the Kathā-vatthu dialogues are concerned with views built up, according to the Commentary, on failure to distinguish amid ambiguities in terms, *e.g.*, I. 3; IV. 4; V. 1; VII. 4; XII. 8, and many others. The heretics, in short, fail in the sagacity of the Vibhajjavādin. And the reader may often feel he would willingly exchange the stereotyped 'eight-faced method' of argument for discussion on the meanings of terms, such as lends great interest to parts of the Commentary. Had this been the method followed, we should have learnt to what extent the scholastic logic of definition had taken shape when the Kathā-vatthu was being completed. It can hardly have been invented when the Dhamma-saṅgaṇi and Vibhanga were compiled.

A final note on our work. It is, I believe, the first translation of the Kathā-vatthu in any European language. Mr. Aung, at my request, took it in hand as soon as his labours on the *Compendium of Philosophy* were completed, *i.e.* in 1911. In about six months, working with both a Burmese printed text, Dr. Arnold Taylor's text (PTS 1894-5), Minayeff's (PTS) Commentary, and Burmese translations of both text and Commentary, he had typed a draft MS. of the first five discourses, amounting in bulk to one half of the whole work. 'I leave it to you,' he wrote, with his wonted modesty, 'to revise my very rough draft in any manner you please. A wholesale revision may be necessary.' . . . For nearly three years, however, I could not see

[1] See my preface to *Vibhanga*, and *Buddhist Psychology* (1914), pp. 139, 188.

my way to carry through the translation without a break. Nor was my distant fellow-labourer thenceforth able to find leisure in which to finish the remaining eighteen vaggas. Meanwhile we corresponded as to the form in which to present the translation and experimented therein for many months, with mutual suggesting and criticizing. Mr. Aung was anxious that so historical a document as the 'Points of Controversy' should be presented in a relatively attractive form, freed as much as was justifiable from tedious repetitions. We were not compiling a 'crib' for learners of Pali. He agreed, however, that the first and most important Kathā should be presented with all its back-and-forth of dialogue exactly as it is in the original. It would serve as a model of the dialectical method of the whole work. But in the remaining discourses we decided to 'go one better' than the editors of the Canon. We would not only take, as they do, the various formulæ of refutation 'as read,' signified in the original by the ever-recurring . . . pe . . . (etc.).' We would further compress the form by extracting its perpetual restatement of the controverted point, and put the substance of the dialogue in the mouth of the refuter, whether he were the orthodox or the heterodox speaker.

In venturing on this departure, we may have incurred blame from purists, but we have saved readers some tedium and loss of time. We have also saved the funds of the Society the expense of a second volume. The pages of the PTS Pali text run to 637, in two volumes.

In allocating all that is spoken to Theravādin or opponent, we have incurred here and there some risk of error. Even Burmese students of Abhidhamma do not always find it easy to judge which is speaking. My colleague wrote in 1912: 'The late Paya Gyi Sadaw of Henzada remarked to me, that it is extremely puzzling at times to find out, in the K.V., which is speaking. The book is not taught regularly in Burmese Vihāras, but is only read by Theras (seniors, presbyters). Moreover the Burmese translations are not well arranged, and are not divided into sections. Hence I do not guarantee my accuracy in every case, and trust you will also be careful, and correct me whenever I have slipped.'[1] As a rule the Commentary indicates which is the querist, and which the respondent, but not always.

It was not till May, 1914, that we were able to resume work on our translation. Our parts were reversed. Mr. Aung revised my draft translation of books VI.-XXIII., as well as the proofs of books I.-V. Each has contributed footnotes. Among those of my colleague, when some on points of great interest bulked too large, I consigned them, with a few additions of my own, to the Appendix. The Indexes, Tables, Diagrams, are mine; the Corrigenda mostly his.

On this wise, and for a third time it has been my good fortune—or 'the result of my good deeds in a former birth'—to complete, with such efficient help from the East, a first English version of a work of Eastern thought. Where we have failed to make the argument appear convincing, the fault may lie in our grasp of the meaning, or in the rendering selected. Or the cause may lie deeper than this. It is no simple task to enter on to the standpoints of the ancient Indian mind. Our apparent equivalents in terms are not always coincident in meaning with what that mind saw.

And further and finally, it should never be forgotten that, in the Canonical books, we are not encountering the relatively easeful and pliant play of an individual intellect—of some Oriental Plato, Augustine, Aquinas—wielding a habile stylus on his palmleaf, marshalling his points, breaking off to discuss a term, adapting his pace and his diction to refute, convince, inspire. The word-architecture of the Canon suggests the work of a race who, having for centuries built only with wood and wattle and clay, producing, it might be, quite artistic if transient edifices, were suddenly to build their shrines and temples in marble or granite. Something of the stiff and jejune qualities, which we actually see in archaic stone and marble constructions, characterizes the late enshrining in the written word of the orally transmitted doctrinal thesauri of Buddhism. Most strongly is this the case with the intentionally bare and formal presentment of

[1] For one such *lapsus calami* of ours, see Corrigenda, p. 47.

abstract tenets in the Abhidhamma books. The wood and clay structures of the exegetical accompaniments—the Commentaries—were continued probably for one or two centuries side by side with the new stone and marble buildings. Then they, too, were written. But *they* were suffered to *grow*. To drop metaphor, as the habit of *writing* literature grew, the power not only of intellectual expression, but also of the play of intellect itself grew. The great constructive ideas did not necessarily increase. They belong to the 'creative evolution' of life itself. But the power to exploit them, through visibly registered statements of and about them, increased. Hence the advance in this direction that we meet with in the Commentaries. The mind that could express in words anything so relatively modern as the sentence on p. 193:—'That "what lies between" any two visible objects, in the absence of other visible objects, is "space":—*this* is an act of ideation, not of sense-cognition'—how differently would a mind, thus trained on a culture of term-and-concept, have *written* out the 'heads' of the K a t h ā - v a t t h u, as compared with the archaic achievement of Moggalīputta-Tissa and his foregoers!

C. A. F. RHYS DAVIDS.

CHIPSTEAD, SURREY,
September, 1915.

SOME CORRIGENDA

Page 2, *l.* 15 : *For* uncompleted by just, *read* which is not quite.
Page 3 ? Note is modified in the Prefatory Notes, p. xl.
Page 4 : *Read* Channāgarikas.
Page 7 : Note 1 is modified in the Prefatory Notes, p. xxxviii.
Page 7, *n.* 2 : See rather Appendix, Note 4.
Page 19, *n.* 1 : *Read* **Ājānāhi paṭikammaŋ.**
Page 24, § 156 : *After* and 'body,' *add* 'as a whole.' Cf. p. 87, *n.* 2.
Page 24, *n.* 3 : *After* taking, *delete, and read* the body as a simple, indivisible unit.
Page 34, § 175 : *Understand the question,* If the concept . . . *as being first negatively, then affirmatively answered, as in* § 176.
Page 45, *n.* 2 : *Read* **puggalaparamparā.**
Page 47 [210, 211] : *For Th., read P*[uggalavādin].
Page 63, *n* 2 : *Between* transient *and* aggregates *insert* collocation of.
Page 82, *l.* 27 : *Read* concentrations and understandings.
Page 92, *n.* 1 : *Read* (§ 1), the ten.
Page 103 [6] : *For* (i.) *read* (ii.).
Page 120, *l.* 4 : *For* It was held, *read* It is held at the present day.
Page 124, *l.* 21 : *Before* belief *read* present.
Page 127, *n.* 5 : *Read* **Āsava's.**
Page 128, *l.* 22 : *For* opposite *read* adapted.
Page 143, *l.* 21 : *Delete* and its contradictory.
Page 143, *l.* 31 : *For* two powers, *read* nine powers.
Page 146, *l.* 22 : *For* of, *read* now held by.
Page 157, *l.* 5 : *After* Uttarāpathakas *add* at the present day.
Page 157, *n.* : *For* houser, *read* 'house-r.'
Page 158, *l.* 23 : *For* had come, *read* have come.
Page 166, *l.* 5 : *After* about *insert* present.
Page 167, *l.* 27 : *After* shared *insert* at present.
Page 170, *l.* 22 : *After* shared *insert* at present.
Page 173, *ll.* 6, 7 : *Invert* or *and* intuition.
Page 182, *n.* 4 : *For* intuition, *read* foresight.

Page 187, *l.* 25: *For* both of these, *read* both this and that ignorance also is unconditioned?

Page 188, *n.* 4: *Add* The fact stated is taken objectively by the Theravādin, subjectively by the opponent.

Page 193, *l.* 10: *Read* That that which lies.

Page 214, *n.* 4: *Read* Kāmaguṇārammaṇo.

Page 215, *l.* 27: *Add* ?.

Page 255, *n.* 1: *For* turn *read* term.

Page 272, *l.* 21: *Delete figure after* deny.

Page 272, *l.* 22: *For* [3] *read* [5].

Page 276, *l.* 21: *Read* Uttarāpathakas.

Page 280, *l.* 28: *For* immoral *read* unmoral.

Page 311, *n.* 2: *After* Desire *read* (rāga); *delete* lower or higher.

Page 325, *l.* 5: *Read* must he not too . . ., etc.?

Page 329, *ll.* 24, 25: *Read* sustained thought (vicāra), without initial application (avitakka), they hold that the form sustained thought only, without initial application (avitakkavicāramatta), intervenes merely as an interim stage between First and Second Jhāna.

Page 323, *l.* 7: *Read* now hold.

Page 338, *n.* 1: *Read* -sankhātā.

Page 343, *l.* 10: *Delete* two of.

Page 345, *l.* 3: *For* learned *read* accompanied.

Page 345, *l.* 8: *For* recognize the truth about, *read* intuit the reality of Ill.

Page 346, *n.* 3: *Delete the sentence*—The Br., etc.

POINTS OF CONTROVERSY;

OR

SUBJECTS OF DISCOURSE

(*KATHĀ-VATTHU*)

THE COMMENTATOR'S INTRODUCTION.

Honour to the Exalted One Arahant Buddha Supreme.

Seated in heavenly mansions, by devas surrounded,
Teacher of earth and of heaven, Person unrivalled,
Skilled in the term and the concept, ending his discourse
Called the 'Description of Persons,[1] *he, supreme Person,*
Set forth in outline the Book of the 'Subjects of Discourse,'
Giving account of the 'soul' and such points controverted.
By the mere heads thus laid down in delectable mansions
Moggalī's son filled out, here on earth, the full detail.
Now inasmuch as achieved is the way for the comment,
I will discourse on the matter. Listen attentive!

Now when he had wrought the Twin-Miracle, the Exalted One repaired for the rains to the City of the Thrice Ten Devas. And there beneath the Coral Tree, seated on the Paṇḍukambala Rock, making his mother chief witness, he discoursed to the assembly of Devas on matters philo-

[1] Puggala-Paññatti. Paññatti signifies both the idea or concept of any cognizable thing or group of things, and also the verbal expression of the same. See *Compendium of Philosophy*, p. 4 f., 198, 264.

sophical [Abhidhamma-kathā]. After he had taught them the Dhamma-Sangaṇi, the Vibhanga, the Dhātu-Kathā, and the Puggala-Paññatti, he thought:—'When in the future the turn for setting forth the Kathāvatthu shall have arrived, my disciple, the greatly wise Elder, Tissa son of Moggalī, will purge the blemishes that have arisen in the Religion,[1] and calling a Third Council, will, seated in the midst of the Order, divide this compilation into a thousand sections,[2] five hundred being assigned to our views, five hundred to views of others.' For this occasion, beginning with an eight-sectioned inquiry into the theory of person or soul, in four questions each of two fivefold divisions, he drew up, with respect to the course to be adopted in all the discourses, a list of heads in a text uncompleted by just one section for recitation. Then delivering in detail the remainder of the Abhidhamma discourse,[3] his rains-season sojourn being over, he descended by the jewelled stairway that was in the midst of the gold and silver stairways from the deva world to the city of Sankassa,[4] and so accomplishing the welfare of all beings and establishing it as long as he lived, he completed existence, leaving no remaining basis of future life.

Thereupon the company of his adherents, headed by Great Kassapa, made friendship with Ajātasattu the king, and drew up a compendium of the body of Doctrine and Discipline.[5] After a hundred years had expired, the Vajji-puttaka bhikkhus declared for the 'ten bases' of relaxation of rules. When they heard of this, Elder Yasa, son of the brahmin Kākaṇḍaka, making friendship with the king named Asoka, son of Susunāga, selected seven hundred from among the twelve thousand

[1] Sāsana, meaning practically what 'in the Church' or 'in the Faith' or 'in Doctrine' would mean for Christendom.

[2] Suttāni.

[3] This can only refer to the two last books Yamaka and Paṭṭhāna.

[4] *Vin. Texts*, iii. 396.

[5] Dhamma-Vinaya-sarīraŋ, not -kāyaŋ, as we might have expected (cf. 24, *n.* 2). But the term was pre-empted; see *Dīgha-Nik*, iii. 84.

bhikkhus, and quashing the ten bases, drew up a compendium of the body of Doctrine and Discipline. Refuted by those Elders who had performed this task, ten thousand of the Vajjiputtaka bhikkhus seeking adherents, and gaining but a weak following among themselves, formed the school called (1) Mahāsanghika.[1] From this arose the secession of two other schools:—the (2) Gokulikas and the (3) Ekabbohārikas. From the former of these arose the secession of yet two other schools:—(4) Paṇṇattivādins and (5) Bāhulikas, or as they were also called, Bahussutikas. Among just these arose other teachers:—the (6) Cetiyavādins. Thus from the school of the Mahāsanghikas, in the second century, five schools arose, making with the Mahāsanghikas six.

In that second century only two schools seceded from the Theravāda:—(i.) Mahiŋsāsakas and (ii.) Vajjiputtakas.

Now, from the Vajjiputtakas four other seceding schools arose, to wit, the (iii.) Dhammuttariyas, the (iv.) Bhadrayānikas, the (v.) Channāgarikas, and the (vi.) Sammitiyas. Again, from the Mahiŋsāsakas, in the second century only, two seceding schools arose:—the (vii.) Sabbatthivādins and the (viii.) Dhammaguttikas. From the Sabbatthivādins in their turn the (ix.) Kassapikas split off, and the Kassapikas again, splitting later in two, the (x.) Sankantikas were formed, and yet again, the Sankantikas splitting in two, the (xi.) Suttavādins.

Thus from the Theravāda arose these eleven seceding bodies, making twelve in all. And thus these twelve, together with the six schools of the Mahāsanghikas, constitute the eighteen schools which arose in the second century. They are also known as the eighteen groups, and as the eighteen sects. But of the eighteen, seventeen schools are to be understood as being schismatics, the

[1] Literally, formed the 'teachers' clan, called the Great-Orderers.' Each of the names of the seceding schools is a crux which we have no means of finally resolving. Some—e.g., Gokulika—may derive from the teacher's name, some—e.g., Cetiyavādins—from a place—here probably Sāñchi, called the Cetiya or shrine—some from the view professed—e.g., Sabbatthivādin.

Theravāda only being non-schismatic. Moreover, it is said in the Dīpavaŋsa :

'The wicked bhikkhus, the Vajjiputtakas, who had been excommunicated by the Theras (Elders), gained another party ; and many people, holding the wrong doctrine, ten thousand assembled and [also] held a council. Therefore this Dhamma Council is called the Great Council.

The Bhikkhus of the Great Council settled a doctrine contrary [to the true faith]. Altering the original redaction, they made another redaction. They transposed Suttas, which belonged to one place [of the collection], to another place ; they destroyed the [true] meaning and the Faith in the Vinaya and in the five Collections [of Suttas]. Those Bhikkhus who understood neither what had been taught in long expositions, nor without exposition, neither the natural meaning nor the recondite meaning, settled a false meaning in connection with spurious speeches of the Buddha. These bhikkhus destroyed a great deal of [true] meaning under the colour of the letter. Rejecting single passages of the Suttas and of the profound Vinaya, they composed other Suttas and another Vinaya which had [only] the appearance [of the genuine ones]. Rejecting the other texts—that is to say, the Parivāra, which is an abstract of the contents [of the Vinaya]—the six sections of the Abhidhamma, the Paṭisambhidā, the Niddesa, and some portions of the Jātaka, they composed new ones. They changed their names, their appearance, requisites, and gestures, forsaking what was original.[1]

Those who held the Great Council were the first schismatics ; in imitation of them many heretics arose. Afterwards a schism occurred in that [new school] ; the Gokulika and Ekabyohāra Bhikkhus formed two divisions. Afterwards two schisms took place amongst the Gokulikas : the Bahussutaka and the Paññatti bhikkhus formed two divisions. And opposing these were the Cetiyas, [another] division of the Mahāsangītikas. All these five sects, originating from the Mahāsangītikas, split the [true] meaning and the doctrine and some portions of the Collection ; setting aside some portions of difficult passages, they altered them. They changed their names, their appearance, requisites, and gestures, forsaking what was original.

In the orthodox school of the Theras again a schism occurred : the Mahiŋsāsaka and Vajjiputtaka bhikkhus formed two sections. In the school of the Vajjiputtakas four sections arose, to wit, the Dhammuttarikas, Bhaddayānikas, Channagarikas, and Sammitis. In later times two divisions arose among the Mahiŋsāsakas : the Sabbatthivāda and Dhammagutta bhikkhus formed two divisions. From the Sabbatthivādins the Kassapikas, from the Kassapikas the Sankantivādins, and

[1] In Dr. Oldenberg's translation this sentence is made to refer to grammatical innovations.

subsequently another section, the Suttavādins, separated in their turn. These eleven schools which separated themselves from the Theravāda split the [true] meaning and the doctrine and some portions of the Collection; setting aside some portions of difficult passages, they altered them. They changed their names, their appearance, requisites, and gestures, forsaking what was original.

Seventeen are the schismatic sects, and there is one that is not schismatic; together with that which is not schismatic, they are eighteen in all. The most excellent one of the Theravādins, which is even as a great banyan tree, is the complete doctrine of the Conqueror, free from omissions or admissions. The other schools arose as thorns grow on the tree. In the first century there were no schisms; in the second century arose the seventeen schismatical schools in the religion of the Conqueror.'[1]

The Hemavatikas, Rājagirikas, Siddhatthas, Pubbaseliyas Aparaseliyas, Vājiriyas—other six schools arose one after the other. To them no reference is here made.

Now the Sāsana held on its way as these eighteen early schools. And when Asoka,[2] the righteous ruler, had received faith, he bestowed daily a sum of 500,000 on the worship of the Buddha, the Norm, the Order, the maintenance of his own teacher, the Elder Nigrodha, and on the dispensaries at the four gates, and so brought notable honour and patronage to the Sāsana. Then the teachers of other faiths, being deprived of honour and patronage, so that they had not even enough to eat, sought that honour and patronage by entering the Order, and set forth each his own heresies, saying: 'This is the Norm, this is the Discipline, this is the religion of the Master.' Some, even without joining the Order, themselves cut off their hair, donned the yellow robes and went about among the Vihāras, entering the assemblies at the time of the feast-services.

These bhikkhus, albeit they were confuted by Norm, Discipline, and the Master's Word, lacking steadfastness, in the right order[3] of Norm and Discipline, wrought divers cankers, stains, and nuisance in the Sāsana. Some practised [holy] fire-cult: some the five-fold heat-asceticism;[4]

[1] *Dīpavaŋsa*, v. 30-54; pp. 140-2 in Oldenberg's translation.

[2] Called also Dhammāsoka; the earlier king was Kālāsoka.

[3] °anulomāya.

[4] *Psalms of the Brethren*, p. 120.

some turned the way of the sun; some deliberately strove in one way or another, saying, 'We shall break up your Doctrine and Discipline.'

Thereupon the Order would not, with such as these, hold festival or confession.[1] For seven years the fortnightly feast was suspended in the Asoka Park. The king strove by a decree to bring it to pass, but could not. Nay, he was filled with remorse when, through the misunderstanding of a stupid delegate, some bhikkhus were slain. And fain to allay both his regret and the plague in the Sāsana, he asked the Order: 'Who now is sufficient for this business?' When he heard the answer: 'The Elder Tissa Moggalī's son, sire,' he invited the Elder to come from the Ahoganga hill. And when he saw the Elder show a miracle, he was filled with confidence in the Elder's powers, and consulted him on that which distressed him, and procured assuaging of his remorse.[2] Moreover, the Elder dwelt seven days in the royal gardens teaching the king doctrine.

Thus instructed, the king on the seventh day convened the Order in the Asoka Park, and seated himself in a pavilion which he had had erected. Marshalling the bhikkhus into separate groups according to the views they professed, he sent for each group in turn, and asked: 'What was the doctrine of the Buddha?' Then the Eternalists said: 'He was an Eternalist'; others that he taught limited eternalism, immortality of the soul, eel-wriggling, fortuitous origins, consciousness [of soul after death], unconsciousness of the same, neither. Annihilationists said he taught annihilation of soul; those who held with Nibbāna in this life only claimed him no less.[3]

The king, through the priming in doctrine previously dealt him, discerned that these were none of them [proper]

[1] *Mahāvaŋsa*, v. 234-282.

[2] *Ib.*, 264: 'The thera taught the king: "There is no resulting guilt without evil intent."'

[3] Various forms of soul-theory, dealt with in the Brahmajāla Suttanta, *Dialogues*, i. 27 f.

bhikkhus, and ejecting them from the Order, he bestowed white lay-raiment upon them. And there were 60,000 of them in all. Then he sent for other bhikkhus and asked them: 'Sir, what was the doctrine of the Buddha?' 'Sire,' they replied, 'he was an Analyst.'[1] At this reply the king asked the Elder, saying: 'Was he an Analyst?' 'Yes, sire.' Then said the king: 'Now, sir, the Sāsana is purged. Let the Order of bhikkhus hold the fortnightly feast.' And, providing a guard, he entered the city. In concord the Order assembled and held the feast. And sixty hundred thousand bhikkhus were present.

At that congress Elder Tissa Moggalī's son, to avert all bases of heresy that had arisen, and that might in the future arise, analyzed in detail the heads of discourse, by the method which had been delivered by the Master, into 500 orthodox statements and 500 heterodox statements, and so uttered the book of the bases of discourse, the salient feature in which had been the future crushing of all dissentient views.

Thereupon, selecting one thousand bhikkhus who were learned in the Three Piṭakas and versed in the Four Paṭisambhidās,[2] just as the Elder, Kassapa the Great [at the First Council, had] recited Dhamma and Vinaya, so did he, reciting, after purging the religion of its stains, hold the Third Council. And in reciting the Abhidhamma, he incorporated this book even as he uttered it. As it is said:—

Set forth in outline the Book of the 'Subjects of Discourse,'
Giving account of the 'soul' and such points controverted.
By the mere heads thus laid down in delectable mansions
Moggalī's son filled out, here on earth, the full detail.
Now, inasmuch as achieved is the way for the comment,
I will discourse on the matter. Listen attentive!

[1] Or a Particularist, as against the superficiality and inaccuracy of sweeping generalizations. See *Majjhima*, ii. 197 (Subhasutta); cf. 'The Value of Life in Buddhism,' by Mrs. Rh. D., *Buddhism*, Rangoon, ii. 193. The name became synonymous with Theravādin.

[2] Meaning text, origins, exposition.

Honour to the Exalted One Arahant Buddha Supreme

POINTS OF CONTROVERSY

BOOK I

1. *Of the Existence of a Personal Entity.*

Controverted Point.—That the 'person' is known in the sense of a real and ultimate fact.

From the Commentary.—The Theravādin[1] questions a Puggalavādin (one who believes in the existence of a personal entity, soul, or perduring immortal essence in man) concerning his position. Who among the eighteen schools of thought were Puggalavādins? In the Sāsana the Vajjiputtakas and Sammitiyas, and many other teachers besides, not belonging to the Sāsana. 'Person'[2] means soul, being, vital principle. 'Is known':[3] is approached and got at by the understanding, is cognized. 'Real': not taken as an effect of magic or mirage, actual. 'Ultimate': highest sense, not taken from tradition, or hearsay. 'Known' as one of the fifty-seven ultimates of our conscious experience.[4]

I.—THE EIGHT REFUTATIONS.

The First Refutation.

(i.) *The Fivefold Affirmative Presentation.*

[§ 1] *Theravādin.*—Is 'the person' known in the sense of a real and ultimate fact?

[1] More literally, 'one of ours':—sakavādin.

[2] Used in its popular sense = homo in the Nikāyas; puggălă in the Abhidhamma Piṭaka largely supersedes attā and other terms for soul.

[3] Literally, is got or found. Cf. *Dialogues*, ii. 166; *Psalms of the Sisters*, 190: 'Mayest thou obtain.'

[4] Five aggregates, twelve sense-organs and objects, eighteen elements, twenty-two controlling powers. See *Compendium of Philosophy*, Part VII.

Puggalavādin.—Yes.[1]

Th.—Is the person known *in the same way*[2] as a real and ultimate fact is known?

P.—Nay, that cannot truly be said.

Th.—Acknowledge your refutation: (i.) If the person be known in the sense of a real and ultimate fact, then indeed, good sir, you should also say, the person is known in the same way as [any other] real and ultimate fact [is known].

(ii.) That which you say here is wrong, namely, (1) that we ought to say, 'the person is known in the sense of a real and ultimate fact,' but (2) we ought not to say, the person is known in the same way as [any other] real and ultimate fact [is known].

(iii.) If the latter statement (2) cannot be admitted, then indeed the former statement (1) should not be admitted.

(iv.) In affirming the former statement (1), while (v.) denying the latter (2), you are wrong.

(ii.) *The Fourfold Rejoinder.*

[2] *P.*—Is the 'person' not known in the sense of a real and ultimate fact?

Th.—No, it is not known.[3]

P.—Is it unknown in the same way as any real and ultimate fact is [known]?

Th.—Nay, that cannot truly be said.

P.—Acknowledge the rejoinder:[4] (i.) If the person be not

[1] 'Yes,' because the Exalted One, whose utterances were mutually consistent, who taught no mere *on-dits*, and who himself had universal knowledge, said in the Suttas handed down, that 'there is for instance the person who is working for his own advantage,' and so on.—*Comy.*

[2] Tato. This is an 'instrumental' phrase: kin te 'puggalo pi ten' ākārena upalabbhatīti?' 'In the same way,' that is, either as the factors of mind and body are known, by immediate consciousness, or under one of the twenty-four relation-categories.—*Comy.*

[3] English idiom requires that the affirmative Āmantā! be rendered negatively.

[4] Paṭi-kammaŋ, 're-action'; hence, retort, rejoinder, rebutting, repartee.

known in the sense of a real and ultimate fact, then indeed, good sir, you should also say : not known in the same way as any real and ultimate fact is known.

(ii.) That which you say here is wrong, namely, that (1) we ought to say 'the person is not known in the sense of a real and ultimate fact,' and (2) we ought not to say: 'not known in the same way as any real and ultimate fact is known.'

If the latter statement (2) cannot be admitted, then indeed the former statement (1) should not be admitted either.

In affirming (2), while denying (1), you are wrong.

(iii.) *The Fourfold Refutation.*

[3] *P.* (*continues*).—But if you imagine we ought to affirm that (1) the person is not known in the sense of a real and ultimate fact, but we ought not also to affirm that (2) the 'person' is not known in the same way as [any] real and ultimate fact [is known], then you, who have actually assented to the very proposition contained in that negative question,[1] must certainly be refuted in the following manner :—let us then refute you, for you are well refuted !

(i.) If (1) the 'person' is not known in the sense of a real and ultimate fact, then indeed, good sir, you should have said [as well] that (2) the 'person' is not known[2] in the same way as any real and ultimate fact is known.

(ii.) What you affirm is false, namely, that the former statement (1) should be affirmed, but that the latter (2) should not be affirmed.

If the latter statement (2) is not to be affirmed, then neither truly can the former (1) be affirmed.

That which you say here—(1) should be affirmed, but not (2); this statement of yours is wrong.

[1] Implied in t a t t h a, there.

[2] In P.T.S. ed. read n'u p a l a b b h a t i.

(iv.) *The Fourfold Application.*[1]

[4] *P.* (*continues*).—If this be a faulty refutation, look at the parallel procedure in your own argument (§ 1). Thus, according to us (1) was true (the person is known, etc.); but (2) was not true (. . . known in the same way, etc.). Now we, who admitted these propositions, do not consider ourselves to have been refuted. [You say] you have refuted us; anyway we are not well refuted. Your argument ran that if we affirmed (1), we must also affirm (2); that if we did not admit the truth of (2), neither could we admit the truth of (1); that we were wrong in assenting to (1), while denying (2).

(v.) *The Fourfold Conclusion.*[2]

[5] *P.* (*continues*).—Nay (I repeat), we are not to be refuted thus, (i.) namely, that my proposition compels me to assent to your 'known in the same way,' etc.; (ii.) your pronouncement that my proposition (1) coupled with my rejection (2) is wrong;[3] (iii.) that if I reject (2), I must also reject (1); (iv.) that I must affirm both or none. This refutation of yours is badly done. I maintain, on the other hand, that my rejoinder was well done, and that my sequel to the argument[4] was well done.

The Second Refutation.

(i.) *The Fivefold Adverse Controversy.*

[6] *P.*—Is the person not known in the sense of a real and ultimate fact?

Th.—No, it is not known . . . (*continue as in* § 1, *reversing the speakers, and substituting* 'not known' *for* 'known.'

[1] Upanaya, or Upanayana, is the technical term in Buddhist logic for the minor premiss, and means the leading-up-towards, the subsumption.

[2] Niggamana, 'going down or away': a technical term in Buddhist logic.

[3] In the P.T.S. ed. n'upalabbhati, in this paragraph, according to B^{r}, should be upalabbhati.

[4] Paṭipādanā—i.e., kathā-magga-paṭipādanā.—*Comy.*

(ii.) *The Fourfold Rejoinder.*

[7] *Th.*—Is the person known in the sense of a real and ultimate fact?

P.—Yes . . . (*continue as in* § 2, *reversing the speakers, and substituting* 'known' *for* 'not known.'

(iii.) *The Fourfold Refutation.*

[8] *Th.*—But if you imagine we ought to affirm that 'the person' is known in the sense of a real and ultimate fact, but that we ought not to affirm as well that the person is known in the same way as [any other] real and ultimate fact [is known], etc. . . . (*continue as in* § 3, *reversing the speakers, and substituting* 'known' *for* 'not known').

(iv.) *The Fourfold Application.*

[9] *Th.* (*continues*).—If this be a faulty refutation, look at the parallel procedure in your own argument (§ 6). Thus, according to us (*a*) was true (a soul is not known, etc.); but (*b*) was not true (. . . not known in the same way, etc.). Now we, who admitted these propositions, do not consider ourselves to have been refuted, etc.

(v.) *The Fourfold Conclusion.*

[10] *Th.* (*continues*).—Nay, I repeat, we are not to be refuted as you claim to have refuted us . . . wherefore your refutation was ill done, etc.[1]

The Third Refutation.

[11]. *Th.*—Is the person known in the sense of a real and ultimate fact?

[1] So far for what the *Comy.* calls paṭhama-suddhisacchikaṭṭho:—the 'first' controversy 'merely' relating to the 'reality' of the personal entity considered absolutely, or in itself. Its reality is next considered in relation to space, to time, and, lastly, to things in general. And under each of these four aspects, as we have already seen above under the first, the argument is presented affirmatively and negatively, thus making up the eight-faced views, or aṭṭha-mukha-vādā, of the controversy.

P.—It is.

Th.—Is the person known *everywhere* in that sense?

P.—Nay, that cannot truly be said.

Th.—Acknowledge the refutation: If the person be known in the sense of a real and ultimate fact, then indeed, good sir, you ought to admit that the person is known in that sense everywhere. You are wrong to admit the one proposition (*A*) and deny the other (*C*). If (*C*) is false, (*A*) is also false.[1]

The Fourth Refutation.

[12] *Th.*—Is the person known in the sense of a real and ultimate fact?

P.—It is.

Th.—Is the person known *always* in that sense?

P.—Nay, that cannot truly be said . . . (*continue as above, substituting* 'always' *for* 'everywhere').[2]

The Fifth Refutation.

[13] *Th.*—Is the person known . . . (*as in* § 11) . . . *in everything*[3] in the sense of a real and ultimate fact? (*continue as in* § 11, *substituting* 'in everything' *for* 'everywhere').

[1] Complete, as in §§ 2-5. This section is termed okāsasacchikaṭṭho, or reality in respect of place. It deals with the errors (1) that the soul or person is in the rūpa or material qualities (rūpasmiŋ attānaŋ samanupassanadosaŋ), so often repudiated in the Nikāyas; and (2) the living thing or principle (jīvo) is different from the body (sarīraŋ), also frequently mentioned in those books. —*Comy.*

[2] This section is known as 'reality in respect of time.' According to the *Comy.* the adherent's question refers to both the former and later lives (of any given person), to the present remainder of life, and to its final close (dharamāna-parinibbutakālañca).

[3] That is, in all the mental and bodily constituents, the organs and objects of sense, etc. *Comy.* (for Khandhesūti, P.T.S. ed., p. 15, read sabbesūti).

The Sixth Refutation.

[14] *P.*—Is the person *not* known . . . (*otherwise as in* § 11) . . . everywhere in that sense? . . . (*substituting* 'not known' *for* 'known').[1]

The Seventh Refutation.

[15] *P.*—Is the person *not* known . . . always in that sense? . . .

The Eighth Refutation.

[16] *P.*—Is the person not known . . . in everything in that sense? . . .

II. COMPARATIVE INQUIRY.

Comparison with other Realities, simply treated.[2]

[17] *Th.*—Is the person known in the sense of a real and ultimate fact, and is material quality[3] also known in the sense of a real and ultimate fact?

P.—Yes.

Th.—Is material quality one thing and the person another?

P.—Nay, that cannot truly be said.

Th.—Acknowledge the refutation: If the person and material quality be each known in the sense of real and ultimate facts, then indeed, good sir, you should also have admitted that they are distinct things. You are wrong to

[1] This and the next two sections, opened by the opponent, are to be completed as in §§ 6-10.

[2] Suddhika-sacchikaṭṭha-saŋsandanā.

[3] Rūpaŋ, i.e., the material khandha, or aggregate in the constituents of personality; the twenty-eight properties of matter considered as qualities of body mentally presented. On the rendering cf. *Compendium*, Part VI., and p. 271 f.

admit the former proposition and not the latter. If the latter cannot be admitted, neither should the former be affirmed. To say that the person and material quality are both known in the sense of real and ultimate facts, but that they are not mutually distinct things, is false.

[18-78] *The same form of controversy is then pursued concerning fifty-five other real and ultimate facts, or aspects of them, namely :—*

[18] feeling
[19] perception [1]
[20] coefficients (*saṅkhāra's*) [2]
[21] consciousness ; — the other aggregates (*khandha's*) ;

[22] the organ of sight
[23] ,, of hearing
[24] ,, of smell
[25] ,, of taste
[26] ,, of touch
[27] visible object
[28] sound
[29] odour
[30] taste
[31] tangible object
[32] mind (*sensus communis*)
[33] cognizable object ; — the twelve sense factors (*āyatana's*) ; [3]

[34] eye as subjective element
[35-8] ear, nose, tongue, body as subjective element — the eighteen elements (*dhātu's*) ; [4]

[39-43] sights, sounds, odours, tastes, touches as objective element ;

[44-8] visual, auditory, olfactory, gustatory, tactile cognition as subjective element,

[49] mind as subjective element,

[50] mind-cognizing as subjective element,

[51] cognizables as objective element ;

[1] On the import of this term cf. *Compendium*, p. 15.

[2] *Ib.*, p. 182, *n.* 2.

[3] *Ib.*, p. 183 f.

[4] *Ib.*

[52-7][1] the eye, ear, nose, tongue, body, mind as controlling power,

[58-60] female sex, male sex, life as controlling power,

[61-5] pleasure, pain, joy, grief, hedonic indifference as controlling power,

[66-70] the controlling powers: faith, energy, mindfulness, concentration, understanding,

[71-3] the controlling powers [known as] (i.) the thought, 'I shall come to know the unknown,' (ii.) the coming to know, (iii.) the having known.

} the twenty-two controlling powers (*indriya's*).[1]

[74] *P.*—Is the person not known in the sense of a real and ultimate fact?

Th.—It is not.

P.—Did the Exalted One say: 'There is the person who works for his own good?'[2] And is material quality known in the sense of a real and ultimate fact?

Th.—Yes.

P.—Is material quality one thing and the person another?

Th.—Nay, that cannot be truly said.

P.—Acknowledge this rejoinder:[3] If the Exalted One said: 'There is the person who works for his own good,' and if material quality be known in the sense of a real and ultimate fact, then indeed, good sir, you should also have admitted that material quality and the person are two distinct things. You are wrong in admitting the truth of the former statement while you deny that of the latter. If material quality and person are not two distinct facts, then neither can you also say that the Exalted One predicated anything concerning a 'person.' Your position is false.[4]

[75-129] *The controversy is now repeated with the succes-*

[1] *Compendium*, p. 175 f.

[2] From a category of four sorts of persons (p u g g a l ā), occurring in three of the four *Nikāyas* (e.g., *Dīgha*, iii. 232; *Majjhima*, i. 341, 411; *Anguttara*, ii. 95), though not with the phrase A t t h i, 'There is.'

[3] Namely, to § 17.

[4] Complete as in §§ 3-16.

sive substitution of each of the real and ultimate facts named in §§ 18-73 *for* 'material quality.'

Comparison with other Realities continued by Way of Analogy.

[130] *Th.*—Material quality is (you have admitted) known as a real and ultimate fact. Feeling, too, is known as such. Now, is material quality one thing and feeling another?

P.—Yes.

Th.—Is the person known also in the sense of a real and ultimate fact, as material quality is known?

P.—Yes.

Th.—Then, is material quality one thing, person another thing?

P.—Nay, that cannot truly be admitted.

Th.—Acknowledge the refutation: If material quality and feeling are both known as real and ultimate facts, and yet are two different things, then analogously, if the person and material quality are both known as real and ultimate facts, they, good sir, can equally be two different things. Your position in admitting the first pair of propositions, but not the second pair, is false. If you cannot admit the second pair, neither should you have admitted the first pair. Your position is false.[1]

[131-133] *The same argument is then applied to the case of each of the other three* khandhas, *substituted for* feeling.

[134] *The permutations of the five aggregates (khandhas) are proceeded with as in* § 130, *thus:*

material quality and feeling,
the person and material quality } *are replaced by*

feeling and perception,
the person and feeling } , *next by*

feeling and the coefficients,
the person and feeling } , *next by*

feeling and consciousness,
the person and feeling } ; *after which*

[1] This discourse may be completed as in §§ 2-16.

perception, coefficients, *and* consciousness *in their turn replace* feeling.

[135] *Next each of the* 12 Āyatanas, *the* 18 Dhātus, *and the* 22 Indriyas *is used in turn to illustrate the analogy, thus :*

organ of sight and organ of hearing,
the person and organ of sight, } *etc., is the first*

grouping in the Āyatana-analogies, the last grouping in the Indriya-analogies being

the controlling power of 'one who has come to know,' and that of 'the coming to know,'

the person and the controlling power of 'one who has come to know.'

[136] *P.*—Material quality is known [you have admitted] in the sense of a real and ultimate fact. Is material quality one thing, feeling another thing?

Th.—Yes.

P.—Was it said by the Exalted One: 'There is the person who works for his own good?'[1] And is material quality known in the sense of a real and ultimate fact?

Th.—Yes.

P.—[Well then,] is material quality one thing, the person another?

Th.—Nay, that cannot truly be said.

P.—Acknowledge the rejoinder:[2] If material quality and feeling are known as real, ultimate facts, and are different things, then why are not 'the person'—a term used by the Exalted One—and material quality also two different things? Your position is false. You admit the truth of the first pair of propositions, but not that of the analogous second pair. If you deny the truth of the second pair, you should not admit the truth of the analogous first pair.

(*The discourse may be completed as in* §§ 3-16.)

[1] Cf. § 74. The opponent still assumes that the Buddha used the word '**puggala**' in the sense of a permanent ultimate entity.

[2] I.e., to § 130.

[137] *The 'wheel'* (cakka)[1] *of all the other ultimate facts—other khandhas, āyatanas,* etc.—*now revolves about this quotation, as it revolved in* §§ 131-135.

Comparison by the Fourfold Method.

[138] *Th.*—Is 'the person' known in the sense of a real and ultimate fact?

P.—Yes.

Th.—(i.) Is material quality the person?

P.—Nay, that cannot truly be said.[2]

Th.—Acknowledge the refutation: If the former proposition is true, you should also, good sir, have admitted the latter. If you cannot affirm that material quality is the person, neither should you have admitted that the person is known in the sense of a real and ultimate fact. Your position is false.

[139] *Th.*—You admit the former proposition. (ii.) Now, is the person [known as being] in material quality? (iii.) Is it known as being apart from material quality? (iv.) Is material quality known as being in the person?[3]

P.—Nay, that cannot truly be said.

Th.—Acknowledge the refutation: If the person is indeed known in the sense of a real and ultimate fact, then, good sir, you should also have admitted one of these other three propositions. Your position is false. If you cannot admit any one of those three propositions [as to where or how the person is known], then indeed, good sir, you should not assent to the original proposition—that the person is known in the sense of a real and ultimate fact.

[140-141] *The 'wheel' is then turned for all the remaining* 'real and ultimate facts' *in relation to* 'person' . . . is

[1] Commentarial term (pron.: chakka) for a repeated formula. In the text, p. 20, l. 1, read Ājānāhipaṭikammaŋ.

[2] The opponent sees he is in danger of admitting himself a Nihilist (ucchedavāda, or materialist), and negates.—*Comy.*

[3] The opponent here fears to assent to the sakkāyadiṭṭhi, or heresy of individuality, often condemned in the Suttas. See below, pp. 44 *n.*, 45 *n.* 3.

feeling the person? . . . is the person . . . in feeling? . . . apart from feeling? . . . is feeling . . . in the person? . . . is the organ of sight the person? . . . *and so on.*

[142] *P.*—Is the person not known in the sense of a real and ultimate fact?

Th.—It is not so known.

P.—(i.) Is material quality the person?

Th.—Nay, that cannot truly be admitted.

P.—Acknowledge the rejoinder:[1] If the person is not so known as you state, then you should have admitted that material quality and person are the same.[2] If you cannot admit the latter proposition, neither can you assert the former. . . .

[143] *P.*—Is the person not known in the sense of a real and ultimate fact?

Th.—It is not so known.

P.—(ii.) Is the person known as being in material quality? (iii.) Or as being apart from material quality? (iv.) Or is material quality known as being in the person?

Th.—Nay, that cannot truly be admitted.

P.—Acknowledge the rejoinder:[3] If the person is not known in the sense of a real and ultimate fact, then, good sir, you should admit that it is known [in association with material quality] as advanced in the other propositions. If one of these cannot be admitted, neither should you have asserted the first proposition.[4]

(*This and the preceding* § *may be completed as in* §§ 3-16.)

[144-145] *The 'wheel' is then turned as indicated in* §§ 140-141.

[1] I.e., to § 138.

[2] 'Material quality,' *or* any other of the fifty-seven ultimates. If 'puggala' is not a separate ultimate, it must be identifiable with one of them—admitting the fact that puggala *is*—did not the Exalted One say so?

[3] I.e., to § 139.

[4] It being still asserted (by P.) that puggala is a real, etc., fact. The Burmese editions repeat the supposed evidence given in § 74.

Associated Characteristics.

[146] *Th.*—Is 'the person' known in the sense of a real and ultimate fact?

P.—Yes.

Th.—Is 'the person' related, or is it absolute? Is 'the person' conditioned, or is it unconditioned? Is it eternal? or is it temporal? Has it external features? or is it without any?

P.—Nay, these things cannot truly be predicated about it. . . . (*Continue as in* § 1: 'Acknowledge the refutation,' etc.[1]

[147] *P.*—Is 'the person' unknown in the sense of a real and ultimate fact?

Th.—It is.

P.—Was it said by the Exalted One: 'There is the person who works for his own good' . . . ?

Th.—Yes.

P.—Is the person related, or is it absolute? conditioned or unconditioned? eternal or temporal? with the marks or without them?

Th.—Nay, these things cannot truly be predicated about it.[2]

P.—Acknowledge, etc.[3] . . . (*complete as in* § 2 *and in* §§ 3-16).

[1] The text has here the eliding . . . p e . . . The *Comy.* remarks: Inasmuch as anything considered in its real, ultimate sense is, except Nibbāna, bound up in relations (p a c c a y ā), happens only as conditioned by relations, arises, ceases, and has no perduring essence, and, finally, has the character known as (*leg.* s a n k h ā t a s s a) the reason for happening, therefore it is asked: Has the person also these characteristics?

[2] Because (1) as an entity 'person' is non-existent; (2) with 'person' as a concrete bundle of phenomena (the 'person' of the quotation) the original thesis is not really concerned.

[3] The text again breaks off with its . . . p e . . . (etc.).

To clear the Meaning of the Terms.[1]

[148] *Th.*—Is 'the person' known, and conversely, is that which is known the person?

P.—The person is known. Conversely, of that which is known some is 'person,' some is not 'person.'

Th.—Do you admit this with respect to the subject also: of that which is person, is some known and some not known?

P.—Nay, that cannot truly be said . . . (*continue as before*).

[149] *Th.*—Does 'person' mean a reality and conversely?

P.—'Person' is a reality. Conversely, reality means in part person, in part not person.

Th.—Do you admit this with respect to the subject also: that 'person means in part reality, in part non-reality'?

P.—Nay, that cannot truly be said. . . .

[150] *Th.*—Does the person exist, and conversely?

P.—The person exists. Conversely, of the existent some is person, some is not person.

Th.—Of the person is some existent, some non-existent?

P.—Nay, that cannot truly be said. . . .

[151] Query repeated with an equivalent major term.[2]

[152] *Th.*—Is person something that is, and conversely?

(*Reply similar to the foregoing.*)

[1] An inquiry into how far the middle term, such as 'that which is known,' is 'distributed' with respect to the subject, or is coincident with it. The *Comy.* explains that k e - h i - c i, 'some,' is [not instrumental, but] equal to k o c i, h i being merely a particle. 'For me the person is, and the Buddha said so, but not all that is known [as ultimately real] is person.' The fact that 'a t t h i,' 'is,' 'exists,' is not used in Pali merely as a copula, gives the term, as meaning separate existence in fact, not only in thought, a greater emphasis than our own 'is.'

[2] S a ŋ v i j j a m ā n o, an equivalent of the preceding v i j j a m ā n o. All are equivalents for u p a l a b b h a t i, 'is known,' or found.—*Comy.*

[153] *Th*:—Does the person exist, and conversely, is that which exists *not all* person?[1]

P.—Yes.

Th.—Can you substitute 'not exist(s)' for 'exist(s)'?

P.—No. . . .

Inquiry into Term-or-Concept.[2]

[154] *Th*.—Is one who has material quality in the sphere of matter[3] a 'person'?

Yes.

Is one who experiences desires of sense in the sphere of sense-desire 'a person'?

Nay, that cannot truly be said. . . .

[154[a]] Are those who have material qualities in the sphere of matter 'persons'?

Yes.

Are those who experience desires of sense in the sphere of sense-desire 'persons'?

[1] On this section the Commentator as follows: The opponent has just admitted that the existent [the real ultimate existent] is greater in extension than 'soul.' The Theravādin, having his assent to this, now connects it with his assertion about the Buddha's statement: You quoted that saying: 'There are (souls or) persons working for their own good' . . . only on account of the term, and this you took as implying that soul exists [as a real ultimate]. But the Bhagavā also said, in the Sutta Nipāta (1116): 'Consider, Mogharāja, that the world is empty of soul (attā).' . . . Hence, by the quotation, it is as easy to deny soul (puggalo natthi) as to affirm it (puggalo atthi), or, to say 'that which exists not is all persons (natthi sabbo puggalo), as to say that 'that which exists is not all persons' (atthi na sabbo puggalo). The Comy. explains this last clause as equivalent to 'some existent things are persons, some not.' The converse in English is better expressed by 'all existent things are not persons.'

[2] Paññatti. See p. 1, *n*.

[3] Dhātu stands here, spatially considered, for loka, hence 'sphere' for 'element.' Cf. *Yam*, i. 374. Henceforth the text gives only the opening of the 'first refutation' in each controversy, the Theravādin putting the question. To indicate the speakers is therefore unnecessary.

Nay, that cannot truly be said. . . .

[154b] Is one who is without material qualities in the sphere of the Immaterial a 'person'?

Yes.

Is one who experiences desires of sense in the sphere of sense-desire a person?

Nay, that cannot truly be said. . . .

[154c] Are those who have no material qualities in the Immaterial sphere 'persons'?

Yes.

Are those who experience sense-desires in the sphere of of sense-desire 'persons'?

Nay, that cannot truly be admitted.

[155] *Th.*—According to you one who has material qualities in the sphere of matter is a 'person'; one who has no material qualities in the Immaterial sphere is a 'person': does anyone deceasing from the Rūpa sphere get reborn in the Immaterial sphere?

Yes.

Is the 'person' who had material qualites [then] annihilated, and does the person with no material qualities come into being?

Nay, that cannot truly be admitted. . . .

Queries repeated, substituting 'being'[1] *for* 'person.'

[156] Applying the terms 'physical frame,'[2] and 'body'[3] indiscriminately to our body, are these identical, one in meaning, the same, the same in denotation, the same in origin?

Yes.

[1] Satto. Both are equivalent expressions for 'soul.' See § 1, *n.* 2.

[2] Kāyo, literally, as in nikāyo, a group, collection, congeries. In psychology, the whole sentient surface, organ and seat of touch. We lack a synonym for 'body'; cf. *Körper*, *Leib*.

[3] The unusual phrase kāyaŋ appiyaŋ karitvā is, in the *Comy.*, paraphrased by kāyaŋ appetabbaŋ alliyāpetabbaŋ ekībhāvaŋ upanetabbaŋ avibhajitabbaŋ katvā 'taking [the two terms as applied to] body not in a separate but a cohesive sense, *i.e.*, in one and the same sense, without distinguishing.'

Are the terms 'personal entity,'[1] or 'soul,'[2] as applied without distinction to the individual, identical, one in meaning, the same, the same in denotation, the same in origin?

Yes.

Is 'physical frame' different from 'personal entity' (or 'individual')?

Yes.

Is 'soul' one thing, 'body' another?

Nay, that cannot truly be said.

Acknowledge the refutation: If there be this identity and coincidence between[3] 'physical frame' and 'body'; and if there be this identity and coincidence between 'individual' (or personal entity) and 'soul'; if, further, 'physical frame' is different from 'individual' (or personal entity), then indeed, good sir, it should also have been admitted that 'soul' is different from 'body.'

You are wrong in (1) admitting the identity between 'physical frame' and 'body,' (2) admitting the identity between 'personal entity' and 'soul,' (3) admitting the difference between 'physical frame' and 'personal entity,' while (4) you deny the difference between 'body' and 'soul.'

If you cannot admit (4), neither should you have admitted (1), (2), (3). You cannot admit (1), (2), (3), while denying (4).

[157] *P.*—Are the terms 'physical frame' and 'body' applied to body without distinction of meaning, identical, one in meaning, the same, the same in denotation, the same in origin?

Th.—Yes.

P.—Was it said by the Exalted One: 'There is the individual [or person] who works for his own good?'

[1] Puggalo.

[2] Jīvo. The etymology of jīvo—'living' thing—reveals, better than our ambiguous 'soul,' the difficulty of denying jīvo of a living or live body.

[3] The text here and below [§ 157] repeats the details of the identity, intensive and extensive.

Th.—Yes.

P.—Is 'physical frame' one thing, 'individual' (or 'personal entity') another?

Th.—Nay, that cannot truly be said.

P.—Acknowledge my rejoinder:[1] If there be this identity and coincidence between 'physical frame' and 'body'; and if it was said by the Exalted One 'There is the individual, *etc.*[2] . . .,' then indeed, good sir, it should also have been admitted that 'physical frame' is one thing and 'individual' or 'personal entity' another. You are wrong in admitting the first two propositions and denying the third. If you cannot admit the third, neither should you have admitted the first two . . . (*complete the discourse as in* §§ 8-16).

Examination continued by way of Rebirth.[3]

[158] *Th.*—Does (a person or) soul[4] run on (or transmigrate) from this world to another and from another world to this?[5]

P.—Yes.

Is it the identical soul who transmigrates from this world to another and from another world to this?[6]

Nay, that cannot be truly said . . . (*complete as above*).

Th.—Then is it a different soul who transmigrates. . . .

P.—Nay, that cannot truly be said.[7] . . . (*complete as above*).

Th.—Then is it both the identical and also a different soul who transmigrates . . .?

P.—Nay, that cannot truly be said. . . .

1 Namely, to § 156.

2 Puggalo.

3 Gati-anuyogo.—*Comy.* The PTS. text omits the title after § 170.

4 Puggalo is now rendered by soul, that term being in eschatological discussion more familiar to us than 'person.'

5 This question eliciting an essential feature in the Puggala-vādin's or animistic position is repeated, as a matter of form, before each of the four following questions.

6 The Eternalist view.—*Comy.* See *Dialogues*, i. 46 f.

7 He fears lest he side with the Annihilationists.—*Comy.*

Th.—Then is it neither the identical soul, nor yet a different soul who transmigrates . . . ?[1]

P.—Nay, that cannot truly be said. . . .

Th.—Is it the identical, a different, both identical and also different, neither identical, nor different soul who transmigrates . . . ?

P.—Nay, that cannot truly be said. . . .

[159] *P.*—Then is it wrong to say, 'The soul transmigrates from this world to another world, and from another world to this?'

Th.—Yes.

P.—Was it not said by the Exalted One:—

> '*When he hath run from birth to birth*
> *Seven times and reached the last, that soul*
> *Endmaker shall become of ill,*
> *By wearing every fetter down*' ?[2]

Is the Suttanta thus?

Th.—Yes.

P.—Then surely the soul does transmigrate from this world to another world and from another world to this. Again (*repeating his first question*) was it not said by the Exalted One: '*Without a known beginning, O bhikkhus, is the way of life ever renewed; unrevealed is the origin of souls* (lit. beings) *who, shrouded in ignorance and bound by the fetters of natural desire, run on transmigrating.*'[3] Is the Suttanta thus?

Th.—Yes.

P.—Then surely the soul does transmigrate as was said.

[160] *Th.*—Does the soul transmigrate from this world, etc.?

P.—Yes.

Th.—Does the identical soul so transmigrate?

[1] He fears in this and the next question lest he side with certain Eternalists and the 'Eelwrigglers' respectively.—*Comy.* Cf. *Dialogues*, i. 87 f.

[2] *Iti-vuttaka*, § 24.

[3] *Saṃyutta-Nikāya*, iii. 149.

P.—Nay, that cannot truly be said . . . (*complete as usual*).

Th.—I repeat my question.

P.—Yes.

Th.—Is there any soul who after being human becomes a deva?[1]

P.—Yes.

Th.—Is the identical man the deva?

P.—Nay, that cannot truly be said . . . (*complete as usual*).

Th.—[I repeat], is the identical man the deva?[2]

P.—Yes.

Th.—Now you are wrong to admit as true that, having been man he becomes deva, or having been deva he becomes man, and again that, having become man, a deva is different from a human being, [and yet] that this identical soul transmigrates. . . .

Surely if the identical soul, without [becoming] different, transmigrates when deceasing hence to another world, there will then be no dying; destruction of life will cease to take place. There is action (karma); there is action's effect; there is the result of deeds done. But when good and bad acts are maturing as results, you say that the very same [person] transmigrates—this is wrong.[3]

[161] *Th.*—Does the self-same soul transmigrate from this world to another, from another world to this?

P.—Yes.

Th.—Is there anyone who, having been human, becomes a Yakkha, a Peta, an inmate of purgatory, a beast, for example a camel, an ox, a mule, a pig, a buffalo?

[1] We have let d e v a stand. It includes all that we mean by spirit, god, angel, and even fairy. (Pronounce d a y - v ă.)

[2] When he is [first] asked this, he denies for a mere man the state of godship. When asked again, he admits the identity because of such Sutta-passages as '*I at that time was Sunetta, a teacher.*' (*Petavatthu*, iv. 7, 3).—*Comy.*

[3] By the orthodox view, the newly reborn is not 'the same,' nor different, but a resultant of the deceased one's karma (acts). Hence the notion of an identical entity persisting is in conflict with that law of karma which the otherwise-dissenting Puggalavādin would accept.

P.—Yes.

Th.—Does the self-same human become anyone of these, say, a buffalo?

P.—Nay, that cannot truly be said . . . (*complete the refutation as usual*).

Th.—[I repeat] is the self-same human the buffalo?

P.—Yes.

Th.—[But all this, namely, that] having been man, he becomes a buffalo, or having been buffalo he becomes man, again, that having become a man, he is quite different from the buffalo, and yet that the self-same soul goes on transmigrating, is wrong . . . (*complete as usual*).

Surely if the identical soul, when deceasing from this world and being reborn in another, is nowise different, then there will be no dying, nor will taking life be possible. There is action; there is action's effect; there is the result of deeds done. But when good and bad acts are maturing as results, you say that the identical person transmigrates, —this is wrong.

[162] *Th.*—You say that the identical soul transmigrates.[1] Is there anyone who having been a noble becomes a brahmin?

Yes.

Is the noble in question the very same as the brahmin in question?

Nay, that cannot truly be said . . . . (*complete the discourse*).

Is there anyone who, having been noble, becomes reborn in the middle, or in the lower class?

Yes.

Is the noble in question the very same as the person so reborn?

Nay, that cannot truly be said. . . .

The other alternatives, substituting 'brahmin,' etc., in turn for 'noble,' are treated similarly.

[1] Repeating the original question, § 160, second query.

[163] You say that the identical soul transmigrates. . . . Is then one who has had hand or foot cut off, or hand and foot, or ear or nose, or both cut off, or finger or thumb cut off, or who is hamstrung, the same as he was before? Or is one whose fingers are bent or webbed[1] the same as he was before? Or is one afflicted with leprosy, skin disease, dry leprosy, consumption, epilepsy, the same as he was before? Or is [one who has become] a camel, ox, mule, pig, buffalo, the same as he was before?

Nay, that cannot truly be said. . . .

[164] *P.*—Is it wrong to say: 'The identical soul transmigrates from this world to another, etc.?'

Th.—Yes.

P.—But is not one who has 'attained the stream' (*i.e.*, the first path towards salvation), when he is deceasing from the world of men, and is reborn in the world of devas, a stream-winner there also?

Th.—Yes.

P.—But if this man, reborn as deva, is a stream-winner also in that world, then indeed, good sir, it is right to say: 'The identical soul transmigrates from this world to another.' . . .

Th.—Assuming that one who has attained the stream, when deceasing from the world of men, is reborn in the world of devas, does the identical soul transmigrate from this world to another and from another world to this in just that manner?

P.—Yes.

Th.—Is such a stream-winner, when reborn in deva-world, a man there also?

P.—Nay, that cannot truly be said. . . . (*complete the 'refutation'*).

[165] *Th.*—Does the identical soul transmigrate from this world to another, etc.?

Yes.

[1] Like the wings of a bat.

Is the transmigrator not different, still present?

Nay, that cannot truly be said. . . .

I repeat, is the transmigrator not different, still present?

Yes.

If he has lost a hand, a foot, . . . if he is diseased . . . if he is an animal . . . is he the same as before?

Nay, that cannot truly be said . . . (*complete*).

[166] *Th.*—Does the identical soul transmigrate? . . .

Yes.

Does he transmigrate with his corporeal qualities?

Nay, that cannot truly be said. . . .

[Think again!] Does he transmigrate with these?[1]

Yes.

Are soul and body the same?

Nay, that cannot truly be said. . . .[2]

Does he transmigrate with feeling, with perception, with mental coefficients, with consciousness?[3]

Nay, that cannot truly be said. . . .

Think again . . . does he transmigrate with consciousness?

Yes.

Is soul the same as body?

Nay, that cannot truly be said. . . .

[167] *Th.*—If, as you say, the identical soul transmigrates, . . . does he transmigrate without corporeal qualities, without feeling, perception, mental coefficients, without consciousness?

Nay, that cannot truly be said. . . .

[1] He first rejects because the material frame does not go with the soul (*Comy.* P.T.S. text: read a g a m a n a ŋ), then accepts because there is no interval of gestation.—*Comy.* See below, VIII. 2.

[2] The opponent rejects this, inasmuch as, in transmigrating, the body is held to be abandoned; moreover, he would not oppose the Suttas.—*Comy.*

[3] According to the *Comy.*, this is denied because of possible rebirth in the sphere known as the unconscious, but is admitted with respect to other spheres.

[4] Because without the five aggregates (mind, body) there is no individual.—*Comy.*

Think again . . . without corporeal qualities . . . without consciousness?

Yes.

Is then the soul one thing, the body another?

Nay, that cannot truly be admitted. . . .

[168] *Th.*—If, as you say, the identical soul transmigrates, . . . do the material qualities transmigrate?

Nay, that cannot truly be admitted. . . .

Think again. . . .

Yes.

But is this soul (x) the same as this body (x)?

Nay, that cannot truly be said. . . .

Does feeling . . . or perception . . . or do mental coefficients . . . or does consciousness transmigrate?

Nay, that cannot truly be saïd. . . .

Think again . . . does consciousness transmigrate?

Yes.

But is this soul (x) the same as this body (x)?

Nay, that cannot truly be said. . . .

[169] *Th.*—Then, the identical soul, according to you, transmigrating . . . does none of the above-named five aggregates transmigrate?

Nay, that cannot truly be said. . . .

Think again. . . .

Yes, they do.

Is, then, soul one thing, body another?

Nay, that cannot truly be said. . . .

[170] *At dissolution of each aggregate,*
If then the 'person' doth disintegrate,
Lo! by the Buddha shunned, the Nihilistic creed.
At dissolution of each aggregate,
If then the 'soul' doth not disintegrate,
Eternal, like Nibbāna,[1] *were the soul indeed.*

[1] Samasamo—'i.e., exceedingly like, or just resembling by the state of resemblance. Just as Nibbāna is neither reborn nor dissolved, so would the soul be.'—*Comy.*

III.—DERIVATIVES.

Examination continued by Way of Derivative Concepts.[1]

[171] *Th.*—Is the concept of soul derived from the corporeal qualities?

P.—Yes.[2]

Are material qualities impermanent, conditioned, do they happen through a cause? Are they liable to perish, to pass away, to become passionless, to cease, to change?

Yes.

But has soul also any or all of these qualities?

Nay, that cannot truly be said. . . .

[172] Or is the concept of soul derived from feeling, from perception, from mental coefficients, from consciousness?

Yes (*to each 'aggregate' in succession*).

Is any mental aggregate impermanent, conditioned? does it happen through a cause? is it liable to perish, to pass away, to become passionless, to cease, to change?

Yes.

But has soul also any or all of these qualities?

Nay, that cannot truly be said. . . .

[173] You said that the concept of soul is derived from material qualities. Is the concept of blue-green[3] soul derived from blue-green material qualities?

Nay, that cannot truly be said. . . .

Or is the concept of yellow, red, white, visible, invisible, resisting, or unresisting soul derived from corresponding material qualities, respectively?

Nay, that cannot truly be said. . . .

[174] Is the concept of soul derived from feeling?

[1] This chapter is still largely eschatological, hence 'soul' is retained for puggala, though individual, person, or ego would serve equally well in the more psychological considerations.

[2] He will have it that the concept or notion of soul, or personal entity, is derived from material and mental qualities, just as the shadow (read PTS. ed., chāyāya) is derived from the tree, and fire from fuel.—*Comy.*

[3] Nīla is both blue and also green, Indian writers applying it to both sky and trees. In these replies the animist rejects a pluralistic state for the soul.—*Comy.*

Yes.

Is the concept of good soul derived from good feeling?

Nay, that cannot truly be said. . . .

I repeat my question.

Yes.[1]

Now, does feeling entail result or fruit, fruit that is desirable, pleasing, gladdening, unspotted, a happy result, and such as conveys happiness?

No.

I repeat my question.

Yes.

But does 'good soul' entail result or fruit of like nature with the above?

Nay, that cannot truly be said.[2] . . .

[175] If the concept of soul is derived from feeling, is the concept of bad soul derived from bad feeling?

Yes.

Now does bad feeling entail result or fruit, fruit that is undesirable, unpleasing, spotted, an unhappy result, and such as conveys unhappiness?

Yes.[3]

But does bad soul entail result or fruit of like nature to the above?

Nay, that cannot truly be said. . . .

[176] If the concept of soul is derived from feeling, is the concept of indeterminate soul—one to be termed neither good nor bad—derived from indeterminate feeling?

Nay, that cannot truly be said. . . .

Is the concept [I repeat] of an ethically indeterminate soul derived from an ethically indeterminate feeling?

Yes.[4]

[1] He now assents, taking 'good' in the sense of expertness, proficiency.—*Comy.*

[2] He rejects because it is not customary to speak thus of 'soul.' —*Comy.*

[3] Taking 'bad' analogously to 'good' above.—*Comy.*

[4] He now assents, because of the indeterminateness [of soul] with respect to the Eternalist or Nihilist heresies. The changed replies are to evade the imputation of Eternalism, etc.—*Comy.*

Is indeterminate feeling impermanent, conditioned? Does it happen through a cause? Is it liable to perish, to pass away, to become passionless, to cease, to change?

Yes.

Has an ethically indeterminate soul any or all of these qualities?

Nay, that cannot truly be said. . . .

[177] Is the concept of soul derived from any of the other three aggregates:—perception, mental co-efficients, consciousness?[1]

Yes.

[Taking the last]:—is the concept of good soul derived from good consciousness?

Nay, that cannot truly be said.

Now does good consciousness entail result or fruit—fruit that is desirable, pleasing, gladdening, unspotted, a happy result, such as conveys happiness?

Yes.

And does a good soul also entail the like?

Nay, that cannot truly be said. . . .

[178] You say that the concept of soul is derived from consciousness—is the concept of bad soul derived from bad consciousness?

Nay, that cannot truly be said. . . .

[I repeat] is the concept of bad soul derived from bad consciousness?

Yes.

Now does bad consciousness entail result or fruit, fruit that is undesirable, etc. (*the reverse of what is entailed by good consciousness*)?

Yes.

And does a bad soul also entail the like?

Nay, that cannot truly be said. . . .

[179] Again, since you admit that the concept of soul is derived from any or all of the aggregates, e.g., conscious-

[1] Elaborate, as with the two preceding aggregates (k h a n d h ā).

ness, is the concept of an ethically indeterminate soul derived from indeterminate consciousness?

Nay, that cannot truly be said. . . .

I repeat my question.

Yes.

But is the ethically indeterminate soul impermanent, conditioned, arisen through a cause, liable to perish . . . to change?

Nay, that cannot truly be said. . . .

[180] Ought it to be said that a soul who sees[1] is derived from sight (or eye)?[2]

Yes.

Ought it to be said that, when sight (or eye) ceases, the seeing soul ceases?

Nay, that cannot truly be said. . . .

(*The pair of queries is applied, with like replies, to the other four senses, and also to the* sensus communis, *mano.*)

[181] Ought it to be said that a soul of wrong views is derived from wrong views?

Yes.

Ought it to be said that when the wrong views cease to exist, the soul having wrong views ceases to exist?

Nay, that cannot truly be said. . . .

Ought it, again, to be said that when any other parts of the Wrong Eightfold Path[3] cease to exist, the soul, said by you to be derived from that part, ceases to exist?

Nay, that cannot truly be said. . . .

[182] Similarly, ought it to be said that a soul of right views, or right aspiration, right speech, right action, right livelihood, right endeavour, right mindfulness, right concentration, is derived from the corresponding part [of the Eightfold Path]?

[1] The *Comy.* notes the ambiguity, in the argument, of moral and physical vision in this word cakkhumā.

[2] Cakkhu is both 'eye' and 'sight.'

[3] The opposites to the qualities prescribed in the Ariyan Eightfold Path are so termed—e.g., in *Majjhima-Nik.*, i. 118.

Yes.

Ought it, again, to be said that when the given part ceases, the soul so derived ceases?

Nay, that cannot truly be said. . . .

[183] Is the concept of soul derived from material qualities and feeling?

Yes.

Then could the concept of a double soul be derived from the pair of aggregates?

Nay, that cannot truly be said. . . .

Or could the concept of a double soul be derived from material quality coupled with any of the other three aggregates . . . or the concept of five souls be derived from all five aggregates?[1]

Nay, that cannot truly be said. . . .

(184) Is the concept of soul derived from the organs of sight (eye) and hearing (ear)?

Yes.

Then could the concept 'two souls' be derived from the two organs? . . . (*and so on as in* § 183, *to include all the twelve* āyatanas—*i.e., organs and objects of sense and the organ and object of sense co-ordination*, m a n o, d h a m m ā.)

[185] Is the concept of soul derived from the elements of sight (or eye) and hearing (or ear)?

Yes.

Could the concept of a double soul be derived from these two?

Nay, that cannot truly be said. . . .

Is the concept of soul derived from the element of sight and any other of the eighteen elements?[2]

Yes.

[1] The idea is that, there being a plurality of aggregates in the individual organism, and soul a derivative of anyone, there might conceivably be five souls cohering in one individual's life-continuum (e k a s a n t ā n e n a)—which the Animist denies.—*Comy.*

[2] See p. 15.

Could the concept of eighteen souls be derived from the eighteen elements?

Nay, that cannot be truly said. . . .

[186] Is the concept of soul derived from the controlling powers[1]—eye and ear?

Yes.

Could the concept of a double soul be derived from these two?

Nay, that cannot truly be said. . . .

Could the concept of soul be derived from the controlling power, eye, and from any other of the twenty-two controlling powers?

Yes.

Could the concept of twenty-two souls be derived from these?

Nay, that cannot truly be said. . . .

[187] Is the concept of one soul derived from the becoming of one aggregate?[2]

Yes.

Could the concept of four souls be derived from the becoming of the four (mental) aggregates?

Nay, that cannot truly be said. . . .

Or again, by your assenting to the former question, could the concept of five souls be derived from the becoming of the five aggregates (mental and bodily)?

Nay, that cannot truly be said. . . .

[188] Is there only one soul in the becoming of one aggregate?

Yes.

Then are five souls in the becoming of all five aggregates?

Nay, that cannot truly be said. . . .

[189] Is the concept of soul derived from material

[1] Indriya (see p. 16). Cf. Ledi Sadaw, *JPTS.*, 1914, p. 162.

[2] Here the term vokāra replaces khandha, as it often does in the Yamaka. Becoming (bhava) in our idiom would be 'lifetime.'

qualities just as the idea of shadow is derived[1] from a tree? And just as the idea of its shadow is derived from the tree, and both tree and shadow are impermanent, is it even so that the concept of soul is derived from material qualities, both soul and material qualities being impermanent?

Nay, that cannot truly be said. . . .

Are material qualities one thing and the concept of soul derived therefrom another, in the same way as the tree is one thing, and the idea of shadow derived from it another?

Nay, that cannot truly be said. . . .

[190] Is the concept of soul derived from material qualities just as the notion 'villager' is derived from village? And if that is so, is material quality one thing, soul another, just as village is one thing, villager another?

Nay, that cannot truly be said. . . .

[191] Or—just as a kingdom is one thing, a king another?[2]

Nay, that cannot truly be said. . . .

[192] A jail[3] is not a jailer, but a jailer is he who has the jail. Is it just so with material qualities and one who has them? And accordingly, just as the jail is one thing, the jailer another, are not material qualities one thing, and one who has them another?

Nay, that cannot truly be said. . . .

IV.—CONSCIOUSNESS.

[193] Is there the notion of soul to each [moment of] consciousness?

Yes.

[1] U p ā d ā y a is only now defined in the *Comy.* as 'having come (or happened) because of, not without such and such.' And as from the impermanent only the impermanent can come, this idea of p u g g a l a as 'derived from' impermanent aggregates, bodily and mental, is obviously unfavourable for its upholder.

[2] Worded analogously to § 190.

[3] More literally a fetter or chain, and a 'fetterer' or 'chainer,' n i g a ḷ o, n e g a ḷ i k o.

Does the soul undergo birth, decay, death, disease and rebirth in each [moment of] consciousness?

Nay, that cannot truly be said. . . .[1]

[194] When the second [moment of] consciousness in a process of thought arises, is it wrong to say: 'It is the same, or something different'?[2]

Yes.

Then, when the second moment arises, is it not also wrong to say: 'It is a boy' or 'it is a girl'?[3]

It may be so said.

Now acknowledge the refutation: If at the second moment of consciousness it could not be said, 'It is the same or something different,' then indeed, good sir, neither can it be said, at that moment, that 'It is a boy, or a girl.' What you say, namely, that the former may not, the latter may be affirmed, is false. If the former proposition may not be affirmed, the second cannot be affirmed. Your rejecting the one and accepting the other is wrong.

[195] According to you it is wrong to say, when the second moment of consciousness arises, 'It is the same or something different.' Can it not then, at such a moment, be said: 'It is male or female, layman or religious, man or deva.'

Yes, it can be . . . (*complete as in* § 194).

V.—THE FIVE SENSES.

[196] *P.*—Is it wrong to say: 'The soul or person is known in the sense of a real and ultimate fact'?

Th.—Yes, it is wrong.

[1] This the Puggalavādin, not approving of a momentary state for the soul, rejects.—*Comy.*

[2] I.e., same as the first moment or different from it.

[3] Should one say 'a man,' 'a woman' instead. The Animist has admitted constant becoming, change, in the previous reply. The child at each moment is becoming more adult, but *popular usage* lets him become 'man' or 'woman,' so to speak, by a sudden transition from one static condition to the next. The Animist, who mixes such usage with his philosophy, is constrained to justify the former and assents. Cf. Mrs. Rh. D.'s *Buddhism*, p. 132.

P.—Is it not the case that when someone sees something by means of something, a certain 'he' sees a certain 'it' by a certain 'means'?[1]

Th.—Yes.

P.—But if that is so, then surely it should be said that the person is known in the sense of a real and ultimate fact?

Analogous questions are asked concerning the other four senses. Again:

Is it not the case that when someone knows something by means of something, a certain 'he' knows a certain 'it' by a certain 'means'? If so, then surely it may be said that the person is known in a real and ultimate sense.

[197] *Th.*—Is the person known in the sense of a real and ultimate fact?

P.—Yes.

Th.—Is it not the case that when someone does not see something by means of something, a certain 'he' does not see a certain 'it' by a certain 'means'?

P.—Yes.

Th.—Then it is equally the case that the person is not known in a real and ultimate sense.

Analogous questions are asked concerning the other four senses and cognition generally.

[198] *P.*—Is it wrong to say the person is known in the sense of a real and ultimate fact?

Th.—Yes.

P.—Was it not said by the Exalted One: '*O bhikkhus, I see beings deceasing and being reborn by the purified vision of the eye celestial, surpassing that of men. I discern beings in spheres sublime or base, fair or frightful, of happy or woeful*

[1] The Animist, or Entity-theorist, seeking to establish his view by another method, now says: 'Why are you so concerned with all this inquiry about derived concept? Tell me this first: Why may we not say, that a person is really and ultimately known, etc. . . .' Here 'someone' is the puggalo, 'something' is the visible object, 'means' is the eye. But the orthodox says it is only eye, depending on visual consciousness, that sees, and so on. But in *conventional usage* we say 'someone sees,' etc.—*Comy.*

doom, faring according to their actions'?[1] Is the Suttanta thus?

Th.—Yes.

P.—Surely then the person[2] is known in the sense of a real and ultimate fact?

[199] *Th.*—Granting that the Exalted One said that which is quoted, is that a reason for affirming that the person is known in the sense of a real and ultimate fact?

P.—Yes.

Th.—Does the Exalted One, by the purified vision of the eye celestial surpassing that of man, see visible objects, and does he also see the person or soul?

P.—He sees visible objects.[3]

Th.—Are visible objects the person? Do *they* end one life and reappear? Do *they* fare according to Karma?

P.—Nay, that cannot truly be said. . . .

Th.—I repeat my former question.

P.—He does see the person or soul.[4]

Th.—Is then the soul visible object? Is it object of sight, objective element of sight, blue, green, yellow, red, white? Is it cognizable by sight? Does it impinge on the eye? Does it enter the avenue of sight?[5]

P.—Nay, that cannot truly be said. . . .

Th.—I repeat my former question.

P.—He does see both.

Th.—Are both then visible objects? Both objective element of sight? Are both blue, green, yellow, red, white? Are both cognizable by sight? Do both impinge

[1] Cf. *Majjhima-Nik.*, i. 482. The wording of this passage above differs very slightly from about some twenty references in the Nikāyas. When adequate indexes to the first two Nikāyas are finished, we may be able to trace one exactly like this.

[2] Satto, 'being,' is synonymous with 'puggalo.'—*Comy.*

[3] The affirmative replies are not distinctly assigned in the P.T.S. text.

[4] By the quotation: 'I see beings.' . . .—*Comy.*

[5] Things that are perceptible are apprehended in a fourfold synthesis of seeing, hearing, reflection, understanding.—*Comy.* Hence the soul cannot be identified with external objects as seen.

on the eye? Do both enter the avenue of sight? Do both disappear, reappear in rebirths, faring according to Karma?

P.—Nay, that cannot truly be said. . . .

VI. ETHICAL GOODNESS.

Examination continued by Reference to Human Action, called also 'The Section on Ethical Goodness.'

[200] *P.*—Are ethically good and bad actions known [to exist]?[1]

Th.—Yes.

P.—Are both the doer of ethically good and bad deeds, and he who causes them to be done[2] known [to exist]?

Th.—Nay, that cannot truly be said . . .[3] (*complete in the usual way, viz., that the former admission involves acceptance of what is denied*).

[201] *Th.*—Admitting that ethically good and bad deeds are known [to exist], do you assert that the doer and the instigator are also known [to exist]?

P.—Yes.

Then is he who made the doer, or inspired the instigator, known [to exist]?

Nay, that cannot truly be said.[4] . . .

I ask you again.

Yes.[5]

But if the one be thus maker, etc., of the other, is there then no making an end of ill, no cutting off the cycle of life renewed, no final Nibbāna without residual stuff of life?[6]

[1] This might, less literally, run: Are there such things as ethically good, etc., actions? Sceptical views in the age of the Nikāyas denied the *inherent* goodness and badness of conduct—denied their happy and painful *results*. These are stated in Abhidhamma also.—*Bud. Psych. Ethics*, § 1215, p. 325, *n.* 1; *Vibhanga*, p. 392.

[2] I.e., by commanding, instructing, and other methods.—*Comy.*

[3] I.e., not as a persisting, identical, personal entity.

[4] Denial from fear of the heresy of creation by a god (*Anguttara-Nik.*, i. 173 f.; *Vibhanga*, 367).—*Comy.*

[5] Assented to because parents 'make' doers, teachers also.—*Comy.*

[6] The idea is that 'each previous soul would be the *inevitable* maker of its successor.'—*Comy.*

Nay, that cannot truly be said. . . .

If good and bad deeds are known [to take place], is the doer, is the instigator, of those deeds known to exist?

Yes.

Is the person or soul known to exist, and his maker or inspirer also?

Nay, that cannot truly be said. . . .

I repeat my question:—if good and bad deeds. . . .

Yes.

Then is Nibbāna [also] known to exist, and the maker and the maker's maker as well?

Nay, that cannot truly be said. . . .

Then, again, if these things be as you say, is the earth known to exist, and its maker and *his* maker also?

Nay, that cannot truly be said. . . .

Or the ocean?—or Sineru, chief of mountains?—or water?—or fire?—or air?—or grass, brush, and forest? and the maker of each and *his* maker also?

Nay, that cannot truly be said. . . .

Again, if good and bad deeds being known to exist, doer and instigator are also known to exist, are those deeds one thing, and doer and instigator quite another thing?

Nay, that cannot truly be said.[1] . . .

[202] *P.*—Is the effect of ethically good and bad deeds known to take place?

Th.—Yes.

P.—Is one who experiences the effect of such deeds known to exist?

Th.—Nay, that cannot truly be said. . . .

[203] *Th.*—Admitting that both these propositions are true, is one who enjoys the first-named person known to exist?

P.—Nay, that cannot truly be said. . . .

Th.—I repeat the question.

[1] Denied lest assent be shown to the heresy: the soul is that which *has* mental properties or co-efficients (cf. *Majjh.-N.*, i. 299: *Bud. Psych. Eth.*, p. 257 f.).—*Comy.*

P.—Yes.[1]

Th.—If the one and the other be so, is there no making an end of ill, no cutting off the cycle of life renewed, no final Nibbāna without residual stuff of life?

P.—Nay, that cannot truly be said. . . .

Th.—Again, admitting both those propositions to be true, does the person exist, and the enjoyer of that person also exist?[2]

Nay, that cannot truly be said. . . .

Again, admitting both those propositions to be true, is Nibbāna known to exist, and one who experiences it also?

Nay, that cannot truly be said. . . .

Or again, is the earth, the ocean, Sineru chief of mountains, water, fire, air, grass, brush, and forest, known to exist, and one who experiences any of them known also to exist?

Nay, that cannot truly be said. . . .[3]

Or [finally] is the result of ethically good and bad deeds one thing and he who experiences those results another?

Nay, that cannot truly be said. . . .[4]

[204] *P.*—Is celestial happiness known to exist?

Th.—Yes.

P.—Is one who is experiencing celestial happiness known to exist?

Th.—Nay, that cannot truly be said. . . .

[205] *Th.*—Assuming both propositions to be true, is one who enjoys that experiencer known to exist?

P.—Nay, that cannot truly be said. . . .

[1] Reflecting that a mother may embrace her child, a wife her husband, who has experienced, or felt, and thus meet the question.—*Comy.*

[2] If effects be not only external phenomena, if one subjectively experiencing, or enjoying them be assumed, this enjoyer, now as himself in turn an effect, would be enjoyed by another experiencer. In this way there would be an endless series of persons or souls (puggalā paramparā).—*Comy.*

[3] It is not clear why the *P.* should here negate. The *Comy.* adds that these questions are put with ordinary meaning (sāmaññena). Cf. p. 46, *n.* 1.

[4] Lest he be accused of that feature in the heresy of individuality: The soul *has* feeling.'—See 56 (fol.), *n.* 1.

I repeat the question.

Yes.

If the one and the other be so, is there no making an end of ill, no cutting off the cycle of life, no final Nibbāna without residual stuff of life?

Nay, that cannot truly be said. . . .

Again, assuming both those propositions to be true, is the person known to exist and the enjoyer of the person also?

Nay, that cannot truly be said. . . .

Again, assuming that celestial happiness and those enjoying it are both known to exist, is Nibbāna known, and one enjoying it known also to exist?

Nay, that cannot truly be said. . . .

Or again, assuming as before, are the earth, the ocean, Sineru chief of mountains, water, fire, air, grass, brush, and forest known to exist and those enjoying them? [1]

Nay, that cannot truly be said. . . .

Or again, assuming as before, is celestial happiness one thing, the enjoyer another thing?

Nay, that cannot truly be said. . . .

[206] *P.*—Is human happiness known to exist?

Th.—Yes.

Is the enjoyer of human happiness known to exist?

Nay, that cannot truly be said. . . .

[207] *Th.*—Is both human happiness and the enjoyer of it known to exist?

P.—Yes.

Is one who enjoys the enjoyer known to exist?

Nay, that cannot truly be said. . . .

I repeat my question.

Yes.

If the one and the other be so, is there no making an end of ill, no cutting off the cycle of life, no final Nibbāna without residual stuff of life?

Nay, that cannot truly be said. . . .

(*The dialogue is then completed, as in* § 205, *on celestial happiness.*)

[1] *As such* they are objects of consciousness, but not subjective ultimates.—*Comy.*

[208] *P.*—Is the misery of the lower planes[1] known to exist?

Th.—Yes.

Is the experiencer of that misery known to exist?

Nay, that cannot truly be said. . . .

[209] *Th.*—Do you admit both these propositions?

P.—Yes.

Is the enjoyer of the sufferer of that misery known to exist?

Nay, that cannot truly be said. . . .

I repeat my question.

Yes.

If the one and the other be so, is there no making an end of ill, etc.? (*complete in full as in* §§ 205, 207).

[210, 211] *Th.*—Is the misery of purgatory known? (*Complete as in* §§ 204, 205, 207.)

[212] *Th.*—Are ethically good and bad acts (karmas) known to exist? And the doer of them also? And the instigator also? And the enjoyer of the effect—is he also known to exist?

P.—Yes.

Is he who does the acts the same as he who experiences the effect?

Nay, that cannot truly be said.[2] . . .

I repeat my question.

Yes.[3]

Then, are happiness and misery self-caused?

Nay, that cannot truly be said. . . .

Then, admitting you still assent to my first propositions, is the doer a different [person] from the enjoyer [of the effect]?

[1] Apaya, i.e., purgatory, animal kingdom, Petas, or unhappy, hungry 'shades,' and Asūras, or titans.

[2] He fears to contradict the Suttas.—See *Saṃyutta Nik.*, ii. 94: 'To say, one-and-the-same both acts and is affected by the result, is not true.'—*Comy.*

[3] In the Suttas it is said: he has pleasure both here and hereafter. —*Comy.*

Nay, that cannot truly be said.[1] . . .

I repeat my question.

Yes.[2]

Then, are happiness and misery caused by another?

Nay, that cannot truly be said. . . .

Admitting you still assent to the first propositions, does the same and another do the deeds, does the same and another enjoy (the results)?

Nay, that cannot truly be said. . . .

I repeat my question.

Yes.

Then is happiness and is misery both self-caused and produced by another?

Nay, that cannot truly be said. . . .

Admitting that you still assent to the first propositions, does neither the same [person] both do the deeds and experience the results, nor one [person] do the deeds and another experience the results?

Nay, that cannot truly be said. . . .

I repeat my question.

Yes, neither the same, nor two different persons.

Then are happiness and misery not self-causing nor caused by something else?

Nay, that cannot truly be said. . . .

Admitting, finally, that you still assent to the first propositions, namely, that ethically good and bad actions; as well as the doer of them, and the instigator of the doer, are known to exist, [I have now asked you four further questions:]

(1) Is he who does the act the same as he who experiences the effect?

(2) Are doer and experiencer two different persons?

(3) Are they the same and also different persons?

(4) Are they neither the same nor different persons?

[You have answered to each:] No. [I have then repeated

[1] *Saŋyutta-Nik.*, ii. 94: 'To say, one acts, another reaps the fruit, is not true.'

[2] Fancying that as deva he surely enjoys the result of his actions when a man.—*Comy.*

the question. You have then said]: Yes. I have then put four questions:

(1) Are happiness and misery self-caused?

(2) Are they the work of another?

(3) Are they both one and the other?

(4) Are they, arising through a cause, self-caused, or the work of another? [And you have replied]: No. . . .

[213] *P.*—Is there such a thing as karma (action taking effect)?

Th.—Yes.

P.—Is there such a thing as a maker of karma?

Th.—Nay, that cannot truly be said. . . .

[214] *Th.*—Is there such a thing as both karma and the maker of karma?

P.—Yes.

Is there a maker of that maker?

Nay, that cannot truly be said. . . .

I repeat the question.

Yes.

Then if the one and the other exist, is there no making an end of ill, no cutting of the cycle of life, no final Nibbāna without residual stuff of life?

Nay, that cannot truly be said. . . .

Again, since you assent to both the first propositions, is there both a person and a maker of the person?

Nay, that cannot truly be said. . . .

Or . . . is there both Nibbāna and a maker thereof? . . . or the earth, ocean, Sineru, water, fire, air, grass, brush and forest, and the maker thereof?

Nay, that cannot truly be said. . . .

. . . Or is karma one thing, the maker of it another?

Nay, that cannot truly be said. . . .

[215] *P.*—Is there such a thing as result of action?

Th.—Yes.

P.—Is there such a thing as an enjoyer of the result?

Th.—Nay, that cannot truly be said. . . .

[216] *Th.*—Do you maintain then that there are both results and enjoyer thereof?

P.—Yes.

Is there an enjoyer of that enjoyer?

Nay, that cannot truly be said. . . .

I repeat my question.

Yes.

Then, if this and that be so, is there no making an end of ill, no . . . etc. (*complete in full similarly to* § 214, *and ending:*—)

You maintaining that there is both result and enjoyer thereof, is then result one thing, and the enjoyer of it another?

Nay, that cannot truly be said . . . (*complete as usual*).

VII. SUPERNORMAL POWER.

Examination into 'Soul' continued by reference to Super-intellectual Power.

[217] *P.*—Is it wrong to say 'the person [or soul] is known in the sense of a real and ultimate fact'?

Th.—Yes.

P.—Have there not been those who could transform themselves by magic potency?[1]

Th.—Yes.

P.—If that be so, then indeed, good sir, it is right to say 'the person [or soul] is known in the sense of a real and ultimate fact.' Again, have there not been those who could hear sounds by the element of celestial hearing, . . . or know the mind of another, or remember previous lives,

[1] On iddhi, and this kind of it, called vikubbanā-iddhi see *Compendium*, p. 61; *Paṭisambhidā-magga*, ii. 210; *Atthasālinī*, 91; *Visuddhi-magga*, ch. xii. The opponent fancies a soul or inner principle can achieve magical efficacy only with respect to such matter as is bound up with human power of control. In the third question are enumerated the other five forms of the so-called chaḷ-abhiññā, or 'sixfold super-knowledge.'—*Comy.*

or see visible objects by the celestial eye, or realize the destruction of the 'intoxicants'?

Th.—Yes.

P.—If these things be so, then indeed, good sir, it is right to say 'the person is known in the sense of a real and ultimate fact.'

[218] *Th.*—Granting that there have been those who could transform themselves by magic potency, is it *for that reason* that the person is known in the sense of a real and ultimate fact?

P.—Yes.

Th.—When one has through magic potency transformed himself, was he then the personal entity, and not when not so transforming himself?

P.—Nay, that cannot truly be said. . . .

This question is asked, and so answered, in the case of the other five modes of super-intellectual faculty named above.

VIII. APPEAL TO THE SUTTAS.[1]

[219] *P.*—Is it wrong to say 'the person is known in the sense of a real and ultimate fact'?

Th.—Yes.

P.—Is there not [one whom we call] mother?

Th.—Yes.

P.—If there be, then indeed, good sir, it is right to say 'the person is known in the sense of a real and ultimate fact.' Again, is there not [one whom we call] father, are there not brothers, sisters, nobles, brahmins, merchants, serfs, householders, religious, devas, humans?

Th.—Yes.

P.—If there be, then indeed, good sir, it is right to say 'the person is known,' etc.

[220] *Th.*—Granting there are mothers, fathers, etc.,

[1] The final citations are led up to by several preliminary inquiries. These, says the *Comy.*, bear on kinship, status, career, rebirth, etc.

is it for this reason that you insist thus respecting the personal entity?

P.—Yes.

Th.—Is there anyone who, not having been a mother, becomes a mother?

P.—Yes.

Th.—Is there anyone who, not having been a personal entity, becomes one?

P.—Nay, that cannot truly be said. . . .

(*This pair of questions is then put concerning* 'father,' 'brother' . . . 'deva,' 'human,' *and answered as above.*)

Th.—Granting the existence of a mother, is it for this reason that the person is known in the sense of a real and ultimate fact?

P.—Yes.

Th.—Is there anyone who, having been a mother, is no longer a mother?

P.—Yes.

Th.—Is there anyone who, having been a personal entity, is no longer one?

P.—Nay, that cannot truly be said. . . .

This last pair of questions is then put with respect to 'father' *and the rest, and answered as above.*

[221] *P.*—Is it wrong to say 'the person is known in the sense of a real and ultimate fact'?

Th.—Yes.

P.—Is there no such thing as a 'stream-winner' (or one who has entered the first stage of the way to salvation)?

Th.—Yes.

P.—If there be such a thing, then indeed, good sir, it is right to assent to the original proposition. Again, is there no such thing as a 'once-returner,' a 'no-returner,' an arahant,[1] one who is freed in both ways,[2] one who is

[1] Or those who are in the second, third, and ultimate stages respectively of the way to salvation.

[2] Cf. *Dialogues*, ii. 70; *Puggala-Paññatti*, I., § 30; viz., both temporarily and permanently, from both body and mind, by Jhāna and the Path respectively.

emancipated by understanding,[1] one who has the testimony within himself,[2] one who has arrived at right views, one who is emancipated by faith, one who marches along with wisdom,[3] one who marches along with faith?

Th.—Yes.

P.—Then surely, good sir, it is right to affirm the first proposition.

[222] *Th.*—Granted that there is such a thing as a 'stream-winner,' is it for that reason that the 'person' is known in the sense of a real and ultimate fact?

P.—Yes.

Th.—Is there anyone who, not having been a stream-winner, is one now?

P.—Yes.

Th.—Is there anyone who, not having been a 'person,' is one now?

P.—Nay, that cannot truly be said. . . .

Th.—Again, granted that there is such an one as a stream-winner, and that this is the reason for your affirmation as to the personal entity, is there anyone who having been a stream-winner, is so no longer?

P.—Yes.

Th.—Is there anyone who, not having been a person, is one now?

P.—Nay, that cannot truly be said. . . .

These questions are now put regarding the other designations, and are answered similarly.

[223] *P.*—If [as you say] it be wrong to assert 'the person is known, etc., . . .' are there not [the accepted terms of] 'the Four Pairs of men,' 'the Eight Individuals'?[4]

[1] Or intuition (paññā).

[2] Namely, that he has certain of the intoxicants destroyed. *Pugg. Paññ.*, I. § 32. For the remaining designations see *op. cit.*, § 33, f.

[3] The *Pugg. Paññ. Comy.* so paraphrases dhammānusārī: 'paññā is borne along and goes before.' *JPTS.*, 1914, p. 194. These are all terms apparently involving a permanent personal entity, from the opponent's point of view.

[4] I.e., those in the four paths (see above, § 221), and these divided into those who have attained one or other of the four paths and the four 'fruits' or fruitions (see prev. page).

Th.—Yes.

P.—But if that be so, surely it is right to speak of the 'person' as known in the sense of a real and ultimate fact.

[224] *Th.*—Granting that there are the Four, the Eight, is it *for this reason* you assert the first proposition?

P.—Yes.

Th.—Do the Four, the Eight, appear because of the Buddha's appearing?

Yes.

Does the 'person' appear because of the Buddha's appearing?

Nay, that cannot truly be said. . . .

I repeat the question.

Yes.

Then at the Buddha's final Nibbāna, is the 'person' annihilated, so that no personal entity exists?

Nay, that cannot truly be said. . . .

[225] *Th.*—The person [you say] is known in the sense of a real and ultimate fact—is the person conditioned?[1]

Nay, that cannot truly be said. . . .

Is the person unconditioned?

Nay, that cannot truly be said. . . .

Is he neither?

Nay, that cannot truly be said. . . .

I repeat my question.

Yes.

Apart from the conditioned or the unconditioned, is there another, a third alternative?[2]

Nay, that cannot truly be said. . . .

I repeat my question.

[1] This is an inquiry into the nature of 'a real and ultimate [or self-dependent] fact.' *Comy.* 'Conditioned' (sankhata) is, in Buddhist tradition, what has been prepared, brought about by something else, made, has come together by conditions (*Comy.* on A., i. 152). The opponent's desire to get puggala outside the category of all phenomena brings him into a somewhat 'tight place.'

[2] Koṭi, literally extreme, or point, or end.

Yes.

But was it not said by the Exalted One: '*There are, bhikkhus, these two irreducible categories—what are the two? The irreducible category of the conditioned, the irreducible category of the unconditioned. These are the two*'?[1]

Is the Suttanta thus?

Yes.

Hence it is surely wrong to say that apart from the conditioned and the unconditioned, there is another, a third alternative.

[226] *Th.* (*continues*).—You say that the person is neither conditioned nor unconditioned? Are then the conditioned, the unconditioned, the person, entirely different things?

Nay, that cannot truly be said. . . .

Are the aggregates conditioned, Nibbāna unconditioned, the person neither conditioned nor unconditioned?

Yes.

Then are the aggregates, Nibbāna, and the person, three entirely different things?

Nay, that cannot truly be said. . . .

(*The last two questions are then applied to each aggregate taken separately*:—material qualities, feeling, perception, mental co-efficients, consciousness).

[227] *Th.*—Is the genesis of the person apparent, and its passing away also, and is its duration distinctively apparent?

Yes.

[Then] is the person conditioned?

Nay, that cannot truly be said. . . .

It was said by the Exalted One: '*Bhikkhus, there are these three characteristics of the conditioned: of conditioned things the genesis is apparent, the passing away is apparent, the duration*[2] *amidst change is apparent.*' Hence if these three are characteristics of the person, this is also

[1] Cf. *Dīgha-Nik.*, iii. 274.

[2] Ṭhitassa aññathattaŋ, literally 'duration's *other-ness*.' Buddhaghosa paraphrases by jarā, decay. *Anguttara-Nik.*, i. 152. See Note on *Ṭhiti*, Appendix.

conditioned. Are these three characteristics *not* apparent in the person?

No, they are not apparent.

Then is the person unconditioned?

Nay, that cannot truly be said. . . .

It was said by the Exalted One: '*Bhikkhus, there are these three characteristics of the unconditioned: of unconditioned things, bhikkhus, the genesis is not apparent, the passing away is not apparent, the duration amidst change is not apparent.*'[1] Now if all these [as you say] do not characterize the [notion of] 'person,' the person is unconditioned.

[228] *Th.*—The person who has attained final Nibbāna, does he exist in the Goal,[2] or does he not exist therein?

He exists in the Goal.

Is then the person who has finally attained eternal?

Nay, that cannot truly be said. . . .

Is the person who has attained final Nibbāna and does not exist in the Goal annihilated?

Nay, that cannot truly be said. . . .

[228*a*] *Th.*—On what does the person depend in order to persist?

P.—He persists through dependence on coming-to-be.[3]

Th.—Is [the state of] coming-to-be impermanent, conditioned, arisen through a cause, liable to perish, to pass away, to become passionless, to cease, to change?

P.—Yes.

[1] *Op. et loc. cit.*

[2] Parinibbuto puggalo atth' atthambinatth' atthambi? The idiom is unusual for the Piṭakas, and in this connection, we believe, unique. The *Comy.* explains: 'atthaŋ pucchati nibbānaŋ, "He asks about the goal (or the Good), Nibbāna." P. rejects both the following questions, lest he be thought either an Eternalist or an Annihilationist.' 'Attained final Nibbāna' could of course be rendered more literally 'has utterly become extinct.'

[3] Bhavaŋ, or existence; but 'existence' is better reserved for atthitā. The *Comy.* paraphrases by upapattibhāvaŋ, the state of being reborn.

Th.—Is the person also impermanent, conditioned, arisen through a cause, liable to perish, to pass away, to become passionless, to cease, to change?

P.—Nay, that cannot truly be said. . . .

[229] *P.*—Is it wrong to say 'the person is known in the sense of a real and ultimate fact'?

Th.—Yes.

P.—Is there no one who, on feeling pleasurable feeling, knows that he is feeling it?[1]

Th.—Yes.

P.—Surely, if that be so, good sir, it is right to say 'the person is known in the sense of a real and ultimate fact' . . . and if he, on feeling painful feeling, knows that he is feeling it—you admit this?—it is right to say 'the person is known,' etc. So also for neutral feeling.

[230] *Th.*—I note what you affirm. Now is it *for this reason* that you maintain the person to be known in the sense of a real and ultimate fact?

P.—Yes.

Th.—Then is one who, on feeling pleasurable feeling, knows he is feeling it, a personal entity, and is one who, on that occasion, does not know, *not* a personal entity?

P.—Nay, that cannot truly be said. . . .

Th.—You deny this also in the case of painful and neutral feeling?

P.—Yes, that cannot truly be said. . . .

Th.—But you maintain, *because of this self-awareness*, that the person is known in the sense of a real and ultimate fact?

P.—Yes.

Th.—Is then pleasurable feeling one thing and the self-conscious enjoyer another?

P.—Nay, that cannot truly be said. . . .

(*Same query and answer in the case of painful and neutral feelings.*)

[1] 'The earnest student (y o g ā v a c a r a) knows; the fool and average man does not.'—*Comy.*

[231] *P.*—You deny that the person is known in the sense of a real and ultimate fact:—Is there then no one who may be occupied in contemplating the [concept of] body with respect to his physical frame?

Yes.

. . . or in contemplating [the concept of] feeling, or consciousness, or certain mental properties[1] with respect to these in himself, respectively?

Yes.

Then surely, good sir, it is right to say as I do with respect to the person.

[232] *Th.*—Granting the carrying out by anyone of the four applications in mindfulness, is it *for this reason* that you say as you do with respect to the personal entity?

Yes.

Then is anyone when so engaged a person, and not, when he is not so engaged?

Nay, that cannot truly be said. . . .

[233] *Th.*—Or again, granting [as above] . . . is 'body' one thing, the contemplator another? and so for 'feeling,' etc.?

Nay, that cannot truly be said. . . .

[234] *Th.*—Is the person known in the sense of a real and ultimate fact?

Yes.

Was it not said by the Exalted One:

'O Mogharājan! look upon the world
As void [of soul],[2] and ever heedful bide.

[1] The reference is to the religious exercise in self-knowledge known as the four Sati-paṭṭhāna's, or 'applications in mindfulness.' These properties are traditionally explained as the cetasika-dhammā (see below . . .), but Ledi Sadaw judges otherwise. See *Compendium*, 179, *n*, 3. The Animist holds that introspective exercise involves a persisting identical subject.

[2] Cf. *Saṃyutta-Nik.*, iv. 54. 'Void' implies 'of soul.' 'Contemplate the world of aggregates as void of entities.'—*Comy.*

Cut out the world's opinions as to soul.
So shalt thou get past death; so an thou look,
The king of death shall no more look on thee'? [1]

Is it thus in the Suttanta?

Yes.

Hence it is surely wrong to say that the person is known in the sense of a real and ultimate fact.

[235] *Th.*—Is it the person [or soul] here who 'looks upon'?

Yes.

Does he contemplate with or without material qualities?

With them.

Is that soul the same as that body?

Nay, that cannot truly be said. . . .

But if he contemplates without material qualities, is that soul quite different from that body?

Nay, that cannot truly be said. . . .

Th.—[I ask again] is it the [soul or] person who contemplates?

Yes.

Does he contemplate when he has gone within, or does he contemplate from without [the organism]?

He contemplates when he has gone within.

Is that soul that body?

Nay, that cannot truly be said. . . .

Supposing he contemplates from without, is the soul one thing, the body another?

Nay, that cannot truly be said. . . .

[236] *P*—Is it wrong to say 'the person is known in the sense of a real and ultimate fact'?

Th.—Yes.

P.—Was not the Exalted One a speaker of truth,[2] a speaker in season,[3] a speaker of facts,[3] a speaker of words that are right,[4] that are not wrong, that are not ambiguous?

[1] *Sutta-Nipāta*, ver. 1119.

[2] *Dialogues*, i. 4; *Psalms of the Sisters*, lxvi.

[3] *Digha-Nik.*, iii. 175; *Anguttara-Nik.*, v. 205.

[4] *Anguttara-Nik.*, ii. 24; *Iti-vuttaka*, § 112.

Th.—Yes.

P.—Now it was said by the Exalted One: '*There is the person who works for his own good . . .*'[1]

Is the Suttanta thus?

Th.—Yes.

P.—Hence surely the person is known in the sense of a real and ultimate fact.

[237] . . . again, it was said by the Exalted One: '*There is one person, bhikkhus, who, being reborn in this world, is born for the good, for the happiness of many, to show compassion on the world, for the advantage, the good, the happiness of devas and of men.*'[2]

Is the Suttanta thus?

Th.—Yes.

P.—Hence surely the person is known in the sense of a real and ultimate fact.

[238] *Th.*—Granting this, and also the veracity, etc., of the Exalted One:—it was said by the Exalted One: '*All things are without soul.*'[3]

Is the Suttanta thus?

P.—Yes.

Th.—Hence surely it is wrong to say the person is known in the sense of a real and ultimate fact.

[239] . . . again, it was said by the Exalted One: '*He does not doubt that misery arises, comes to pass, that misery ceases, passes away, nor is he perplexed thereat. And thereupon independent insight*[4] *comes herein to him. Now this, Kaccāna, thus far is right views.*'[5]

Is the Suttanta thus?

[1] See § 74.

[2] *Anguttara-Nik.*, i. 22; quoted in *Questions of King Milinda*, ii. 56.

[3] Attā. *Dhammapada*, ver. 279; *Saṃyutta-Nik.*, iv. 28.

[4] A-para-paccaya-ñāṇaṃ, 'insight not conditioned by others.'

[5] *Saṃyutta-Nik.*, ii. 17; iii. 135. The quotation does not obviously bear on the controverted point to us, but to a Buddhist versed in his Suttas the context (*apparently a familiar one*) arises: Insight comes to him who has rejected the theories that the world is a persisting entity, or a concourse of fortuitous illusions, being convinced that it is, in its essentials, a cosmos of conditioned becoming.

P.—Yes.

Th.—Hence surely it is wrong to say 'the person is known,' etc.

[240] *Th.*—. . . again, was it not said by Bhikkhunī Vajirā to Māra the evil one:

> '"*Being*"?[1] *What dost thou fancy by that word?*
> *'Mong false opinions, Māra, art thou strayed.*
> *This a mere bundle of formations is.*
> *Therefrom no "being" mayest thou obtain.*
> *For e'en as, when the factors are arranged,*
> *The product by the name "chariot" is known,*
> *So doth our usage covenant to say:*
> *"A being," when the aggregates are there.*
> *'Tis simply Ill that riseth, simply Ill*[2]
> *That doth persist, and then fadeth away.*
> *Nought beside Ill there is that comes to be;*
> *Nought else but Ill there is that fades away'?*[3]

Is the Suttanta thus?

P.—Yes.

[241] *Th.*— . . . again, did not the venerable Ānanda say to the Exalted One: '*It is said, lord, "the world is void, the world is void." Now in what way, lord, is it meant that the world is void?*' [and did not the Exalted One reply:] '*Inasmuch, Ānanda, as it is void of soul*[4] *and of what belongs to soul,*[5] *therefore is the world called void. And wherein, Ananda, is it void of soul and of what belongs to soul? The eye, Ānanda, is verily void of soul and of what belongs to soul, so is visible object and the sense and contact of sight. So are the other organs, and objects of the senses, and the other senses. So is the co-ordinating organ, cognizable objects, mental consciousness and contact. All are void of soul and of what belongs to soul. And whatever pleasurable, painful, or neutral feeling*

[1] Satta.

[2] On this term see Ledi Sadaw, *J.P.T.S.*, 1914, 133 f., and Mrs. Rh. D., *Buddhist Psychology*, 1914, p. 83 f.

[3] *Saṃyutta-Nik.*, i. 134 f.; *Pss. Sisters*, 190. Her verses are not in the Anthology of the Therīs or Senior Sisters. She is not called Therī, but only Bhikkhunī.

[4] Attā.

[5] Attaniya.

arises, in relation to the senses, and the sense-co-ordinating mind, that too is void of soul and of what belongs to soul. It is for this, Ānanda, that the world is said to be void' ? [1]

Is the Suttanta thus?

P.—Yes.

[242] *Th.*—. . . again, whereas you affirm that the person is known, etc. . . . and we know the veracity, etc., of the Exalted One, it was said by the Exalted One: '*Bhikkhus, if there were soul, should I have that which belongs to a soul?*[2] *Or if there were that which belongs to soul, should I have a soul? In both cases ye would reply: "Yea, lord." But both soul and that which belongs to soul being in very truth and for ever impossible to be known, then this that is a stage of opinion, namely : "* that *is the world,* that *is the soul, this I shall hereafter become, permanent, constant, eternal, unchangeable—so shall I abide even like unto the Eternal—is not this, bhikkhus, absolutely and entirely a doctrine of fools?" "Whatever it be not, lord, it surely is, absolutely and entirely a doctrine of fools."* ' [3]

Is the Suttanta thus?

P.—Yes.

[243] *Th.*— . . . again, it was said by the Exalted One: '*There are these three teachers, Seniya, to be found in the world—who are the three? There is first, Seniya, that kind of teacher who declares that there is a real, persistent soul in the life that now is, and in that which is to come; then there is the kind of teacher, Seniya, who declares that there is a real, persistent soul in the life that now is, but not a soul in a future life; lastly, there is a certain teacher who does not declare that there is a soul either in the life that now is, nor in that which is to come. The first, Seniya, of these three is called an Eternalist, the second is called an Annihilationist; the third of these, he, Seniya, is called the teacher, who is Buddha supreme.*[4] *These are the three teachers to be found in the world.*'[5]

[1] *Saṃyutta-N.*, iv. 54.

[2] Attā, attaniya.

[3] *Majjhima-Nik.*, i. 138.

[4] More literally, perfectly enlightened (sammā sambuddho).

[5] We cannot trace this quotation.

Is the Suttanta thus?

P.—Yes.

Th.— . . . again, did the Exalted One speak of 'a butter-jar'?[1]

P.—Yes.

Th.—Is there anyone who can make a jar out of butter?

P.—Nay, that cannot truly be said. . . .

Th. . . . finally, did the Exalted One speak of an oil-jar, a honey-jar, a molasses-jar, a milk-pail, a water-pot, a cup, flask, bowl of water, a 'meal provided in perpetuity,' a 'constant supply of congey'?[2]

P.—Yes.

Th.—Is there any supply of congey that is permanent, stable, eternal, not liable to change?

P.—Nay, that cannot truly be said. . . .

Th.—Hence it is surely wrong to say 'the soul is known in the sense of a real and ultimate fact.'

[1] Nor this. But the *Comy.* remarks: 'The following is adduced to show that meaning is not always according to the form of what is said. A gold jar is made of gold; a butter-jar is not made of butter, nor is an oil-jar made of oil, and so on. A meal instituted in perpetuity by charity is not eternal and permanent as is Nibbāna.

[2] E.g., *Vinaya*, iv. 74; *Jātaka*, i. 178 (trans., i. 60). The argument is that to use such terms as p u g g a l a, being, etc., in their popular conventional sense, as the Buddha did when teaching the laity, by no means confers upon the transient aggregates so called any ultimate or philosophical reality, any more than to speak of a constant supply of food implies any eternal, immutable source. 'Given bodily and mental aggregates,' concludes the Commentator in his peroration, 'it is customary to say such and such a name, a family. This by popular convention means "a person." Hereon it was said by the Exalted One: "These are merely names, expressions, turns of speech, designations in common use in the world" (*Dialogues*, i. 263). . . . The Buddhas have two kinds of discourse, the popular and the philosophical. The latter is, as a rule, too severe to begin with, therefore they take the former first. But both first and last they teach consistently and in conformity with truth according to the method selected.'

2. *Of Falling Away.*

Controverted Point.—That an Arahant can fall away from Arahantship.

From the Commentary.—Because of such statements in the Suttas as 'liability to fall away, and the opposite, these two things, bhikkhus, are concerned with the falling away of a bhikkhu who is training';[1] and 'these five things, bhikkhus, are concerned with the falling away of a bhikkhu who now and then attains emancipation,'[2] certain sects in the Order incline to the belief that an Arahant can fall away. These are the Sammitiyas, the Vajjiputtiyas, the Sabbatthivādins, and some of the Mahāsanghikas. Hence, whether it be their view or that of others, the Theravādin, in order to break them of it asks this question.'[3]

I.—APPLYING THE THESIS.

[1][4] *Th.*—Your assertion that an Arahant may fall away from Arahantship involves the admission also of the following: that he may fall away *anywhere;* [2] *at any time;* [3] that *all* Arahants are liable to fall away; [4] that an Arahant is liable to fall away not only from Arahantship, but from all four of the Path-fruitions. [5] Just as a man may still be rich if he lose one lakh in four lakhs, but must, you would say, lose all four to lose his title to the status given him by the four.

1 *Anguttara-Nikāya*, i. 96.

2 *Ibid.*, iii. 173.

3 'Falling away' is, more literally, declined, the opposite of growth. See *Dialogues*, ii. 82 f. The *Comy.* continues: '"Falling away" is twofold—from what is won, and from what is not yet won. "The venerable Godhika fell away from that emancipation of will which was intermittent only" (Br., sāmayikāla, or, PTS, samādhikāyā: which comes of concentrative exercise, *Saŋyutta-Nikāya*, i. 120), illustrates the former. "See that the reward of your recluseship fall not away for you who are seeking it, [while yet more remains to be done!]" (*Majjhima-N.*, i. 271) illustrates the latter.'

4 We have, for the remainder of the work, applied just sufficient condensation to eliminate most of the dialogue as such, with its abundant repetitions of the point controverted, and have endeavoured to reproduce all the stages of argument and the matter adduced therein.

II. REFUTATION BY COMPARING CLASSES OF ARIYANS.[1]

[6] If an Arahant may fall away, then must those in the three lower Stages or Paths—the Never-Returners, the Once-Returners, the Stream-Winners—also be held liable to fall away and lose their respective fruits.[2]

[7] If an Arahant may fall away, so as to be established only in the next lower fruit, then must an analogous falling away be held possible in the case of the other three classes, so that those in the first stage who fall away are 'established' only as average worldlings. Further,

If the Arahant fall away so as to be established in the first fruit only, then must he, in regaining Arahantship, realize it next after the first fruit.[3]

[8] If an Arahant may fall away from Arahantship who has admittedly put away more corruptions[4] than any of those in the three lower stages, surely these may always fall away from their respective fruits. Why deny this liability in their case (9-13), and assert it only with respect to the Arahant?

[14-20] If an Arahant may fall away from Arahantship who admittedly excels all others in culture of the [Eightfold] Path, of the Earnest Applications of Mindfulness, of the Supreme Efforts, the Four Steps to Potency of Will, the Controlling Powers and Forces, and of the Seven Factors of Enlightenment, why deny that those who have cultivated these [thirty-seven matters pertaining to Enlightenment[5]] in a lesser degree may no less fall away from their respective fruits?

[21-32] Similarly, if each and all of the Four Truths —the fact of Ill, the Cause of it, the Cessation of it, the Way to the cessation of it—have been seen by the Arahant

[1] Viz., all who are graduating or have graduated in Arahantship.

[2] Or fruition; the conscious realization or assurance (to borrow a Christian term) of the specified attainment.

[3] Thus violating the constant four-graded order.

[4] Literally, torments, k i l e s ā, i.e., vices causing torment. On these ten see below, and *Bud. Psych. Ethics*, p. 327 f.

[5] On these see *Dialogues*, ii. 129 f.; *Compendium*, pt. vii., § 6.

no less than by the three lower Paths, why maintain only of the Arahant that he can fall away?

[33] You cannot assert that the Arahant, who has put away lust[1] and all the other corruptions, may fall away from Arahantship, and yet deny that the Stream-Winner, who [on his part] has put away the theory of soul,[2] may also fall away from his fruit; or deny either that the latter, who [on his part] has also put away doubt, the contagion of mere rule and ritual, or the passions, ill-will and nescience, all three entailing rebirth on planes of misery, may also fall away. Or [34], similarly, deny that the Once-Returner, who [on his part] has put away the theory of a soul, doubt, the contagion of mere rule and ritual, gross sensuous passions, coarse forms of ill-will, may also fall away from his fruit. Or [35], similarly, deny that the Never-Returner, who [on his part] has put away the theory of soul, doubt, the contagion of mere rule and ritual, the residuum[3] of sensuous passion and ill-will, may also fall away from his fruit. Or analogously [36] assert that the Never-Returner can fall away, but that the Stream-Winner cannot, or [37], that the Once-Returner cannot. Or, analogously [38], assert that the Once-Returner can fall away, but that the Stream-Winner cannot.

Conversely [39], you cannot maintain that the Stream-Winner, who has [of course] put away theory of soul, etc., cannot fall away from his fruit, without maintaining as much for the Arahant who [on his part] has put away the passions of appetite and all the other corruptions.[4] Nor, similarly [40-4], can you maintain that anyone of the four

[1] Rāga, or lobha, understood as appetite or greed in general.

[2] Sakkāyadiṭṭhi. On this term see *Bud. Psy. Ethics*, 247, *n.* 2. This and the next two vices are the first three 'fetters' destroyed by those in the first Path. Rhys Davids, *American Lectures*, p. 146 f.

[3] Literally, accompanied by a minimum of (aṇu-sahagato). In the *Dhammasangaṇi*, and below (iv. 10), this work of diminishing is worded differently. See *Bud. Psy. Ethics*, p. 96, and *n.* 1.

[4] Namely, hate, nescience, or dulness, conceit, error, doubt, stolidity, excitement, unconscientiousness, disregard of blame, or indiscretion.

Classes cannot fall away, without maintaining as much for any other of the four.

[45] You admit all the achievements and qualifications conveyed by the terms and phrases associated [in the Suttas] with the position of Arahant :—

That he has 'put away passion or lust, cut it off at the root, made it as the stump of a palm tree, incapable of renewing its existence, not subject to recrudescence,'[1] and has also so put away the remaining [nine] corruptions—hate, nescience, conceit, etc.

[46] That, in order so to put away each and all of the corruptions, he has cultivated—

the Path,
the Earnest Applications of Mindfulness,
the Supreme Efforts,
the Steps to Potency of Will,
the Controlling Powers and Forces,
the Factors of Enlightenment ;[2]

[47] That he has [consummated as having] 'done with lust, done with hate, done with nescience,'[3] that he is one by whom

'that which was to be done is done,'
'the burden is laid down,
the good supreme is won,
the fetter of becoming is wholly broken away,'

one who is 'emancipated through perfect knowledge,'[4] who has 'lifted the bar,' 'filled up the trenches,' 'who has drawn out,' 'is without lock or bolt,' an Ariyan, one for whom 'the banner is lowered,' 'the burden is fallen,' who is 'detached,'[5] 'conqueror of a realm well conquered,'[6] who

[1] *Anguttara-Nik.*, i. 218 (elsewhere connected with taṇhā, natural desire).

[2] See above, §§ 14-29.

[3] *Pss. Brethren*, p. 193.

[4] The epithets named thus far recur frequently as one of the refrains of Arahantship, e.g., *Anguttara-Nik.*, iii. 359.

[5] These are all discussed in *Majjhima-Nik.*, i. 139.

[6] We cannot trace this simile *verbatim*. Differently worded, it occurs, e.g., in *Iti-vuttaka*, § 82.

has 'comprehended Ill, has put away its cause, has realized its cessation, has cultivated the Path [thereto],'[1] who has 'understood that which is to be understood,[2] comprehended that which is to be comprehended, put away that which is to be put away, developed that which is to be developed, realized that which is to be realized.'[3]

How then can you say that an Arahant can fall away from Arahantship?

[48] With respect to your modified statement, that only the Arahant, who now and then [*i.e.*, in Jhāna] reaches emancipation, falls away, but not the Arahant who is at any and all seasons emancipated:—

[49-51] I ask, does the former class of Arahant, who has put away each and all of the corruptions, who has cultivated each and all of the matters or states pertaining to enlightenment, who deserves each and all of the aforesaid terms and phrases associated with Arahantship, fall away from Arahantship?

[52-54] For you admit that the latter class of Arahant, who has done and who has deserved as aforesaid, does not fall away. If you admit also, with respect to the former class, that all these qualities make falling away from Arahantship impossible, then it is clear that the matter of occasional, or of constant realization of emancipation does not affect the argument.

[55] Can you give instances of Arahants falling away from Arahantship? Did Sāriputta? Or the Great Moggallāna? Or the Great Kassapa? Or the Great Kaccāyana? Or the great Koṭṭhita? Or the Great Panthaka?[4] Of all you admit that they did not.

[1] The noble or Ariyan Eightfold Path.

[2] Esp. the five aggregates. *Saŋyutta-Nik.*, iii. 26, etc.

[3] On all these four see *Dīgha Nik.*, iii. 280 f.

[4] On all of these *Pss. of the Brethren* may be consulted. Koṭṭhita in some MSS. is Koṭṭhika.

PROOF FROM THE SUTTAS.

[56] You say that an Arahant may fall away from Arahantship. But was it not said by the Exalted One :—

'*Both high and low the ways the learners wend :*
So hath the Holy One to man revealed.
Not twice they fare who reach the further shore,
Nor once [alone that goal] doth fill their thought ?'[1]

Hence you are wrong.

[57] . . . Again, is there to be a 'cutting of what has been cut ?' For was it not said by the Exalted One :—

'*He who with cravings conquered grasps at naught,*
For whom no work on self is still unwrought,
Is need for cutting what is cut yet there ?
All perils swept away, the Flood, the Snare.'[2]

[58] . . . Again, your proposition implies that there is a reconstructing of what is already done. But this is not for the Arahant, for was it not said by the Exalted One :—

'*For such a Brother rightly freed, whose heart*
Hath peace, there is no building up again,
Nor yet remaineth, aught for him to do.
Like to a rock that is a monolith,
And trembleth never in the windy blast,
So all the world of sights and tastes and sounds,
Odours and tangibles, yea, things desired
And undesirable can ne'er excite
A man like him. His heart stands firm, detached,
And of all that he notes the passing hence ?'[3]

Hence there is no reconstructing what is already done.

[1] *Sutta-Nipāta*, ver. 714. The *Comy.* explains 'high and low ways' by easy or painful progress, as formulated in *Bud. Psy. Eth.*, p. 54.

[2] Untraced except the first line, for which see *Sutta-Nipāta*, ver. 741; *Anguttara-Nik.*, ii. 10; *Iti-vuttaka*, §§ 15, 105.

[3] *Anguttara-Nik.*, iii. 378; *Pss. of the Brethren*, vers. 642-4.

[59] *S.V.S.M*:[1]—Then our proposition according to you is wrong. But was it not said by the Exalted One:—

'*Bhikkhus, there are these five things which conduce to the falling away of a bhikkhu who is intermittently emancipated:—which are the five? Delight in business, in talk, in sleep, in society, absence of reflection on how his heart is emancipated?*'[2]

Hence the Arahant may fall away.

[60] *Th.*—But does the Arahant delight in any of those things? If you deny, how can they conduce to his falling away? If you assent, you are admitting that an Arahant is affected and bound by worldly desires—which of course you deny.

[61] Now if an Arahant were falling away from Arahantship, it would be, you say, because he is assailed by lust, or hate, or error. Such an attack, you say further, is in consequence of a corresponding latent bias.[3] Yet if I ask you whether an Arahant harbours any one of the seven forms of latent bias—sensuality, enmity, conceit, erroneous opinion, doubt, lust for rebirth, ignorance—you must deny such a thing.

[62] Or if, in his falling away, he is, you say, accumulating lust, belief in a soul, doubt, or the taint of mere rule and ritual, these are not vices you would impugn an Arahant withal.

[63] In fact you admit that an Arahant neither heaps up nor pulls down, neither puts away nor grasps at, neither scatters nor binds, neither disperses nor collects, but that, having pulled down, put away, scattered, dispersed, so abides.

Hence it surely cannot be said that 'An Arahant may fall away from Arahantship.'[2]

[1] Any of the four sects holding the controverted view.

[2] *Anguttara-Nik.*, iii. 173.

[3] See below, ix. 4.

3. *Of the Higher Life.*

Controverted Point.—That there is no higher life among the devas.[1]

From the Commentary.—'The higher life[2] is of twofold import: path-culture and renunciation of the world. No deva practises the latter. But the former is not forbidden them, except to those of the unconscious plane. But some, for instance the Sammitiyas, do not believe in any path-culture among the higher devas of the Kāmaloka, and, beyond them, of the Rūpaloka, justifying themselves by the Suttanta passage cited below.'

The Theravādin speaks:—

[1] You deny the practice of the higher life among devas; yet you deny also [that they are physically, mentally, or morally defective]:—that they are, any of them, stupid, deaf and dumb, unintelligent, communicating by signs,[3] and incapable of discerning the meaning of what is well or badly spoken; that they all lack faith in the Buddha, the Doctrine, the Order; that they did not attend the Exalted Buddha; ask him questions and delight in his answers; that they are all of them handicapped by their actions, by the corruptions, by the effect of their actions; that they are all faithless, devoid of purpose and understanding, incapable of reaching the right Order of the Path[4] in things that are good; that they are matricides, parricides, murderers of saints, shedders of holy blood, schismatics; that they all take life, steal, are unchaste, liars,

[1] On 'deva' see above, p. 28, *n.* 1.

[2] Brahmacariyavāsa, or best-conduct-living. The Sammitiya holds by the externals; the Therāvadin is more concerned with the essential ethical career.

[3] Explained in the *Comy.* by mugā viya hattha muddāya vattāro, 'like dumb speakers by signs made by the hands.' On such language cf. *Dialogues*, i. 21, *n.* 4, or *Dīgha-Nik.*, i. 11, § 25.

[4] Sammattaŋ (Sansk., samyaktva, abstract noun of sammā; ref. wrongly given in *JPTS*, 1910, p. 116, *s.v.*, § II.). Sammatta-niyāmo (opposed to micchatta-niyāmo, the wrong, vicious order of things), the right law or order, insuring against rebirth in purgatory, involving final salvation. Cf. v. 4; xii. 5.

slanderers, revilers, idle talkers, given to covetousness, ill-will and erroneous opinion.

[2] Nay, you maintain on the other hand that they are, and practise the opposite of all this. How then can you say there is no religious life among them?

The Sammitiya speaks :—

[3] You maintain the thesis in the affirmative, and yet you deny that devas practise renouncing the world, the tonsure, wearing the yellow robes, carrying the beggar's bowl; you deny that either a Supremely Awakened one, or those enlightened for self only,[1] or the pair of chief disciples,[2] appear among the devas. Where then is their 'religious life'?

Theravādin speaks :—

[4-7] We agree that among the gods these practices and advents are not found. But is the religious life found only where these things are observed—the renunciation, the tonsure and the rest—and not where they are not observed? Only there, you say; and yet when I ask: 'Does he who renounces the world, and so forth, lead the religious life, and does he who does not renounce the world, etc., not lead the religious life,' you do not agree.[3]

[8] Again, do you maintain that only where Buddhas arise is there religious life, and that where they do not arise, there is none? You vacillate in your reply. Now the Exalted One was born in Lumbinī, became supremely enlightened at the foot of the Bodhi Tree, and set turning the Norm-Wheel at Benares. Is the religious life to be observed in those places only and not elsewhere?

[9] I ask a similar question with regard to the Middle Country,[4] where there have been advents of those awakened

[1] Pacceka-Buddhas, who did not teach the world.

[2] On these, believed to attend every Buddha, see *Dialogues*, ii. 7.

[3] Because of the attainment of the Path by laymen, and by some of the devas.—*Comy.*

[4] Roughly speaking, the Ganges valley, or the whole of Aryan North India. See Rhys Davids in *JRAS*, 1904, 83 f.

for self alone, and [10] with regard to the Magadhese,[1] where there was the advent of a chief pair of disciples.

[11] *S.*—You claim that the religious life is practised among devas, yet you deny that it is universally practised, for instance, among the devas of the 'unconscious sphere.'

Th.—This is only what we should both claim and deny for mankind, for instance, that whereas the religious life is practised among men, it is not practised among the untutored barbarians of the border countries, where there is no rebirth of such as become religieux of either sex, or of believing laymen and laywomen.

[12] *S.*—You say with respect to the religious life in deva-worlds, 'There are spheres where it exists, there are other spheres where it does not':—are both these conditions represented in the unconscious sphere, and both in the worlds of conscious devas? If not, then where does it exist and where does it not exist?

Th.—The religious life exists only among such devas as are conscious.

[13] *Th.*—You admit that the religious life is practised among men.

S.—In certain places only, not in others.

Th.—Do you mean to say that both kind of places are represented in the outlying border countries, among untrained barbarians, where none are born who become religieux or pious laymen and laywomen? If not, how can you claim that the religious life is practised at all? Where is it practised?

S.—In the Middle Country, not in the outlying border countries.

[14] *S.*—But was it not said by the Exalted One: '*In three respects, bhikkhus, do the people of India excel both those of North Kuru and the Three-and-Thirty gods: —in courage, in mindfulness, and in the religious life*?'[2]

[1] Cf. *Vinaya Texts*, i. 144 f.; *Pss. of the Brethren*, 340 f.

[2] *Anguttara-Nik.*, iv. 396.

Is the Suttanta thus? Does it not show there is no religious life among devas?

Th.—Did not the Exalted One say at Sāvatthī: '*Here the religious life is practised?*'[1] And does this show that it was only practised at Sāvatthī, and not elsewhere?

[15] Again, the Never-Returner, for whom the five 'lower fetters' are done away with, but not, as yet, the five 'upper fetters,' deceases 'here,' is reborn 'there'[2]— where for him does the fruit [of his works] arise? 'There,' and only there, you say. How then can you deny religious life among the devas?

[16] For when such an one is reborn 'there,' it is there that he 'gets rid of the burden,' there that he comprehends the nature of Ill, there that he puts away the corruptions, there that he realizes the cessation [of Ill], there that he has intuition of the immutable. What then do you mean when you say, 'There is no religious life among the devas?'

S.—Because it was *here* that he practised that Path of which he *there* realizes the fruit.

[17] *Th.*—If you admit that the Never-Returner realizes fruit *there* by the Path practised *here*, you must also admit that the Stream-Winner realizes fruit *here* by path-practice *there*. You must, similarly, admit that the Once-Returner and the person completing existence[3] *here*, realize *here* the fruit won by path-practice *there*.

Further, since you do admit that the Stream-Winner realizes fruit *here* won by path-practice *here*, you must admit that the Never-Returner may, similarly, realize fruit

[1] We cannot trace this quotation.

[2] I.e., in the heavens called 'Pure Abodes.'—*Comy*. There, and and not on earth, he was believed to complete existence (parinibbāyati). In the Suttanta phrase, he became a '*there*-utter-going-outer' (tattha-parinibbāyī), e.g., *Majjh. Nik.*, ii. 146; *Anguttara-Nik.*, i. 232, etc. The Pure Abodes were the summit of the Rūpa-heaven, the limit of *material*, if ethereal, rebirth. See *Compendium*, p. 138 f.

[3] Parinibbāyī puggalo. The latter word is now used in its common or popular meaning—the only meaning accepted in Theravāda.

there won by path-practice *there*. Again, just as you admit that the Once-Returner and the person completing existence may, by path-practice *here*, realize fruit *here*, so must you similarly admit that the Never-Returner may realize fruit *there* won by path-practice *there*.

[18] If you declare that a person who, 'leaving this life, attains consummation [in the Pure Abodes],'[1] practises the path without putting away the corruptions, you must admit it no less in the case of a person who has worked for the realization of the fruit of Stream-Winning, or the fruit of the One-Return, or the fruit of Arahantship.

Again, if you declare that a person who has worked for the realization of the fruit of Stream-Winning, or for the fruit of the One-Return, or for that of Arahantship, practises the path and puts away the corruptions simultaneously, you must also admit as much in his case who, leaving this life, attains consummation [in the Pure Abodes].

[19] You are admitting [by the position taken up with regard to the thesis], that a Never-Returning person, when he is reborn *there*, has 'done that which was to be done,'[2] is in the condition of having practised. But this is tantamount to declaring that the Arahant is reborn,—that the Arahant goes from one life to another, goes from one destination to another, goes from one cycle to another of renewed life, goes from one rebirth to another—which of course you deny.

You cannot, again, admit those qualifications in the Never-Returner and deny him those of 'one who has got rid of the burden,'[2] when he is reborn *there*; for then you must admit that he will [there] practise the path again[3] to get rid of the burden

[20] Similarly, whatever other attainments in the re-

[1] Idha-vihāya-niṭṭho puggalo='a Never-Returner who consummates after leaving this life.'—*Comy.*

[2] A phrase always associated with Arahantship. See above, 2, § 47.

[3] This would bring 'the religious life' into the life of the devas, the Never-Returner being then reborn, finally, as a deva of the Pure Abodes.

ligious life you withhold from the Never-Returner on his final rebirth there:—understanding of Ill, putting away of corruptions, realization of the cessation of Ill, intuition of the immutable—you compel him, in order to win them, to 'practise the path' [among the devas as deva]. Else you declare implicitly that he there completes existence without winning one or the other of them.

[21] *S.*—Just as a deer wounded by an arrow, though he may run far, yet dies of his hurt, even so does the Never-Returner, by the path here practised, realize there the fruit thereof.

Th.—The deer wounded by an arrow, though he run far, yet dies of his hurt with the arrow in him. But does the Never-Returner, when by the path here practised he there realizes the fruit thereof, bear the arrow with him?[1]

S.—Nay, that cannot truly be said.

---

4. *Of Purification Piecemeal.*

Controverted Point.—That [the converted man] gives up the corruptions piecemeal.[2]

From the Commentary.—'This discussion is to break down the opinion, held now by the Sammitiyas and others, that when Stream-Winners and those in the other paths, through the higher comprehension gained in jhāna, attain insight into the nature of Ill and so on,

---

[1] The simile is not apt in so far as the Non-Returner's final birth 'there' is likened to the dying only of the deer, and not to the last, expiring run before it sinks dying. The arrow, for the Never-Returner, has still work to do. Only for the Arahant is its work done. The former, as *deva*, has one more spell of running to do.

[2] Odhis-odhiso. This term is applied also, in the *Paṭisambhidā-magga* (ii. 130), to the more specialized variety of the 'love-irradiating' contemplation prescribed as a religious exercise, anodhiso being the more catholic form of the same. As we pointed out, in reviewing this work (*JRAS*, 1908, p. 591), in a corresponding differentiation in the *Jātaka Atthakathā* (i. 80 f.; ii. 61), the word appears as an-odissaka. We have not found either variant elsewhere in the Piṭakas.

the putting away of corruptions [or vices] goes on piecemeal, that is, by one portion at a time.'

[1-4] *Theravādin.*—You affirm this because, you say, when a person[1] who has worked to realize the fruit of the First Path (Stream-Winning) wins insight into the nature of Ill and its cause, he gives up these [three of the ten] fetters[2]—theory of a soul, doubt, and the contagion of mere rule and ritual—and the corruptions involved in these, in part; further, that when such a person wins insight into the cessation of Ill, he gives up the latter two of those fetters and the corruptions involved in them, in part; further, that when such a person wins insight into the Path [leading to that cessation], he gives up those corruptions involved, in part.

But then you should also admit—what you deny—that one part of him is Stream-Winner, one part is not; that he attains, obtains, reaches up to, lives in the realization of, enters into personal contact with the fruition of Stream-Winning with one part of him, and not with the other part of him; that with one part only of him has he earned the destiny of but seven more rebirths, or the destiny to be well reborn only twice or thrice, as man or deva, or the destiny of but one more rebirth;[3] that in one part of him only is he filled with faith in the Buddha, the Norm, the Order; that with one part only of him is he filled with virtues dear to Ariyans.

[5-8] Again, you say, that when a person who has worked to realize the fruition of the Once-Returner, wins insight into the nature of Ill and its cause, he gives up gross sensuous passions, the coarser forms of ill-will, and the corruptions involved in these, in part; further, that

[1] Puggala, again used in its popular or non-metaphysical sense.

[2] Cf. above, p. 66, *n.* 2.

[3] Satta-kkhattuparamo, kolankolo, ekabījī. Cf. *Anguttara-Nik.*, i. 233; *Puggala-Paññatti*, p. 15 f.; and *Commentary, JPTS*, 1914, p. 195 f., in all of which these terms are explained. The last—the 'one-seeder'—differs from the Once, and the Never-Returners, in that he is already in his last life, and that on earth.

when such a person wins insight into the cessation of Ill, he gives up the coarser forms of ill-will and the corruptions involved therewith, in part; further, that when such a person wins insight into the Path [leading to the cessation of Ill], he gives up the corruptions referred to.

But then you should also admit—which you deny—that one part of him is Once-Returner, one part is not; that he attains, obtains, reaches up to, lives in the realization of, enters into personal contact with the fruition of the Once-Returner, with one part of him and not with the other part.

[9-12] Again, you say, that when a person who has worked to realize the fruition of the Never-Returner, wins insight into the nature of Ill and its cause, he gives up the little residuum of sensuous passion, the little residuum of ill-will and the corruptions involved therewith, in part; further, that when such a person wins insight into the cessation of Ill, he gives up the little residuum of ill-will and the corruptions involved therewith, in part; further, that when he wins insight into the path [leading to the cessation of Ill], he gives up the corruptions aforenamed in part.

But then you must also admit—which you deny—that one part of him is Never-Returner, one part is not; that he attains, obtains, reaches up to, lives in the realization of, enters into personal contact with the fruition of the Never-Returner with one part of him, and not with the other part of him; that with one part of him only does he complete existence within the term between birth and middle life, or within the term between middle life and death, or without external instigation,[1] or with it; that with one part of him only does he become 'an upstreamer,' bound for the senior deva-world,[2] and not with the other part of him.

[1] Asankhārena. The *Puggala-Paññatti Comy.* explains this to mean 'effected with little trouble, without much contriving' (*JPTS*, 1914, p. 199). Sa-sankhārena implies of course the opposite: 'dukkhena, kasirena, adhimattapayogaŋ katvā.

[2] Akaniṭṭha, the fifth and topmost plane of the 'Pure Abodes.' The 'stream,' according to the *Comy.* quoted, may be understood *either* as 'natural desire,' *or* the 'round' of rebirth, *or* as the 'Path-stream.'

[13-16] Again, you say that when a person who has worked to realize Arahantship wins insight into the nature of Ill and its cause, he gives up the lust of life with material quality, the lust of life of immaterial quality, conceit, distraction, ignorance, and the corruptions involved therein, in part; further, that when such an one wins insight into the cessation of Ill, he gives up the last three of those fetters and the corruptions involved therein, in part; further, that when he wins insight into the path [leading to the cessation of Ill], he gives up the last two of those fetters—distraction and ignorance—and the corruptions involved in them, in part.

But then you must also admit—what you deny—that one part of him is Arahant, and one part is not; that he attains to, obtains, reaches up to, lives in the realization of, enters into personal contact with Arahantship with one part of him, and not with the other part of him; that with one part only has he done with passions, hate, dulness; that with one part only has he 'done that which was to be done,'[1] 'got rid of the burden,' 'won the good supreme,' 'wholly destroyed the fetter of becoming,' with one part only is he emancipated by perfect knowledge, is 'one for whom the bar is thrown up,' 'the trenches are filled,' 'one who has drawn out,' 'for whom there is no lock or bolt,' with one part only is he Ariyan, 'with lowered banner,' 'with burden fallen,' 'detached,' 'conqueror of a realm well conquered,' with one part only has he understood Ill, put away its cause, realized its cessation, practised the path, comprehended that which is to be comprehended, learnt that which should be learnt, put away that which is to be eliminated, developed that which is to be developed, realized that which may be realized, and not any of this with the other part.

[17] *S.*—But if it be wrong to deny that my thesis is true, why did the Exalted One say thus:—

> '*Little by little, one by one, as pass*
> *The moments, gradually let the wise,*

[1] Cf. I. 2, § 47.

Like smith the blemishes of silver, blow
The specks that mar his purity away' ?[1]

Is the Suttanta thus? Does this not justify my answering 'Yes'?[2]

[18] *Th.*—But was it not said by the Exalted One:—

'*For him, e'en as insight doth come to pass,*
Three things as bygones are renounced for aye:
Belief that in him dwells a soul, and doubt,
And faith in rule and rite—if aught[3] *remain.*
Both from the fourfold doom[4] *is he released,*
And ne'er the six fell deeds are his to do' ?[5]

Is the Suttanta thus?

[19] Again, was it not said by the Exalted One:—

'*Whenever, O bhikkhus, for the Ariyan disciple there doth arise the stainless, flawless Eye of the Norm—that whatsoever by its nature may happen, may also by its nature cease—then with the arising of that vision doth he put away these three fetters:—belief in a soul, doubt, and the contagion of mere rule and ritual' ?*[6]

Is the Suttanta thus? Hence it must not be said that the religious man gives up the corruptions piecemeal.

---

5. *Of Renouncing Evil.*

Controverted Point.—That the average man[7] renounces sensuous passions and ill-will.

[1] *Dhammapada*, verse 239; latter half also in *Sutta-Nipāta*, verse 962.

[2] Omit na in Tenahi, etc.

[3] Read yad' for yadi.

[4] Rebirth in purgatory, as demon, as 'shade,' or as beast.

[5] Matricide, parricide, Arahanticide, wounding a Buddha, schism, heresy. *Sutta-Nipāta*, verse 231.

[6] Cf. *Vinaya Texts*, i. 97; *Saŋy-Nik.*, iv. 47, 107; *Anguttara-Nik.*, iv. 186.

[7] Puthujjano, literally 'one-of-the-many-folk,' a worldling, *l'homme moyen sensuel*, to quote the famous phrase of Quetelet.

Commentary.—This question is asked to break down the opinion held, for instance, at present by the Sammitiyas, that an average man who achieves Jhāna, who understands the Truths and becomes a Never-Returner, renounced sensuous passions and ill-will while he was as yet only an average man of the world.

[1, 2] *Theravādin.*—You maintain that, *as* average man, he does renounce them. Now by 'renouncing' I imply that he renounces for ever, without remainder,[1] severing all connection with them, them and their roots, and all desire for them, and all latent bias toward them; renounces them by Ariyan insight, by the Ariyan path; renounces them while experiencing the immutable; renounces them while realizing the Fruit of the Never-Returner. This you deny.

And if, for 'renouncing,' you substitute 'arresting,' I claim the same implications, and you deny them.

[3, 4] The person who works for the realization of the Never-Returner's Fruit:—he renounces, he arrests in this thorough-going way—on that we are agreed. But does the average man? You deny this [no less than I].

[5, 6] But if you apply these words 'renounce,' 'arrest' [in your limited meaning] to the average man, you must also apply them, as meaning just so much and no more, to the candidate for the Fruit of the Never-Returner.

[7, 8] By what path (or means) does your average man renounce sensuous passions and ill-will?

S.—By the path that belongs to the Rūpa-sphere [2]

Th.—Now does that path lead men out [of the round of rebirth]? [3] does it go to extinction [of Ill], to Enlightenment, to disaccumulation? [3] Is it clear of intoxicants,

[1] The orthodox view is of a gradual giving up, from the First Path onward, residua lingering till the Third Path is past. See above, p. 66 [83]. The Stream-Winner is no longer 'average man.'

[2] I.e., to the plane of a sublimated material existence, to wit, a more ethereal frame, sight and hearing. Man and the lower devas occupy the Kāma-sphere of full sensuous endowment as we know it. On this 'path,' *Bud. Psy. Eth.*, p. 43 f. The Rūpa-sphere, or sublimated material heavens, would be the limit of the average man's aspirations.

[3] On this term see *Bud. Psy. Ethics*, 82, *n* 2

fetters, ties, floods, bonds, hindrances, uninfected,[1] clear of what makes for grasping and for corruption?[2] Is it not true, on the other hand, that this path is not any of these things? How, then, can you say that by it an average man renounces sensuous passions and ill-will?

[9, 10] You agree that the path practised by the person who works for the realization of the Never-Returner's Fruit possesses all those qualities. But you should agree that that path belonging to the Rūpa-sphere possesses the same qualities [since you claim that by it the average man renounces even as the Never-Returner renounces]. But you admit it has the opposite qualities? Then, by parity of reasoning, you should find those opposite qualities in the path practised by the Never-Returner [since you claim that by it the latter arrives at the same renunciation as does the average man].

[11] You say that an average man, who is done with lusting after sensuous pleasures,[3] as soon as he has comprehended the truth,[4] becomes forthwith established in the fruition of the Never-Returner[5]—why not add in Arahantship? Why stop short of this?

You must also admit that he has been practising the First, Second, and Third Paths at the same time, realizing the respective Fruits at the same time, and experiencing a combination of the respective contacts, feelings, perceptions, volitions, cognitions, believings, endeavours, reflections, and concentrations [all at different stages of evolution] which characterize each upward step.

[12] Or, if he does not arrive [at the Third Fruit] in this way, by what path does he arrive? 'By the path of the Never-Returner,' say you? Yet you deny that the renouncing of the three fetters—theory of a soul, doubt,

[1] Read aparāmaṭṭho.

[2] On all these terms see *op. cit.*, 291-317.

[3] Kāmesu vītarāgo. The latter word is one of the stock of Arahant terms; see above, p. 67 [47].

[4] Dhamma, or Norm.

[5] In other words, you make him leap at a bound from No-path to the consummation of the Third Path.

and the contagion of mere rule and ritual—belongs to the work of the Never-Returning Path. Nay, you must admit it [since you leave your average man no other path], although it was said, was it not, by the Exalted One that the Fruit of the *First* Path was got by the renouncing of those three fetters?[1]

[13] Once more, you deny that, by that Third Path, gross, sensuous desires and the coarser forms of ill-will are renounced. Nay, but you are bound to admit this, for was it not said by the Exalted One that the Fruit of the *Second* Path was got by the reducing sensuous passions and ill-will to a minimum?[2]

Finally, by your previous assertion concerning the average man's comprehending the truth (§11), you are bound to admit, though you deny it, that all who comprehend the truth, the Norm, are established in the Never-Returner's Fruit as soon as that comprehension arises.

[14] *S.*—But if the controverted question is to be answered by 'No,' was it not said by the Exalted One:

'*In days of old on earth there lived*
Six teachers whom men flocked to hear.
No flesh they ate for pity's sake,
Freed from the bonds of sense-desires.
No taste had they for fleshly lusts.
In Brahma-heaven they found rebirth.

'*Disciples too of them there were,*
Souls by the hundred not a few.
No flesh they ate for pity's sake,
Freed from the bonds of sense-desires.
No taste had they for fleshly lusts.
In Brahma-heaven they found rebirth'?[3]

[1] *Anguttara Nik.*, i. 231; ii. 89, etc.

[2] *Saŋyutta-Nik.*, v. 357, etc.; *Anguttara-Nik.*, i. 232; ii. 89.

[3] *Anguttara-N.*, iii. 373. The Opponent's argument is obscured, in English, by the want of association between the terms Kāma-(loka) and Brahma—i.e., Rūpa-loka. 'Sense,' 'fleshly,' belong to the former term. Renouncing all that, the persons of the poem are reborn, like Never-Returners, in the upper heavens.

Is the Suttanta thus?

[15] *Th.*—Yes. But was it not said by the Exalted One:—

'*Verily, bhikkhus, I say unto you that this teacher, Sunetta, though he lived long maintaining life on earth, did not get released from birth, decay, death, grief, lamentation, suffering, sorrow, and despair. Why was he not released from ill? Because he had not enlightenment nor penetration concerning four things. What were they? The virtue, the concentration, the understanding, the emancipation of the Ariyan. Once, bhikkhus, these four are understood and penetrated, then is the thirst for becoming cut off, then is the lust for becoming perished, then is there no more coming back to be. . . .*

'*The virtuous habit and the mind intent,*
Insight and utmost range of liberty:
All these are known to GOTAMA *renowned.*
His understanding mastering all its truth,
The Buddha to the Brethren taught the Norm;
Our Teacher, Seer, Ender of all Ill,
Perfected life and wholly passed away'?[1]

Is the Suttanta thus? Hence it is not right to say 'the average man [as such] renounces sensuous passions and ill-will.'

---

6. *Of Everything as persistently existing.*

Controverted Point.—That everything exists.

From the Commentary.—This question was asked by one of ours, in order to break down an opinion, held at present by the Sabbatthivādins,[2] that, judging by the Suttanta passage: 'Whatever is material quality,

---

[1] *Anguttara-Nik.*, iv. 104 f. (The last line expands the one Pali word: parinibbuto.)

[2] Sansk. Sarvāsthivādins, literally, 'everything-exists-believers.' On the history and literature of this influential school, see Professor Takakusu in *JPTS*, 1905, 67 f.; T. Watters, *On Yuen Chwang* (in which consult Index).

past, present, future,' etc., all phenomena, past, present, future [once they arise among the aggregate constituents of personal life and experience] persist in that state,[1] and that therefore all go on existing.

TO PURGE [ABSTRACT TIME-]IDEAS.

[1] *Theravādin.*—You say that 'all'[2] exists. Hereby you are involved in these further admissions:—

All exists everywhere,[3] at all times, in every way,[4] in all things, not in a combined state, the non-existent exists,[5] the right view which looks upon your wrong view as wrong exists.

[2] Again, taking all in terms of time, you affirm that the past exists, the future exists, the present exists. But is not the past [something that has] ceased—that is, departed, changed, gone away, gone utterly away? How then can you say 'the past exists'? Again, is not the future [something that is] not yet born, not yet come to be, not yet come to pass, has not happened, not befallen, is not manifested? How then can you say 'the future exists'?

The present, you say, exists; and the present is [something that has as yet] not ceased, not departed, not changed, not gone away, not utterly gone away. And the past, you say, 'exists'; then you should say of the past also that it has not ceased, not departed, and so on.

Again, the present, you say, exists—that is, it is born,

1 Literally, 'do not abandon that state.'

2 'All,' in the Nikāyas, stands for everything accessible to sentient experience. '*I will teach you the "all"'—what is that? The sense-organs and their objects and the co-ordinating mind. If anyone say: '"I reject this all, and teach you another all," he could not explain . . . he would be out of his range.*' *Saṃyutta-Nik.*, iv. 15; cf. *Majjhima-Nik.*, i. 3.

3 'In the whole body.'—*Comy.*

4 'In various colours,' is the illustration given by the Burmese translator.

5 I.e., chimæras, such as a sixth personal aggregate (one more than the orthodox five constituents mental and bodily), or horns in a hare, etc.—*Comy.*

has become, has come to pass, happened, befallen, is manifested. And the future, you say, 'exists'; then you should say of the future also that it is born, has become, and so on.

Again, the past, you say, exists, and yet that it has ceased, departed, and so on. And the present, you say, exists; then you should say of the present also that it has ceased, departed, and so on.

Once more, the future, you say, exists, and yet that it is not born, not become, and so on. And the present, you say, exists; then you should say of the present also that it is not born, not become, and so on.

[3] Do past material qualities[1] exist? 'Yes,' you say. But if you describe these in terms of what 'has ceased,' and so on, as aforesaid, how can you say 'those past qualities exist'? Similarly, for future material qualities—if they [in common with all that is future] are not born, and so on, how can they be said to exist?

[Similarly, the other more general admissions aforestated apply also to material qualities in particular:] if in saying 'present material qualities exist,' you mean they have 'not ceased to be,' etc., then if past material qualities 'exist,' they also have 'not ceased to be,' etc. And if, in saying present material qualities 'exist,' you mean they are 'born, are come to be,' etc., then, if future material qualities 'exist,' they also are 'born, are come to be,' etc. Again, if in saying 'past material qualities exist,' you mean that they have 'ceased, departed,' etc., then, if present material qualities 'exist,' they also have 'ceased,' etc. And if, in saying 'future material qualities exist,' you mean they are 'not yet born,' etc., then, if present material qualities 'exist,' they also are 'not yet born,' etc.

[4] And all these arguments apply equally to each of the other four aggregates—to feeling, to perception, to mental coefficients, to consciousness.

For instance, if, in saying, 'present consciousness exists,' you mean it has not ceased to be, not departed, etc., then,

[1] Rūpaŋ. 'The time-reference is now connected with the aggregates (khandha's, mental and bodily constituents).'—*Comy.*

if past consciousness [still] 'exists,' it also has not 'ceased to be, departed,' etc. And if, in saying 'present consciousness exists,' you mean it is born, is come to be, etc., then, if future consciousness, as you say, 'exists,' it also 'is born, is come to be,' etc. Again, if, in saying 'past consciousness exists,' you mean it has ceased, departed, etc., then, if present consciousness, as you say, 'exists,' it also has 'ceased, departed,' etc. And if, in saying 'future consciousness exists,' you mean it is not yet born, has not come to be, etc., then, when you say 'present consciousness exists,' it also is 'not yet born, has not come to be, etc.

[5] In the expression 'present material-aggregate,'[1] in whichever order you use the two terms, if no distinction is made[2] between each, if they are used as identical, of one import, as the same, as of the same content and origin, then when you say, that (A) present material-aggregate, on ceasing, gives up its present state, you must also admit that (A_1) material-aggregate gives up its materiality. Similarly, when you say, that (a) present material-aggregate on ceasing does not give up its materiality, you must also admit that (a_1) it does not give up its presence (present state).

[6] *S.*—But in the expression 'white cloth,' in whichever order you use the terms, if no distinction is made between each, if they are used as identical, of one import, as the same, as one in content and origin, then when you say (A) 'white cloth when it is being dyed loses its whiteness,' you must also admit (A_1) it loses its 'clothness.'

Again, in the expression 'white cloth,' in whichever order you use the terms, if no distinction is made between each, if they are used as aforesaid, then when you say (a) 'white cloth when it is being dyed does not give up its clothness,' you must also admit that (a_1) it does not give up its whiteness. . . .

[7] *Th.*—If you assert that the material-aggregate retains its materiality, you must admit that the material-

[1] Paccuppannaŋ rūpaŋ.

[2] Appiyaŋ karitvā. Ekaṭṭhatā anuññātā.—*Comy.*

aggregate is permanent, persistent, eternal, not subject to change. You know that the opposite is true; hence it should not be said that materiality is retained.

[8] Nibbāna does not abandon its state as Nibbāna—by this we mean Nibbāna is permanent, persistent, eternal, not subject to change. And you ought to mean this, too, in the case of material-aggregate, if you say that the latter does not abandon its materiality.

Do you mean by 'material-aggregate does not abandon its materiality,' that the aggregate is impermanent, non-persistent, temporary, subject to change? You assent. Well, then, you should affirm the same with regard to Nibbāna when you say: Nibbāna does not abandon its state as Nibbāna. . . .

[9] If, in your statement 'the past exists' (§ 2), you mean it retains its pastness or preterition, then in your statement 'the future exists' (§ 2) you ought to mean: it retains its futurity, and in your statement 'the present exists,' you ought to mean: it retains its presentness, or presence. [10] Each of these affirmations involves a similar affirmation respecting the other two divisions of time.

[11] If the past 'exists' and retains its preterition, then must it be permanent, persistent, eternal, not subject to change; and this, you admit, is not right. [12] When you say Nibbāna exists, and retains its state as Nibbāna, you mean: it is permanent and so on. So much also must you mean if you predicate the same respecting 'the past.' Or, if you do not mean that the past is permanent and so on, when you say 'it exists and retains its preterition,' then when you say this of Nibbāna, you imply that Nibbāna is impermanent and so on.

[13-20] All the foregoing (§§ 9-12) applies equally to the particular past, future, and present things called 'the five aggregates'—e.g. :—

If, in your statement 'past consciousness exists,' you mean: it retains its preterition, then, in your statement 'future consciousness exists,' you must mean: such consciousness retains its futurity; also, in your statement 'present consciousness exists,' you must mean such consciousness retains its presence. And each of these affirmations involves a similar affirmation respecting the other two divisions of time. Again, if past consciousness exists and retains its preterition, then must it be permanent, persistent, eternal, not subject to change—and this you admit is not right. When you say, 'Nibbāna exists and retains its state as Nibbāna,' you mean it is permanent and so on. So much also must you mean, if you predicate the same respecting past consciousness. Or, if you do not mean that past consciousness is permanent and so on, when you say 'it exists and retains its preterition,' then when you say this of Nibbāna, you imply that Nibbāna is impermanent, not persistent, temporary, subject to change. . . .

[21] Is the past a non-existent thing? If you say 'yes,' you must reject your view that the past exists. If you say 'the non-past exists,' then to say 'there exists a past,' is equally wrong.

Again, is the future a non-existent thing? If you say 'yes,' you must reject your view that the future exists. If you say 'the non-future [alone] exists,' then to say 'there exists the future,' is equally wrong.

[22] Does that which has been future become present? If you assent,[1] you must admit that that which was future is *the same* as that which is now present. You admit this? Then you must admit that anything which having been [future], is [present], will in turn, having been [future], become once more [present].[2] You admit this? Then you must also admit that that which, not having been [future], is not [present], will not in turn have been [future] only to become [present] again.[3]

[1] He first denies because the future was then not yet present ; he then assents, because an anticipated thing when realized is present.—*Comy.*

[2] The translation from Pali into Burmese has: 'Having become present, does it become future and then again present?' The *Comy.* explains that the opponent admits the repetition of this imaginary process of becoming, because he thinks he can speak of an anticipated thing realized as 'having been, is.'

[3] E.g., a chimæra like the horn of a hare.—*Comy.* Or as we might say, a unicorn.

[This series of dilemmas is also applicable to 'present and 'past,' thus:] Does that which has been present become past? If so, *you* must admit that that which was present is *the same* as that which is past.[1] If you do admit this, you must also admit that anything which having been [present], is [past] will in turn have been [present] only to become [past *once more*][2] If you do admit this, you must also admit it as true for their contradictories.

Similarly for future, present, past:—Does the future, having been, become present, and the present, having been, become past? If so, *you* must admit that these three are identical, and that the process of becoming the one after having been the other is repeated. If you do admit this, you must admit it as true for their contradictories.

APPLICATIONS OF THE PURGED TIME-IDEAS.

[23] Do [all the conditions of an act of visual perception:—] eye, visible objects, visual consciousness, light, attention, when *past*, exist? If you say 'yes,' you should also admit that one sees the object that is past with an eye that is past. Similarly, for all the conditions of all other varieties of sense-perception that are past—to wit: ear, audible objects, auditory consciousness, space,[3] attention; the nose, odours, olfactory consciousness, air, attention; the tongue, sapid objects, sapid consciousness, liquid, attention; body, touches, body-consciousness, extensity, attention; mind, objects of consciousness, reflection, the seat [of mental activity],[4] attention. For instance, taking the last: you should then also admit that one perceives the 'past' object of consciousness with the 'past' mind.

[1] In the Burmese translation: Is [just] this 'past' that present, or that (present) this past?

[2] The opponent invests time with objective reality, but practically rejects all time distinctions. According to him 'will be' becomes 'is,' merges into 'was.' The Theravādin tests this by inverting the time-process, and showing the endlessness of such imaginary processes.

[3] *Sic*, presumably conceived as full of air (v ā y o); cf. smell below.

[4] V a t t h u. Note the silence as to the heart.—*Compendium*, 277.

[24] Similarly, if the conditions of a future act of sense-perception exist—e.g., eye, visible objects, visual consciousness, light, attention, then one should see future object with future eye, and so on. [25] For if you say that the conditions of present visual and other perception exist, and that you see present objects with an eye, etc., that is present, so, if you maintain that the past conditions of sense-perception 'exist,' must you say that with the past eye one sees past objects, etc.; [26] and similarly for future conditions of sense-perception.

[27] If you deny that with the past eye, visible objects, visual consciousness *existing*, one does not see past objects with past eyes, equally must you deny that, with the conditions for present vision existing, one does not see present objects with present eyes. Similarly for the other senses.

[28] Similarly for future vision.

[29] Does past coming-to-know[1] exist? If you assent, you must admit that the function of knowing is done by that same [past] coming-to-know. And if you admit that, you must also admit that by that same [past] coming-to-know one understands Ill, puts away its cause, realizes its cessation, practises the Path [not by present cognition].

[30] The same argument applies to future coming-to-know.

[31] Does present coming-to-know, or cognition, exist, and is the function of knowing performed by that same present cognition? If you assent, you must admit that, past coming-to-know *also existing* [§ 29], the function of knowing is performed by *that* same past cognition. So that if, by that present cognition, the nature of Ill be understood, its cause put away, its cessation realized, the path leading thereto be practised, it is no less by that past cognition that all this is effected. [32] The same reasoning precisely holds good to the extent to which you maintain that present coming-to-know exists. [33] But you maintain that,

[1] Ñ ā ṇ a ŋ :—the process is meant, not the 'body' of knowledge, or knowing conceived as a product.

whereas the past process-of-knowing *exists*, it is impossible to perform the function of knowing with it. Then, by parity of reasoning, surely it is equally impossible to know with the *existing* present process-of-knowing. More particularly, if you cannot carry out the Four Truths concerning Ill [§§ 29, 31] with past *existing* cognition, neither can you do so with present *existing* cognition—which is absurd. [34] Future knowing and present knowing are mutually involved in just the same way.

[35] Do the corruptions of [his] past exist for the Arahant?[1] You reply 'yes.' But is the Arahant [now] lustful with [that past, yet existing] lust, hostile with that hate, ignorant with that dulness, vain with that conceit, errant with that error, perplexed with that doubt, torpid with that sloth, distracted with that excitement, shameless with that impudence, reckless with that indiscretion, all of which are past and yet 'existing'?

[36] Similarly, you say that the past [five lower] fetters and corruptions exist for the Never-Returner. But is he now holding that theory of soul, perplexed with that doubt, infected by that contagion of mere rule and ritual, subject to residual sensuous passions and ill-will, that are past and yet 'existing'?

[37] Similarly, you say that the same past fetters, and grosser sensuous passions and coarser forms of ill-will 'exist' for the Once-Returner. But is he now bound by those fetters, and subject to those grosser passions and coarse forms of ill-will?

[38] Similarly, you say that the past three fetters[2] and lust, hate and dulness entailing the rebirths of misery, exist for the Stream-Winner. But is he now bound by those fetters and those vices?

[39] Granting that past lust exists for an average man, is he affected by that same lust? Yes? Then, surely, if past lust 'exists' for an Arahant, he also is affected by that same lust? Similarly for the other nine corruptions

[1] *A fortiori*, since 'all exists' (§ 1). The ten corruptions (pp. 65, *n.* 4; 66, *n.* 4) follow.

[2] Soul-theory, doubt, ritualism.

[§ 35]. [40-42] If you say that the average man is still subject to corruptions or fetters, past, yet 'existing,' you must also admit that past corruptions and fetters, in so far as they 'exist' in those who have reached any stago of the path, involve their being subject to them at present. [43-6] Conversely, if it is impossible for an Arahant, or one in any lower stage of the path, to be now subject to certain corruptions or to fetters which 'exist' for him *as past*, it is equally impossible for the average man to be subject to a corruption or fetter which 'exists' for him as 'past.'

[47] Do past hands exist?[1] Then must you also admit that taking and laying down by them is also apparent [as existences]. Similarly for legs, feet, and their going to and fro, for joints of limbs, and their contracting and extending, for the stomach, and its hunger and thirst.

[48] Does the past body exist? Then must you also admit that the past body undergoes lifting and lowering, annihilation and dissolution, the being shared by crows, vultures, and kites; also that poison, weapons, fire may get access to the body; also that this past body may be liable to be bound by confinement by rope or chain, by village, town, or city jail, by fourfold restraint, and by the fifth, to wit, strangling.[2]

[49] Do the [other] past elements [of the past body] exist — its cohesiveness, heat, mobility?[3] If you assent, then you must admit that with each past element the past body still performs the corresponding function.

[50] Do past and future as well as present material aggregates exist? If so, then there must be three material aggregates. And if you say that past and future as well as present fivefold aggregates exist, you must admit that there are fifteen aggregates. [51] Similarly, you must admit three organs of sight, or thrice twelve organs and objects

[1] As part of 'everything' (§ 1).

[2] Literally, by the neck.

[3] The first, 'hardness' (or solidity), has been implicitly dealt with under § 47. 'Cohesiveness' may be rendered fluidity. The four elements are the philosophic or abstract conceptions of the popular four elements: earth, water, etc.

of sense.[1] [52] Similarly, you must admit three elements of sight, or eighteen elements multiplied by three time-divisions, fifty-four in all. [53] Similarly, you must admit three visual controllers,[2] or sixty-six controllers in all.

[54] Would you say that a Wheel-turning monarch[3] of the past or of the future, as well as one of the present, 'exists'? But this amounts to saying that three Wheel-turning monarchs are actually living.[4] The same implication lies in a similar assertion respecting Perfectly Enlightened Ones [Buddhas].

[55] Does the past exist? 'Yes' you reply. Then, is the existent the past? You reply 'the existent may be past, and may be not-past.' But herein you make out that the past may be the past and may be the not-past. Your position is wrong, and you are refuted.[5]

[56] You are similarly involved if you say that, whereas the future exists, the existent may be future [and] may not be future. [57] So also for 'the present.' [58] Similarly, if you affirm that Nibbāna exists, but that the existent may be Nibbāna,[6] may not be Nibbāna:—this amounts to saying that Nibbāna [is or may be] not Nibbāna, not-Nibbāna [is, or may be] Nibbāna.

[1] The six senses and their objects multiplied by three time-divisions.

[2] *Indriya's.* See p. 16; *Vibhanga*, 122; *Yamaka*, ii. 61, 283.

[3] Or world-emperor.

[4] Literally, there is for them the state of being face to face. It is orthodox to hold that there can neither be two such monarchs, nor two Buddhas (Saviour-Buddhas) at the same time. *Dīgha-Nik.*, iii. 114; *Vibhanga*, 336.

[5] The position of the Theravādin is, of course, by European logic, only tenable if the major term 'exist,' 'the existent,' be distributed: does (A) the past = (B) all that exists. But since, in Buddhist or natural logic, B coincides with A in one and the same object, we can substitute B for A; and we may then follow the argument. But that such an argument as that above could be introduced in serious dialectical discussion shows how the Indian mind grasped particular concepts in philosophical discussion.

[6] Read, for a t ī t a n, n i b b ā n a n (t i), in PTS. edition.

[59] *S.*—Is it wrong to say 'the past exists,' 'the future exists'?

Th.—Yes.

S.—But was it not said by the Exalted One: '*Whatsoever material quality, bhikkhus, whether past, future, or present, is either internal or external, gross or subtle, common or excellent, distant or near, is called the material aggregate. Whatsoever feeling, whether past, future, or present, of which the foregoing may be said, is termed the aggregate of feeling. So also are the other three aggregates*'?[1] Surely then the past exists, the future exists.

[60] *Th.*—But was it not said by the Exalted One: '*These three modes in word, term, or name, bhikkhus, which have been distinct in the past, are now distinct, and will be distinct, are not condemned by recluses and brahmins who are wise. Which three?* (1) *That material aggregate which is past, which has ceased, which is changed, is reckoned, termed, named "has been"; it is not reckoned as "exists," nor as "will be." And so for the aggregates of feeling, perception, mental coefficients, consciousness.* (2) *That material aggregate which is not yet born, and which has not appeared, is reckoned, termed, named "will be," but is not reckoned as "exists," nor as "has been." And so for the mental aggregates.* (3) *That material body which has come to birth, has appeared, is reckoned, termed, named "exists," but is not reckoned as "has been," nor as "will be." And so for the mental aggregates. Verily these three modes in word, term, or name, bhikkhus, are distinct, have been distinct in the past, are not, will not, be condemned by recluses and brahmins who are wise.*

'*Bhikkhus, the folk of Ukkala, Lenten speakers of old,*[2]

[1] *Majjhima-Nik.*, iii. 16 f.; *Saṃy.-Nik.*, iii. 47.

[2] Ukkala-vassa bhaññā. In B[h] Okkalā. . . . The Br. translation renders this by ādipurisā, men of old. But that the district so-called (? identified with Orissa) is referred to is Buddhaghosa's opinion: 'Those dwelling in the country Ukkala.' He divides the rest: vasso (*sic*) ca bhaññā ca—'for these causation-theorists are two.' Presently, however, he refers to them collectively

Casualists, Deniers of the Deed, Sceptics—even they, too, judged that these three modes of reckoning, terming, or naming, should not be condemned or repudiated. And why was that? Because they were afraid of blame, of unpopularity, of incurring opposition'?[1]

[61] Again, did not the venerable Phagguna say to the Exalted One: '*Does the eye (or sight), lord, still exist by which past Buddhas, who have completed existence, have cut off the multipliers of life,*[2] *have cut off its cycle, have exhausted it, and utterly passed beyond all Ill, might be revealed? Or does the ear, the nose, the tongue, the co-ordinating sense, still exist with which one might do this'? 'Nay, Phagguna, the eye does not exist, nor any sense by which past Buddhas, who have so wrought, might be revealed'?*[3]

Is the Suttanta thus? Then it must surely not be said that 'the past is,' 'the future is.'

[62] Again, was it not said by the venerable Nandaka: '*Formerly there was greed [within him], that was bad; that this no longer exists is good. Formerly there were hate and dulness, that was bad; that these no longer exist, that is good'?*[4]

Is the Suttanta thus? Surely then it should not be said that 'the past exists.'

[63] *S.*—But was it not said by the Exalted One: '*If, bhikkhus, there be lust after, pleasure in, craving for, edible food,*[5] *consciousness establishes itself and grows there. Wherever*

---

as jana, people, thus: 'These two (classes of) people and these three views.' These three views he tersely characterizes by referring to (1) Makkhali Gosāla's formula (*Dialogues*, i. 71; *Majjh.-Nik.*, i. 407); (2) the words karoto na kariyati pāpaŋ—'evil result befalls not the doer' (*Angutt.-Nik.*, i. 192); (3) Ajita Kesakambali's view (*Dialogues*, i. 73). *Sāratthappakāsinī*, VI. 437. Cf. *Vin. Texts*, i. 81; Rhys Davids, *Bud. Birth Stories*, 110. Cf. *JRAS.*, 1910, 526 f., where the reviewer, E. Müller, overlooks this passage.

[1] *Saŋyutta-Nik.*, iii. 71.

[2] Natural desires (taṇhā)—so Buddhaghosa's Commentary; elsewhere conceit and erroneous views are added.

[3] *Op cit.*, iv. 52.

[4] *Anguttara-Nik.*, i. 197 (III. 66).

[5] Support, proximate cause; see next page, *n.* 4.

consciousness establishes itself and grows, there doth exist an entry[1] *for mind and body. Wherever an entry for mind and body doth exist, there do grow*[2] *mental coefficients. Wherever mental coefficients do grow, there re-becoming in the future doth exist. Wherever re-becoming in the future doth exist, there do follow future birth, decay, and dying. Wherever future birth, decay, and dying do exist, I, bhikkhus, do declare that to be accompanied by grief, anguish,*[3] *and despair. And whether the "food" be [edible, or] contact, or act of will, or consciousness,*[4] *I declare it to be accompanied by grief, anguish, and despair'?*[5]

Is the Suttanta thus? Hence must it not surely be said 'the future exists'?[6]

[64] *Th.*—But was it not also said by the Exalted One: '*If there be no lust after, pleasure in, craving for, edible food, consciousness doth not establish itself or grow there. Wherever consciousness doth not establish itself and grow, there doth not exist an entry for mind and body. Wherever an entry for mind and body doth not exist, there doth exist no growth of mental coefficients. Wherever growth of mental coefficients doth not exist, there doth exist no future re-becoming. Wherever future re-becoming doth not exist, there doth exist no future birth, no decay and dying. Wherever there doth exist in the future no birth, decay, or dying, I declare, bhikkhus, that such edible food is not attended by grief, anguish, and despair. Or whether the "food" be contact, or act of will,*

[1] Avakkanti, an opportunity for rebirth as the resultant of foregoing consciousness, i.e., in a previous life.

[2] The Burmese translation also reads vuddhi, though Br. has buddhi.

[3] Sadaraŋ. So Singhalese MSS. PTS edition and Br. read sarajaŋ (with) 'dust,' a figure for the passions which cause obscurity of 'vision.' Cf. *Dialogues*, ii. 32.

[4] As one of the four 'foods' or proximate causes taught in the Dhamma, viññāṇa (consciousness), functioning at death, is the *cause* of fresh effect-viññāṇa beginning in the conceived germ. Cf. Mrs. Rh. D., *Bud. Psychology*, 1914, 22, 61; also *Bud. Psy. Eth.*, 30, *n.* 1.

[5] *Saŋyutta-Nik.*, ii. 101.

[6] In PTS edition either na must be suppressed, or ? must be inserted. The Hanthawaddy Br. edition omits na vattabbaŋ.

or consciousness, I declare it to be unattended by grief, anguish, and despair'?[1]

Is the Suttanta thus? Surely then it should not be said that 'the future exists.'

---

7. *Of what does my 'Past' Consist?*

Controverted Point.—That one's past consists in [bodily and mental] aggregates.[2]

[1] *Opponent.*—If you affirm that [my] past consisted in aggregates—as you do—you must also admit that the past *exists*[3]—which you deny. This is also the position in the case of the organs and objects of sense, the elements,[4] or all of the three taken together. [2] Again, if you admit that [my] future will consist in aggregates—as you do—you must also admit that the future exists—which you deny.

This is also the position in the case of the organs and objects of sense, the elements, or all of the three taken together.

[3] If you admit—as you do—that [my] present consists in aggregates and that it exists, you must also admit that

[1] This passage in the Sutta quoted, follows immediately on the previous quotation. The Opponent's emphasis lies on the a t t h i, 'doth exist,' of the solemn categorical declaration in the Sutta. The Theravādin, by completing the declaration, shows that the future, so far from existing, depends entirely, for its coming-to-exist at all, on the circumstances attending the occurrence of a certain pre-requisite, or antecedent condition. *Before* it exists, certain conditions must have come to pass. So the *Comy.*: 'the words "there doth exist in the future re-becoming," etc., do not amount to a "state of existing," but refer to certainty of result, given the consummation of the conditions.'

[2] This is a supplementary discussion to the foregoing, the Opponent, in the absence of any new allocation by the Commentator, being doubtless still a Sabbatthi vādin. His 'opinion is that past and future both exist, because the aggregates and other factors of our experience retain their state [as a sort of complex soul]. The Theravādin's "yes" summarizes the past as k h a n d h a s (read k h a n d h a s a n g a h ī t a t t ā, as in Br.).'—*Comy.*

[3] The factors of individual life—in their ultimate terms—were among the 'phenomenal realities' of orthodox doctrine.

[4] The elements were the physical irreducibles in the organism, and the sentient apparatus 'derived' from them. *Vibhanga*, 82-5.

my past, which consisted in aggregates, exists. Similarly for other present factors of experience. [4] Similarly, again, for my future.

[5] Again, if you admit a past consisting in aggregates —or other factors, such as sense-organs, etc.—which does not [now] exist, you must admit that the present consisting (as you agree) in aggregates, etc., no longer exists. [6] Similarly as to a future consisting in aggregates, etc., but not existent.

[7] Again, a little more specifically, if you admit that material qualities in the past formed my aggregates, sense-organs and objects, elements, or all of these together, then you must also admit that past material qualities exist. [8] And if you admit that material qualities in the future will form my aggregates, etc., you must also admit that future material qualities exist.

[9] Again, if you admit that material qualities in the present form my bodily aggregate and the other factors, and that the present exists, you must also admit that my past material qualities, having consisted in bodily aggregate, etc., exist.

[10] The same reasoning holds good, if, for 'past, 'future' material quality be substituted.

[11] Again, if you admit past material qualities existing as an aggregate, and hold the view that those past qualities do not exist, then you must admit that present material qualities existing as an aggregate, and other present factors, do not exist. [12] Similarly as to future material qualities existing as an aggregate, and other future factors, held by you to be non-existent.

[13] This also holds good if, for 'material qualities,' any of the four *mental* aggregates be substituted. For instance,[1] if you admit that consciousness in the past formed my aggregate, sense-organs and objects, or elements [all of which you would call real], then you must also admit that past consciousness exists. [14] Similarly, if you admit that future consciousness will form my aggregate,

[1] §§ 13-18 are parallel to §§ 7-11.

etc., you must also admit that future consciousness exists. [15] Again, if you admit that present consciousness forms my aggregate, with other factors, and that the present exists. you must also admit that my past consciousness, consisting in aggregate, sense-organ, and the rest, exists. So again for future consciousness.

[17] Once more, if you declare, of past consciousness existing as an aggregate, and the rest, that that consciousness does not exist, then you must admit that present consciousness, existing as an aggregate, does not exist. [18] Similarly as to future consciousness.

[19] *Th.*—Is it then wrong to say that my past and my future consisting in aggregates, elements, sense-organs and -objects, do not exist?

Opp.—Yes.

Th.—But was it not said by the Exalted One: '*These three modes in word, in term, or in name, bhikkhus, which are, and were, formerly held distinct, are not mixed, will not be confused, are not condemned by recluses and brahmins who are wise:—which three?* (1) *Those aggregates, material and mental, which are past, have ceased, are changed, are reckoned, termed, named "have been"; they are not reckoned as "are" (or "exist"), nor yet as "will be." Similarly,* (2) *for those aggregates that "will be," and* (3) *for those that "are."* . . .'?[1]

Is the Suttanta thus? Then it should surely[2] be said that my past and future consisting in aggregates, elements, sense-organs and -objects, exist.

[20] *Opp.*—But was it not said by the Exalted One: '*Whatsoever material qualities, bhikkhus, whether past, future, or present, are either internal or external, gross or subtle, common or excellent, distant or near, are called the material aggregate. Whatsoever feeling, or other mental aggregate, whether past, etc.* . . .'?[3]

[1] This quotation, cut short in the original, is that of § 60 in the preceding discourse.—*Saṃy.-Nik.*, iii. 71.

[2] In the PTS text n a should be omitted. Br. reads n a both here and in the final sentence. The *Comy.* assigns the question and citation in [20] to the Opponent. Hence the two conclusions must differ.

[3] *Saṃyutta-Nik.*, iii. 47; quoted also above, I. 7, § 59.

Is the Suttanta thus?

Th.—Yes.

Opp.—Hence it should certainly not be said that 'my past and future consisting in aggregates,' etc., do not exist.

---

8. *Of Some of the Past and Future as still Existing.*

Controverted Point.—That (i.) some of the past exists, some does not; (ii.) some of the future exists, some does not.

From the Commentary.—The Theravādin by his questions seeks to break down the opinion, held by those seceders from the Sabbatthivādins known as Kassapika's, that the past survives, as presently existing, in part.

[1] (i.) *Th.*—Does the past exist? Some of it exists, you reply, some does not exist. You must then admit, [in equivalent terms], that some of it has ceased, departed, passed away, utterly passed away; some of it has not ceased, departed, passed away, utterly passed away. Yet you deny this.

[2] You must also admit, more specifically, that of past things of which the results are not yet matured some are existent, some not—you deny this—and that of past things of which the results are matured, some are existent, some not—you deny this—further, that of things which are without result,[1] some exist, some do not. This also you deny.

[3] Again, referring to your declaration that the past exists in part, which of the past exists, which not?

K.—Those past things of which the effect is not matured exist; those past things of which the effect is matured do not.

Th.—But if you admit the existence of the former part, you must also admit the existence of the latter part, and also the existence of those past things that are without

[1] Avipākā = avyākatā (or abyākatā). These include all classes of consciousness which happen as moral effects or resultants (vipākacittā), and are morally inoperative, also all material qualities, and Nibbāna. Cf. *Compendium*, pp. 19, 20; *Bud. Psych. Eth.*, p. 156, *n.* 1; 168.

effect.[1] Again, if those past things of which the effect is matured are non-existent, no less are those past things of which the effect is not matured existent, as well as those things which are without effect. Once more, you say, those past things the effect of which is not matured exist, but might not such past things be said to have ceased? You admit this? But you cannot say that a thing both is and has ceased.

[4] Do you contend that those past things, the effect of which is not yet matured, but which have ceased, exist? Then must you also admit that those past things, the effect of which is matured and which have ceased, exist, as well as those past things which are without effect—that these, too, exist.

If, on the other hand, you say that those past things, the effect of which is matured, and which have ceased, do not exist, then must you also admit that those past things, the effect of which is not yet matured, and which have ceased, do not exist [contradicting what you have previously affirmed], as well as those things which are without effect.

Or do those past things, the effect of which is not yet matured, but which have ceased, exist? And are those past things, the effect of which is matured, but which have ceased, non-existent? Then you hereby affirm also that some of those past things, the effect of which is in part matured, and in part not yet matured, but which have ceased, exist, while some do not exist—which you deny.

[5] *K.*—Is it then wrong to say 'those past things, the effect of which is not yet matured, exist'?

Th.—Yes.

K.—Is it not a fact that past things, the effect of which is not yet matured, will become mature as to effect?

Th.—Yes.

[1] 'Queries and answers all revolve about these three groups: incomplete results, completed results, and the indeterminate, or absence of results. Of the act producing rebirth, life and decease are its result, and the maturing of that result, accordingly, lasts from birth to death.' —*Comy.*

K.—If that be so, then it is surely not wrong to say that past things yet immature in their effect exist.

Th.—Granting that such past things will become mature as to their effect, can they be said to exist? Yes, you say; but granting that they will in this respect mature, can they be said to be present? If you admit this,[1] then, granting that present things will perish, are they non-existent?

[6][2] (i.) To the question 'Does the future exist?' you reply 'some of it exists, some does not.' You must then admit [in equivalent terms] that some of it is born, produced, has happened, appeared, some of it not. Yet you deny this. Granting your declaration, do some things that have been inevitably determined[3] exist, and some not? You are committed to this, and also to this: that some future things which are not inevitably determined exist, and some not.

[7] Referring to your declaration (ii.):—which of the future exists, which does not exist? You reply: 'Those future things which are inevitably determined exist, those that are not so determined do not.' You deny then that those future things not inevitably determined do exist, though you are really committed to this by the former half of your reply. Again, if future things not inevitably determined are non-existent, then also future things which are inevitably determined are also non-existent.

With regard to those future things inevitably determined which you say 'exist,' would you not admit that such future things have not been born? Yes? Then how can you say that things not yet born exist?

[8] Or, if inevitably determined future things, which are not yet born, do exist, then future things not so determined, which are not yet born, exist. Or again, if future things

[1] Namely, that past things are present things.

[2] §§ 6-10 correspond to §§ 1-5.

[3] Uppādino. Cf. *Bud. Psy. Eth.*, § 1037, *n.* 4. They will certainly arise from the fact that their conditions are stable, however long the maturing may take, e.g. the consummation to be achieved in the coming of Metteyya Buddha. *Atthasālinī*, 361.

not inevitably determined, which are not yet born, are non-existent, then you must say no less of similar but inevitably determined things.

[9] *K.*—Then is it wrong to say 'those future things which are inevitably determined exist'?

Th.—Yes.

K—But will not future things which are inevitably determined happen?

Th.—Yes.

K.—Surely then things inevitably determined exist.

[10] *Th.*—Granting that future things, if inevitably determined, will happen, do they exist?

K.—Yes.

Th.—Granting they will happen, are they present?

K.—No [the future is not the present].

Th.—I repeat my question.

K.—Yes [since, if they are existent, they are present].

Th.—And granting that present things will cease, are they non-existent?

K.—Nay, that cannot truly be said.

Th.—But you have already admitted this.

---

9. *Of Applications in Mindfulness.*

Controverted Point.—That all mental states are applications in mindfulness.

From the Commentary.—The groups holding special views who arose later, to wit, the Andhakas, comprising the sub-groups of the Pubbaseliyas, Aparaseliyas, Rājagirikas, and Siddhatthikas, held the opinion that the *objects* of mindfulness, namely, the body and the rest, were themselves [the conscious *subject*:] mindfulness. This they deduced from the passage in the 'Satipaṭṭhāna-Saŋyutta': 'I will show you, bhikkhus, the induction and the cessation of applications in mindfulness.'[1] To break down this opinion, the Theravādin puts the question.

---

[1] *Saŋyutta-Nikāya*, v. 184. The controversy turns upon the double sense, subjective and objective, of the term sati-paṭṭhānā, or mindfulness-applications. The Opponent confuses the objects of this important fourfold religious exercise with the mental exercise itself,

[1] *Th.*—Do all cognizable things constitute applications in mindfulness ?[1]

Andhaka.—Yes.

Th.—Then must you also admit that all cognizable things constitute mindfulness, the controlling faculty and force of mindfulness, mindfulness that is perfect, that is a factor of enlightenment, the 'sole conveying' path 'leading to extinction,' to 'enlightenment,' to 'disintegration,' are 'not [bound up with] the intoxicants,' not akin to the fetters, ties, floods, bonds, hindrances, contagions, graspings, corruptions'; you must admit that all cognizable things constitute the 'ten recollections,' namely of the Buddha, the Norm, the Order, morals, pious liberality, the devas, 'mindfulness in respiration,' 'reflection on death,' 'mindfulness concerning the body,' 'reflection on peace.'[2] But this you deny.

---

thus merging object in subject, 'subject' in Buddhism being 'con sciousness of object.' We have much the same ambiguity observed in the popular use of object and subject of thought. Etymologically *ob-* and *sub-* scarcely support the distinction prescribed by philosophy. A 'subject for meditation' is an 'object of thought.' A 'hypnotic subject' is for the hypnotizer an object.

The Sutta on which the opinion is based *is* ambiguously worded in the context that follows. This gives not the induction and cessation of the meditating 'mindfulness,' but the cause or genesis (samudayo can mean these or induction) of the four prescribed objects of the meditation—the body, feelings, consciousness, and cognizable objects—the causes being nourishment, contact, mind-and-body, attention, respectively. Hence for the immature thought of the sectarian mind there is thus much of justification.

[1] On this term, which includes 'memory,' the etymological meaning of sati, see *Compendium*, 40, 179; *Buddh. Psy.*, 1914. . . . The quaint comment runs thus: 'Inasmuch as paṭṭhānā mean "those things to which one applies";—applies what? mindfulness . . . thus such mindfulness has paṭṭhānā's as its field; but paṭṭhānās apply—what? mindfulnesses. Thus paṭṭhānā's mean (*a*) objects of mindful application, (*b*) subjects applying mindfulness.'

[2] All of these terms are technical in Buddhist religious culture, and most are associated with applications of mindfulness, in the Suttas concerning it. *Dialogues*, ii. 327 f.; *Majjhima-Nik.*, i. 55 f.; *Saṃyutta-Nik.*, v. 141 f.; 294; also *Vibhanga*, 193 f.; 206.

[2] Again, you must equally admit, given your first affirmation, that the eye-organ constitutes an application in mindfulness. And if you are driven to admit that it does, then you must admit everything for it, which, as I claim, you must admit for all cognizable things. [3] The same argument holds for the four other sense-organs, for the five objects of sense, for lust, hate, dulness, conceit, error, doubt, sloth, distraction, impudence, indiscretion.

[4] Is mindfulness itself an application of mindfulness, and conversely? If you admit this, then must you also admit that each of the foregoing cognizable things is an application of mindfulness, and that application of mindfulness is each of those things.

You deny; then do you hold that each of those cognizable things is an application of mindfulness, but not conversely? You assent; then you must equally admit that mindfulness itself is an application in mindfulness, but that application in mindfulness is not mindfulness.

[5] *A.*—Then is it wrong to say 'all things are applications in mindfulness'?

Th.—Yes.

A.—But is not mindfulness established[1] concerning all cognizable things?

Th.—Yes.

A.—How then, good sir, can you deny what I affirm: 'All cognizable things are applications of mindfulness'?

Th.—We have said that mindfulness is established concerning all cognizable things: now, are all cognizable things applications of mindfulness?

A.—Yes.

Th.—Contact[2] is established with respect to all cognizable things: are then all such things applications in contact? For this is that to which you have committed yourself. Again, feeling, perception, volition, consciousness, each of

[1] Santiṭṭhati, literally translated, but 'actualized' may possibly be a truer rendering.

[2] Contact (phassa) may be physical or mental. If mental, it takes place without *impact* (saṅghaṭṭana). *Bud. Psy. Eth.*, 5, *n.* 2.

these is established with respect to all cognizable things: are then all such things applications in feeling, in perception, etc.? For this must equally be admitted.

[6] Again, if your proposition is to stand, then you equally admit for all beings[1] that they have mindfulness at hand, are endowed and set up with[2] mindfulness, having it ever in readiness.[3]

Moreover, was it not said by the Exalted One: '*They, bhikkhus, who do not enjoy mindfulness regarding the body, do not enjoy the Ambrosial; they, bhikkhus, who enjoy mindfulness regarding the body, enjoy the Ambrosial*'?[4]

Is the Suttanta thus? You admit it is; but do 'all beings' enjoy, obtain, practise, develop, and multiply mindfulness regarding the body? You know they do not.

[7] Again, was it not said by the Exalted One: '*There is a way, bhikkhus, that leads only to the purification of beings, to the passing beyond sorrow and grief, to the extinction of ill and sadness, to the attainment of right method,*[5] *to the realization of Nibbāna, and that way is the four applications of mindfulness*'?[6]

Is the Suttanta thus? You admit it is; but have 'all beings' this one and only way so leading? You are bound to admit that they have not.

[8] Again, was it not said by the Exalted One: '*When a Wheel-turning Monarch appears, bhikkhus, then doth there appear seven treasures. What are the seven? The treasure of the Wheel doth appear, and the treasures of the Elephant, the Horse, the Jewel, the Woman, the Householder, the Heir-apparent; yea, bhikkhus, on the appearance of a Wheel-turning Monarch do these seven treasures appear. When*

[1] Who are all 'cognizable things' (dhammā).

[2] Samohitā.

[3] This term, in the original, is an intensive form of the attribute first named in this sentence: upaṭṭhita, paccupaṭṭhita.

[4] *Anguttara-Nik.*, i. 45. 'The Ambrosial' in its literal meaning, the Not-dead, is a name for Nibbāna.

[5] Cf. *Saŋyutta-Nik.*, v. 388.

[6] *Saŋyutta-Nik.*, v. 141; cf. *Dialogues*, ii. 327: *Majjhima-Nik.*, i. 55.

a Tathāgata appears, bhikkhus, Arahant Buddha Supreme, then doth there appear these seven treasures of enlightenment. What are the seven? The treasures of those factors of enlightenment: Mindfulness, Search for Truth, Energy, Zest, Serenity, Concentration, Equanimity; yea, bhikkhus, on the appearance of a Tathāgata Arahant, Buddha Supreme, do these seven treasures appear'? [1]

Is the Suttanta thus? You admit it is. But do 'all things' become that treasure of Mindfulness which is a factor of enlightenment, when a Tathāgata appears? You know they do not, yet you are bound to admit they do.

[9] Lastly, if all things are applications of mindfulness, they must be equally other of the (thirty-seven) things pertaining to enlightenment,[2] such as the supreme efforts, the steps to magic potency, the controlling faculties and forces, the factors of enlightenment. To this admission are you committed.

---

10. *Of Existence in Immutable Modes.*

Controverted Point.— That things exist so and not otherwise.

From the Commentary.—This is an opinion now held by the Andhakas and others, such as the Pubbaseliyas, etc., named above. They declare that all things exist, in time, by way of material and other qualities, as past, present, or future, but that there is no past that is at once future and present, nor any future and present that are also past, and therefore all exists only as thus (*a*), and not as thus (*b*). Then, says the Theravādin, the past both is and is not.

[1] *Th.*—Does the past exist?

A.—It exists on this wise, it does not exist on that wise.

Th.—Does the past, as you describe it, both exist and not exist? You deny,[3] then affirm[4]—for you must affirm. And

[1] *Saŋyutta-Nik.*, v. 99. [2] See p. 65, *n.* 5.

[3] Because it cannot, in its character as past, be both existent and non-existent.

[4] Because it can exist in its own character only.

if this same past both exists and does not exist, then is also existence non-existence and conversely, then is the state of being a state of non-being and conversely, then are 'is' and 'is not' convertible terms, identical, one in meaning, the same, same in content and in origin. And this of course you do not admit.

[2] Similarly, you say the future exists only on this wise, not on that wise. This is to say it both exists and does not exist; and that involves the same antinomy.

[3] Similarly, you say the present exists only on this wise, not on that wise—and you are landed as before.

[4] If the past exists only as you say it does, how is it existent, how non-existent?

A.—The past exists only as past; it does not exist as future, it does not exist as present.

Th.—But this still commits you to saying that the same both is and is not, and thus to the same antinomy.

[5, 6] Similarly as regards the 'how' of such future and present as you hold to exist.

[7] *A.*—Then is it wrong to say 'the past or the future or the present exists only on this wise, not on that wise'?

Th.—Yes.

A.—Do you mean then that the past exists also as future and as present, the future also as past and as present, the present also as past and as future—for to this you are committed? Hence I am surely right.

[8] *Th.*—Do material qualities exist?

A.—They exist on this wise, they do not exist on that wise.

Th.—Here again you are committed to saying 'the same both exists and does not exist,' and to the same antinomy as before. [9] Similarly in the case of the other four aggregates—feeling, etc. [10-11] Again, with reference to *how* they exist on this wise, and how they do not, when you reply, 'the one aggregate, e.g., the bodily, exists as such, but not as any of the four mental aggregates,' you are equally committed to the antinomy stated above.

[12] *A.*—Then is it wrong to say 'any aggregate exists only on this wise, not on that wise'?

Th.—Yes.

A.—But this commits you to saying that each aggregate exists equally *as* any of the other four. Surely then I am right in saying that each aggregate exists in a specific fashion, and not otherwise.[1]

[1] The peculiar phraseology of this dialogue:—the 'S'ev'atthi s'eva n'atthīti' of the Theravādin, and the h'ev'atthi h'eva natthīti of the Andhaka,—calls up, as Mr. Beni M. Barua has pointed out to us, the Sapta-bhangī-naya of the Jains, by which they sought to meet the uncompromising scepticism of Sañjaya Belaṭṭhiputta and his school. However that may be, the object here is rather to shake rigid dogma, than to meet a series of negations. See H. Jacobi, *Jaina-Sūtras*, SBE, XLV., pp. xxvi-viii; *Dialogues of the Buddha*, i. 75.

BOOK II

1. *Of Conveyance by Another.*

Controverted Point.—That an Arahant has impure discharge.

From the Commentary.—This was asked concerning a notion entertained by the Pubbaseliyas and Aparaseliyas. These had noted seminal discharge among those who professed Arahantship in the belief that they had won that which was not won, or who professed Arahantship, yet were overconfident and deceitful. And they wrongly attributed to devas of the Māra group the conveyance, to such, of an impure discharge. This leads to the second question, since even a pure discharge is caused by passion.

[1] *Th.*—You contend that he may have. Yet you deny that in the Arahant there remains any lust, sensuous desires or assailing passion, any 'fetter,' 'flood,' 'bond,' or 'hindrance of sensuality.' But this denial commits you to negate your proposition.

[2] You admit that the average worldling may have both the one and the other, both the desires and the physical result. But then you must also admit both as true in the case of the Arahant.

[3] What is the cause of that physical impurity which you impute to the Arahant?

P. A.—The devas of the Māra group convey it to the Arahant.

Th.—Have then these devas themselves that physical impurity?

P. A.—No, in them it is non-existent.

Th.—Then you should not say that they convey it to the Arahant. [4] From whom do they convey it? Not, you affirm, from their own bodies, nor from the Arahant himself, nor from other beings [which is absurd]. [5] You deny also that they effect the conveyance through the pores of the body. Then you should also deny that they convey it at all. What [do you allege] is the reason of their conveying it?

P. A.—Their idea is: 'we shall cause doubt as to his attainment to be laid hold of.'[1]

Th.—Is there doubt in an Arahant? If you reply 'No,' then your argument falls through. Or if you reply 'Yes,' then must you herein admit that an Arahant may hold doubts about the Teacher, the Doctrine, the Order, the ethical training, the beginning and end of time—either or both—and about things as happening through assignable causes—which is absurd. [6] The average man holds doubts about such things, but an Arahant does not [else is he like the average man]. Or if both hold doubts not on any of these eight points, but on other matters,[2] then again the Arahant is no better than the average man.

[7] Granting your proposition, to what is the impurity due? You reply, to eating, drinking, chewing, tasting. But you deny that the proposition is true of all who eat, drink, chew, taste. Or, if you maintain the opposite conclusion, you must admit that children, eunuchs, devas eat, drink, etc., yet that the proposition is not true in their case. [8] Nor can you refer to any specific repository for that impurity which you call a result of eating, drinking, etc., similar to that which is provided for the natural results of eating, drinking, etc.

[9] If your proposition were true, then the Arahant would pursue and produce things relating to sexual intercourse, live a family life, use Kāsi sandalwood preparations,

[1] Vimatiŋ gāhayissāmāti. A Singhalese *v.l.* has gahissāmāti.

[2] 'Such as the name, family, etc., of a given woman or man, and the like.'—*Comy.* The 'eight points' constitute a stock formula even up to the present. See 'Some Points in Buddhist Doctrine,' by Ledi Sadaw, *JPTS*, 1913-14, p. 119. *Bud. Psy. Ethics*, § 1004.

adorn himself with wreaths, perfumes, and cosmetics, hoard gold and silver, like any average man, concerning whom your proposition were true. [10] But how can it be true of the Arahant who, as you admit, has put away passion, has cut it off at the root, and made it as the stump of a palm tree, made it incapable of rising up again in future renewal?—of the Arahant who has treated in like manner hate, ignorance, conceit, error, doubt, sloth, distraction, impudence, and indiscretion?

[11, 12] How, again, should it be true of one who, like the Arahant, has cultivated the means for the putting away of passion, etc., and all the other factors of enlightenment.[1] [13] How should it be true of one who, like the Arahant, has [consummated as having] done with lust, done with hate, done with nescience, by whom that which was to be done is done, by whom the burden is laid down, by whom the good supreme is won, and the fetter of becoming is wholly broken away, who is emancipated through perfect knowledge, who has lifted the bar, has filled up the trenches, is a drawer-out, is without lock or bolt, an Ariyan, of one for whom the banner is lowered, the burden is fallen, who is detached, conqueror of a realm well-conquered, who has comprehended Ill, has put away the cause thereof, has realized the cessation thereof, has cultivated the Path thereto, who has understood that which is to be understood, comprehended that which is to be comprehended, put away that which is to be put away, developed that which is to be developed, realized that which is to be realized?[2]

[14-20] Do you still maintain your proposition?

P. A.—Yes, but only in the case of an Arahant who is proficient in his own field, not of an Arahant who is proficient in other things.[3]

[1] These are enumerated under heads in the text as above, I. 2, § 47.

[2] See II., § 47 (p. 67).

[3] This curious distinction is explained by the *Comy.* as that between the Arahant who is 'freed by reason' (paññāvimutto) and one who is freed by the 'eight attainments' (or stages in deliverance), or who is 'freed both ways.' See *Dialogues,* ii. 69, 70. The modified position may be compared with a similar recourse above, p. 68.

Th.—But how can you maintain it in the one case without admitting it as true in the other? [15] The former has the qualities and requisites of Arahantship no less than the other; both have equally put away passion, and so on.

[21] How can you maintain your proposition when you admit that there is a Suttanta in which the Exalted One said: '*Bhikkhus! those bhikkhus who are but average men, yet are proficient in virtue and are mindful and reflective, can go to sleep without impure discharge. Those Rishis who are outsiders, yet are devoid of passion in matters of sense, have also no impure discharge. That an Arahant should have impure discharge is anomalous and unnatural*'?[1]

[22] *P.A.*—Is the proposition untrue?

Th.—Yes.

P.A.—But if you admit that others may convey to the Arahant clothing, alms, bedding, or medicine, surely my proposition [as involving conveyance of something by another] is tenable?

[23] *Th.*—But is everything beyond those four requisites conveyable? Could others convey to the Arahant the fruition of Stream-Winning, of Once-Returning, of Never-Returning, or of Arahanship? No? Then your argument cannot hold.

---

2. *Of the Knowledge of the Arahant.*

Controverted Point.—That the Arahant may lack knowledge.[2]

[1] *Vinaya*, i. 295. Aṭṭhānam, anavakāso—this idiomatic pair of words means literally [something] out of place, without occasion.

[2] Añ-ñāṇa. This is less often used as a technical term in religion than avijjā, ignorance, and moha, but see *Saṃy.-Nik.*, ii. 4; v. 127, 429; *Dhamma-saṅgaṇi*, § 1061, etc. This and the two following propositions are based on the vague, loose extension of three several terms.

From the Commentary.—The Pubbaseliyas hold that, because he was liable to be ignorant and to get perplexed about facts concerning every-day life, and to be surpassed in such knowledge by others, an Arahant might be considered as lacking knowledge or insight, as given to doubt, and as inferior to some. These views are refuted in this and the next two discourses.

[1] *Th.*—You maintain that he does. Then you must also admit that the Arahant has ignorance—ignorance as flood, bond, latent bias, attack, fetter, hindrance.[1] If you deny this, you cannot say he lacks knowledge.

[2] You would certainly admit lack of knowledge, ignorance as 'flood,' etc., in the case of the average man. [3] How can you assert the former and deny the latter in the case of the Arahant?

[4] You would deny that an Arahant from lack of knowledge would kill living things, take what is not given, speak lies, utter slander, speak harshly, indulge in idle talk, commit burglary, carry off plunder, be a highwayman, commit adultery,[2] and destroy village or town; yet you would admit an average man might from lack of knowledge do such things. [5] In fact you assert that an Arahant from lack of knowledge would pursue the opposite course from what an average man would do from lack of knowledge.

[6] You deny that an Arahant lacks knowledge in respect of the Teacher, the Doctrine, the Order, of the ethical training, of the beginning of time, the end of time, both beginning and end, and of things as happening by way of assignable causes. You deny that herein he lacks knowledge. Yet you maintain your proposition. . . .

[7] You admit that an average man who lacks knowledge lacks it in those respects, but that an Arahant who lacks knowledge does not lack it in those respects. Must you not also admit that an average man, lacking in knowledge, does not lack it in those respects?

[8-10] Can you maintain that the Arahant—one who

[1] Six metaphors constantly applied to spiritual ignorance and other failings in the Suttas. Cf. I., 5, § 8.

[2] Cf. *Dialogues*, i. 69.

has so put away passion,[1] hate, ignorance, conceit, error, doubt, sloth, distraction, impudence, and indiscretion, that they are cut off at the root and made as the stump of a palm tree, incapable of rising again in future renewal, who has cultivated the means for putting away passions and all the other factors of enlightenment to that end, who has consummated as having done with lust, hate, and nescience, and to whom all the terms for the Arahant may be applied —that such an one lacks knowledge?

[11-16] Or how can you maintain your proposition with regard to one class of Arahant only—to those who are proficient in their own field—and not to another class—to those who are proficient in other things?

[17] Did not the Exalted One say in the Suttanta: '*In him who knows, O bhikkhus, who sees do I declare the intoxicants to be extinct, not in him who knows not neither sees. And what, bhikkhus, in him who knows who sees, is the extinction of intoxicants? "Such is body, such its cause, so is its cessation; such are the four mental factors, such their cause, so is their cessation"—even this, O bhikkhus, is the extinguishing of intoxicants*'?[2]

How then can the Arahant [who knows who sees] lack knowledge?

[18] Again, did not the Exalted One say in the Suttanta: '*In him who knows, O bhikkhus, who sees do I declare the intoxicants to be extinct, not in him who knows not, neither sees And what, bhikkhus, in him who knows who sees is the extinguishing of intoxicants? "This is Ill!" herein, bhikkhus, for him who knows who sees is that extinguishing. "This is the cause of Ill . . . this is the cessation of Ill . . . this is the course leading to the cessation of Ill"—herein, bhikkhus, for him who knows who sees is the extinguishing of intoxicants*'?[3]

How then can the Arahant [who knows who sees] lack knowledge?

[1] §§ 8-16 are given more fully in the preceding discourse, §§ 10-20.

[2] *Saṃyutta-Nikāya*, ii. 29.

[3] *Ibid.*, v. 434.

[19] Again, did not the Exalted One say in the Suttanta: '*The man, O bhikkhus, who does not understand and comprehend all, who has not emptied himself of all, and given up all, is not capable of extinguishing Ill. And he, O bhikkhus, who understands, comprehends, empties himself of, and gives up all, he is capable of extinguishing Ill*'?[1]

How then can the Arahant [who knows who sees] lack knowledge?

[20] Again, did not the Exalted One say in the Suttanta:

'*For him e'en as insight doth come to pass,*
Three things as bygones are renounced for aye:
Belief that in him dwells a soul,
And faith in rule and rite—if aught remain.
Both from the fourfold doom is he released,
And ne'er the six fell deeds are his to do'?[2]

How then can the Arahant be said to lack knowledge?

[21] Again, did not the Exalted One say in the Suttanta: '*Whenever, O bhikkhus, for the Ariyan disciple there doth arise the stainless, flawless eye of the Norm—that whatsoever is liable to happen is also liable to cease—together with the arising of that vision are these three fetters: belief in a soul, doubt, and the contagion of mere rule and ritual put away by him*'?[3]

How then can the Arahant be said to lack knowledge?

[22] *P.*—Is it wrong to say 'the Arahant lacks knowledge'? May he not be ignorant of the name and lineage of a woman or a man, of a right or wrong road, or of how grasses, twigs, and forest plants are called? If this is so, surely, good sir, it is right to say that he lacks knowledge.

[23] *Th.*—If you say that, in not knowing such things, the Arahant lacks 'knowledge,' would you also say he lacks knowledge as to the fruition of Stream-Winning, Once-Returning, Never-Returning, Arahantship? Of course not; hence it should not be said that he lacks knowledge.

[1] *Saŋyutta-Nikāya*, iv. 17. The Br. translator renders the second line—aviràjayaŋ appajahaŋ—by 'is not free from "dust," has not given up the corruptions.'

[2] See above (I. 4), p. 80.

[3] See *ibid.*

3. *Of Doubt in the Arahant.*

Controverted Point.—That an Arahant may have doubts.

From the Commentary.—This discourse resembles the foregoing, sentence for sentence—substituting 'doubt' (kankhā) for lack of knowledge and 'perplexity' (vicikicchā) for ignorance—but with the following exceptions: (1) The expressions (from the religious metaphors of the Suttas) 'flood,' 'bond,' 'latent bias,' are not used in the case of doubt (see above, §§ 1, 2). (2) The sections (§§ 4, 5) where it is argued that, if an Arahant lacked knowledge, he might, like any average man, offend against law and morality, are omitted. (3) An additional passage is adduced from the Suttas (following the others as § 20) as follows:

[20] Again, did not the Exalted One say in the Suttanta:

'*Whene'er in sooth ardently meditating*
The brahmin sees [the truth of] things[1] *revealèd,*
All doubts are rolled away, for now he knoweth
That which befalls and likewise its conditions.[1]

'*Whene'er in sooth ardently meditating*
The brahmin sees [the truth of] things revealèd,
All doubts are rolled away, for he discerneth
That which doth make befall may be abolished.

'*Whene'er in sooth ardent and meditating*
The brahmin sees the truth of things revealèd,
He standeth victor o'er the hosts of evil,
E'en as the sun that lighteth up the heavens.'[2]

'*All doubts soever as to here or yonder,*
Felt by themselves, or doubts that torture others
Thinkers renounce in ardent meditation,
Choosing to follow after holy conduct.'[3]

[1] Dhammā and sa-hetu-dhamman, meaning in the (plural) form things given, or data, phenomena, mental objects. But the Burmese translation paraphrases dhammā by either bodhipakkhiyā dhammā or saccādhammā. In the context the Buddha has just evolved the formula of causation as expressing a universal law.

[2] *Vin. Texts*, i. 18. The triṣṭhubh metre of the text has been imitated.

[3] *Udāna*, v. 7.

'They who 'mong souls beset by doubts, past all doubt
Have won, and now unswayed, from bonds enfranchised
Abide, to them a great reward is given.'[1]

'How should disciple ever doubt
That by the kind who here abide
The truth may yet be realized?
All hail to Buddha who hath crossed
The flood and severed every doubt,
Great Conqueror and Lord of all'?[2]

---

4. *Of the Arahant being excelled by Others.*

Controverted Point.—That the Arahant is excelled by others.

From the Commentary.—Here again the argument resembles that in II. 2, section for section, substituting 'excelled by others' for 'lack knowledge,' and revealing the following exceptions:

(*a*) [1] *Th.*—You maintain that he is. Then you must also admit that the Arahant is led by others, attains through others, is conditioned by others, exists in dependence upon others, and knows not sees not, being baffled and without thoughtfulness. If you deny this, you cannot affirm that he is excelled by others, etc. . . .

(*b*) *The argument in* 2, §§ 4, 5, *is omitted.*

(*c*) *To the five quoted Sutta passages in* 2, §§ 17-21, *a sixth is added:*

[20] Again, did not the Exalted One say in the Suttanta:

'Nay, Dhôtaka, to no one upon earth who doubts
Is't mine to go that I may set him free.
'Tis in the learning of the noble Norm
That thou thyself shalt journey o'er this Flood'?[3]

[1] We have not been able as yet to trace this stanza. The *Udānavarga* has the 'enfranchised' phrase in its last stanza of seven imitating those above. Rockhill's transl., xxxii. 91.

[2] *Dīgha-Nik.*, ii. 275 (*Dialogues*, ii. 309).

[3] *Sutta-Nipāta*, 1064.

5. *Of Articulate Utterance [during Ecstasy].*

Controverted Point.—That there is articulate utterance[1] on the part of one who has entered into Jhāna.

From the Commentary.—It was held by the Pubbaseliyas and others that anyone in First Jhāna, at the moment of attaining the [first or] Stream-Winner's Path, uttered the truth : 'Sorrow!'[2] This is refuted by the Theravādin.

[1] You affirm this [in general]. Your statement should hold good for such an one everywhere, always, for all such persons, and for all such attainments in ecstatic meditation. But you do not admit all such cases. Then you cannot affirm it at all.

[2] Does such an one make utterance by bodily movements? You deny that he does so, but why not, if your thesis is true? If he make no bodily expression, you should not affirm that he makes vocal expression.

[3] If one during Jhāna having [the power of] speech, gives vocal expression, it follows that, having a body, he may also make bodily expression.

[4] You affirm that, knowing the fact of Ill, he utters the word 'Sorrow,' yet you deny that, knowing the fact of Cause [of Ill], he utters the word 'Cause.'[3] But why? Why, again, deny that he, knowing the facts of 'Cessation' [of Ill], and 'Path' [leading to that Cessation],[4] utters those words?

[5] Or, taken negatively, why deny that he utters any of the last three terms, yet not deny that he utters the first?

[6] You say that the object of such an one's insight is the [Ariyan] truth. But you deny that the object of

[1] B h e d o is literally a breaking or dividing off or up. The *Commentary* paraphrases by v i ñ ñ a t t i, intimation. See *Bud. Psy. Eth.*, 192 f.; *Compendium*, 22, 264. We have also rendered it by 'expression.'

[2] I.e., the first of the four Ariyan Truths: that everything in life is liable to undergo suffering or ill in general (d u k k h a).

[3] I.e. the second of the four Ariyan Truths.

[4] I.e., the third and fourth of these four.

such an one's ear[1] is truth. This, you say, is sound. But you deny that the object of his insight is sound. [7] No, you say, the truth is the object of his insight, sound the object of his ear. But if his insight has the truth as its object, and his ear has sound as its object, then, good sir, you should not affirm that such an one makes articulate utterance.

[7*a*] If you say, that while his insight is concerned with the [first] truth and his ear with the sound, the attainer makes articulate utterance, you must admit a combination of two contacts, two feelings, two perceptions, two volitions, two consciousnesses [at a given moment], (which is absurd).

[8] You affirm your thesis, yet you deny that it applies to one who has attained Jhāna by any one of the eight artifices,[2] to wit, earth, water, fire, or air; blue-green, yellow, red, or white colour, or by [any of the four immaterial conceptual inductions, to wit,] infinity of space or of consciousness, 'nothingness,' or 'neither perception nor non-perception.'[3] How is this intelligible? [9] If you deny each of these possibilities, you cannot affirm your proposition.

[10] You deny, further, that one who practises Jhāna for merely mundane objects makes articulate expression, whether he attain any of the four stages. Neither then can you affirm your proposition. [11] If you deny the former, you must deny the latter.

[12] You affirm your proposition only of one attaining the first supramundane Jhāna, not the second, third, or fourth. But if you affirm it of the first stage, what is there to make you deny it of the other three stages?

[14] *P.*—Is it wrong to say that there is articulate utterance on the part of one who has entered Jhāna?

Th.—Yes.

P.—But was it not said by the Exalted One that initial

[1] Or, hearing (sotaṃ).

[2] *Bud. Psy. Eth.*, 43, *n.* 4; 58.

[3] *Ibid.*, p. 71 f.

and sustained application of mind was vocal activity?[1] And does not such application belong to one in first Jhāna? Surely then my proposition is true.

[15] *Th.*—Granting that you quote correctly, and that one in first Jhāna is engaged in such application, I say, you have just denied that anyone attaining Jhāna by any of the eight artifices does make articulate utterance. How then can you also affirm your proposition?

[16] *P.*—But was it not said by the Exalted One that speech arises from initial application [or directing] of thought? And does not such movement of thought belong to one in first Jhāna?

[17] *Th.*—That is no good reason. The Exalted One also said that speech is caused by perception.[2] Now one in second, third, or fourth Jhāna has perception, but [we know that] he no longer applies or sustains thought. So also for the four more abstract Jhāna states (see § 8).

[18] Moreover, is it not said in the Suttanta: '*In one who has entered first Jhāna speech has ceased*'?[3]

[19] If you maintain your proposition in the teeth of this one, you must cease to hold [in accordance with the next words] in the Suttanta: that '*in one who has entered second Jhāna, thought initial and sustained has ceased.*'[4] Similarly you must contradict the remaining words: '*in one who has entered third Jhāna, zest has ceased; in one who has induced fourth Jhāna, respiration has ceased; in one who has induced ecstasy of infinite space, perception of bodily qualities has ceased; in one who has induced ecstasy of infinite consciousness, perception of space infinity has ceased;*

[1] *Majjhima-Nik.*, i. 301: 'vitakka-vicārā vacī-sankhāro quoted in *Yamaka*, i. 229). The context in the Sutta (the Cūḷa-Vedalla) shows that Dhammadinnā teaches, not identity between the two terms, but causal sequence. Thinking leads to speaking. This is probably the reference made in § 16, or it may be to *Dhamma-sangaṇi*, §§ 981, 982.

[2] See again *Dhamma-sangaṇi*, *ibid.* Perception (saññā) is awareness without the more ratiocinative procedure implied in 'applied and sustained thought.'

[3] *Saṃyutta-Nik.*, iv. 217.

[4] *Ibid.*

in one who has induced ecstasy of nothingness, perception of infinity, of consciousness, has ceased; in one who has induced ecstasy wherein is neither perception nor non-perception, perception of nothingness has ceased; in one who has induced trance,[1] *both perception and feeling have ceased.'*[2]

[20] *P.*—But if my proposition is wrong, why did the Exalted One say that '*for first Jhāna sound is obnoxious*'?[3] Does not this show that one who has attained Jhāna can emit speech?

[21] *Th.*—You accept both the Suttanta dictum and your proposition. But, by the same Sutta, that which is eliminated successively, as each further stage of Jhāna[4] is reached, was pronounced to be obnoxious in its turn. Does that therefore indicate that one who attained each stage, practised each obstacle to that stage?

[22] *P.*—But did not the Exalted One say in the Suttanta: *O Ananda, Abhibhu, disciple of Sikhin, the Exalted One, Arahant Buddha Supreme, standing in the Brahma-world, lifted up his voice over ten thousand worlds, saying*[5]:

> '*Arise and strive! go forth and give*
> *Yourselves unto the Buddha's Rule!*
> *Sweep ye away the hosts of Death*
> *As elephant a rush-built shed.*
> *Who in this Norm and Discipline*
> *Earnest and zealous shall abide,*
> *Casting away the round of births,*
> *He shall make utter end of Ill*'?[6]

Surely then an attainer does utter articulate sounds during ecstasy.

[1] Literally, the cessation of perception and sensation.

[2] *Op. cit.*, *ibid.*

[3] *Anguttara-Nik.*, v. 133 f.

[4] *Ibid.* The stages are here given as those in § 19, but in the Sutta, only the four Jhānas and trance are given.

[5] *Ibid.* i. 227.

[6] *Saṃyutta-Nik.*, i. 157.

6. *Of inducing [Insight] by saying 'Sorrow!'*

Controverted Point.—That induction [of insight] by the word 'sorrow!' is a factor of and included in the Path.

From the Commentary.—An opinion of the Pubbaseliyas is that repeating the word 'dukkha!' induced insight (ñāṇaŋ), and was thus a factor and part of the Path [of salvation].[1] They admit it as true for those only who are qualified to win insight (vipassakā).

Th. Then you must also affirm that all who utter that word are practising[2] the Path, which is absurd.

Or if you do affirm this, notwithstanding, then you must also affirm that the average foolish person, in uttering that word, is practising the Path, and, again, that matricides, parricides, murderers of Arahants, those that shed blood [of Buddhas], those that cause schism in the Order, in uttering the word 'sorrow!' are practising the Path, which is absurd.

---

7. *Of the Duration of Consciousness.*[3]

Controverted Point.—That a single [unit of] consciousness lasts for a day.

From the Commentary.—The Theravādin puts this question to correct the belief of the Andhakas, whose secession is narrated above, that, judging by the apparent continuity both of consciousness in Jhāna and of sub-consciousness, a single state of consciousness lasted for a length of time.

[1] *Th.*—If your proposition is true, does one-half of the day belong to the 'nascent moment,' and one-half to the

[1] I.e., the Four-staged Path: Stream-Winning, etc., not the Ariyan Eightfold Path. Cf. *Dhamma-saṅgaṇi*, §§ 283-92. (This is incorrectly stated to be the latter path in the translation, p. 84, *n.* 1.)

[2] Bhāventi, making to become, developing.

[3] In the appended title, p. 208, of PTS text, read cittaṭṭhiti-kathā, as in the *Commentary*.

'cessant moment'?[1] You say no; but you have implied it. A similar admission is involved in affirming that a state of consciousness lasts two days, or four days or eight, ten, or twenty days, or a month, or two, four, eight, or ten months, or a year, or any number of years, or any number of æons.

[2] Are there other phenomena beside mind which arise and cease many times during one day? Yes, you say? Then do you contend that they come and go as quickly as mind? If you say no, then your proposition falls. If you say they do, was it not said by the Exalted One: '*I consider, bhikkhus, that there is no phenomenon that comes and goes so quickly as mind. It is not easy to find a simile to show how quickly mind comes and goes*'?[2]

Again: '*Just as a monkey faring through the dense forest catches one bough, and, letting it go, catches another, and then another, even so, bhikkhus, with what is called thought, or mind, or consciousness, by day as by night, one arises when another perishes*'?[3]

[4] [Take the content of a state of consciousness:] does any visual consciousness or other sense-consciousness last a whole day, or any bad thought, such as consciousness accompanied by passion, hate, ignorance, conceit, error, doubt, sloth, distraction, impudence, or indiscretion? If not, then neither can consciousness be said to last a day.

[5] Does one hear, smell, taste, touch, apprehend mentally by means of the same [unit of] consciousness as one sees? Or see, hear, etc., or touch by means of the same [unit of] consciousness as one apprehends mentally? You

[1] Any citta (unit of consciousness) came to be orthodoxly considered as consisting of *three* 'moments': nascent, static, cessant. This grew apparently out of the older *twofold* division of nascent (uppāda) and cessant (vaya, bhanga), such as is here alone adduced.

[2] *Anguttara-Nik.*, i. 10.

[3] *Saṃyutta-Nik.*, ii. 95. Cf. Hume: perceptions 'succeed each other with an inconceivable rapidity, and are in a perpetual flux and movement. . . .' (p. 534, Green and Grose ed.).

say 'no.' Then you cannot affirm that one [and the same unit of] consciousness lasts a whole day.

[6] Similarly, if you deny that one moves backward with the same [unit of] consciousness as one moves forward, and *vice versâ*, you cannot affirm your proposition. A similar argument applies to looking backward, looking forward, and to bending, extending by means of the same unit of consciousness.[1]

[7] In the case of the devas who have reached the realm of space-infinity, does any unit of consciousness last their whole lifetime? You affirm it does, yet you deny a similar duration in the case of humanity. You deny it also in the case of all devas of the plane of sense-desires, and of all devas of the higher or Rūpa plane,[2] why not of those of the first-named non-Rūpa plane?

[8] You affirm, I say, this duration of a unit of consciousness during the 20,000 æons of the Arūpa-deva's life, yet you deny an analogous duration in a unit of human consciousness, lasting, say, for 100 years, and you deny it in the case of all those devas of the Kāmaloka and Rūpaloka, whose lifetime varies from 500 years in the Four Great Kings to 16,000 æons of years in the senior[3] devas.

[9] *A.*—Does then the mind of the devas who have reached the plane of space-infinity arise and cease moment by moment?

Th.—It does.

[1] Cf. again Hume's unconscious plagiarism: 'Our eyes cannot turn in their sockets without varying our perceptions. Our thought is still more variable than our sight; . . . nor is there any single power of the soul which remains unalterably the same, perhaps for one moment . . . several perceptions successively make their appearance; pass, re-pass, glide away, and mingle in an infinite variety of postures and situations' (p. 534, Green and Grose ed.).

[2] The groups of devas are all enumerated in the text: of the heavens of the Four Kings, of the Thirty-Three, of the Yāmā's, of Delight, etc., of the Brahmās, etc., as enumerated in the accurately preserved tradition recorded in the *Compendium*, pp. 138, 142.

[3] Literally, the non-younger devas. Cf. *Compendium*, pp. 140, 142.

A.—But do these devas themselves decease, and are they reborn moment by moment?

Th.—Nay, that cannot truly be said.

A.—Surely this momentary living and dying is involved in the momentary happening of consciousness?

[10] *Th.*—But if you affirm that in the case of these devas a unit of consciousness lasts as long as they live, then you must also admit that they die with the same unit of consciousness as that wherewith they are reborn; but you are not prepared to admit this. . . .

---

8. *Of [the World as only a] Cinderheap.*

Controverted Point.—That all conditioned things are absolutely[1] cinderheaps.

From the Commentary.—The opinion of the Gokulikas, from grasping thoughtlessly the teaching of such Suttas as 'All is on fire, bhikkhus!'[2] 'All conditioned things [involve] ill,'[3] is that all conditioned things are without qualification no better than a welter of embers whence the flames have died out, like an inferno of ashes. To correct this by indicating various forms of happiness, the Theravādin puts the question.

[1] *Th.*—You affirm this; but is there not such a thing as pleasurable feeling, bodily pleasure, mental pleasure, celestial happiness, human happiness, the pleasures of gain, of being honoured, of riding-and-driving,[4] of resting, the pleasures of ruling, of administrating, of domestic-and-secular life, of the religious life, pleasures involved in the intoxicants[5] and pleasures that are not, the happiness [of Nibbāna], both while stuff of life remains and when none remains,[6] worldly and spiritual pleasures, happiness with

[1] Anodhikatvā, 'not having made a limit, without distinction. —*Comy.*

[2] *Vin. Texts*, i. 134.

[3] *Dialogues*, ii. 175.

[4] Yāna-sukhaŋ, literally, vehicle-pleasure.

[5] Asava's: sensuality, desire for rebirth, erroneous opinions; ignorance was added as a fourth.

[6] Upadhisukhaŋ nirupadhisukhaŋ.

zest and without zest, Jhāna-happiness, the bliss of liberty, pleasures of sense-desire, and the happiness of renunciation, the bliss of solitude, of peace, of enlightenment?[1] Of course. How then can you maintain your general affirmation?

[2] *G.*—My proposition then is wrong? But was it not said by the Exalted One: '*All is on fire, O bhikkhus! How is everything on fire? The eye is on fire; visible objects, visual consciousness, visual contact and the pleasure, the pain, the neutral feeling therefrom—all is on fire. On fire wherewithal? I tell you, on fire with the fires of passion, hate, and ignorance; with the fires of birth, decay, and death; with the fires of sorrow, lamentation, ill, grief, and despair. All the field of sense, all the field of mind, all the feeling therefrom is on fire with those fires*'?[2] Surely then all conditioned things are mere cinderheaps absolutely.

[3] *Th.*—But was it not also said by the Exalted One: '*There are these five pleasures of sense, bhikkhus—namely, visible objects seen through the eye as desirable, pleasing, delightful, lovely, adapted to sense-desire, seductive; audible objects, odorous, sapid, tangible objects, desirable, pleasing, delightful, lovely, opposite to sense-desire, seductive*' . . .?[3]

[4] *G.*—But was it not also said by the Exalted One:—'*A gain is yours, O bhikkhus! well have ye won, for ye have discerned the hour*[4] *for living the religious life. Hells have I seen, bhikkhus, belonging to the six fields of contact. Hereof whatsoever object is seen by the eye is undesired only, not desired; whatsoever object is sensed by ear, smell, taste, touch, mind, is undesired only, not desired; is unpleasant only, not pleasant; is unlovely only, not lovely*'?[5]

[1] The invariable generic term in each of the Pali compounds is sukhaŋ. On its pregnant import see *Compendium*, 277; cf. *JPTS* 1914, 134.

[2] *Vin. Texts*, i. 134.

[3] *Majjhima-Nik.*, i. 85, 92 *passim*.

[4] Literally, moment.

[5] *Saŋyutta-Nik.*, iv. 126. The 'hour' is the crucial time when a Buddha is living on earth. Cf. the passage with frequent allusions in the *Psalms of the Early Buddhists*, I. 13, 167; II. 162, 213, 280, 347 also *Anguttara-Nik.*, iv. 225 f.

[5] *Th.*—But was it not also said by the Exalted One: '*A gain is yours, bhikkhus! well have ye won, for ye have discerned the hour for living the religious life. Heavens have I seen, bhikkhus, belonging to the six fields of contact. Hereof whatsoever object is seen by the eye, or otherwise sensed, is desired only, not undesired; is pleasing only, not unpleasing; is lovely only, not unlovely*'?[1]

[6] *G.*—But was it not said by the Exalted One: '*The impermanent involves Ill; all conditioned things are impermanent*'?[2]

[7] *Th.*—But take giving:—does that bring forth fruit that is undesired, unpleasant, disagreeable, adulterated? Does it bear, and result in, sorrow? Or take virtue, the keeping of feastdays, religious training, and religious life:—do they bring forth such fruit, etc.? Do they not rather have the opposite result? How then can you affirm your general proposition?

[8] Finally, was it not said by the Exalted One:

'*Happy his solitude who, glad at heart,*
Hath learnt the Norm and doth the vision see!
Happy is that benignity towards
The world which on no creature worketh harm.
Happy the freedom from all lust, th' ascent
Past and beyond the needs of sense-desires.
He who doth crush the great "I am"-conceit:
This, even this, is happiness supreme.
This happiness by happiness is won,
Unending happiness is this alone.
The Threefold Wisdom hath he made his own.
This, even this, is happiness supreme'?[3]

You admit the Suttanta says this? How then can you maintain your proposition?

[1] *Saŋyutta-Nik.*, iv. 126.

[2] *Anguttara-Nik.*, i. 286; *Dialogues*, ii. 232; *Saŋyutta-Nik.*, *passim.*

[3] *Udāna*, II. 1. Line 9 (slightly different) also occurs in *Psalms of the Brethren*, ver. 220; *cf.* ver. 63; and line 11 occurs often in the *Psalms*, Parts I. and II. See *ibid.*, II., pp. 29, 57.

9. *Of a specified Progress in Penetration.*

Controverted Point.—That penetration is acquired in segmentary order.

From the Commentary.—By thoughtlessly considering such Suttas as—

> '*Little by little, one by one, as pass*
> *The moments, gradually let the wise,*' etc.,[1]

the Andhakas, Sabbatthivādins, Sammitiyas, and Bhadrayānikas have acquired the opinion that, in realizing the Four Paths, the corruptions were put away by so many slices as each of the Four Truths was intuited (cf. I. 4).

[1] *Th.*—If you affirm that there is a definite graduation in penetration, you must also affirm that the first Path (Stream-Winning) is gradually developed.[2] If you refuse, your first proposition falls. If you consent, you must also admit gradual realization of the fruition of that Path. But you cannot. [2-4] Similarly for the realization of the second, third, and fourth Fruits.

[5] [But tell me more of this gradual piecemeal acquiring:] when a person is working to be able to realize the fruition of Stream-Winning, and wins insight into [the first Truth, namely] the fact of Ill, what does he give up?

A. S. S. Bh.—He gives up the theory of soul, doubt, the infection of mere rule and ritual,[3] and a fourth part in the corruptions that are bound up with them.

Th.—This fourth part:—do you maintain that he [thereby] becomes one quarter Stream-Winner, one quarter not? Has one quarter of him won, attained to, arrived at, realized the Fruit? Does a quarter of him abide in personal contact with it, and a quarter not? Does a

[1] *Sutta-Nipāta*, verse 962; *Dhammapada*, verse 239; quoted already, I. 4, § 17; and below, § 18.

[2] Development in Path-attainments is considered as essentially a momentary flash of insight. Each *phala-citta* (unit of fruitional consciousness) is, for instance, momentary, albeit the *flow* of such units may persist awhile. Cf. *Compendium*, pp. 25, 161, *n.* 5, 215.

[3] The first three 'Fetters.' See above, p. 66, *n.* 2.

quarter of him get seven more rebirths only, rebirths only among gods and men, or one more rebirth only?[1] Is one quarter of him endowed with implicit faith in the Buddha, the Norm, the Order? Is a quarter of him endowed with virtues dear to Ariyans, and a quarter of him not? You deny this, yet it follows from your proposition.

[6] Again, when he wins insight into [the second, third, and fourth Truths, namely] the cause of Ill, its cessation, and the Path leading to that, what does he give up? The same things, say you? Then the same objection applies.

[7-9] Or what does a person who is working to be able to realize the fruition of the other three Paths give up?

A. S. S. Bh.—He gives up respectively (1) the bulk of sense-desires, intense ill-will, and a quarter of the corruptions bound up with them; (2) the residuum of sense-desires and of ill-will, and one quarter of the corruptions bound up with them; (3) lusting after life in any of the higher heavens, conceit, distraction, ignorance, and one quarter of the corruptions bound up with them.

Th.—Then the same objection applies, namely, you must say whether, for example, he is one quarter Arahant,[2] one quarter not, and so on.

[10] When a person who is practising to be able to realize the fruition of Stream-Winning is beginning to see the fact of Ill, would you call him 'a practiser'?

A. S. S. Bh.—Yes.

Th.—Would you, when he has seen it, call him 'established in the fruit'? No, you reply, but why not? So again, in the case of the three other Truths—why not?

[11] Again, you allow that such a person, when he is coming to see the [first] Path, may be called a practiser, and you allow that when he has seen that Path, he is to be called 'established in fruition.' Yet you do not allow that such a person who, when he is coming to see the fact

[1] On these terms, see above, p. 77, *n.* 3.

[2] The detailed replies to (1), (2), and (3) enumerate the respective rewards of the Second, Third, and Fourth Paths stated fully in I. 4, §§ 5, 9, and 13.

of Ill, may be called practiser, may, when he has seen the fact of Ill, be called 'established in fruition'—why not? Again, you allow that such a person, when he is coming to see the [first] Path, may be called practiser, and when he has seen the fact of Ill, may be called established in fruition. Yet you do not allow that such a person who, when he is coming to see the cause, or the cessation of Ill, may be called practiser, may, when he has seen either of these Truths, be called established in fruition—why not?

[12] Once more, you allow that such a person, when he is coming to see the fact of Ill, may be called practiser, while you refuse, when he has seen that fact, to call him established in fruition (as in § 10). Then you must allow, and refuse similarly, if we substitute any other of the Four Truths—but to this you did not agree [§ 11]. [13] With reference to your position (in § 12): you compel yourself to admit, that insight into the fact, or the cause, or the cessation, of Ill is really of no value.[1]

[14] *A. S. S. Bh.*—You affirm then that, when once [the first Truth, viz., the fact and nature of] Ill is seen, the Four Truths are seen?

Th.—Yes.

A. S. S. Bh.—Then you must admit also that the First Truth amounts to the Four Truths.

Th.—[Ah, no! for you as for us] if the material aggregate (khandha) is seen to be impermanent, all five are seen to be so.[2] Yet you would not therefore say that the material aggregate amounts to all the others. [15] A similar argument may be applied to the twelvefold field of sense and the twenty-two 'controllers' or faculties.

[16] If you believe that the fruition of the First Path is realized by [insight considered as divided into so many integral portions, for example,] the Four Insights, the

[1] Since the discerner may not be called 'established in fruition.'

[2] 'Just as the presence of the sea may be known by the taste of one drop of sea-water.'—*Comy.* See Appendix: Paramattha.

Eight, Twelve, Forty-four, Seventy-seven Insights,[1] then you must admit a corresponding number of Fruits of the First Path—which of course you do not.

[17] *A. S. S. Bh.*—You say our proposition that there is a gradual sequence in penetration is wrong. But was it not said by the Exalted One: '*Even, O bhikkhus, as the ocean slopes gradually, inclines gradually, has gradual hollows, without abrupt precipices, so, in this Norm and Discipline, is there gradual training, gradual achievement, gradual practice, but no sudden discernment of gnosis*'?[2]

[18] Again, was it not said by the Exalted One:

> '*Little by little, one by one, as pass*
> *The moments, gradually let the wise*
> *Like smith the blemishes of silver, blow*
> *The specks away that mar his purity*'?[3]

[19] *Th.*—That is so. But did not the venerable Gavampati address the brethren thus: '*Brothers, I have heard this from the Exalted One, and learnt it from his lips:—O bhikkhus! whoso sees the fact of Ill, sees also its cause, its cessation, and the course of practice leading thereto. Whoso sees the cause of Ill, sees also Ill itself, its cessation, and the course of practice leading thereto. Whoso sees the cessation of Ill, sees also Ill itself, its cause, and the course of practice leading to its cessation. Whoso sees the way, sees also Ill, sees its cause, sees its cessation*'?[4]

[20] Again, was it not said by the Exalted One:

> '*For him e'en as insight doth come to pass,*
> *Three things as bygones are renounced for aye:*

[1] These are explained as insight into (*a*) the Truths, (*b*) the Truths *plus* the four Sections of analytic knowledge (paṭisambhidā's), (*c*) the Causal formula (paṭicca-samuppāda), (*d*) the Truths each applied to items 2 to 12 of that formula (as in *Saŋyutta-Nik.*, ii. 56 f.; ñāṇassa vatthūni), and, similarly applied, these seven terms: 'impermanent, conditioned, causally arisen, subject to perish, to pass away, to lose passion, to cease' (*Saŋyutta-Nik.*, ii. 26).

[2] *Vinaya Texts*, iii. 303.

[3] See above (I. 4, § 17), from the *Comy.*

[4] *Saŋyutta-Nik.*, v. 436.

Belief that in him dwells a soul, and doubt,
And faith in rule and rite—if aught remain.
Both from the fourfold doom is he released
And n'er the six fell deeds are his to do' ?[1]

Again, was it not said by the Exalted One: '*Whenever, O bhikkhus, for the Ariyan disciple there doth arise the stainless, flawless Eye of the Norm—that whatsoever by its nature may happen, may all by its nature cease—then with the coming of that vision doth he put away these three fetters: belief in a soul, doubt, and the contagion of mere rule and ritual*' ?[2]

---

10. *Of a Buddha's Everyday Usage.*

Controverted Point.—That the Exalted Buddha's ordinary speech[3] was supramundane.[4]

From the Commentary.—The Andhakas hold that his daily usages were supramundane usages.

[1] Does this not involve the further statement that his speech impinged only on the spiritual, but not on the mundane ear; and that the spiritual, not the mundane, intelligence responded to it, and thus that disciples alone were aware of it, not average persons? You do not admit this. . . . Nay, you know that the Exalted Buddha's speech struck on the mundane hearing of men, was responded to by mundane intelligence, and that average persons were aware of it.

[2] [The terms he used, are they supramundane—] Path, Fruit, Nibbāna, Path and Fruit of Stream-Winning, Once-Returning, Never-Returning, Arahantship, earnest

[1] Quoted above, I. 4, § 18. *Sutta-Nipāta*, verse 231.

[2] Quoted above, I. 5, § 19; see references.

[3] Vohāro refers to common, worldly matters in general, but reference is confined throughout to speech.

[4] Lōk-uttara, a wide term meaning all unworldly thought and ideals, and including supernormal powers of mind, when occupied with such ideals only. Jhāna, e.g., *may* be lokiya, mundane. The Opponent over-emphasizes the supernormal side of it.

application in mindfulness, supreme endeavour, steps to magic potency, controlling power or faculty, force, factor of enlightenment?

[3] Were there any who heard his everyday speech? But you deny that a supramundane object is known by way of the ear, impinges on the ear, comes into the avenue of hearing. Therefore you cannot affirm that men 'heard' his everyday speech.

[4] Were there any who were ravished by his everyday speech? [We know that there were such.[1]] But is a supramundane thing an occasion of sensuous desire, ravishing, entrancing, intoxicating, captivating, enervating? Is it not rather the opposite? . . .

[5] Further, there were some who were offended by his habitual speech[2] But is a supramundane thing an occasion of hate, of anger, of resentment? Is it not rather the opposite? . . .

[6] Further, there were some who were baffled by his habitual speech.[3] But is a supramundane thing an occasion of obfuscation, causing want of insight and blindness, extinguishing understanding, provoking vexation, not conducing to Nibbāna? Is it not rather the opposite? . . .

[7] Now those who heard the Exalted Buddha's habitual speech, did they all develop the paths? Yes, you say? But foolish average people heard him—matricides, too, and parricides, slayers of Arahants, shedders of holy blood, schismatics—therefore you are affirming that these developed the paths! . . .

[8] *A.*—But you may with one golden wand point out both a heap of paddy and a heap of gold. So the Exalted One, with his supramundane habitual speech, habitually spoke about both mundane and supramundane doctrine.

Th.—It is no less possible to point out both paddy and

[1] Cf. *Psalms of the Brethren*, verse, 1270; *Dialogues*, ii. 16.

[2] Cf. *Saŋyutta-Nik.*, i. 160; *Dīgha-Nikāya*, Pāṭhika-Suttanta, etc.

[3] E.g., disciples were asked to explain concise pronouncements by the Master (*Saŋyutta-Nik.*, iv. 93 f., etc.).

gold with a wand of castor-oil wood. So the Exalted One, with his mundane habitual speech, habitually spoke about both mundane and supramundane matter.

[9] Now some of you[1] say that the habitual speech of the Exalted One the Buddha was mundane when speaking to one so conversing, supramundane when speaking to one so conversing. But this implies that his words impinged on mundane hearing when he spoke of worldly things, and on the supramundane hearing when he spoke of supramundane things; also that his hearers understood with their mundane intelligence in the former case, and with their supramundane intelligence in the latter; also that average persons understood in the former case, disciples in the latter. To which you do not agree.

[10] *A.*—It is wrong then, according to you, to say that the Exalted Buddha's customary speech was mundane when he spoke of mundane matters, supramundane when he spoke of supramundane matters. But did he not use both kinds of speech? You assent. Then surely what you maintain is untenable.

[11] Again, your proposition involves this further admission: that the speech of anyone becomes that of which he is speaking—that if you speak of Path, your word becomes Path; similarly of what is not Path, of Fruit, of Nibbāna, of the Conditioned, of matter, of mind and their opposites.

---

11. *Of Cessation.*

Controverted Point.—That there are two cessations [of sorrow].

From the Commentary.—It is a belief of the Mahiŋsāsakas and the Andhakas that the Third Truth (as to the Cessation of Ill), though constructed as one, relates to two cessations, according as sorrow ceases through reasoned or unreasoned reflections about things.

---

[1] So the *Comy.*

[1] If you assert that there are two kinds of cessation,[1] you must also assert this duality with respect to the cessation of Ill, the Truth about the cessation of Ill, the Truth about the nature of Ill, its cause, and the path leading to the cessation of Ill—to none of which you consent.

Further, you must assert that there are two shelters, two retreats, two refuges, two supports, two deathlessnesses, two ambrosias, two Nibbānas[2]—which you deny. Or if you admit that there are, say, two Nibbānas, you must admit some specific difference, say, of high, low, base, sublime, superior, inferior—some boundary, division, line or cleavage[3] in these two Nibbānas—which you deny.[4]

[2] Further, you admit, do you not, that things[5] which have ceased without deep reflection,[6] may also be made

[1] Nirōdha. In religious import, the term is a synonym of Nibbāna, whether it refers to cessation of Ill (dukkha), or to the conditions of rebirth which inevitably result in Ill. In the medically inspired formula of the four Truths, nirōdha is tantamount to 'health,' i.e., to the 'cessation' of disease. Hence it suggests happiness, rather than the reverse. Hence the English word 'riddance' might often be a better rendering.

[2] These terms are all similes for Nibbāna, from the Suttas.

[3] To the different readings of this word (see text, 226, *n.* 3), we would add antarikā, 'interstice in threads,' from *Vinaya Texts*, III. 94.

[4] The somewhat scholastic insistence on the oneness of Nibbāna in the mediæval *Compendium* (p. 168) is here shown to have early authority, but we cannot quote any Suttanta support for it.

[5] Sankhārā. On the meaning in this context, cf. *Compendium*, 211, *n.* 3. It should not be concluded that on any idealistic view 'things' are made no longer to exist now for the individual thinker through his thought. According to the Commentarial tradition, 'to cease' means here prospective cessation; 'to make to cease= to cause to go into a state of not re-arising (anuppattibhāvaŋ)'—the negative of the term used to express future rebirth.

[6] Paṭisankhā, literally, re-reckoning. On this term, large, if vague in import, yet rarely used in the Nikāyas, see *Bud. Psy. Eth.*, p. 354, *n.* 2. In popular diction its use in negative form is well shown in the simile of the thirsty, exhausted man drinking 'rashly, unreflectingly,' from a cup against the contents of which he had been warned. *Saŋyutta-Nik.*, ii. 110. See *Compendium*, *loc. cit.* Deep reflection of spiritual insight, through its purity and the absence of statements and questionings, is *said* to make worldly things cease.—*Comy.*

to cease by deep reflection? But this does not involve two (final) cessations.

[3] *M. A.*—Surely it does, if you admit, as do you not, that things which have ceased without, and those that have ceased by, deep reflection are both annihilated for ever?[1]

[4] *Th.*—You admit that the latter class of things ceases because the Ariyan [eightfold] Path has been attained? Then must you also admit that the former class of things ceases for the same reason—but you do not.

[5] Again, the latter class (i.e., things which have ceased by deep reflection) does not, according to you, ever arise again. Then you must also admit this of the former class—but you do not.[2] . . . Hence cessation is really one, not two.

[1] *Comy.* PTS edition, p. 61, line 1: for sakavādissa read paravādissa. The Theravādin assents to the asserted annihilation, partly because there is no need to destroy what has been destroyed, partly because the things that have ceased without paṭisankhā continue as non-existent when the Path is developed.—*Comy.*

[2] *Contra* the Theravādin's view, § 3.

BOOK III

1. *Of Powers.*

Controverted Point.—That the powers of the Buddha are common to disciples.

From the Commentary.—This is an opinion among the Andhakas, derived from a thoughtless consideration of the ten Suttas in the Anuruddha Saŋyutta,[1] beginning: '*I, brethren, from practice and development of the Four Applications of Mindfulness, understand even as it really is the causal occasion*[2] *as such, and what is not the causal occasion,*' *etc.* Now of a Tathāgata's 'ten powers,' some he holds wholly in common with his disciples, some not, and some are partly common to both. All can share insight into extinction of intoxicants (ā s a v ā); he alone discerns the degrees of development in the controlling powers (i n d r i y ā n i). The causal occasion of anything, as well as seven other matters, a Tathāgata knows without limit, the disciple knows them only within a certain range.[3] The latter can state them; the former can explain them. But the Andhakas say that the whole of his power was held in common with his [leading] disciples.

[1] *Th.*—If your proposition is true, you must also affirm that power of the Tathāgata is power of the disciple and conversely, whether you take power in general, or this or that power, or power of this or that sort. And you must also affirm that the disciple's previous application, previous line of conduct, instruction in the Doctrine, teaching of the Doctrine,[4] are of the same sort as those of the Tathāgata. But all these [corollaries] you deny. . . .

[1] *Saŋyutta-Nikāya*, v. 304 f.; Suttas 15-24.

[2] Ṭ h ā n a ŋ ṭ h ā n a t o, paraphrased by Buddhaghosa (*Comy. on A.*, iii. 417) as k ā r a ṇ a ŋ k ā r a ṇ a t o (reason).

[3] P a d e s e n a, cf. *Jāt.*, v. 457 (trans., v. 246, *n.* 3).

[4] The *Comy.* calls these two pairs of terms two pairs of synonyms.

[2] You affirm [of course] that the Tathāgata is Conqueror, Master, Buddha Supreme, All-knowing, All-seeing, Lord of the Norm, the Fountain-head of the Norm.[1] But you would refuse these titles to disciples. Nor will you admit of the disciples, as you do of the Tathāgata, that he brings into being a Way where no way was, produces a Way that had not been called into being, proclaims a Way untold, is knower and seer of the Way and adept therein.

[3] If you affirm that [one of the Tathāgata's powers: that] of understanding as they really are the different degrees of development in our controlling powers (indriyāni) is held by disciples in common with him, you must also allow that a disciple is all-knowing, all-seeing.

[4] *A.*[2]—But you will admit that if a disciple can distinguish a causal occasion from an occasion that is not causal, it were right to say that genuine insight of this kind is common to Tathāgata and disciple. [But you refuse to say this.[3]] . . .

[5] Again, you will admit that if a disciple knows, in its causal occasion and conditions,[4] the result of actions undertaken in the past, future, and present, it were right to say that genuine insight of this kind is common to Tathāgata and disciple. [This, too, you refuse to say.[5]]

[6-11] A similar implication holds good with respect to the power of knowing the tendency of any course of action, of knowing the worlds of manifold and intrinsically different

[1] Dhamma-paṭisaraṇaŋ, the latter half is a neuter substantive applied to the Buddha, when appealed to for guidance and explanatory teaching. It means literally 'resorting to, having recourse to,' and thence the objective of such movement. See *Bud. Psychology*, 1914, p. 69.

[2] The Andhaka is querist to the end.

[3] The Theravādin draws the line at a *coincident range* of power. 'These questions (§§ 4-11) are asked just to establish this: that the powers named are common to disciples just in so far as they know (jānanamatta-sāmaññena).'—*Comy.*

[4] Ṭhānaso hetuso, paraphrased, in *Comy. on Anguttara-Nik.*, iii. 417, by paccayato ceva hetuto ca.

[5] Because the power is not equally supreme in both.

elements; of knowing the manifold things beings have done from free choice, of knowing the attainments in Jhāna or Deliverance or Concentration[1]—their impurities, their purity, and emergence from them; of knowing how to remember former lives; of knowing whence beings are deceasing and where they are being reborn. All these corollaries, namely, that if a disciple knows, where a Tathāgata knows, the knowledge is common to both, you deny. Finally, [12] are not the intoxicants as extinct for a disciple as for a Tathāgata? Or is there any difference between their extinction for a Tathāgata and their extinction for a disciple, or between the [ensuing] emancipation for a Tathāgata and that for a disciple? 'None' you say;[2] then surely my proposition holds.

[13] Again, you have admitted that a Tathāgata shares the power of insight into the extinction as it really is of intoxicants, in common with the disciple. But you will not admit—though you surely must—that this is the case with his knowledge of real causal antecedents and such as are not real . . .[3] and also of the decease and rebirth of beings.

[14] You affirm then that the power of the Tathāgata's insight to discern as it really is a causal antecedent and one that is not, is not held in common by disciples. Yet you refuse to draw this line in the case of the extinction of intoxicants. Similarly, in the case of the remaining eight powers—[which is absurd].

[15] Again, you admit that the power of the Tathāgata's insight to know as they really are the degrees of development in controlling powers is not held in common with the disciples. Yet you will not admit as much with regard to the insight into what are really causal antecedents and what

[1] Buddhaghosa (on *Anguttara-Nik.*, iii. 417) enumerates these as 'the four Jhānas, the eight Deliverances (*Dialogues*, ii. 119), and the three samādhi's (*Dīgha-Nik.*, iii. 219), also the nine grades in elimination (*ibid.*, 266).

[2] Here the Theravādin admits there is no distinction in insight. —*Comy.*

[3] Here supply the remaining powers, §§ 6-11.

are not, . . . nor of the insight into the extinction of intoxicants. (Here, on the contrary, you find powers held in common.)[1]

[16] On the other hand, you admit a common power[1] in the discernment of what is really a causal occasion . . . and of the extinction of intoxicants. But you will not equally admit a common power in discernment of degrees of development in controlling powers—how is this?

---

2. *Of [the Quality called] Ariyan.*

Controverted Point.—(*a*) That the power of a Tathāgata, e.g., in discerning as it really is the causal occasion of anything, and its contradictory, is Ariyan.[2]

From the Commentary.—That, of the foregoing ten powers of discernment or insight, not only the last (insight into extinction of intoxicants), but also the preceding nine were Ariyan, is a view of the Andhakas.

[1] *Th.*—If it be so, you should also affirm of that power that it is the (Ariyan) Path, [or other Ariyan doctrine, such as] Fruit, Nibbāna, one of the Four Paths to Arahantship, or of the Four Fruits thereof, one of the Applications in Mindfulness, Supreme Efforts, Steps to Potency, Controlling Powers,[3] Forces, or Factors of Enlightenment. But you do not agree to this.

[2] Or is [the concept of] Emptiness the object of that power?[4] If you deny, you cannot affirm your proposition. If you assent, then you must affirm that one who is attending to the exercise of this power attends also to Emptiness. If you deny, you cannot affirm that Emptiness is the object of the power in your proposition. If you

[1] To the whole or to a limited extent.—See *Comy.* above.

[2] See Rhys Davids, *Early Buddhism*, 49; Mrs. Rh. D., *Buddhism*, 69.

[3] I.e., ethical or spiritual faculties. Cf. I. 2, § 15; *Compendium*, 179 f.

[4] Suññatā. Cf. *Bud. Psy. Eth.*, p. 91, § 344 f. 'There are two Emptinesses: (1) In the aggregates of a soul (satta); (2) Nibbāna, or detachment from all conditioned things. The Opponent denies because of the latter, assents because of the former.—*Comy.*

assent, then you are claiming a combination of two (mental) contacts, two consciousnesses—which of course you deny.

[3] A similar argument holds good for the other two concepts of the 'Signless' and the 'Not-hankered-after.'[1]

[4] [Or, to argue conversely], you admit that (1) the Applications in Mindfulness are Ariyan, and have as their object the concepts of 'Emptiness,' the 'Signless,' and the 'Not-hankered-after.' But you deny that these are the object of that power of a Tathāgata. Hence that power cannot be classified under things 'Ariyan.'

[5] This argument applies also to (2) the Supreme Efforts and (3-6) the Steps to Potency, etc. (§ 1).

[6] *A.*—You say then that my proposition is wrong—that it is not Ariyan, and has not as its object Emptiness, the Signless, or the Not-hankered-after. Yet you do not deny that the six foregoing doctrines are Ariyan, and also have that Threefold object—why deny the same of that power of which my proposition speaks?

[7] *Th.*—Nay, why do *you* maintain that the power of a Tathāgata, in discerning as it really is the decrease and rebirth of beings and its contradictory, is Ariyan, while you are not prepared to class that power with things we call Ariyan—the Path, and so on?

[8-12] *The arguments in* §§ 2-6 *are then repeated for the Andhaka's propositions:—that the other powers of a Tathāgata discerning the decease and rebirth of beings as they really are, etc., are Ariyan.*

[13] *A.*—You admit then that the tenth of the 'Powers' ascribed to a Tathāgata—insight into the extinction as it really is of intoxicants—is Ariyan, but you deny it in the case of the two powers named above. How can you affirm it of the tenth?

[14] *The Andhaka puts the case negatively.*

[15, 16] *As in* [13, 14], *with the addition of the 'Three Signs,' as 'object,' added to the predicate 'is Ariyan.'*

[1] Animitta, Appaṇihita (*Bud. Psy. Eth.*, p. 91, § 344 f.); *Comp.*, 211.

3. *Of Emancipation.*

Controverted Point.—That 'becoming emancipated' has reference to the heart being [at the time] in touch with lust,[1] etc.

From the Commentary.—Whereas it is true that, in minds or hearts devoid of e.g. lust, there is no need to get emancipated, the opinion held at present by such as the Andhakas is that, just as a soiled garment is released from its stains on being washed, so emancipation means that a heart beset with lust is emancipated from lust.[2]

[1] *Th.*—You affirm this. Then you must equally affirm that 'becoming emancipated' refers to a heart which is accompanied by, co-existent with, mixed with, associated with, has developed with, goes about with, lust; to a heart, again, which is immoral, worldly, in touch with intoxicants, allied with fetters, ties, floods, bonds, hindrances, is infected, allied with grasping, corrupt—which you refuse to do.

[2] If the heart or mind which is in contact be emancipated, are both contact and mind emancipated? 'Yes' you say. But then you must equally affirm that, if the heart which is in touch with lust be emancipated, both lust and heart are emancipated—which you refuse to do.

The same reasoning holds good not only of contact, but also of [the other properties of the mind]—feeling, perception, volition, . . . reason, or understanding.

[1] S a r ā g a ŋ. The prefix s a corresponds to our c o (or affix -f u l). S a implies contact (p h a s s a), and contact was ranked as the essential co-efficient of mind as receptive of, in touch with, sense.

[2] In other words, the climax and crown of Path-graduation is degraded to denote progress in the early stages. Emancipation is technically applied to release from rebirth, through release from the conditions thereof. N i b b ā n a is extinction of lust, hate, and nescience or delusion. Emancipation is the state of purity after the purging was done (cf. III. 4). The opponent holds the serious errors that the Arahant still has lust, etc., to get rid of, and that a preceding unit of consciousness is essentially identical with the succeeding unit. Cf. *Saŋyutta-Nik.*, iv. 251 ; ii. 171 and *passim.*

[3] Once more, if mind which is in contact, and in touch with lust, be emancipated, are both contact and mind emancipated? Yes, you say. But then you must equally affirm that both lust and mind are emancipated—which you refuse to do.

The same reasoning holds good of the other properties of the mind.

[4-6, 7-9] *The same argument is then applied to* 'emancipation' *referred to* 'hate,' *and to* 'nescience or delusion'—*the other two of the fundamental conditions of evil doing.*

[10] *A.*—You say that we are wrong in affirming that a mind full of lust, hate and nescience undergoes emancipation. But your denial that a mind which is devoid of all three undergoes emancipation rather confirms our view.

---

4. *Of Emancipation as a Process.*

Controverted Point.—That spiritual emancipation is a [gradual] process of becoming free.[1]

From the Commentary.—The opinion is questioned of those who confuse the emancipation by partial arrest in the exercise of Jhāna with that emancipation by complete severance experienced in a 'Path-moment.' They think that the mind, partially liberated by the former, completes its emancipation by the gradual process of the latter.

[1] *Th.*—If your proposition is to stand, you must affirm also that such a mind is then in part freed, in part not. And if you assent to the second proposition, you must admit that your subject is part Stream-Winner, part not—in other words, that he has all the attributes of the Stream-Winner in part only.[2]

[2-4] The same argument holds for the other three Paths.

[5] You must also affirm as to whether [each conscious unit] is emancipated at the moment of its genesis, and in process of being emancipated as it ceases.[3] . . .

[1] The heresy seems to be analogous to that in III. 3, and to involve a misapprehension of the orthodox meaning of the term in question (vimutti).

[2] Here and in [2-4] the same lists are given as in I. 4, §§ 1, 5, 9, 13.

[3] Cf. II. 7, § 1: ekaŋ cittaŋ (unit of consciousness).

[6] *Opponent*—You do not assent to my proposition; but was it not said by the Exalted One: '*For him who thus knows thus sees, the heart is set free from the intoxicants of sense-desires, of becoming, and of ignorance*'?[1] Is there no 'being emancipated' here of the emancipated mind?

[7] *Th.*—But is there not also a Suttanta in which the Exalted One said: '*With heart thus made serene, made wholly pure, and very clean, freed from lust and from defilement, become pliant, ready to work and imperturbable, he bends over the mind to insight in the destruction of intoxicants*'?[2] There is no process here of being set free.

[8] You would not speak of a mind partially lusting, hating, being bewildered, being corrupted. How can you then maintain your proposition? Would you not say [straight away] that the mind is lustful or not, malevolent or not, confused or not, suspended or not, destroyed or not, finished or not?[3]

---

5. *Of the Eighth Man.*[4]

Controverted Point.—That for the person in the Eighth Stage, outbursts of wrong views and of doubt are put away.

From the Commentary.—Here the question is raised concerning a certain view of both Andhakas and Sammitiyas, namely, that, at the

---

[1] *Dialogues*, i. 93.

[2] *Ibid.*, 92. It seems a little strange that this is not quoted as 'the same Suttanta.' There are, however, parallels in this work, e.g., p. 96 f. Cf. 98, *n.* 1.

[3] 'The mind' (in our idiom) being, in Buddhist doctrine, a conditioned series of citta's, each as momentary as the 'moments' of its attainments. Here the Theravādin resorts to the principle of Excluded Middle, 'there being no room in philosophic Reality for a third alternative'—paramatthato tatiyā koṭi natthi.—*Comy.*

[4] Aṭṭhama-ko, literally Eighth-er. Of the Four Paths and Four Fruitions, this is the lowest, the first reached, or eighth from Arahantship. The more correct view was that the victories alluded to belonged only to the next stage—to the 'moment' of fruition—making the subject a genuine 'Stream Winner.'

moment of entering on the Path, after qualification and adoption,[1] two of the (ten) corruptions no longer break out in the eighth man—that is, the person who has entered on the stream.

[1] *Th.*—Are you then also prepared to admit that the eighth man is a Stream-Winner, one who has won, obtained, arrived at, and realized the Fruit of Stream-Winning, and that, having achieved, he lives in personal contact therewith? [2, 3] Are you further prepared to admit that he has put away the latent bias of doubt and wrong views? And if these, then also the infection of mere rule and ritual? For your proposition involves all this. [4] Conversely, if you deny that these are put away by him, you must also deny that he has put away wrong views and doubt.

[5] How should he have already put away wrong views and doubt when he has not yet practised the Path wherein they get put away? And not only the Path (the Eightfold), but all the other factors of Enlightenment?[2]

[6] For if he have not put away wrong views and doubt by the Path, or the other factors, he can surely not have put them away by means that is not the Path, but is worldly, co-intoxicant, etc. . . .[3] and corrupt.

[7-8] *A. S.*—Since you deny that a person of the eighth rank has put away the [overt] outburst of wrong views and of doubt, I ask you, will these arise any more in him?

Th.—They will not.

A. S.—Surely then our proposition is true: they *are* put away.

[9, 10] *Th.*—Assuming that the outbursts will not again arise [i.e., become manifest in action], you say they are put away. But is the latent bias of wrong opinions, doubt, and belief in mere rule and ritual equally put away simply because these do not arise? And this you are not prepared to admit.

[11] Once more, you claim that the eighth man has put away wrong views and doubt. But you must then allow

[1] See *Compendium*, pp. 55, 67 f., 129, *n.* 3, 170, *n.* 1.

[2] See above, I. 2, §§ 14-20; III. 2, § 1.

[3] For these elisions in the text, not ours, see above, III. 3, § 7.

that one who has reached the stage in Jhāna-meditation of 'adoption'[1] has put them away, and in this you do not concur.

---

6. *Of the Controlling Powers*[2] *of the Eighth Man.*

Controverted Point.—That the five controlling powers are absent[3] in a person of the Eighth Stage.

From the Commentary.—Among the Andhakas it is held that, at the moment of entering the (first stage of the) Path, the 'Eighth Man' is in process of acquiring, but has not yet attained to, these powers.

[1] *Th.*—You must deny him faith, if you deny in him the controlling power of faith. So also for the other four. But you will not go as far as that. [2] Contrariwise, you do allow that he [as Eighth Man] has faith and the rest, but you go no farther. [3] Yet you are prepared to admit, with respect to other controlling powers—e.g., mind, gladness, etc. . . . and psychic life[4]—that whoso has the attribute, has also the controlling power of it. [4] Why draw the line at those five? [5, 6] as, in fact, you do.

[7] You contend that, whereas the controlling power of faith is absent in him, faith itself is not absent. That whereas the controlling powers of energy, mindfulness, concentration, and reason are absent in him, he is neither indolent, nor heedless, nor unsteady or mentally vacillating, nor stupid, nor deaf, nor dumb.

[8] You acknowledge that his faith, energy, etc., are [of the saving kind called] forth-leading,[5] yet you do not credit him with the controlling powers [in which such attributes consist].

[1] See above, from the Commentary.

[2] The five spiritual (or moral) sense-faculties are faith, energy, mindfulness, concentration, reason, or understanding. We cannot point to any passage where they are, as a pentad., connected with the five 'external' senses. But they were considered, no less than the latter five, as capable of being raised to powers controlling the reciprocal interaction of the human being and his environment.

[3] I.e., of course, not yet developed at this stage.

[4] See *Bud. Psy. Eth.*, p. 4 (xviii.) and p. 19, § 19; *Compendium*, 17.

[5] Niyyānika. Cf. *Bud. Psy. Eth.*, p 82, *n.* 2.

[9-12] You admit the attainment both of the attributes and of these five controlling powers in the person who is practising that he may realize the fruit of Once-Returning, of Never-Returning, of Arahantship, but you deny the latter for the Eighth Man alone; the one goes with the other!

[13] Finally, is there not a Suttanta in which the Exalted One said: '*The five controlling powers, bhikkhus—which are they? The controlling powers that are faith, energy, mindfulness, concentration, understanding. From the completion and perfection of these five, a man becomes Arahant. Held in a weaker degree, the holder becomes one who is practising that he may realize the Fruit of Arahantship; in a yet weaker degree the holder becomes a Never-Returner; in a yet weaker degree, one who is practising that he may realize the Fruit of Never-Returning; in a yet weaker degree, a Once-Returner; in a yet weaker degree, one who is practising that he may realize the Fruit of Once-Returning; in a yet weaker degree, a Stream-Winner; in a yet weaker degree, one who is practising that he may realize the Fruit of Stream-Winning. In whom these five controlling powers are in every way, and everywhere wholly absent, he, I declare, is one who stands without, in the ranks of the average man*'?[1]

Yet you would not say that the Eighth Man stood thus without? Hence you must concede that the five controlling powers are present in him.

---

7. *Of the 'Celestial Eye.'*[2]

Controverted Point.—That the fleshly eye, when it is the medium of an idea,[3] becomes the celestial eye.

From the Commentary.—This is a view held by the Andhakas and Sammitiyas.

---

[1] *Saŋyutta-Nikāya*, v. 202.

[2] Or vision. The power of apprehending, as visualized, things not accessible to the sense of sight.

[3] Dhammupatthaddaŋ. 'Medium' is, more literally, support, basis. Dhamma may stand, as in § 1, for Fourth Jhāna, or for the sensuous idea, or the spiritual idea, according to the context.

[1] *Th.*—If you affirm this, you must also say that the fleshly eye is the celestial eye, and conversely, that the two are like in kind, are, in fact, identical, the one having the same range, power, and field as the other. This you deny.

[2] Again, if you make the two thus on a par, you are affirming that something grasped at [as effect by previous karma][1] becomes something not so grasped at, that experience in the universe of sense is experience in the universe of 'Rūpa,' that experience, analogously reasoning, in the universe of Rūpa is experience in the universe of the remoter heavens, that the things included in these universes are 'the *Un*-included'[2]—which is absurd.

[3] Further, you are, by your proposition, also admitting that the celestial eye, when it is the medium of a sensuous idea [in Jhāna], becomes the fleshly eye. And, again, that, when it is the medium of a [spiritual] idea, it then becomes the eye of understanding—which you must deny.

[4] Further, you are also admitting that there are only two kinds of vision (or 'eye'). If you deny, your proposition falls. If you assent, I would ask whether the Exalted One did not speak of three kinds of vision—the fleshly, the celestial, and the eye of understanding, thus: '*Three, bhikkhus, are the modes of sight*[3]*—which are they? The fleshly eye, the celestial eye, the eye of understanding?*

'*The eye of flesh, the heavenly eye,*
And insight's eye, vision supreme:—
These are the eyes, the visions three
Revealèd by the man supreme.

The genesis of fleshly eye,
The way of eye celestial,
How intuition took its rise:—
The eye of insight unsurpassed.
Whoso doth come that eye to know,
Is from all ill and sorrow freed.'[4]

[1] *See Compendium*, 159, *n.* 6.

[2] Cf. *Bud. Psy. Eth.*, xc.; 254, *n.* 1.

[3] Literally, 'are these eyes.'

[4] Iti-vuttaka, § 61.

8. *Of the Celestial Ear.*

Controverted Point.—That the fleshly ear, when it is the medium of an idea, is the celestial ear.

[1, 2] *correspond exactly to the same sections in* III. 7.

[3] *Th.*—Further, you are, by your proposition, also admitting that the celestial ear, when it is the medium of a [sensuous] idea, becomes the fleshly ear. Further, you are also admitting that there is only one ear, or sense of hearing. If you deny, you cannot maintain your proposition. If you assent, I would ask whether the Exalted One did not speak of two ears—the fleshly ear and the heavenly ear?[1]

---

9. *Of Insight into Destiny according to Deeds.*

Controverted Point.—That the celestial eye amounts to insight into destiny according to deeds.

From the Commentary.—This is an opinion arising from a careless interpretation of the Sutta-passage: '*With purified celestial eye surpassing that of men he sees beings as they pass away from one form of existence and take shape in another . . . he knows their destiny as being according to their deeds,*'[2] namely, that the vision of itself was also an explanation of the things seen.

[1] *Th.*—Your proposition involves this also: that in the act of vision, attention is also paid to the sequence of the Karma—which you did not allow. Or, if you do allow this, you are further implying a combination of two contacts and two consciousnesses—which you do not allow. [2] *Either*, I repeat, you refuse to admit, that the act of seeing with the celestial eye involves judgment:—[3] '*these* beings, sirs, have plenty of evil deeds, words, and thoughts in their past:[4] they are accusers of Ariyans, holders of erratic views, undertakers of actions in conformity therewith; now that their living frame is broken up, they are

[1] Cf. *Dialogues*, i. 89, and elsewhere, e.g., *Majjhima-Nik.*, ii. 19.

[2] *Dīgha-Nik.*, i. 82 (*Dialogues*, i. 91), and elsewhere.

[3] Manasikaroti, or attending.

[4] Literally, 'are endowed with.' So below.

reborn in purgatory, in the abode of the fallen, the destiny of evil-doers, a woeful doom; but *those* folk, sirs, on the other hand, have plenty of good deeds, words, and thoughts to their account: the opposite of the foregoing; they are now reborn in a heaven to a happy destiny'; *or*, you accept this implication in celestial sight, and concede that [in what is really one act of consciousness] there are two contacts (or mental stimuli) and two consciousnesses.

[3] Again, if there have been those who, without this celestial vision, without having obtained, arrived at, and realized it, have had insight into destiny as being according to deeds, your proposition cannot stand. [4] The venerable Sāriputta, as you imagine, was such an one. Did he not say:

> '*Nor to attain the vision of my past,*
> *Nor for the means to see—the eye divine—*
> *The mystic power to read the thoughts of men,*
> *Discern decease, rebirth in earth and heaven,*
> *Nor for the ear celestially attuned*
> *Cared I to strive*' ?[1]

---

10. *Of Moral Restraint.*

Controverted Point.—That there is self-control among devas.

From the Commentary.—The question is raised concerning the view of those who hold that among the devas, beginning above the Thirty-Three, inasmuch as there was no committal of the five vices,[2] there is self-control.

---

[1] *Theragāthā*, 996, 997. Cf. *Psalms of the Brethren*, p. 345. The inference drawn by the translator from the *Commentary* to that work tallies with the tradition. But we may conclude that Sāriputta, who stood foremost in wisdom and insight (*Anguttara-Nik.*, i. 23) could, according to tradition, have exercised those powers, had he cared to. Cf. the contrasted temperament in Moggallāna, verse 1182-84. The verse is cited (*a*) to dissipate (*Comy.*, *lege* vikkhepaŋ karonto) any misinterpretation through a wrong impression that the Thera could not had he wished, (*b*) to refute the opponent on his own ground.

[2] Verāni: taking life, theft, fornication, false, slanderous, idle speech, taking intoxicating drinks.

[1] *Th.*—Since you affirm its existence, you imply also [that there may be] absence of it among devas. You deny this, meaning that there is no want of it among devas. Then you imply that there is no [need of] self-control among them—this again you deny, by your proposition.

[2] Granting that virtue is restraint from absence of self-restraint, does this restraint exist among devas? 'Yes,' you say, but you are hereby implying also the co-existence of absence of self-restraint. And this you deny.

[3] Yet you admit the co-existence among humans. Why not among devas? [4] For instance, you say 'devas abstain from taking life, from intoxicating drinks.' Yet you deny that these vices are found among them. [5] You contend they are not found among them, yet you will not allow that restraint from them is not found either, [6, 7] although you allow the co-existence of both among men.

[8] *Opponent.*—But if moral restraint is absent among devas, surely you are implying that all devas are takers of life, thieves, etc.[1] They are not, hence, etc. . . .

---

11. *Of Unconscious Life.*

Controverted Point.—That there is consciousness among the denizens of the sphere called Unconscious.[2]

From the Commentary.—This belief is of the Andhakas, derived partly from the Word: '*mind* [at rebirth] *is conditioned by previous actions*,'[3] so that, in their view, there is no living rebirth without mind, partly from this other Word: '*those devas decease from that group as soon as consciousness arises in them.*'[4] They concede consciousness to those devas of the unconscious sphere at the moment of rebirth and of decease.

---

[1] Asaṃvara = saṃvaritabbo—that over which self-restraint ought to be used.—*Comy.* Hence, 'a vice.' If there were no vice, self-restraint would be meaningless. Presence of vice denotes absence of self-restraint.

[2] Cf. *Compendium*, p. 136. A sphere in the mid-heavens called Rūpa-loka. Cf. *n.* 4.

[3] *Vibhanga*, 135 f.; *Sanyutta-Nik.*, ii. 2 *passim*.

[4] *Dīgha-Nik.*, iii. 33. 'Mind' (viññāṇa) and consciousness (saññā) are here used in a synonymous and very general sense.

[1] *Th.*—But you surely cannot admit that such a being has conscious life or destiny, dwells among conscious beings, fares onward with conscious continuity from birth to birth, has consciousness as his birthright, has acquired a conscious personality? Is not the opposite of all these terms true of him? [2] Is their life, etc., fivefold in its constituents? Is it not rather a life, destiny . . . acquisition of personality, of a single constituent?[1] Hence, even if we grant your proposition, you cannot say that such a being, when consciously functioning, functions by just that [act of] consciousness you ascribe to him; nor do you claim this.

[3] If, in § 1, you substitute for 'unconscious beings' 'men,' you could and would describe the latter further as 'having conscious life, and destiny, and so on.' And you would describe them, further, as having a life, destiny, habitation, further rebirth, constitution, acquisition of personality [as determined for them] by five organic constituents. But when I say you have committed yourself to all this with respect to unconscious beings, in virtue of your proposition, you deny. Similarly for § 3, if we substitute 'man' for 'such a being.'

[4] Let us assume the truth of your proposition, admitting, of course, that there is consciousness in the human sphere—why do you go on to affirm, for those devas, an unconscious life, destiny, habitation, further rebirth, constitution, acquisition of personality, but deny it for men? And why do you go on, further, to affirm a life, destiny, etc., of one organic constituent for those devas, but deny it for men? Why, finally, do you deny, for the unconscious beings, the functioning in consciousness by just that [quota of] consciousness you assign to them, but affirm it in the case of human beings?

[5] *A.*—If it is wrong to say 'there is consciousness in

[1] I.e., of material quality only, not of this, *plus* the four classes of mental constituents. V o k ā r a is here used for k h a n d h a. Buddhist tradition connects it with k a r - m a. V i v i d h e n a v i s u ŋ v i s u ŋ k a r ī y a t i : 'is made by various ways and alternatives.' Cf. *Vibhanga*, 419; *Yamaka, passim*.

the Unconscious devas,' let me remind you of a Suttanta in which the Exalted One said: *There are devas, bhikkhus, called the Unconscious Beings; now those devas, when consciousness does arise, decease from that group.*[1] But our view really is this, that [6] they are only conscious sometimes.

Th.—That is to say, they are sometimes conscious beings, having conscious life, having fivefold organic life, and sometimes unconscious beings, having unconscious life, having a single organic life—which is absurd.

[7] Again, at what time are they conscious, at what time not?

A.—At decease and at rebirth, but not during life.

Th.—But then the same absurd transformation must happen.

---

12. *Of [the plane] wherein Consciousness neither is nor is not.*[2]

Controverted Point.—That it is wrong to say that, in the plane wherein consciousness neither is nor is not, there is consciousness.

From the Commentary.—This inquiry was directed against those who, like the Andhakas of our time, hold that, from the Word :—'*the sphere of neither consciousness nor unconsciousness*,'[3]—it is not right to say that in that realm of life there is consciousness.

[1] *Th.*—But you would not describe that plane as one of life, destiny, habitation of beings, continued existence, birth, acquired personality that is unconscious? [2] Nor as a life, etc., of one constituent only? Would you not call it a life of *four* constituents?[4]

[1] See p. 153, *n.* 4.

[2] In the Pali summary, at the end of Book III., the title becomes 'of the topmost sphere of life.'

[3] Cf. any account of the more abstract Jhānas (e.g., *Bud. Psy. Eth.*, 74), or of the remoter heavens (e.g., *Vibhanga*, 421).

[4] I.e., of the four *mental* aggregates. We are now concerned with the remotest, Arūpa or immaterial heavens. The PTS ed. has here omitted a sentence. Cf. the next § (2), and also III. 11, § 1. For Hañci asaññabhavo, etc., read . . . saññabhavo.

[3] If we deny consciousness among the Unconscious Beings, and call that sphere a life, destiny . . . personality without consciousness, how can you deny consciousness to this plane where consciousness neither is nor is not, without describing it in the same terms? Or how can we speak of that sphere as a life of a single organic constituent without describing this plane in the same terms? [4] If your proposition be right, and yet you describe this plane as conscious life, etc., then similarly, in refusing consciousness to the Unconscious sphere, you must describe that sphere as conscious life, etc., which is absurd. So also for the fourfold organic life. [5] For if you deny consciousness to this plane, and yet call it a life of four [mental] constituents, then your proposition obviously falls through.

[6] You grant me that this plane, wherein consciousness neither is nor is not, is a life of four constituents, saying the while that there is no consciousness in this plane—you allow, do you not, that in the [lower] plane called 'infinity of space' there is consciousness? And that there is consciousness in the [next higher] planes: 'infinity of consciousness,' and 'nothingness.' Why not then for our [fourth and highest] plane? [7] How can you admit consciousness for those three and not for this, while you allow that each is a life of four [mental] constituents?

[8-10] Do you object to this:—in this plane consciousness either is or is not? Yes? but why, when you admit the co-presence of those four constituents? Why, again, when you admit them in the case of the other three planes, and allow that there, too, consciousness either is or is not?

[11] You admit that the plane in question is that wherein is neither consciousness nor unconsciousness, and yet you maintain that it is wrong. to say: in that plane consciousness neither is nor is not! [12] But take neutral feeling—is it wrong to say that neutral feeling is either feeling or not feeling? 'Yes,' you admit, 'that cannot truly be said.' Then how can the other be said?

BOOK IV.

1. *As to whether a Layman may be Arahant.*

Controverted Point.—That a layman may be Arahant.

From the Commentary.—This concerns the belief of those who, like the Uttarāpathakas, seeing that Yasa, the clansman's son, and others attained Arahantship while living amid the circumstances of secular life, judge that a layman might be an Arahant. Now the meaning in the Theravādin's question refers to the spiritual 'fetters' by which a layman is bound. But the opponent answers 'yes,' because he sees only the outward characteristics. Now a layman is such by the spiritual fetter, and not merely by the outward trappings, even as the Exalted One said:

> '*Though he be finely clad, if he fare rightly,*
> *At peace and tamed, by right law nobly living,*
> *Refrain from scathe and harm to every creature;—*
> *Noble is he, recluse is he and bhikkhu!*'[1]

[1] *Th.*—You say the layman may be Arahant. But you imply therewith that the Arahant has the layman's fetters. 'No,' you say, 'they do not exist for him.' Then how can a layman be Arahant? [2] Now for the Arahant the lay-fetters are put away, cut off at the root, made as the stump of a palm tree, incapable of renewed life or of coming again to birth. Can you say that of a layman?

[3] You admit that there was never a layman who, [as such] without putting away his lay-fetters, made an end in this very life of all sorrow. [4] Is there not a Suttanta in which the Wanderer Vacchagotta addressed the Exalted One thus: '*Is there now, O Gotama, any layman who,*

[1] *Dhammapada*, ver. 142. 'Layman' is literally house-ʳ, householder (gihī).

without having put away the layman's fetters, makes at death an end of Ill?' [And to whom the Exalted One said:] '*Nay, Vacchagotta, there is none*'?[1]

[5] Again, in affirming your proposition, you imply that an Arahant may carry on sexual relations, may suffer such matters to come into his life, may indulge in a home[2] encumbered with children,[2] may seek to enjoy sandalwood preparations of Kāsi, may wear wreaths, use perfumes and ointments, may accept gold and silver, may acquire goats and sheep, poultry and pigs, elephants, cattle, horses and mares, partridges, quails, peacocks and pheasants,[3] may wear an attractively swathed head-dress,[4] may wear white garments with long skirts, may be a house-dweller all his life—which of course you deny.

[6] *U.*—Then, if my proposition be wrong, how is it that Yasa of the clans, Uttiya the householder, Setu the Brahmin youth, attained Arahantship in all the circumstances of life in the laity?[5]

---

2. *Of* [*Arahantship as conferred by*] *Rebirth* [*alone*].

Controverted Point.—That one may become Arahant at the moment of rebirth.

From the Commentary.—This question is raised to elicit an opinion of the Uttarāpathakas. They namely had come to the conclusion that at the very outset of reborn consciousness, one might be an Arahant, they having either carelessly applied the Word, '*becomes born without parentage in the higher heavens and there completes existence*,'[6] or,

---

[1] *Majjhima-Nik.*, i. 483.

[2] Literally couch. With this and the next four clauses, cf. *Milinda*, ii. 57, 244 of the translation. Also above, p. 112 f.

[3] Kapiñjala, -jara, we have not met with elsewhere. It *may* mean 'dove.'

[4] Read citta-, as in footnote, PTS.

[5] The inference is that the layman, under exceptional circumstances, may attain Arahantship, but to keep it, must give up the world.

[6] *Dīgha-Nikāya*, iii. 182 and elsewhere.

converting the word 'upahacca' into 'uppajja,' and changing the meaning, 'completed existence *during the second half of the term*,'[1] into 'completed existence *on being reborn*.'

[1, 2] *Th.*—You affirm this proposition; yet you deny that one can become at birth either a Stream-Winner, Once-Returner, or Never-Returner.

[3] And you can name none—not even the greatest—who were Arahants from the time of birth—Sāriputta, or the Great Theras: Moggallāna, Kassapa, Kaccāyana, Koṭṭhika or Panthaka. [4] You deny it in fact of all of them.

[5, 6] Consider our consciousness at rebirth: it arises because rebirth has been desired.[2] Now such a mind is worldly, co-intoxicant . . .[3] corrupt. Can it realize Arahantship? Is it of the kind that is called forthleading,[4] that goes toward extinction,[5] enlightenment, disaccumulating,[4] is free from intoxicants . . . and corruptions? Can one by it put away lust, and hate, delusion . . . indiscretion? Is it the Ariyan Path, the applications of mindfulness and the rest of the thirty-seven factors of enlightenment? Can it understand Ill, put away its cause, realize its cessation, develop the path thereto? All this you, of course, must deny.

[6*a*] Or is the last act of consciousness at death the realization of the Topmost Path (of Arahantship) and the ensuing act of consciousness at rebirth the Fruit of that Path (or full realization of Arahantship)? You deny again. Then your proposition is proved false.

[1] *Saṃyutta-Nik.*, v. 201, etc.; *Anguttara-Nik.*, i. 233, f., etc. 'Completes (-ed) existence' is parinibbāyi, have become completely extinct, passed utterly away—a climax only effected by an Arahant.

[2] Literally, 'Does one by a rebirth-seeking consciousness realize,' etc.

[3] For these elisions, not ours, in the text, see above III. 3, § 7.

[4] See p. 148, *n*. 5.

[5] Khayagāmī, either of lust, hate, delusion (*Saṃyutta-Nik.*, iv., 251, or of the conditions of rebirth).

---

3. *Of the Arahant's Common Humanity.*

Controverted Point.—That all that belongs to the Arahant is devoid of intoxicants.

From the Commentary.—It is an opinion of the Uttarāpathakas that everything about or belonging to an Arahant, he being devoid of intoxicants,[1] is free from these.

[1] *Th.*—The things devoid of intoxicants are the Four Paths, the Four Fruits, Nibbāna, and the [thirty-seven] factors of enlightenment; but these do not constitute everything belonging to an Arahant. [2] His five sense-organs, for instance, you do not call free from intoxicants[2]—hence your proposition falls through.

[3] His body, again, is destined to be seized and coerced,[3] cut off and broken up, and shared by crows, vultures, and kites—is anything 'free from intoxicants' to be so described?

[4] Into his body poison may get, and fire and the knife—is anything 'free from intoxicants' to be so described?

His body may get bound by captivity,[4] by ropes, by chains, may be interned in a village, town, city, or province, may be imprisoned by the fourfold bondage, the fifth being strangling[5]—is anything 'free from intoxicants' liable to this?

[5] Moreover, if an Arahant give his robe to a man of the world, does that which was free from intoxicants thereby become co-intoxicant? You may admit this in general terms, but do you admit that that which is free from intoxicants may also be the opposite? If you say 'yes,' then, by the analogy of the robe, anything else about the Arahant—his religious characters: Path,

[1] The Āsavas or cardinal vices were in the Abhidhamma reckoned as four: sensuality, rebirth (lust after), erroneous opinion, ignorance.

[2] 'Co-intoxicant' is an essential of rūpa, or material quality.

[3] Paggaha-niggahūpago, 'liable to be raised, lowered.'

[4] Addubandhanena.

[5] For kaṇha read kaṇṭha. See I. 6, § 48.

Fruit, etc.—having been free from intoxicants, may become co-intoxicant. [6] The analogy may also be based on the gift of food, lodging, or medicine.

[7] Or, conversely, if a man of the world give a robe or [8] other requisite to an Arahant, does that which is co-intoxicant become thereby the opposite? Does that which has been co-intoxicant become free from intoxicants—lust, for instance, hate, delusion . . . indiscretion [such as beset and characterize the man of the world]?

[9] *U.*—You condemn my proposition. But is not the Arahant free from intoxicants? If he is, then I say that everything connected with him is so.

---

4. *Of [the Retaining of Distinctive] Endowments.*

Controverted Point.—That one who realizes a fruition retains the attributes thereof after realizing a higher fruition.

From the Commentary.—There are two kinds of spiritual acquisitions, namely, acquisition at the present moment and acquisition accruing at rebirth hereafter. But some, like the Uttarāpathakas, believe that there is one other, namely, the holding of past acquirements as a permanent acquisition[1] in some Rūpa or Arūpa heaven. The latter kind is retained as long as the Jhānic achievement has not spent its force.' The Theravādin view is that there is no such quality, but that all personal endowments are only held, as distinct acquisitions, until they are cancelled by other acquisitions.

[1, 2] *Th.*—You say, in fact, that an Arahant is endowed with all the Four Fruits, a Never-Returner with three, a Once-Returner with two. Then you must also admit that an Arahant is endowed with four contacts, four feelings, four perceptions, four volitions, four thoughts, four faiths, energies, mindfulnesses, concentrations, understandings;

[1] Pattidhammo. An Arahant is the resultant of his earlier spiritual victories, but these are transcended and cancelled by subsequent attainments. Nothing is permanent. Spiritual growth is analogous to physical growth. The heterodox view is that of a transference of something persisting. Cf. with this discourse, IV. 9.

the Never-Returner with three of each, the Once-Returner with two of each—which you must deny.[1]

[3] Again, if an Arahant is endowed with the first fruition, the second, and the third, he must be one of whom the characteristics of all three classes of the first, of the second, and of all five classes of the third stages are true.[2] Then he would be rightly described as in one and all at the same time—which is absurd. [4] The same argument holds for those who have realized the Third and the Second Fruit.

[5] Again, you admit that one who is endowed with the Fruit of Stream-Winning is rightly called 'Stream-Winner.' But is the same person both Stream-Winner and Arahant? Similarly for the two other fruitions. [6] Similarly, is the same person both Never-Returner and Stream-Winner, or both Once-Returner and Never-Returner?[3]

[7] Would you not admit that the Arahant had evolved past[4] the Fruit of the First Path? Yes, you say; then you cannot maintain your proposition;

[7-18] Because, if you are to maintain consistently that the Arahant is yet endowed with that Path and that Fruit out of and past which he has evolved, you must further ascribe to him all those corruptions out of which the Stream-Winner evolves—which is absurd. Similarly for the other Paths and Fruits. And similarly for the Never-Returner and the Once-Returner.

[19-21] *U.*—But if it be wrong to say that an Arahant is endowed with four Fruits, not one, a Never-Returner with three, not one, a Once-Returner with two, not one, do you deny that the Arahant has acquired four Fruits and has not fallen away from them, the Never-Returner three, and so on? You do not deny this. Hence it is right to say: They 'are endowed with' four, three, two Fruits.

[1] The 'Fruit' or fruition is one psychic act, in which the whole being is engaged. This act 'informs' the next, etc., but does not *itself* persist.

[2] See pp. 77, 78. [3] A clause omitted in the PTS edition.

[4] Vītivatto, vi-ati-vatto, away-beyond-turned; 'in-trans-volved' for 'e-volved,' our 'in' having, like *vi*, a double import. Cf. with this argument, III. 4.

[22-4] *Th.*—I grant they have acquired them, and have not fallen away from them. But I say that, if you affirm that they are endowed with the Fruits, you must no less affirm *a fortiori* that they are endowed with the respective Paths. [But by pushing the argument a step further, we have seen that you were landed in the absurdity of ascribing corruptions to saints.]

---

5. *Of the Arahant's Indifference in Sense-Cognition.*

Controverted Point.—That an Arahant is endowed with six indifferences.

From the Commentary.—The Arahant is said to be able to call up indifference with respect to each of the six gates of sense-knowledge. But he is not in a state of calling up indifference with respect to all six at the same moment.[1]

[1] *Th.*—In affirming this proposition, you imply that the Arahant experiences [simultaneously] six contacts [between sense-organ (and sense-mind) and their objects], six feelings, perceptions, volitions, . . . insights—which you deny; that [2] he is using his five senses and mental co-ordination at [the same instant]; that [3] he, being continually, constantly, uninterruptedly in possession of, and made intent with six indifferences, six indifferences are present to him[2]—both of which you deny.

[4] *Opponent.*—Yet you admit that an Arahant is gifted with sixfold indifference.[3] Is this not admitting my proposition?

[1] In Theravāda, sensations, however swift in succession, are never simultaneous.

[2] Literally, 'recur to him' (p a c c u p a ṭ ṭ h i t ā).

[3] C h a ḷ u p e k k h o, a phrase we have not yet traced in the Piṭakas. The six, however, are mentioned in *Dīgha-Nik.*, iii. 245; *Majjhima-Nik.*, iii. 219.

---

6. *Of becoming 'The Enlightened'* (*Buddha*) *through Enlightenment* (*bôdhi*).

Controverted Point.—That through Enlightenment one becomes 'The Enlightened.'[1]

From the Commentary.—Bôdhi is an equivalent for (1) insight into the Four Paths; (2) insight into all things, or the omniscience of a Buddha. And some, like the Uttarâpathakas at present, [do not distinguish, but] hold that, as a thing is called white by white-coloured surface, black by black-coloured surface, so a person is called 'Buddha' because of this or that aspect of bôdhi.[2]

[1] *Th.*—If it is in virtue of 'enlightenment' that one becomes 'The Enlightened,' then it follows that, in virtue of the cessation, suspension, subsidence of enlightenment, he ceases to be The Enlightened—this you deny, but you imply it.

[2] Or is one The Enlightened only in virtue of *past* enlightenment? Of course you deny this[3]—[then my previous point holds]. If you assent, do you mean that one who is The Enlightened exercises the work of enlightenment by that past enlightenment only? If you assent, you imply that he understands Ill, puts away its cause, realizes its cessation, develops the Eightfold Path thereto, by that *past* enlightenment—which is absurd.

[1] It is difficult for those who are not readers of Pali to follow the intentional ambiguity of the terms in the argument. To the noun bôdhi corresponds the deponent verb bujjhati, to awake, to be enlightened, to be wise, to know. And buddho is the past participle. One who is buddho is graduating, or has graduated in the Fourfold Path. If he become sammâ sambuddho, supremely and continually (or generally) enlightened, or sabbaññu-buddho, omnisciently enlightened, he is then a world-Buddha, saviour of men. To keep this double sense in view, we have not used 'Buddha' for this latter meaning.

[2] Here (1) and (2) are applied indiscriminately to one and the same person; again, there is still a sect in Burma who identify the Buddha with bôdhi itself, ignoring his distinctive personality. The Theravâdin takes account of both views.

[3] 'Because of the absence now of that past moment [of enlightenment.']—*Comy.*

[3] Substitute for 'past,' 'future' enlightenment, and the same argument applies.

[4] Let us assume that one is called The Enlightened through present enlightenment: if you assert that he exercises the work of enlightenment through present enlightenment, you must also affirm [by analogy] that if he is called The Enlightened through past, or [5] through future enlightenment, it is by that that he understands Ill, puts away its cause, and so on—which you deny.

[6] For if an enlightened person, so-called in virtue of past, or [7] of future enlightenment, does not exercise the work of enlightenment, through one or the other respectively, then [by analogy] one who is enlightened by present enlightenment does not exercise enlightenment through that present enlightenment—which is absurd.

[8] Do you then affirm that one is called The Enlightened through past, present, and future enlightenment?[1] Then are there three enlightenments? If you deny, your affirmation [by the foregoing] cannot stand. If you assent, you imply that he, being continually, constantly, uninterruptedly gifted with and intent through three enlightenments, these three are simultaneously present to him—which you of course deny.[2]

[9] *U.*—But surely one who is called The Enlightened is one who has acquired enlightenment? How is my proposition wrong?[3]

[10] *Th.*—You assume that one is called The Enlightened from having acquired enlightenment, or by enlightenment—is enlightenment the same as the acquiring of enlightenment?[4]

[1] 'This is assented to as being the proper thing to say.'—*Comy.*

[2] Cf. IV. 5, § 3.

[3] In that it would mean: a Buddha, in the absence of Bôdhi, would no longer be a Buddha, a distinct personality. The person is merged in the concept of Bôdhi.—Cf. *Comy.*

[4] The opponent denying, the argument finishes according to the stereotyped procedure.

7. *Of One gifted with the Marks.*

Controverted Point.—That one who is gifted with the Marks is a Bodhisat.

From the Commentary.—This and the two following discourses are about Uttarāpathaka views. This one deals with a belief derived from a careless interpretation of the Sutta: 'for one endowed as a superman there are two careers.' [1]

[1] *Th.*—By your proposition you must also admit [*a fortiori*] (*a*) that anyone who is gifted with the Marks to a limited extent,[2] with one-third, or one-half of them, is a limited, one-third, or half Bodhisat, respectively—which you deny.

[2] And (*b*) that a universal emperor[3]—who is also gifted with the Marks—is a Bodhisat, and that the previous study and conduct, declaring and teaching the Norm[4] in the Bodhisat's career, are the same as those in the universal emperor's career; that (*c*) when a universal emperor is born, devas receive him first, and then humans, as they do the new-born Bodhisat; [3] that (*d*) four sons of the devas receiving the new-born imperial babe place it before the mother, saying: 'Rejoice, O queen! to thee is born a mighty son!' even as they do for the new-born Bodhisat; that (*e*) two rain-showers, cold and warm, come from the sky, wherewith both babe and mother may be washed, even as happens at the birth of a Bodhisat; [4] that (*f*) a new-born imperial babe, standing on even feet, and facing north, walks seven paces, a white canopy being held over him, and looking round on all sides speaks the trumpet[5] notes: 'I am the foremost, I am chief, I am the highest in the world. This is my last birth; now is there no more coming again to be!' [5] that (*g*) there is manifested at

[1] See below. On the thirty-two Marks and the Bodhisat—i.e., Bodhisatta, 'enlightenment-being,' or one who in the same life becomes a Buddha, i.e., a Sammā-sambuddha—see *Dialogues*, ii. 14 f.

[2] Padesa. See above, III. 1, *n.* 8.

[3] Literally, a Wheel-Turner, disposer of the symbol of empire. *Dialogues*, ii. 11 f.

[4] Cf. above, III. 1, § 1.

[5] Literally, bull-speech.

the birth of the one as of the other a mighty light, a mighty radiance, a mighty earthquake; that (*h*) the natural body of the one as of the other lights up a fathom's space around it; that (*i*) one and the other see a great dream[1]—all of which you deny.

[6] *U.*—But if you reject my proposition, tell me: is there not a Suttanta in which the Exalted One said: '*Bhikkhus, to one endowed with the thirty-two marks of a Superman, two careers lie open, and none other. If he live the life of the house, he becomes Lord of the Wheel, a righteous Lord of the Right, Ruler of the four quarters, conqueror, guardian of the people's good, owner of the Seven Treasures; his do those seven treasures become, to wit, the Wheel treasure, the Elephant, the Horse, the Jewel, the Woman, the Steward, the Heir Apparent. More than a thousand sons are his, heroes, vigorous of frame, crushers of the hosts of the enemy. He, when he has conquered this earth to its ocean bounds, is established not by the scourge, not by the sword, but by righteousness. But if he go forth from his home to the homeless, he becomes an Arahant Buddha Supreme, rolling back the veil from the world*'?[2]

Is not therefore my proposition true?

---

8. *Of entering on the Path of Assurance.*

Controverted Point.—That the Bodhisat had entered on the Path of Assurance and conformed to the life therein during the dispensation[3] of Kassapa Buddha.[4]

From the Commentary.—This discourse deals with a belief, shared by the Andhakas,[5] with reference to the account in the Ghaṭīkāra Sutta of Jotipāla joining the Order,[6] that [our] Bodhisat had entered the

---

[1] On the five 'great dreams' see *Anguttara-Nik*, iii. 240 f.

[2] *Dīgha-Nik.*, iii. p. 145. Cf. *Dialogues*, ii. 13.

[3] Literally, teaching or doctrine (p a v a c a n a).

[4] This was the Buddha next before 'our' Buddha. See *Dialogues*, ii., p. 6. On 'Assurance,' see V. 4, and Appendix: 'Assurance.'

[5] See preceding extract.

[6] *Majjhima-Nik.*, ii. p. 46 f. Jotipāla was a Brahmin youth who,

Path of Assurance under Kassapa Buddha. Now Assurance (n i y ā m a) and the 'higher life therein' (b r a h m a c a r i y a) are equivalents for the Ariyan [Fourfold] Path. And there is no other entering upon that Path for Bodhisats save when they are fulfilling the Perfections;[1] otherwise our Bodhisat would have been a disciple when Stream-Winner, etc. The Buddhas prophesy 'he will become a Buddha' (as Kassapa is said to have prophesied concerning Gotama Buddha, then alive as this Jotipāla) simply by the might of their insight.

[1] *Th.*—If so, [our] Bodhisat must have been a disciple —i.e., one in the Ariyan Way—of Kassapa Buddha. You deny. For if you assent, you must admit that he became Buddha after his career as disciple. Moreover, a 'disciple' is one who learns through information from others, while a Buddha is self-developed.[2]

[2] Further, if the Bodhisat became Kassapa's disciple, [entering on the first Path and Fruit], it follows that there were only three stages of fruition for him to know thoroughly when under the Bôdhi Tree. But we believe that all four were then realized.[3]

[3] Further, would one who had entered on the Path of Assurance [as a disciple] have undergone the austerities practised by the Bodhisat [in his own last life]? And would such an one point to others as his teachers and practise their austerities, as did the Bodhisat in his last life?[4]

[4] Do we learn that, as the Venerable Ānanda, and the householder Citta and Hatthaka the Āḷavakan entered into Assurance and lived its higher life as disciples under the Exalted One, so the Exalted One himself, as Bodhisat, acted under Kassapa Buddha? You deny, of course. [5] If they did so enter, under the Exalted One, as his disciples, you cannot affirm that the Bodhisat entered on the Path of Assurance, and lived its higher life under Kassapa Buddha without being his disciple. Or can a

---

against his will, was brought by Ghaṭikāra, the potter, to hear Kassapa Buddha, and became a bhikkhu. Gotama Buddha affirmed that Jotipāla was a former impersonation of himself.

[1] Cf. *Buddhist Birth Stories*, p. 18 f.

[2] S a y a m - b h u.

[3] *Op. cit.*, 109.

[4] *Majjhima-Nik.*, i. 80, 245.

disciple who has evolved past one birth become a non-disciple afterwards? You deny, of course.

[6] *A. U.*—But if our proposition is wrong, is there not a Suttanta in which the Exalted One said: '*Under the Exalted One Kassapa, Ānanda, I lived the higher life for supreme enlightenment in the future*'?[1]

[7] *Th.*—But is there not a Suttanta in which the Exalted One said:

> '*All have I overcome. All things I know,*
> *'Mid all things undefiled. Renouncing all,*
> *In death of craving wholly free. My own*
> *The deeper view. Whom should I name to thee?*
> *For me no teacher lives. I stand alone*
> *On earth, in heav'n rival to me there's none.*
> *Yea, I am Arahant as to this world,*
> *A Teacher I above whom there is none.*
> *Supreme enlightenment is mine alone.*
> *In holy Coolness I, all fires extinct.*
> *Now go I on seeking Benares town,*
> *To start the Wheel, to set on foot the Norm.*
> *Amid a world in gloom and very blind,*
> *I strike the alarm upon Ambrosia's Drum*'?

'*According to what thou declarest, brother, thou art indeed Arahant,* [*"worthy" to be*][2] *conqueror world without end.*'

> '*Like unto me indeed are conquerors*
> *Who every poisonous canker have cast out.*
> *Conquered by me is every evil thing,*
> *And therefore am I conqueror, Upaka*'?[3]

[8] And is there not a Suttanta in which the Exalted One said: "*O bhikkhus, it was concerning things unlearnt before that vision, insight, understanding, wisdom, light arose in me at the thought of the Ariyan Truth of the nature and*

[1] We cannot trace this, but cf. *Majjhima-Nik.*, ii., p. 54; *Buddha-vaṃsa*, xxv. 10.

[2] Br. and PTS editions read arahā 'si; *Majjhima-Nik.* (Trenckner) has arahasi.

[3] *Vinaya Texts*, i. 91; *Majjhima-Nik.*, i. 171; *Pss. Sisters*, 129.

fact of Ill, and that this Truth was to be understood, and was understood by me. It was concerning things unlearnt before that vision, insight, understanding, wisdom, light arose in me at the thought of the Ariyan Truth as to the Cause of Ill, and that this Truth was concerning something to be put away, and was put away by me. It was concerning things unlearnt before that vision, insight, understanding, wisdom, light arose in me at the thought of the Ariyan Truth as to the Cessation of Ill, and that this Truth was concerning something to be realized, and was realized by me. It was concerning things unlearnt before that vision, insight, understanding, wisdom, light arose in me at the thought of the Ariyan Truth as to the Course leading to the cessation of Ill, and that this truth was to be developed, and was developed by me' ?[1]

How then can you say that the Bodhisat entered on the Path of Assurance and lived the higher life thereof [as far back as] the age of Kassapa Buddha ?

---

9. *More about Endowment.*[2]

Controverted Point.—That a person who is practising in order to realize Arahantship possesses [as a persistent distinct endowment] the preceding three fruitions.

From the Commentary.—This discourse deals with the belief, shared by the Andhakas,[3] that a person as described holds the three Fruitions as an acquired quality (patta-dhamma-vasena). It is to be understood as like that on 'the four Fruits.'

[1] *Th.*—You say, in fact, that such a person is endowed with, or possesses four contacts, four feelings, four perceptions, volitions, thoughts, four faiths, energies, mindfulnesses, concentrations, understandings[4]—which cannot be.

[2] Do you make an analogous assertion as to one who is practising for the Third or Second Paths? An analo-

[1] *Saŋyutta-Nik.*, v. 422.

[2] This discourse is practically the same as IV. 4.

[3] See Commentary on IV. 7.

[4] The five spiritual-sense controls. See above, p. 148, *n.* 1.

gous paradox will apply in that case; and you must [3, 4] be able to describe such persons in terms of lower stages, e.g. one practising for the topmost stage in terms of one who has only got to the first—which is anomalous.[1]

[5] But can a person who is a proximate candidate for Arahantship be described in terms of a Stream-Winner? Can he *be* both at the same time? Even if he be a Never-Returner, is he rightly so described when he is in process of becoming Arahant?[2] [6] Similarly for a candidate for the Third and Second Fruitions.

[7] Would you not rather maintain that a person practising in order to realize Arahantship had evolved past[3] the fruition of Stream-Winning?

[8] Or do you maintain that one so evolved was still holding that first Fruit [as a distinctive quality]? For then you must also hold that he also remains possessed of those evil qualities which as Stream-Winner he has evolved out of—which is absurd.

[9-18] A similar argument applies to a proximate candidate for Arahantship (Fourth Fruit) and the Second Path and Fruit; to such a candidate and the Third Path and Fruit; to a proximate candidate for the Third Fruit and the First and Second Paths and Fruits; and to a proximate candidate for the Second Fruit, and the First Path and Fruit.

[19] *U. A.*—If our proposition is wrong, surely you would nevertheless say that a person who is a proximate candidate for realizing Arahantship had both won the preceding three Fruits, and had not fallen away from them?

Th.—Yes, that is true.

U. A.—Surely then he is still possessed of them. [20-21] And so for candidates in the Third, Second and First Paths.

[22] *Th.*—Assuming that he is still possessed of the three Fruits, do you also admit that, having attained to all four Paths, he is still possessed of all the Paths? Of course you do not; [*there* at least you see my point]

[1] Cf. above, I. 2, I. 6, and subsequently.

[2] I.e., in the Fourth Path, striving to realize its Fruit.

[3] See IV. 4, 8.

[23, 24], neither do you admit a similar possession in other candidates.

---

10. *Of putting off the Fetters.*

Controverted Point.—That the putting off of all the Fetters *is* Arahantship.

From the Commentary. — This is an opinion of the Andhakas—namely, that Arahantship means the [simultaneous], unlimited putting off of all the fetters.[1]

[1] *Th.*—By your proposition you must admit that all the Fetters are put off by the Path of Arahantship (the Fourth)—which is not correct, you allow. The proximate candidate for the Fruit of that Path is not occupied in again getting rid of the theory of individuality, doubt, or the infection of mere rule and ritual, already rejected in the First Path. Nor [2] in getting rid of the grosser sensuality and enmity conquered already in the Second Path; nor [3] of the residual sensuality put away without remainder in the Third Path. [4] Was not his work pronounced by the Exalted One to be the putting off without remainder of lust for corporeal, and for incorporeal rebirth, conceit, distraction and ignorance?[2]

[5] *A.*—But if my proposition is wrong, do you not nevertheless admit that for an Arahant all Fetters are put off? Surely then I may say that Arahantship is a putting off all the Fetters?

[1] These were ten vicious states or qualities, to be put away gradually by progress in the 'four paths,' and not all at once. See *Compendium*, 172 f.; *Bud. Psy. Eth.*, pp. 297-303. In the thesis there is no copula, much less an emphatic one. But the two substantival clauses are in apposition as equivalents.

[2] *Dialogues*, ii. 98 f.

BOOK V

1. *Of Emancipation.*

Controverted Point.—That the knowledge of emancipation has itself the quality of emancipation.

From the Commentary.—Four sorts of knowledge (or insight, ñ ā ṇ a) are grouped under knowledge of emancipation, to wit, insight or intuition, path-knowledge, fruit-knowledge, reflective knowledge. In other words, emancipation considered as (1) freedom from perceiving things as permanent or persisting, or through perceiving the opposite ; (2) the severance and renunciation effected by the Paths; (3) the peace of fruition[1] ; (4) contemplation of emancipation as such. Now only the peace of fruition is abstract, unqualified emancipation. The rest cannot be called emancipated things. But the Andhakas say that all four are such.

[1] *Th.*—Does not your proposition imply that any knowledge of emancipation whatever has the quality of emancipation? For instance, has reflective knowledge[2] that quality? Is such knowledge of emancipation as is possessed by one who has attained to the stage of Ariyan adoption[3] of that quality? You deny both. [Then your proposition is too general.]

[2] Again, it includes that knowledge of emancipation possessed by one who is practising in order to realize the Fruit of the First, Second, Third, Fourth Paths.[4] But do you mean to convey that the knowledge of one in the

[1] Phalaŋ paṭipassaddhi-vimutti.

[2] Or retrospective. Cf. *Compendium*, 58, 69 ; 132, *n.* 6 ; 207, *n.* 7.

[3] Gotrabhū puggalo ; cf. *Anguttara-Nik.*, iv. 373; v. 23 ; *Compendium*, 55, 215, *n.* 5 ; the preparatory stage to the First Path.

[4] On this wider extension of the term cf. III. 3 and 4.

First Path is equal to the knowledge of one who has won, acquired, arrived at, realized the Fruit of that Path, and so for the Second, Third, and Fourth? Of course you deny.

[3] Conversely, do you mean to convey that, if the knowledge of emancipation belonging to one who possesses the Fruition of a Path has the quality of emancipation, the knowledge of emancipation of one who is only practising in order to realize that Fruition has the same quality? Of course you deny.

[4] Or in other words, let us assume, as you say, that when a person has realized the fruition of any of the Four Paths his knowledge of emancipation has itself the quality or nature of emancipation. Now you admit that the knowledge in question is the knowledge of one who has won the Fruit, do you not?

But do you maintain as much, if the person has not yet realized, but is only practising to realize a given fruition? Of course you deny. . . .

---

2. *Of the Knowledge of an Adept.*[1]

Controverted Point.—That a learner has the insight of an adept.

From the Commentary.—This is an opinion of the Uttarāpathakas, namely, that learners, as Ānanda and others were, showed by their confessions about the Exalted One, etc., that they knew who were adepts, [and therefore understood that knowledge, the possession of which made them adepts].

[1] *Th.*—Then you imply that the learner knows, sees[2] the ideas of the adept, lives in the attainment of having seen, known, realized them, lives in personal contact therewith. If not—and you do deny this—then you cannot maintain your proposition.

[2] We grant of course that the adept knows, sees the ideas of the adept, lives in the attainment . . . and so on.

[1] A-sekha, literally, non-learner, proficient, expert; in this case, an Arahant. Sekha is one who is being 'trained.'

[2] This idiom applies to those who arrive at their knowledge by themselves.—*Comy.*

But, as you have admitted, you cannot impute this knowledge to the learner.[1]

Your position then is, that you credit the learner with the insight of an adept, yet you deny that the learner knows, sees the ideas of the adept, etc. But, the adept having also of course the insight of the adept, if he be as to insight on a level only with the learner, you must add of the adept also that he knows not, sees not the ideas of the adept, does not live in the attainment of having seen, known, realized them, does not live in personal contact therewith. Which is absurd, as you by your denial admit.

[3] You are ready to deny that a person in a lower Stage of the Path has the insight as yet of the next higher Stage, or that one who is adopted[2] has yet the insight of even the First Stage. How then can you ascribe the insight of those who have finally attained to those who as yet have not?

[4] *U.*—If my proposition is wrong, then how is it that a learner, as Ānanda was, *knew* the sublimity of the Exalted One, or of the Elder Sāriputta, or of the Elder Moggallāna the Great?

---

3. *Of Perverted Perception or Hallucination (in Jhāna).*

Controverted Point.—That in one who has attained Jhāna through the earth-artifice, etc.,[3] knowledge [of what is seen] is perverted.

From the Commentary.—It is a belief among the Andhakas, that when anyone has induced Jhāna by the [self-hypnotizing] process of gazing on [a portion of] earth and being conscious of earth, the content of consciousness becoming other than earth [though his gaze is still fixed thereon], his cognition may be called perverted, seeing one thing, namely, the physical earth, and being conscious of something else, to wit, the percept, or concept.[4] The Theravādin's position is the

---

[1] The PTS edition should read a *negative* reply here and at the end of this section. [2] Gotrabhū, V. 1, § 1.

[3] This, as heading the list of 'artifices' (kasiṇa) for self-hypnosis, is always cited as representing artifice in general. See p. 121; also *Bud. Psy. Eth.*, p. 48, and *passim*; *Vibhanga*, 171, 178.

[4] The opponent's position is that the subject is really conscious of an idea, which is never the original object, the mind being referred to that by a process of hallucination.

specialization of the meaning of 'earth.' It may mean the ultimate quality of extension, physical (literally, structural) earth, a percept or concept, a [nature-] deva. The only real perversion of cognition is to see permanence, persistence in the impermanent. There is no hallucination or illusion, etc., properly so called, in Jhāna.[1]

[1] *Th.*—If your proposition is right, then do you imply that this 'perversion' is the same as that involved in seeing the permanent in the impermanent, happiness in Ill, a soul in what is not soul, the beautiful in the ugly? Of course you deny.

[2] Again, you imply that such a person's knowledge during Jhāna is not proficient. But you do not wish to imply this, but the opposite.

[3] You admit that the reversal of judgment which sees permanence in impermanence is a bad judgment, and those other judgments above-stated also. Yet you will not admit that cognition during Jhāna is badly accomplished.

[4] You hold on the contrary that it is well accomplished. Yet a similar perversion in the case of those other four judgments you consider bad.

[5] If it were an Arahant who so accomplished Jhāna, would you claim a perverted cognition for him? You could not. [6] Or, if you could, you would have to make him liable to reversals of perception, consciousness, and views in general.[2]

[7] *A.*—But if my proposition is wrong, do you hold that, when any one attains Jhāna by earth-cognition, everything becomes earth to him?[3] No, you reply. Then surely his judgment is upset.

[1] Because, when the subject is conscious of the percept or concept of earth, the content of his consciousness is just that percept or concept.

[2] Cf. *Compendium*, p. 216, *n.* 4; 67. Vipariyesa, viparīta here used are tantamount to the term [preferred in later idiom] 'vipallāsa.'

[3] There is even now a tendency among Burmese Buddhists, if not well trained, to believe that Jhānic practice by any given 'artifice'—say earth-gazing—is only successful when every external thing seems to become earth. This would be true hallucination. But here the opponent thinks that the mind of the Jhānic subject is upset, because the Theravādin's denial in general includes the specific denial that the content of consciousness becomes 'earth.'

[8] *Th.*—But you will admit that the earth is there, and that the subject enters Jhāna by regarding earth as earth? Where then is the perversion of cognition?

You say that the earth is actually there, and that in entering Jhāna by the consciousness of earth as earth, perception is perverted. Substitute for earth Nibbāna: would you still say that perception was perverted? . . .

---

4. *Of Assurance.*

Controverted Point.—That one who has not made sure has the insight for entering the Path of Assurance.[1]

From the Commentary.—Some, like the Uttarāpathakas, at present hold this view on these grounds: The Exalted One judged that 'anyone who will enter on the right Path of Assurance[2] is capable of penetrating the Truths.' Therefore only the average worldling who has not made sure has the religious insight requisite for entering.

[1] *Th.*—If one who has not made sure has the insight for entering the Path of Assurance, then his opposite—one who has made sure—must have the insight for *not* entering it.[3] If you deny, your proposition falls through. If, by it, you maintain that one who *has* made sure has *not* the insight for *not* entering that Path, then you imply that one who has *not* made sure has *not* the insight for entering thereon. Which, by your proposition, is wrong.

[2] Again, if one who has not made sure has the insight for entering the Path of Assurance, do you then admit that one who has made sure is in the same intellectual stage?[4] You deny. And if you admit, on the contrary, that one who has made sure has not [i.e., no longer] the insight

[1] 'Assurance (niyāma) is a synonym of the Path' [to Arahantship].—*Comy.* The expression 'made sure,' niyato, is applied to those who have entered on it, and are 'assured of' eventual attainment.

[2] Sammatta-niyāma. Cf. *Saṃyutta-Nik.*, iii. 225 (the last clause is different); and *Anguttara-Nik.*, i. 121.

[3] Literally, for entering the opposite path of non-assurance.

[4] 'Inasmuch as for the *initial* purpose of the Path he no longer needs the requisite insight.'—*Comy.*

for entering, then you must surely deny that insight also to one who has not made sure.

[3] Again, in affirming that one who has not made sure has the insight for entering the Path of Assurance, do you admit that he has also the insight for not entering it? You deny, that is, you affirm he has *not* the insight for not entering it. Do you equally admit then that he has *not* the insight for entering it? You deny. . . .[1]

[4] Does your proposition mean that there is a Path of Assurance for one who has not made sure of entering?[2] You deny. Yet you admit that there is insight for entering upon it! Does this insight consist in applications of mindfulness and all the other factors of Enlightenment? You must deny, and [5] affirm that there is no such Assurance. How then can your proposition stand?

[6] You do not grant to one who is only in the prior stage of adoption[3] the insight of the First Path? Or to one who is practising for the insight of the First . . . Fourth Fruition the insight of that Fruition? How then can you allow the insight of entering on the Path of Assurance to one who has not made sure?

[7] *U.*—If I am wrong, you must on the other hand admit that the Exalted One knows that a person, M or N, will enter the true Path of Assurance, and is capable of penetrating the Truths.

[1] We have given a full, if slightly free, rendering of this curious bout of ancient dialectic. At the end of each section the sectary is brought up against the same rejoinder, compelling him either to contradict his proposition or to withdraw it. This may be shown diagrammatically, A = one-who-has-made-sure; B, entering-on-the-'Path'; C, insight-for; a, b, c standing for the respective contradictories. We then get,

§ 1 { aBC (thesis), AbC, Abc, aBc }   § 2 { aBC, ABC, ABc, aBc }   § 3 { aBC, abC, abc, aBc }

[2] The Path proper being reserved for one who *has* made sure.

[3] Gotrabhū puggalo. See V. 1, § 1.

5. *Of Analytic Insight.*[1]

Controverted Point.—That all knowledge is analytic.

From the Commentary.—It is a belief of the Andhakas that in an Ariyan (that is, one who has 'made sure,' is in some Stage of the Path or Way) all 'knowledge' whatsoever is supramundane or transcendental.[2] Hence they conclude that it is also analytic.

[1] *Th.*—Then you must admit that popular knowledge is analytic—which you deny. For if you assent, then all who have popular, conventional knowledge, have also acquired analytic insight—which you deny. The same argument holds good if 'knowledge in discerning the thought of another' be substituted for 'popular . . . knowledge.'[3]

[2] Again, if all knowledge is analytic, then *a fortiori* all discernment is analytic. Or, if you can assent to that, you must therewith admit that the discernment of one who attains Jhāna by any of the elemental, or colour 'artifices,' who attains any of the four more abstract Jhānas, who gives donations, who gives to the Order any of the four necessaries of life, is analytic. But this you deny.

[3] *A.*—If I am wrong, you admit that there is such a thing as [spiritual or] supramundane discernment; is that not analytic?

Th.—That I do not deny.[4]

A.—Then my proposition is true.[5]

[1] Paṭisambhidā, or analysis; literally, 'resolving, continued breaking-up.' On the four branches in this organon, see Appendix: Paṭisambhidā.

[2] See p. 184, *n*. 4.

[3] See pp. 180, 181.

[4] The Theravādin does not of course mean that all 'supramundane' knowledge is analytic. There is analytic, and there is intuitive supramundane knowledge.

[5] Namely, for Ariyans. This is another little joust of logomachy: What is the extension of the term ñāṇa, knowledge (see II. 2)? And what is the nature of an 'Ariyan'?

---

6. *Of Popular Knowledge.*

Controverted Point.—That it is wrong to say: Popular knowledge has only truth as its object and nothing else.

From the Commentary.—This discourse is to purge the incorrect tenet held by the Andhakas, that the word 'truth' is to be applied without any distinction being drawn between popular and philosophical truth.[1]

[1] *Andhaka.*—You admit, do you not, that one who attains Jhāna by way of the earth-artifice, has knowledge? Does not that earth-artifice come under popular truth?

Th.—Yes.

A.—Then why exempt popular knowledge from the search for truth?

[2] The same argument applies to the other artifices, and to gifts as stated above (V. 5).

[3] *Th.*—Then according to you, popular knowledge *has* only Truth as its object. But is it the object of popular knowledge to understand the fact and nature of Ill, to put away the Cause, to realize the Cessation, to develop the Path thereto? You must deny. (Hence the need for a distinction between truths.)

---

7. *Of the Mental Object in Telepathy.*

Controverted Point.—That insight into the thoughts of another has no object beyond bare other-consciousness as such.[2]

[1] Literally, truth in the highest or ultimate sense. On this ancient Buddhist distinction, see above, p. 63, *n.* 2; also Ledi Sadaw's exposition, *JPTS*, 1914, 129 f., and note: P a r a m a t t h a.

[2] 'Of another' is filled in, the supernormal power in question being one of the six so-called abnormal knowledges, c h a ḷ - a b h i ñ ñ ā, attainable by gifted disciples. The Buddha is frequently shown, in the Suttas, exercising it. See also *Psalms of the Brethren, passim*; *Compendium*, 63, 209. The psychological point can only be followed

From the Commentary.—Some, like the Andhakas at present, have held this view, deriving it from just the [technical] expression 'insight into a limited portion of the consciousness of another].'[1] But this is untenable, since in knowing consciousness *as* lustful and so on, the object becomes essentially complex.

[1] *Th.*—You admit, do you not, that one may discern a 'lust-ridden consciousness,' and so on[2] as such? Then this disposes of your proposition.

[2] Again, you cannot deny that, in thought-discerning, insight can have as its object contact, feeling, etc. [or any of the concomitants of consciousness]. Where then is bare consciousness as sole object?

[3] Or do you dispute the statement that insight having contact, or feeling, or the rest as its object, comes into thought-discerning? 'Yes' you say?[3] But does not thought-discerning include discerning the course of contact, feeling, etc.? This you now deny.[4]

[4] *A.*—You say my proposition is wrong. But is not this thought-discerning insight limited to a portion of the course of thought [in others]? Then surely I am right.

---

if the Buddhist distinction between (*a*) a bare *continuum* of conscious moments, (*b*) various concomitants or coefficients of that bare consciousness be kept in mind. See *Compendium*, 13. Thus the dispute is really on the meaning or context of the term *citta:* bare fact of consciousness, *or* the concrete, complex psychic unit as understood in European psychology. The discussion is therefore of more than antiquarian interest. See *Buddhist Psychology*, 6 f., 175.

1 Ceto pariyāye ñāṇaŋ is usually so rendered, in this connection, by Burmese translators. The opponent misconstrues 'limited,' holding that thought-reading is limited to the bare flux of consciousness, without its factors.

2 The quoted phrase heads the list usually given in the Nikāyas when the thought-reading power is stated—e.g., *Dialogues*, i. 89 f.

3 Because, he holds, one cannot make a mental object of more than one factor [at once].—*Comy.*

4 'Because there is no Sutta-passage about it.'—*Comy.*

8. *Of Insight into the Future.*

Controverted Point.—That there is knowledge of the future.

From the Commentary.—The future includes both what will happen proximately and what is not just proximate. Concerning the former there is absolutely no knowledge, any more than there is of what is included in a single track or moment of cognition. But some, like the Andhakas, incline to a belief that knowledge concerning any part of the future is possible.

[1] *Th.*—If we can know about the future [in general], it must be [as in other knowledge] through knowing its root, condition, cause, source, origin, upspringing, support,[1] basis, correlation, genesis. But you deny that we know the future thus. . . .[2]

[2] And it must be [as in other knowledge] through knowing how it will be correlated by condition, base, predominance, contiguity, and immediate contiguity.[3] But you deny here again. . . .

[3] Again, if you are right, one in the stage of adoption has insight into the First Path, one in the First Path has insight into the First Fruition, and so on. But you deny here again. . . .

[4] *A.*—If I am wrong, is there not a Suttanta in which the Exalted One said: '*To Patna, Ānanda, three disasters will happen: by fire or by water or by rupture of friendship*'?[4] Surely then the future may be known.

[1] Literally, 'food.'

[2] Presumably, the belief was in an intuitive vision, and not in a process of inference. The ten terms are the 'root' and its nine synonyms of the First Book in the *Yamaka*, I, p. 18.

[3] These are the time-relations assigned in the doctrine of Relations detailed in the *Paṭṭhāna*, or last book of the *Abhidhamma-Piṭaka*.

[4] *Dialogues*, ii. 92. The orthodox position seems to have been, that whereas events indefinitely future may be foretold through a superman's intuition, the exact nature of molecular, or psychical, vital change at any given moment is unpredictable. Cf. M. Bergson on this point: *Creative Evolution*, ch. i., p. 6 *passim*.

9. *Of Knowledge of the Present.*

Controverted Point.—That the present may be known.

From the Commentary.—Because of the Word: When all phenomena are seen to be impermanent, the insight itself, as a phenomenon, is also seen to be impermanent, some, as the Andhakas, have the opinion that there is knowledge of the entire present, without distinction. Now if there be such knowledge, it [as present] must take place at the present instant through itself. But because two knowledges cannot be simultaneous in the one self-conscious subject, knowledge of the present cannot be known by the same act of knowledge.[1]

[1] *Th.*—If there be a knowledge of the present, does one know *that* knowledge by the same act of knowledge? If you deny, your proposition must fall. If you assent, I ask: Does one know that he knows the present by that same act of knowledge? You deny, and your previous assertion falls. If you assent, I ask: Is the conscious act of knowing the object of the knowledge? You deny, and your previous assertion falls. If you assent, then you imply that one touches contact by the contact, feels feeling by that feeling, wills volition by that volition. So for the initial and the sustained application of thought. So for zest, for mindfulness, for understanding. You imply that one cuts a sword with that sword; an axe with that axe; a knife with that knife; an adze with that adze; that one sews a needle with that needle; handles the tip of a finger with that finger; kisses the tip of the nose with that nose; handles the head with that head; washes off impurity with that impurity.

[2] *A.*—I am wrong then? But when all things are seen as impermanent, is not that knowledge also seen as impermanent? Surely then I am right.

[1] In other words, self-consciousness is really an act of retrospection, and its object is not present, but past.

10. *Of Knowing Others' Fruition.*

Controverted Point.—That a disciple can have knowledge concerning fruition.

From the Commentary.—Some, like the Andhakas, have held that, since it was said that both the Buddhas and their disciples teach beings the doctrine of the attainment of Ariyan fruition, disciples can, like the Buddhas, state that this or that being has won some Fruit. Now if that were so, they could also, by their insight, give details concerning that attainment. But they cannot.

[1] *Th.*—This implies that a disciple can make known the property of each fruit;[1] that he possesses a knowledge of the different degrees of development in fruitions, controlling powers, personalities; [2] that he possesses a conception of aggregates, sense-fields, elements, truths, controlling powers, personality; [3] that he is a Conqueror, a Teacher, a Buddha Supreme, omniscient, all-seeing, Master of the Norm, the Norm-Judge of appeal; [4] that he is one who causes a Way to spring up where no Way was, one who engenders a Way not engendered; proclaims a Path not proclaimed, knows the Path, is conversant with the Path, is expert in the Path. All of which of course you deny. . . .

[5] *A.*—Yet you deny that the disciple lacks insight. Surely then he may have insight into others' fruition.

[1] Read phala-ssakataŋ. In line 5, for paññāpetīti read the atthīti of the controverted proposition.

BOOK VI

1. *Of Assurance* [*of salvation*].[1]

Controverted Point.—That 'Assurance' is unconditioned.

From the Commentary.—In the Word: '*Capable of entering into Assurance, the culmination in things that are good,*'[2] the Ariyan Path is meant. But inasmuch as a person therein would not forfeit salvation even if that Path which [for him] had arisen were to pass away, therefore there is an opinion, among Andhakas for instance, that this Assurance is unconditioned in the sense of being eternal.[3]

[1] *Th.*—Then is Assurance [that other unconditioned called] Nibbāna, or the Shelter, the Cave, the Refuge, the Goal, the Past-Decease, the Ambrosial? You deny. Yet you would call both alike unconditioned. Are there then two kinds of unconditioned? If you deny, you cannot affirm; if you assent, then [for all we know] there are two Shelters . . . two Goals . . . two Nibbānas. If you deny, you cannot affirm your proposition; if you assent, then do you allow that of the two Nibbānas one is higher than the other, sublimer than the other, exalted more than the other? Is there a boundary, or a division, or a line, or an interstice[4] between them? Of course you deny. . . .

[2] Again, are there any who enter into and attain Assurance, cause it to arise, to keep arising, set it up, continue to set it up, bring it to pass, to come into being, produce it, continue to produce it? 'Of course,' you say.

[1] Niyāmo, as before (V. 4).

[2] *Anguttara-Nik.*, i. 122. Cf. *Saṃyutta-Nik.*, iii. 225.

[3] Or permanent, nicca.

[4] See above, II. 11.

But are these terms that you can apply to what is unconditioned? Of course not. . . .

[3] Again, is the Path (the Fourfold) unconditioned? 'Nay,' you say, 'conditioned.'[1] Yet you would make Assurance unconditioned; the Path of Stream-Winning, Once-Returning, Never-Returning, Arahantship, conditioned; but Assurance of Stream-Winning, etc., unconditioned! . . .

[4] If then these four stages of Assurance be unconditioned, and Nibbāna be unconditioned, are there five kinds of the unconditioned? If you assent, you are in the same difficulty as before (§ 1).

[5] Finally, is false Assurance[2] unconditioned? 'No, conditioned,' you say. But has true Assurance the same quality? Here you must deny. . . .

[6] *A.*—If I am wrong, would you say that, if Assurance having arisen for anyone and ceased, his work of making sure [his salvation] would be cancelled?

Th.—No.

A.—Then Assurance must be unconditioned [that is, it cannot begin and cease].

Th.—But your argument can be applied to false Assurance. You would not therefore call that unconditioned!

---

2. *Of Causal Genesis.*

Controverted Point.—That the causal elements in the law of causal genesis are unconditioned.

From the Commentary.—Because of the Word in the chapter on causation—'*whether Tathāgatas arise or do not arise, this elemental datum which remains fixed,*' etc., some, as the Pubbaseliyas and the Mahiṃsāsakas, have arrived at the view here affirmed.

[1] This is exactly similar to the opening argument in VI. 1, § 1.

[1] 'Since it is something that has a genesis and a cessation.'—*Comy.*

[2] Micchatta-niyāma, assurance in the wrong direction, applied to the five heinous crimes (p. 71, *n.* 4) which entail retribution in the next existence.

[2, 3] *Th.*—Would you say that any single term in each clause of the formula of causal genesis refers to something unconditioned, for instance, 'ignorance,' or 'karma,' in the clause 'because of ignorance, karma,' etc.? No? Then how can you maintain your thesis?

[4] *P. M.*—If we are wrong, why did the Exalted One say as follows: '"*Because of birth, bhikkhus, comes decay and death":—whether Tathāgatas arise or not, this element stands as the establishing of things as effects, as the marking out of things as effects, as the cause of this or that. Concerning this element a Tathāgata becomes enlightened, and penetrates it. Thus enlightened and penetrating, he declares, teaches, makes known, lays it down, reveals, dispenses, makes manifest, and behold! he saith: "Because of birth, bhikkhus, comes decay and death." "Because of the tendency to become*[1] *comes birth. Because of . . . and so on, back to." "Because of ignorance comes karma." Thus, bhikkhus, this element, stable, constant, immutable, is called a causal term [in the law of causal genesis]*'?[2]

Surely then the causal element in that law is unconditioned.

[5] *Th.*—In the clause 'Because of ignorance karma,' the former is that which establishes, which marks out the latter as its effect. And Nibbāna is unconditioned—you affirm both of these? Yes? Then are there two unconditioneds? . . . two shelters . . . (as in § 1)?

[6] And if in the next clause: 'Because of karma, con-

[1] Or 'be reborn.'

[2] *Saŋyutta-Nik.*, II. 25. 'The sense in which each term (a n g a) of the law of causal genesis is termed Paṭicca-samuppāda is stated in the *Vibhanga* on the P a ṭ i c c a - s a m u p p ā d a.'—*Comy.* See *Vibhanga*, 'Paccayākāra-vibhanga,' pp. 135-192. It is interesting that this term for the P a ṭ i c c a - s a m u p p ā d a, peculiar, it may be, to the *Vibhanga*, is not used by our Commentary. Causes by which d h a m m a ' s (things as *effects*) are established, are marked out, are called the ṭ h i t a t ā, the n i y ā m a t ā, of d h a m m a ' s. These terms, with i d a p p a c c a y a t ā, are synonymous with p a ṭ i c c a - s a m u p p ā d a, and signify, not the abstract statement of the law, but the concrete causal element.

sciousness,' you affirm that karma is unconditioned,[1] are there then three unconditioneds? . . .

[7] And so on, affirming that each of the remaining nine terms and Nibbāna are unconditioned:—are there then twelve unconditioneds? . . . twelve shelters, twelve refuges, etc.?

Of course you deny, hence you cannot affirm that the causal term in the law of causal genesis is unconditioned.[2]

---

3. *Of the Four Truths.*

Controverted Point.—That the Four Truths are unconditioned.

From the Commentary.—Some, like the Pubbaseliyas, hold this belief, deriving it from the Sutta: '*These four, bhikkhus, are stable, constant,*' etc.[3] They draw a distinction between a 'fact' and a 'truth,' considering that the former is conditioned, the latter unconditioned. In the Third Truth they disallow the existence of any corresponding fact.[4]

[1] *Th.*—Do you then also admit [not one, but] four Nibbānas? For if you do, is there among these four a boundary, division, line or interstice, different degrees as to loftiness, excellence or sublimity?[5] . . .

[2] You affirm, do you not, that each Truth is unconditioned. Take the first Truth on [the fact and nature of] Ill: is Ill itself unconditioned? You deny—that is, you mean that bodily ill, mental ill, grief, lamentation, melancholy or despair is conditioned? Or the second Truth on the cause of Ill—is that cause unconditioned? You deny. . . . Then you must equally deny that desires of sense, desire for [after-] life, or desire to end life, is unconditioned? Or the fourth Truth of the Path to Cessation of

[1] The PTS edition gives erroneously a negative reply. Cf. Br. edition, and §§ 5, 7.

[2] The point is that only Nibbāna is unconditioned.

[3] See below.

[4] Lakkhaṇa-saccaŋ (Truth) is the statement of the characteristics of a vatthu-saccaŋ (fact).

[5] See VI. 1, § 1; II. 11.

Ill—is the Path[1] itself unconditioned? You deny. . . . Then you do not mean that right views, right intentions . . . right concentration are unconditioned?

[3] You admit then that Ill, its Cause, the Path are conditioned, and all the factors of those facts are conditioned, but deny that the [abstract] statement of each fact as a 'Truth' is conditioned[2]—which cannot be. . . .

[4] Take now the Third Truth on the Cessation of Ill—is Cessation unconditioned? 'Yes,' you say?[3] Why then, if the First Truth is unconditioned, is not Ill unconditioned? Or the Cause? Or the Path? [5] In all but the Third Truth, you maintain that the true thing is conditioned—why not in the Third?

[6] *P.*—But if I am wrong, why was it said by the Exalted One: '*These four things, bhikkhus, are stable, constant, immutable. Which are the four? "This is Ill!"—this, bhikkhus, is stable, constant, immutable. "This is the cause of Ill . . . the Cessation of Ill . . . the course leading to the Cessation of Ill!"—this, bhikkhus, is stable, constant, immutable. These are the four*'?[4]

Surely then the Four Truths are unconditioned.[5]

---

4. *Of the Four Immaterial Spheres [of Life and Thought].*

Controverted Point.—That the sphere of infinite space is unconditioned.

From the Commentary.—Because of the Word, '*the four Immaterials are imperturbable,*' some hold they are all unconditioned.

[1] *Th.*—Are you implying that it is in this respect identical with Nibbāna, the Shelter, the Cave, the Refuge,

[1] The Ariyan or Noble Eightfold Path, not the Four Paths. The latter are really one, divided into four stages, each of which has eight factors (p. 188, *n.* 5).

[2] In the PTS edition (p. 323) the line Dukkhasaccaŋ asankhataṃ should read . . . sankhataṃ.

[3] 'Cessation' (nirodha) is a synonym for Nibbāna—the extinction of Ill and its Causes. Hence the opponent's view.

[4] *Saŋyutta-Nik.*, v. 430.

[5] In the sense of being eternally, constantly, not occasionally, true.

the Goal, the Past-Decease, the Ambrosial? You deny. . . . Then you cannot so class it. If you affirm, we may then have two Unconditioneds, two Nibbānas. . . .

[2] You admit, do you not, that the sphere of infinite space is a form of rebirth, a destination, an abode of beings, a sequel in living, a matrix of birth, a station for reborn consciousness, an acquiring of individuality? Then is the unconditioned to be so described? Of course not. . . .

Is there karma which brings us to rebirth in that sphere? 'Yes,' you say. Then is there karma which brings about rebirth in the unconditioned? Of course you deny. . . . There are beings who for their deserts are reborn in that sphere of infinite space, but are there any who for their deserts are reborn in the unconditioned? Of course you deny. . . .

[3] Do any beings become born, decay, die, decease, and spring up again in that sphere? Yes? But surely not in the unconditioned. . . .

Does mind in its four constituents[1] exist in that sphere? Yes? But hardly in the unconditioned. . . . You cannot call the latter a plane of life with four constituents, as is the former.

[4] *Opponent.*—But did not the Exalted One say that the four Immaterial spheres are imperturbable?[2] Surely then we may call them unconditioned.

---

5. *Of the attaining to Cessation.*

Controverted Point.—That the attainment of Cessation is unconditioned.

From the Commentary.—By the attainment of Cessation is here meant the suspension of conscious procedure in Jhāna. As something

---

[1] Of the five 'aggregates' of being, only 'body' is absent.

[2] Aneja, anañja; *Anguttara-Nik.*, ii. 184: he who has entered into the Jhānas so called is said to have won the Imperturbable.

done, attained, it is called 'completed,' but it cannot be spoken of as conditioned or unconditioned, since the features of one state or the other are absent. But some, as the Andhakas and Uttarāpathakas, hold that, because it is not conditioned, it is therefore unconditioned.

[1] *Th.*—Does this mean that this state is Nibbāna, the Shelter, etc.? You deny. Then are both similarly described as unconditioned? You affirm? Then are there two unconditioneds . . . two Nibbānas? . . .

[2] Are there any who attain to Cessation, acquire it, cause it to rise, to keep rising, set up, induce, produce, bring to pass, make to be born, to happen? If so, can you so speak of the unconditioned? Of course not. . . .

[3] Is there apparent such a thing as a purging through, emerging from,[1] Cessation? If so, is there the same from the unconditioned? Of course not. . . .

In attaining Cessation, first speech, then action, then consciousness ceases. Can you so speak of attaining the unconditioned?

In emerging from Cessation, first consciousness, then action, then speech occurs. Can you so speak of emerging from the unconditioned?

[4] After emerging from Cessation, one is in touch with three contacts: that of the void, of the signless, of the unhankered-after.[2] Can you so speak of emerging from the unconditioned? Or that, when one emerges from Cessation, consciousness is inclined for, tends to, takes shelter in solitude?

[5] *A. U.*—If we are wrong, we would just ask you, Is Cessation conditioned? No, you say; then it must be unconditioned.[3]

[1] These two terms refer to the attainment of Fruition after emergence.—*Comy.*

[2] See above, pp. 142, *n.* 4, 143, *n.* 1.

[3] Indian logic recognizes four alternatives to our two: is, is not, is and is not, neither is nor is not. The reply here would be in terms of the last. The state is outside that 'universe of thought' which comprises conditioned and its opposite, as much as green is outside music.

6. *Of Space.*

Controverted Point.—That space is unconditioned.

From the Commentary.—Space is of three modes: as confined or delimited, as abstracted from object, as empty or inane. Of these the first is conditioned; the other two are mere abstract ideas. But some, like the Uttarāpathakas and Mahiŋsāsakas, hold that the two latter modes also, inasmuch as [being mental fictions] they are not conditioned, must therefore be unconditioned.

[1] *Th.*—If space is unconditioned, as you affirm, you must class it with Nibbāna, or you must affirm two [sorts of] unconditioned—and so two Nibbānas—all of which you deny. . . .

[2] Can anyone make space where there has been no space? Then one can make that which is conditioned unconditioned—which you deny. . . . So, too, for the reverse process. . . .

[3] Again, if you admit that birds go through space, moon, sun, and stars go through space, supernormal movement is worked in space,[1] the arm or hand is waved in space, clods, clubs, a supernormally moved person, arrows are projected through space, you must state as much about movement through or in the unconditioned—which you cannot. . . .

[4] Again, if people enclose space when they make houses or barns, do they enclose the unconditioned? Or when a well is dug, does non-space become space? Yes? Then does the unconditioned become conditioned? Or, when an empty well, or an empty barn, or an empty jar, is filled, does 'space' disappear? If so, does the unconditioned disappear?

[5] *U. M.*—If then it is wrong to say space is unconditioned, is it conditioned? You deny. Then it must be unconditioned.[2]

[1] Ākāse . . . iddhiŋ vikubbanti.

[2] On space see *Bud. Psy. Eth.*, lviii. 194, and cf. *Milinda*, ii. 103, and 316 f.

7. *Of Space as visible.*

Controverted Point.—That space is visible.

From the Commentary.—This is the view, among the Andhakas for instance, namely, that because we have cognition of enclosed space, such as keyholes, etc., therefore all void space is visible. They argue that in that case space is rūpa, that is, material visible object. In the absence of a Sutta authorizing this, the opponent rejects it, yet insists on the testimony of pillar-interstices, etc., as visible things. In such cases, however, what is *seen* are the pillars, trees, and so forth. That what lies between is space, there being no visible objects, *is an act of ideation, not of sense-cognition.*[1] This applies throughout. Hence the opponent's argument is not conclusive.

[1] *Th.*—If this is so, you commit yourself to saying that space is visible material, visible object and element, and therefore, as such, is either blue-green, yellow, red, or white, is cognizable by the eye, impinges on the eye or organ of vision, enters into the avenue of sight—which you deny. . . .

[2] Substituting 'space' for 'visible object,' you must affirm or deny that 'because of eye and space visual consciousness arises.' If *not*, your proposition falls through. If you agree, you cannot quote any Suttanta to establish this. All that the Suttanta says is: '*Because of eye and visible object visual consciousness arises*,'[2] as you agree. Hence you must either call space visible object (with its properties), or fail to maintain your position.

[3] *A.*—If I am wrong, you must nevertheless admit that you 'see' the interval between two trees or two posts, the space in a keyhole or in a window. Surely then space is visible.

[1] Manodvāraviññāṇaŋ uppajjati, na cakkhuviññāṇaŋ. This advance in psychological explanation is a notable trait in Buddhaghosa's age.

[2] *Saŋyutta-Nik.*, ii. 72; iv. 83; *Majjhima-Nik.*, i. 259.

8. *Of the Four Elements, the Five Senses, and of Action as Visibles.*

Controverted Point.—That each of these is visible.

From the Commentary.—This opinion is also maintained by such as the Andhakas, from the fact that we 'see' oscillations in stones, water, flames, trees, as well as colours of sentient surfaces and the shapes of hands, feet, etc., on occasion of bodily intimations. The rest may be understood by the text.[1]

[1-9] *The discourse is verbatim identical with VI.* 7, *each of the* 'four elements,' 'the organ of sight' *alone, and* 'bodily action' *being substituted for* 'space.' *The opponent's rejoinders are severally as follows :*

A.—But do we not see earth, a stone, a mountain? water? fire blazing? trees waving in the wind? The eye, the ear, the nose, the tongue, the body? anyone advancing, retreating, looking forward, looking backward, stretching forth, retracting?

[1] Pāḷi-anusārena. The psychology is similar. The four 'elements' were not the material compounds, earthy, etc., but the abstract common qualities distinguishing the four groups so-called. Indriya is the controlling power or faculty exercised in sense. Kamma is the notion of 'action' in overt physical movements. All that we actually *see* are changing coloured surfaces. On Dhātu, Indriya, see *Compendium :* Notes *s.vv.*

BOOK VII

1. *Of the Classification [of things]*.[1]

Controverted Point.—That things cannot be grouped together by means of abstract ideas.

From the Commentary.—It is a belief held, for instance, by the Rājagirikas and the Siddhatthikas, that the orthodox classification of particular, material qualities under one generic concept of 'matter,' etc., is worthless, for this reason, that you cannot group things together by means of ideas, as you can rope together bullocks, and so on. The argument seeks to point out a different meaning in the notion of grouping.[2]

[1] *Th.*—But you do not also deny that any things may combine or be included with other things under a concept of totality or universality. Hence, how can you deny that they may be grouped together? [2] The organs of sense [3] and their objects are, you admit, computed under the material aggregate [of a living individual]. [4] Pleasant, painful, or neutral feelings are computed under the aggregate of feeling. [5] Percepts on occasion of sense and ideation come under the aggregate of perception. [6] Volitions on occasion of sense and ideation come under the aggregate of conscious concomitants. [7] Consciousness on occasion of sense and ideation comes under the aggregate of consciousness. Hence, by admitting these inclusions, you must admit that things may be grouped by an idea.

1 The title should, in the Pali, be Sangaha-, not Sangahītakathā.

2 Physical grouping is, of course, the bringing together a number of individuals. But things may be grouped mentally, *i.e.*, included under a concept of totality involved in counting, or a general concept by generalizing.

[8] *R. S.*—Then *you* understand 'things being grouped together by ideas' in the same way as two bullocks may be grouped together by a rope or a yoke, an alms-bowl may be held together by a suspender, a dog may be held in by a leash?

Th.—[Yes;[1] and] hence it is not less right to say that some things may be grouped together by other things (ideas).

---

2. *Of Mental States as mutually connected.*

Controverted Point.—That mental states are not connected with other mental states.

From the Commentary.—This again is a view of some, for instance, the Rājagirikas and Siddhatthikas, namely, that the orthodox phrase 'associated with knowledge'[2] is meaningless, because feeling or other mental states do not pervade each other (anupaviṭṭhā) as oil pervades sesamum-seeds. The argument is to show 'connected' under another aspect.[3]

[1] *Th.*—But you do not also deny that some things are concomitant, co-existent, compounded with other things, arise and cease together with them, have the same physical basis and the same object? Why then except the relation 'connected with'?

[2] One aggregate, for instance, may be co-existent with another: feeling with perception, mental coefficients, consciousness, and so on. Surely then it may be 'connected with' that other.

R. S.—Then do you understand that one such state accompanies, pervades another state, just as oil pervades sesamum, or sugar pervades cane?

Th.—Nay, that cannot truly be said. . . .[4]

[1] Bʳ [rightly] omits this. The Theravādin, concludes the Commentator, neither approves nor disapproves of the [material] simile, but by his rejoinder implies that 'even as you can't deny the physical grouping, so must you admit the mental grouping by general concepts.

[2] *E.g.*, *Dhamma-saṅgaṇi*, § 1, etc.

[3] Bʳ reads, as in the preceding kathā, aññen' ev' aṭṭhena for aññe va sabbe va (PTS). The latter seems meaningless.

[4] 'This, namely, is not a proper parallel. We cannot assign an

3. *Of Mental Properties.*

Controverted Point.—That they do not exist.

From the Commentary.**—Once more, some, like the Rājagirikas and Siddhatthikas, hold that we can no more get 'mentals' (cetasikā) from mind (citta), than we can get 'contactals' from contact, so that there is no such thing as a property, or concomitant, of mind. The Theravādin contends that there would be nothing wrong if custom permitted us to say 'contactal' for what depends on contact, just as it is customary usage to call 'mental' that which depends on mind (citta-nissitako).**

[1] *Th.*—You surely do not also deny that some mental phenomena are concomitant, co-existent, conjoined with consciousness, have their genesis and cessation, physical basis and object in common with it? Why then exclude the 'mental?' [2] Contact, for instance, is co-existent with consciousness; hence it is a 'mental,' i.e., a property or concomitant of mind. So are feeling, perception, volition, faith, energy, mindfulness, concentration, understanding, lust, hate, dulness, . . . indiscretion—all the 'mentals.'

[3] *R. S.*—You allow then that what is co-existent with consciousness is a 'mental.' Do you equally admit that what is co-existent with contact is a 'contactal,' or that what is co-existent with each of those mental phenomena is to be analogously regarded; for instance, that what is co-existent with indiscretion is an 'indiscretional'?

Th.—Certainly. [4] And if you assert that there are no mental phenomena corresponding to our term 'mentals,' was it not said by the Exalted One:

'Yea! verily this mind and mental states
Are void of soul for one who understands.
Whoso discerns the low and high in both,
The seer, he knows that neither can endure'?[1]

---

essential difference between sesamum and its oil as we can between feeling and perception. "Sesamum" is the customary name for something that is kernel, husk, and oil. When the former appearance is changed, we call it oil.'—*Comy.* The MSS. and B[r] are discrepant in detail here, but we believe we have given the intended meaning.

[1] We cannot trace these verses.

[5] Or again, was it not said by the Exalted One: *Suppose in this case, Kevaṭṭa,*[1] *that a bhikkhu can make manifest the mind, and the mental [property], and the direction and application of thought in other beings, other individuals, saying : Such is your mind. This is your mind. Thus and thus are you conscious '?*[2]

Hence there is such a thing as a 'mental' [that is, a property, or concomitant, of conciousness or mind].[3]

---

4. *Of Giving and the Gift*

Controverted Point.—That dāna is [not the gift but] the mental state.

From the Commentary.—Dāna is of three kinds:[4] the will to surrender [something], abstinence, the gift. In the line—

Faith, modesty, and meritorious giving,

we have the will to surrender something when opportunity occurs. In the phrase '*he gives security,*' abstinence, when opportunity occurs, is meant. In the phrase 'he gives food and drink in charity,' a thing to be given on a given occasion is meant. The first is dāna [in an active sense], as that which surrenders, or [in the instrumental sense] as that by which something is given. Abstinence is giving in the sense of severing from, cutting off. When it is practised, one severs, cuts off the immoral will which we consider to be a fearful and dangerous state. And this is a 'giving.' Finally, dāna implies that an offering is given. This *triple* distinction is in reality reduced to two : mental and material. But the view held, for instance, by the Rājagirikas and Siddhattikas, recognizes the *former only.* And the object of the discourse is to clear up the confusion (*lege* sankāra-bhāvaŋ)[5] between the meanings of this dual distinction.

[1] *Th.*—If dāna be a mental state, is it possible to give a mental state away to others? If you deny, your

---

[1] Or Kevaddha. The KV. MSS. read as above.

[2] *Dīgha-Nikāya,* i. 213.

[3] On cetasika see *Compendium,* 237 f.; *Buddh. Psychology,* 175 f.

[4] Dāna means grammatically both giving and gift and liberality. Hence the necessity of retaining the Pali word.

[5] So Br. The readings in the PTS edition are impossible.

proposition falls through. If you assent,[1] you then imply that it is possible to give any mental property to others: contact, feeling, perception, volition, faith, energy, mindfulness, concentration, understanding.

[2] *R. S.*—If we are wrong, we ask you, is giving attended by undesirable, disagreeable, unpleasant, barren consequences?[2] Does it induce, and result in, sorrow? Is not rather the opposite true? Surely then dāna is a mental state.

[3] *Th.*—Granting that giving was pronounced by the Exalted One to produce desirable results, is giving a robe, or alms-food, or lodging, or materia medica and requisites for illness dāna? You admit they are, but you cannot assert that these *directly* bring about desirable, agreeable, pleasant, felicific mental results.

[4] *R. S.*—If we are wrong, let us quote the words of the Exalted One:

> '*Faith, modesty, and meritorious giving:*
> *These are the things that men of worth pursue;*
> *This, say they, is the path celestial,*
> *Hereby we pass into the deva-world.*'[3]

[5] Again: '*Bhikkhus, these five givings, the Great Dāna's,*[4] *are supreme, secular, hereditary; ancient* [*customs*], *unmixed now or in the past; they are not mixed one with the other, nor shall be, and they are not despised by recluses or brahmins, or by the wise. What are the five? First, there is the Ariyan disciple who, having put away taking life, is opposed to it. Such an one gives to all beings without limit security, amity,*

[1] On the ground that anything mental cannot be given as if it were food, etc., the opponent denies; when the question is insisted upon, he recollects the Sutta on 'giving security, etc.,' and assents.—*Comy.*

[2] If dāna means the material gift, and this be, say, a nauseous medicine, the giver must reap corresponding undesirable fruit.—*Comy.*

[3] *Anguttara-Nik.*, iv. 236.

[4] In his Commentary on *Anguttara-Nik.* Buddhaghosa calls these 'the gifts of the will' (cetanā), deliberate, intentional giving.

benevolence. And having thus given without limit, he himself becomes partaker in that security, amity, benevolence. Secondly, the Ariyan disciple, having put away taking what is not given, wrong conduct in sense-desires, lying, and occasions for indulging in strong drinks, is opposed to these. Thus renouncing, bhikkhus, he gives to all beings without limit security, amity, goodwill. And so giving, he himself becomes partaker in that unlimited security, amity, goodwill. These, bhikkhus, are the five Great Dāna's. . . .'[1]

If the Suttanta says thus, then giving is a mental state.

[6] *Th.*—According to you, then, dāna is not something to be given. But was it not said by the Exalted One: '*Take the case of one who gives food, drink, raiment, a carriage, a wreath, a perfume, ointment, a couch, a dwelling, means of lighting*'?[2] Surely then dāna is a thing to be given.

[7] *R. S.*—You say then that giving is a thing to be given. Now you do not admit that the thing to be given has as its direct result something desirable, agreeable, pleasant, felicific, a happy capacity and consequence. On the other hand, the Exalted One said that dāna had such a result. Now you say that a robe, alms-food, and the other requisites are dāna. Hence it follows that a robe and so on has such a result, which cannot be. Therefore it is wrong to say that dāna is a thing to be given.

---

5. *Of Utility.*

Controverted Point.—That merit increases with utility.

From the Commentary.—Some, like the Rājagirikas, Siddhattikas, and Sammitiyas, from thoughtlessly interpreting such Suttas as '*merit day and night is always growing,*' and '*the robe, bhikkhus, which a bhikkhu enjoying the use of . . .,*'[3] hold that there is such a thing as merit achieved by utility.

---

[1] *Anguttara-Nik.*, iv. 246.

[2] *Op. cit.*, iv. 239. This is a 'stock' catalogue; cf. *op. cit.*, i. 107; ii. 85, 208; *Dīgha-Nik.*, iii. 259.

[3] See below.

[1] *Th.*—By your thesis you imply [that other mental experiences are increasing quantities :—] that contact, feeling, perception, volition, cognition, faith, energy, mindfulness, concentration, understanding, can each keep growing[1] —which you deny. . . . And that merit keeps growing just as a creeper, a liana, a tree, grass, or brushwood grows—which you deny. . . .

[2] Again, in affirming it, do you also admit that a giver acquires merit when, having given his gift, he does not consider it further?[2] You do. But this is to imply, in other words, that merit accrues to one who does not consciously advert to, reflect upon, consider, attend to, deliberate, anticipate, aim. Is not the opposite the case? You assent. Then it is wrong to say that merit goes on growing with utility.

[3] Again, in affirming your thesis, do you also admit that a giver may acquire merit who, on giving a gift, entertains sensual, malevolent, or cruel thoughts? 'Yes,' you reply. Then have we here a combination of two contacts, feelings, perceptions, volitions, cognitions? No? Think! 'Yes,' you now reply.[3] Then you are maintaining that good and bad, guilty and innocent, base and noble, sinister and clear mental states, can co-exist side by side [at the same moment]. You deny. Think again! 'Yes,' you now reply.[4] But was it not said by the Exalted One: '*There are four things, bhikkhus, very far away one*

[1] Merit (puñña) is an abstract notion or human estimate of the balance of anyone's chances of a surplus over unhappy experience in the future in consequence of deeds done now. Thus, for both estimator and the subject of the estimate, it is nothing else than a series of mental phenomena, and should be considered as such, and not as some external and mystic entity or continuum.

[2] Na samannāharati, *i.e.*, the 'adverting,' having arrested the subconscious life-flux, does not 'smoothly conduct' the will-to-give (dāna-cetanā) along its own path.—*Comy.*

[3] He now assents, because he includes the consciousnesses of both donor and donee.—*Comy.*

[4] He now assents, because by his opinion that which is derived from sustained enjoyment is not a conscious phenomenon.—*Comy.*

from the other. What are the four? The sky and the earth, the hither and the yonder shore of the ocean, whence the sun rises and where he sinks, the Norm of the good and that of the wicked.

> '*Far is the sky and far from it the earth lies;*
> *Far too the further shore of ocean, say they;*
> *And whence the radiant sun at day-dawn rises,*
> *And where he goes, lightmaker, to his ending.*
> *Yet further than all these asunder, say they,*
> *The Norm of good men's lives and that of bad men.*
> *Co-operation of the good can never perish,*
> *True to its nature while it yet endureth.*
> *But swift dissolves the intercourse of bad men.*
> *Hence far is Norm of good from that of evil*'?[1]

Therefore it is wrong to say that good and bad, etc., mental states, co-exist side by side in anyone.

[4] *R. S. S.*—But, if your rejection is right, was it not said by the Exalted One:

> '*Planters of groves and shady woods,*
> *And they who build causeway and bridge,*
> *And wells construct and watering-sheds,*
> *And to the homeless dwellings give:—*
> *Of such as these by day and night*
> *For ever doth the merit grow.*
> *In righteousness and virtue's might*
> *Such folk from earth to heaven go*'?[2]

Therefore merit goes on growing with utility.

[5] Again, was it not said by the Exalted One: '*Bhikkhus, there are these four streams of merit and of good, sources of happiness and blissful fate, resulting in happiness, conducive to heavenly life, conducive to that which is desirable, agreeable, and sweet, to welfare and happiness. What are the four? When a bhikkhu, enjoying the use of robes, or of alms-food, or of shelter, or of medical requisites*

[1] *Anguttara-Nik.*, ii. 50. [2] *Saŋyutta-Nik.*, i. 33.

given him, is able to attain to and dwell in infinite concentration of mind, to the giver each of these four gifts is an infinite stream of merit and of good . . .'?[1]

Therefore merit goes on growing with utility.

[6] *Th.*—You still affirm your proposition. Now, does a giver who has given a gift acquire merit when the acceptor, having accepted the gift, throws it away, abandons it? 'Yes,' you reply. But you cannot possibly say of that giver's merit that it goes on growing.

[7] Or if, when the gift is accepted, kings, or thieves, take it away again, or fire burns it, or water bears it away, or hostile heirs take it back? The same holds good. Hence merit is not dependent upon utility.

6. *Of the Effect of Gifts given in this Life.*

Controverted Point.—That what is given here sustains elsewhere.

From the Commentary.—It is held by some—for instance, the Rājagiriyas and Siddhatthikas—that because of the Word:

> '*By what is given here below*
> *They share who, dead, 'mong Petas go,*'[2]

gifts of robes, etc., cause life to be sustained there.

[1] *Th.*—Your proposition commits you to the further statement that robes, alms-food, lodging, medical requisites for ailments, hard food, soft food, and drink, given in this life, are enjoyed in the after-life—which you deny. . . . And it commits you further to this [heterodox position], that one person is the agent for another; that the happiness or ill we feel is wrought by others; that one acts, another experiences the consequences[3] — which you deny. . . .

[1] *Aṅguttara-Nik.*, ii. 54. [2] See next page.

[3] *Saṃyutta-Nik.*, ii. 75 f. Judging by the Commentary on the verses just below [§ 8], gifts to the memory of dead kinsfolk were made to the Order, the donor specifying that he made them in the name of

[2] *R. S.*—You deny our proposition. But do not the Petas thank him who gives a gift for their advantage, are not their hearts appeased, are they not interested, do they not obtain gladness? [3] Was it not said by the Exalted One:

'As water rained upon high slope
Doth ever down the hillside run,
E'en so whate'er on earth is given
Doth reach the hapless Peta shades.
And as the brimming rivers run
To keep the mighty ocean full,
E'en so whate'er, etc.
For where they dwell no husbandry
Nor tending dairy kine is there,
No merchant traffic as with us,
No goods to buy with precious coin.
By what is given here below
They share who, dead, 'mong Petas go'?[1]

Therefore our proposition is right.

[4] Again, was it not said by the Exalted One: '*Bhikkhus, there are these five matters which parents, if wishing for a child to be born to them, contemplate. Which are the five? Cared for (they think) he will care for us; or, he will do our work; he will continue our family; he will inherit our property; he will institute offerings to the departed parent shades (Petas).*

'Wise folk who fain a child would have
Have five advantages in view:—
Us by his wages he will keep;
His will it be our work to do;

---

such of his kin as might have been reborn as Petas. *Paramatthajotikā* (PTS, I., p. 204 f.); cf. Spence Hardy, *Buddhism*, p. 59 (Childers, *s.v.* Peta), whose view is that offerings were *exposed* for such ill-plighted shades, not given for the use of the Order. The argument in the Kathā-Vatthu implies that the former procedure was followed. The merit of the gift might avail to bless the Petas, but the material gift itself could not nourish them, as the superstitious deemed.

[1] *Khuddakapāṭha* (PTS), 6 (VII.).

Our family will long endure;
Our heritage to him we leave;
And then again an offering
To Peta-shades he'll institute.
These matters five keep well in view
The wise who fain a child would have.
Wherefore the pious and the good,
Children who know and grateful feel,
Support their mother and their sire,
Remembering all these did for them.
Their tasks they take upon themselves,
E'en as their parents toiled for them;
Do their behests and them maintain,
Nor suffer that their race decay.
Praise to the child of filial heart,
With piety and virtue dight'?[1]

Was it not so said? Then is our proposition right.

---

7. *Of the Earth and Karma.*

Controverted Point.—That land is a result of action.

From the Commentary.—Inasmuch as there is human action directed to gain dominion and sovereignty over the soil, some, like the Andhakas, hold that the earth itself is a resultant of such action (or karma). The argument goes to show that (1) land has nothing in common with the sentient results which are caused by karma;[2] (2) that such results are a matter of individual subjective experience, not shared by others, myriads of whom do not even live upon the earth.

[1] *Th.*—As well say that the earth belongs to feeling[3] pleasant, painful, or neutral, or is conjoined [as mental] with feeling or with perception, or volition, or cognition, that the earth has a mental object, that she can advert to, reflect upon, consider, attend, intend, anticipate, aim. Is not just the opposite true of her? Hence your proposition is wrong.

[1] *Anguttara-Nik.*, iii. 43.

[2] Sukha-vedanīyā, etc.

[3] Kamma-vipāka, or result of actions was, in its ultimate terms, conceived as *feeling* experienced by the agent in this life, or by the resultant of him in another life.

[2] Again, compare her [with something mental]—with contact. Of contact you could say that it is both (i.) a result of action and also that it (ii.) belongs to feeling, and so on (as in § 1). But you cannot say both these things of earth. Or if you affirm the former (i.) and deny the latter predicate (ii.) of earth, you must be prepared to do no less in the case of contact.

[3] Again, the earth undergoes expansion and contraction, cutting and breaking up. Can you say as much of the [mental] result of action?

Again, the earth may be bought and sold, located, collected, explored. Can you say as much of the result of action?

Again, the earth is common to everyone else. But is the result of [my] action common to everyone else? 'Yes,' you say. But was it not said by the Exalted One:

> '*This treasure to none else belongs,*
> *No bandit hence may bear it.*
> *The mortal who would fare aright*
> *Let him work acts of merit*'?[1]

Hence it is wrong to say that a result of action is experienced by everyone else.

[4] Again, you would admit that first the earth is established and afterwards beings are reborn [on it]. But does result first come to pass and afterwards people act to insure result? If you deny, you cannot maintain that earth is a result of action.

[5] Again, is the earth a common result of collective action? Yes, you say? Do you mean that all beings enjoy the use of the earth? If you deny, you cannot affirm your proposition. If you assent, I ask whether there are any who pass utterly away without enjoying the use of it? You assent, of course. But are there any who pass utterly away without exhausting the experienced result of their actions? Of course you deny. . . .

[1] *Khuddakapāṭha*, VIII. 9. The last two lines are discrepant. The work quoted reads 'wise man' for 'mortal,' and, for the third line:

That treasure which doth follow him—viz. merit.

[6] Once more, is the earth a result of the action of a being who is a world-monarch? and do other beings share in the use of the earth? Yes, you reply. Then do other beings make use of the result of his actions? You deny. . . . I ask again, and you assent. But then, do other beings share also in his contact, feelings, perception, volition, consciousness, faith, energy, mindfulness, concentration, understanding? Of course you deny. . . .

[7] *A.*—But if I am wrong, surely there is action to gain dominion [over the earth],[1] action to gain sovereignty [on the earth]? If so, surely the earth is a result of action.

---

8. *Of Decay and Death and Karma.*

Controverted Point.—That old age and death are a result of action.

From the Commentary.—Inasmuch as some action does conduce to that deterioration we call decay or old age, and to that curtailing of life we call death, some, like the Andhakas, hold that old age and death are the 'result (vipāka)' of that action. Now there is between morally bad action and material decay the relation known as karma,[2] but the moral cause and the physical effect differ in kind. Hence the latter is not subjective result (vipāka). It is unlike any mental state:—contact, feeling, etc.—such as is produced by karma. Besides, it is partly due to the physical order (utu).[3]

[1, 2] *Th.—The first two sections are* verbatim *as in the preceding discourse, save that instead of* 'result of action' (kamma-vipāka), 'result' (vipāka) *only is used.*

[3] Again, you admit, do you not, that the decay and dying of bad states of mind is the result of previous bad states? But then you must also admit that the decay and dying of good states of mind is the result of previous good

[1] Literally, lordship, 'here meaning large possessions.'—*Comy.*

[2] Kamma and vipāka (result *in sentience*) are two of the twenty-four paccayas or correlations of things physical or mental. *Compendium*, 191 f.

[3] In the *Comy.* p. 101, last line (PTS), read: Utusamuṭṭhānādibhedena taŋ paṭilābhavasena āyuno ca. . . .

states—which you deny. . . . But in denying the latter, you imply denial of the former statement. . . .

[4] Or do you hold that the decay and dying of good states of mind is the result of previous bad states? You do, you say. Then you imply that the decay and dying of bad states is the result of previous good states—which you deny. . . . But in denying this, you imply denial of the former statement. . . .

[5] Or do you affirm that the decay and dying of both good and bad states of mind are the result of bad states? You do, you say. Then you must say no less: 'is the result of good states'—which you deny. . . .

[6] *A.*—You say my proposition is false. But surely acts conduce to the deterioration and to the curtailment of life? If so, my proposition is true.

---

9. *Of the Ariyan Mind and its Results.*

Controverted Point.—That Ariyan states of mind have no [positive] result.[1]

From the Commentary.—Some, like the Andhakas, hold that the fruits of religious life, being merely the negative putting away of corrupt qualities, are not properly states of mind. By religious life is meant the career of a recluse, or progress in the Paths, as it is said: '*I will show you the religious life and the fruits thereof,*'[2] the former being the Fourfold Path,[3] and the fruits thereof those of Stream-Winner, Once-Returner, Never-Returner, and Arahantship.

[1, 2] *Th.*—But you admit that the career of a recluse or religious student is productive of great rewards—to wit, the fruits of the Four Paths. How then can you deny positive result?

[3] Or, if you deny that these four kinds of fruit are positive result—as you do—then you equally deny that

[1] Vipāka—i.e., are they actions engendering for the subject no positive psychical sequel, such as is always understood by this term?

[2] *Saṃyutta-Nik.*, v. 25.

[3] Each stage of the Path has the eight factors (Eightfold Path) in different degrees.

there is positive result in the fruit of giving or of moral conduct, or of religious exercises, which you maintain. . . .

[4] Now in maintaining these propositions, you must no less maintain that there is positive result in the fruits of the Paths. . . .

[5] Again, you will of course admit that good done in relation to life on earth or in the heavens, material or immaterial, entails result. Does this not commit you to admitting that good done in relation to path-graduating[1] also entails result [though you deny this by your proposition]? Conversely, if you maintain that good done in relation to path-graduating entails no result, must you not also deny result to good done in relation to life on earth or in heaven?

[6] *A.*—[Well, but is not this a parallel case?] You will of course admit that good done in relation to life on earth or in the heavens, material or immaterial, entailing result, makes for accumulation of rebirth.[2] Does this not commit you to admitting that good done in relation to path-graduating, entailing [as you say] result, makes also for accumulation of rebirth [though you of course deny this]?

---

10. *Of Results as again causing Results.*

Controverted Point.—That 'result' is itself a state entailing resultant states.[3]

From the Commentary.—Because one result [of karma] stands in relation to another result by way of reciprocity,[4] etc., some, like the Andhakas, hold that the result is itself necessarily the cause of other results.

---

[1] Literally, non-worldly, or supramundane. The Commentary classes all good done for rebirth as lōkiya, mundane. Path-graduating militated against rebirth.

[2] For Buddhaghosa's definition of this term, see *Bud. Psy. Eth.*, p. 82, *n.* 2.

[3] Vipākadhamma-dhammo. See *Bud. Psy. Eth.*, p. 253, *n.* 1.

[4] Aññamañña-paccayo, or mutuality; one of the twenty-four relations. The statement here is from the Paṭṭhāna.

[1] *Th.*—If your proposition is true it is tantamount to saying that the result of *that* [result] entails [other] results—which you deny. . . . Or, if you assent, then you are asserting that in a given series there is no making an end of ill, no cutting off the round of birth and death, no Nibbāna without residual stuff of life—which is contrary to doctrine.[1]

[2] Again, are you asserting that 'result' and 'state entailing resultant states' are identical, equivalent terms—of one import, the same, of the same content and origin?

[3] That they are concomitant, co-existent, conjoined, connected, one in genesis, in cessation, in basis, and in mental object? All this you deny. . . .[2]

[4] Again, do you mean that a given bad mental state is its own result, a given good state its own result? That the consciousness with which we take life is the very consciousness with which we burn in purgatory? That the consciousness with which we give a gift of merit is the very consciousness with which we rejoice in heaven? . . .

[5] *A.*—You deny my proposition; but are not 'results [of karma]' the four immaterial aggregates in reciprocal relation? If so, surely it is right to say that a result is a mental state resulting from other mental states?

[1] *A.* 'denies this for fear of contravening doctrine.'—*Comy.* Cf. above, I. 1 (p. 48 f.).

[2] The opponent regards any one of the four mental groups as 'result entailing the other three as *its* results' in their mutual relation at any given moment.—*Comy.* But this cannot be, since all four are mutually co-inhering at that moment as an indivisible whole.

BOOK VIII

1. *Of Divers Destinies.*[1]

Controverted Point.—That there are six spheres of destiny.

From the Commentary.—There is an opinion among some schools—the Andhakas and Uttarāpathakas—that the Asuras form a sixth plane of rebirth. The Theravādin contradicts this in virtue of the hair-raising illustration of the five divisions of destiny in the Sutta: '*There are these five destinies, Sāriputta.*'[2] . . . It is true that a troop of Asuras—that of Vepacitti[3]—was freed from the fourfold plane of misery, but not to form a separate plane. They were taken up among the devas. The Kālakañjakas were taken up among the Petas.

[1] *Th.*—Did not the Exalted One name five destinies—purgatory, the animal kingdom, the Peta-realm, mankind, the devas? [2] And did not the Kālakañjaka Asuras, who resembled the Petas in [ugly or frightful] shape, sex-life, diet, and length of life, intermarry with them? [3] And did not Vepacitti's troop, who in the same respects resembled the devas, intermarry with devas? [4] And had not Vepacitti's troop been formerly devas?

[5] *A. U.*—But since there is an Asura-group, it is surely right to speak of it as a [possible] destiny?[4]

[1] Gati, literally, a going, or bourne, a career. On these, concisely stated, see *Compendium*, p. 187.

[2] *Majjhima-Nik.*, i. 73.

[3] *Saṃyutta-Nik.*, i. 221 f. Cf. *Dialogues*, ii. 289; *Pss. of the Brethren*, verse 749.

[4] The *Commentary* includes between 'in shape' and 'sex-life,' the [bracketed] term bībhacchā—Bībhacchā ti virūpā duddasikā. It also paraphrases samānābhogā (rendered as 'resembling . . . in sex-life') by sadisa-methuna-samācārā; and samānāhārā ('resembling . . . in diet') by sadisa-kheḷa-singhānika-pubba-lohitādi-āhārā.

2. *Of an Intermediate State.*

Controverted Point.—That there is an intermediate state of existence.

From the Commentary.—Some (as, for instance, the Pubbaseliyas and Sammitiyas), by a careless acceptation of the Sutta-phrase—'completed existence within the interval'[1]—held that there is an interim stage where a being awaits reconception for a week or longer. The counter-argument is based on the Exalted One's dictum that there are three states of becoming only—the Kāma-, the Rūpa-, and the Arūpa-worlds.[2] And it is because of that dictum that the opponent [in so far as he is orthodox] has to deny so many of the questions.

[1] *Th.*—If there be such a state, you must identify it with either the Kāma-life, or Rūpa-life, or Arūpa-life, which you refuse to do. . . .

[2] You deny that there is an intermediate state between the first and second, or the second and third, of these . . . [3] you affirm, indeed, that is no such thing; how then can you maintain your proposition?

[4] Is it a fifth matrix, a sixth destiny, an eighth station for reborn consciousness,[3] a tenth realm of beings? Is it a mode of living, a destiny, a realm of beings, a renewal of life, a matrix, a station of consciousness, an acquiring of individuality? Is there karma leading to it? Are there beings who approach thither? Do beings get born in it, grow old, die in it, decease from it, and get reborn from it? Do the five aggregates exist in it? Is it a five-mode existence? All this you deny. How then can you maintain your proposition?

[5-7] You admit that every one of these [categories or notions] applies to each of the three planes of life named above, the only difference being that the first two—Kāma-life and Rūpa-life—are five-mode existences; the last—

[1] I.e., died within the first half of the normal life-span in those heavens. See I. 4, § 9.

[2] *Saṃyutta-Nik.*, ii. 3, etc. Cf. *Compendium*, 81, *n.* 2, 138 f.

[3] The seven 'stations' (v i ñ ñ ā ṇ a ṭ ṭ h i t i y o), or opportunities for the *resultant* rebirth-consciousness (the effect of a dying person's consciousness) to happen—are described in *Dialogues*, ii. 66 f.

Arūpa-life—is a four-mode existence (that is, without material qualities). If then there is an intermediate stage of life, you must be able to predicate some or all of these [notions or categories] of it. But you say you cannot. . . .

[8] But you deny also that there is an intermediate life for all beings. Hence your proposition is not universally valid.

[9-11] For whom then do you deny the intermediate state? For the person whose retribution is immediate?[1] If you assent, to that extent your proposition is for you not true. Or is it for the person whose retribution is not immediate that you affirm this state? Yes, you say. Then you must deny it for his opposite.

You deny it also for one who is to be reborn in purgatory, in the sphere of unconscious beings, in the immaterial heavens. Therefore to that extent your proposition is not universally valid. Nevertheless, you maintain that there is an intermediate stage of life for one whose retribution is not immediate, for one who is not to be reborn in purgatory, nor among the 'unconscious beings,' nor in the immaterial heavens. [Concerning these you have yet to state in what respect, as a plane of life, it resembles, or differs from, the three named by the Exalted One.]

[12] *P.S.*[2]—But are there not beings who 'complete existence within the first half of the term?' If so, are we not right?

[13] *Th.*—Granted that there are such beings, is there a separate interval-*state* [between any two recognized existences]? Yes, you say. But granted that there are beings who 'complete existence within the second half of the term,' is there a separate state of life corresponding thereto? If you deny, you must also deny your proposition [since you rest it on this basis].

The same argument applies to such cognate terms as 'beings who complete existence without,' and again, 'with difficulty and striving' (see above, I., 4, § 9, *n*. 1).

[1] On this term, see *Bud. Psy. Eth.*, § 1028.

[2] Pubbaseliya, Sammitiya.

3. *Of the Pleasures of Sense.*

Controverted Point.—That the kāma-sphere means only the fivefold pleasures of sense.

From the Commentary.—This discourse is intended to teach those who, like the Pubbaseliyas, contract the meaning of kāma-dhātu (element or datum of desire) to that of kāma-guṇā (pleasurable sensations), ignoring the difference in the meaning of the two terms. It is true that in the Sutta—'*There are these five kinds of pleasurable sensations, bhikkhus*'[1]—the whole world of kāmadhātu is implied. But generally kāmadhātu may stand for vatthukāmā, objects of sense-desire; kilesakāmā, corrupt, worldly desires; and kāmabhavā, or the eleven lowest planes of existence (from purgatory to the six lowest heavens). In the first term kāma means 'to be desired'; in the second, it means both 'to be desired' and 'to desire.' But in the last term kāma means 'to be desired' or 'desiring,' or 'place where objects of sense happen.' Dhātu, as always, means self-existing ultimate, without entity, non-substantial.[2]

[1] *Th.*—You admit, do you not, that desire, intention, zest, and joy, and the passion or lust[3] that is involved in each, are all bound up with the fivefold pleasures of sense?[4] How then can you maintain that the kāma-life is only those pleasures?

[2] Do you mean that human organs of sense are not co-extensive with kāma-life, the five organs of external sense and the co-ordinating sense, or mind? No,[5] you say (meaning only the pleasures of sense in your proposition); but think again as to mind. . . . Yes, you now say, mind is not kāma-life.[6] But was it not said by the Exalted One:

[1] *Majjhima-Nik.*, i. 85. See *Dīgha-Nik.*, iii. 234, for other references.

[2] The PTS edition of the *Commentary*, through either corrupt MSS., or printing errors, or defective punctuation, is here not always intelligible. A perusal of the Br. edition will make the meaning clearer.

[3] Here kāmadhātu means kilesakāmā.—*Comy.*

[4] As objects, kāmaguṇāramnaṇo.—*Comy.*

[5] The opponent does not reject these as objects of desire (vatthukāmā).—*Comy.*

[6] He recollects the sublimer and also the supramundane or spiritual work of mind.—*Comy.* Read te-bhūmaka-mano (*ib.*).

'Fivefold the world's sense-pleasures be,
And mind as sixth, our lore doth rede.
Whoso therein doth purge desire,[1]
Is thus from ill and sorrow freed'?

Hence it cannot be said that the kāma-life does not include the mind.

[3] Again, can you say that the pleasures of sense amount to a sphere of life,[2] a destiny, a realm of beings, to renewed life, to a matrix, a station for consciousness, an acquiring of individuality? Is there karma leading to them? Are there beings to be reborn in them? Do beings get born, grow old, die, decease, get reborn 'in' sense-pleasures? Are there the five aggregates in them? Are they a five-mode existence? Are Buddhas Supreme, Silent Buddhas, Chief Pairs of disciples[3] reborn in them? [4] All these things you can predicate of the 'kāma-element,' but not one of them of the pleasures of sense.

[5] *P.*—But was it not said by the Exalted One: *Bhikkhus, there are these fivefold kāma-pleasures—which are they? Objects desirable, sweet, agreeable, dear, connected with 'kāma,' and seductive, are cognizable by sight, hearing, smell, taste, and touch—these are the five kinds of kāma-pleasures'?*[4]

Hence surely the kāma-element is only those five.

---

4. *Of Sense-Desires.*

Controverted Point.—Whether the subjective sense-desires or the objective five fields of sense constitute kāma's.

From the Commentary.—Going merely by the Sutta last quoted above, some, like the Pubbaseliyas, hold the latter view. The

---

[1] *Saṃyutta-Nik.*, i. 16.

[2] Here kāmadhātu = kāma-bhava or -loka.

[3] See above, I. 8, §§ 9, 10.

[4] *Anguttara-Nik.*, iii. 411, etc.

Theravādin shows that 'corruptions' alone truly constitute sensualit .[1]

[1] is *verbatim* = § 1 in VIII. 3, and [2] is *verbatim* = § 5, save for the substitution of 'Hence sensuality consists in only the five fields of sense-object.'

[3] *Th.*—But was it not also said by the Exalted One: '*There are these fivefold pleasures of sense, bhikkhus: which are the five? Objects desirable, . . . adapted to sense-desires* (kāmā), *and seductive are cognizable by sight, hearing, etc. . . . five kinds of [objects associated with] sense-pleasure. Nevertheless, bhikkhus, these are not sense-desires; they are called in the Ariyan discipline [objects of] sense-pleasures* [kāmaguṇā]. *For* kāma *is a man's lustful intention*';[2]

'*The manifold of objects*[3] *in the world—*
This in itself is not 'desires of sense.'
Lustful intention[4] *is man's sense-desires.*
That manifold of objects doth endure;
The will thereto the wise exterminate'?[5]

Hence it is wrong to say that just the five kinds of sense-objects constitute sense-desires.

[1] Read kāmabhāvaŋ, 'state of having kāma's.' The translators' difficulties increase in this discourse. But the Indian conception of all the universe, save the higher and highest heavens, in terms of 'desire,' is of great interest. See *Ency. Religion and Ethics*, 'Desire, Buddhist,' by Mrs. Rhys Davids.

[2] *Anguttara-Nik.*, iii. 411. Br. does not support the reading of the PTS text—Te ariyassa . . .—as verse, but agrees with Edmund Hardy's reading in the PTS edition of the *Nikāya*, which we have mainly followed. Cf. *ibid.*, the many differences of reading in the MSS. consulted. The gāthās occur, as above, in *Saŋyutta*, i. 22. In the *Anguttara* line 3 is prefixed to the verses, and *repeated* as line 4 (in translation above, line 3 in text).

[3] The Pāli for this phrase, yāni citrāni—'the varied things which'—is paraphrased in the *Anguttara Commentary* with 'objects': citra-citrārammaṇāni.

[4] *Ib.*, paraphrased as sankappavasena uppannarāge.

[5] Or 'discipline' (vinayanti).

5. *Of the Rūpa-element.*

Controverted Point.—That the ultimate 'datum or element of *rūpa*' is things [cognized as] material.

From the Commentary.—The Theravādin criticizes this view—held, for instance, by the Andhakas—on the ground that the 'Rūpa-element' includes all the spheres of life known as Rūpa-bhava, and is therefore more extensive than just material qualities of things.[1]

[1] *Th.*—Is then *rūpa* a sphere of life, a destiny, a realm of beings, renewed life, a matrix, a station for rebirth-consciousness, an acquiring of individuality? Is there karma leading to it, beings to be reborn in it? Do they get born, grow old, die, decease, get rebirth there? Are the five aggregates 'in' rūpa? Is it a five-mode existence? [2] Now all these you can predicate of the Rūpa-datum, but not of *rūpa*, or material quality. Hence the latter has not all that is implicated in the former.

Again, if the *Rūpa*-datum consists only of material qualities—and, as you will admit, there is material quality in the *Kāma*-datum—is this latter datum the same as *Rūpa*-datum? You say 'no.' But think. *You* must admit it is.[2] Then we get a man in two life-spheres at the same time. . . .

---

6. *Of the Arūpa-Element.*

Controverted Point.—That the ultimate 'datum, or element' of *arūpa* is things [cognized as] immaterial.

From the Commentary.—Here the same method is followed. Instruction is given by taking a certain immaterial notion—'feeling'—and asking if that is a sphere of life, etc.; thus it is showed that in no case are the two identical.

[1] *Th.*—Is then feeling a sphere of life, a destiny, a realm of beings, renewed life, a matrix, a station for rebirth-consciousness, an acquiring of individuality? Is there

[1] Here there is the corresponding difficulty of the ambiguity of rūpa. See *Compendium*, 271 f.; *Bud. Psy. Eth.*, 43 f.

[2] He denies, so as not to contradict the accepted triad of life-spheres. When pushed, he assents, because of his thesis.—*Comy.*

karma leading to it? Are beings to be reborn in it? Do they get old, die, decease from, get reborn in it? Are the five aggregates 'in' feeling? Is it a five-mode existence? [2] Now all these you can predicate of the Arūpa-datum or element, but not of feeling only.

Again, if the Arūpa-element mean only immaterial things —and you will admit there is feeling and other mental aggregates in the Kāma-element—are these two elements or data identical? Either you must deny (which were unorthodox) or assent. In the latter case we get a person in two spheres of life at the same time. The same argument holds good for Arūpa and Rūpa data. And if all three be mutually identical, we get a person in three spheres of life at the same time. . . .

7. *Of the Senses in the Rūpa-Sphere.*

Controverted Point.— That in the Rūpa-sphere[1] the individual has all the six senses.

From the Commentary.—Some (as, for instance, the Andhakas and Sammitiyas), judging by the Sutta-passage—'*having form, made of mind, with all its main and lesser parts complete, not deficient in any organ*'[2]—imagine that the Brahma-group and the rest had sensations of smell, taste, and touch.

[1] *Th.*—If that be so, and one in that sphere have, say, the sense of smell, you must admit odorous objects for him to smell; and so too for the senses of taste and touch. [2] But you deny the existence, in that sphere, of such objects. [3-6] Yet it seems only rational that, admitting, as you do, the existence in that sphere of *both organ and object* in the case of sight, hearing, and [sense-co-ordination or] mind, you should admit no less as to the other fields of

[1] This includes sixteen grades of devas, the Brahma heavens being the lowest (*Compendium*, p. 138).

[2] *Dialogues*, i. 47. In the Rūpa heavens, where 'a subtle residuum of matter is still met with' (*Compendium*, p. 12), only sight, hearing, and intellectual co-ordination of these survives.

sense, once you affirm the existence, in that sphere, of any of the other sense-organs. [7-8] 'No,' you say. You are prepared to admit organs of sight, hearing, and co-ordination, and corresponding objects seen, heard, and cognized by those organs; yet while you admit the other sense-organs, you deny the existence of their objects. [9-10] In fact, even if you were to concede the existence, in that sphere, of objects odorous, sapid, and tangible, you would, you say, deny they were apprehended by the corresponding organs, though you admit the corresponding apprehension in the case of sight, etc.

[11-13] But there are among you some[1] who *would* admit this apprehension of odours, tastes, and touches by the respective organs, the existence of which you affirm. I would ask them whether there exists in that sphere the odour of roots, pith, bark, leaves, flowers, fruit, raw flesh, poisonous, pleasant, or evil odours; whether there exists there also the taste of roots, pith, bark, leaves, flowers, fruit, or sour, sweet, bitter, pungent, saline, alkaline, acrid, astringent, nice, or nauseous tastes; whether there exist there also hard and soft, smooth and rough, pleasant and painful contacts, heavy and light tangibles?[2] *You* deny that any of these does exist in that sphere. . . .

[14] *A. S.*—But is there not in that sphere the wherewithal[3] for smelling, tasting, touching?

Th.—Yes.

A. S.—Surely then it is right to say that in the Rūpa-element the individual has all six senses?

[1] Certain teachers who will have it that the fields of sense are there complete, each organ having its function.—*Comy.*

[2] These are standard formulas of enumeration. See *Bud. Psy. Eth.*, pp. 187-89, 198.

[3] Ghāna-nimittaŋ, etc. But this is only a matter of external appearance, not of organ and mental object, and is therefore a futile reference.—*Comy.*

8. *Of Matter in Arūpa-Sphere.*

Controverted Point.—That there is matter among the Immaterials.

From the Commentary.—Some (as, for instance, the Andhakas), judging by the Word—'*Because of consciousness there comes mind and body*'[1]—imagined that, even in the Arūpa-sphere of existence, there was a subtle, refined matter segregated from grosser matter.

[1] *Th.*—Is then 'matter' (*rūpa*) a sphere of life, a destiny, a realm of beings, renewed life, a matrix, an acquiring of individuality? This you deny; but all this you can predicate truly of Arūpa. Hence you cannot maintain your proposition.

[2] You cannot predicate them truly of a five-mode existence, one mode of which is material qualities. But you can do so respecting a four-mode existence, that is, with the material qualities omitted, as is the case with Arūpa. . . .

[3] You can predicate them truly of the Rūpa-sphere, where there yet is matter. But this sphere is not identical with the Arūpa-sphere. [4] And if you predicate matter of the Arūpa-sphere, you must show that matter agrees with the description you can truly give of the Arūpa-sphere as a state of existence, a destiny, etc.

[5] Again, did not the Exalted One say that the Arūpa was a way of escape from visible or material things? If that is true, do you still maintain your proposition? Yes? Well, then, the Exalted One said that renunciation was a way of escape from sense-desires.[2] Now, according to your reasoning (if there is matter in the Immaterial), there are sense-desires in renunciation, and there are intoxicants in

[1] *Dialogues*, ii. 52 f.; *Saṃyutta-Nik.*, ii. 1, *passim*; *Compendium*, p. 188; *Buddhism* (Mrs. Rhys Davids), p. 91.

[2] Nekkhamma . . . kāmā, a (very poor) word-play of exegetical derivation. The former term = going out or down from. Cf. *Dīgha-Nik.*, iii. 239 f., 275; *Anguttara-Nik.*, iii. 245.

those who are freed from them, there are things 'included' (in intoxicant-infested states of the three spheres) among the 'unincluded'[1] which is absurd.

---

9. *Of Matter as ethically Good or Bad.*

Controverted Point.—That physical actions [involved in bodily and vocal intimations] proceeding from good or bad thoughts amount to a moral act of karma.

From the Commentary.—Some (as, for instance, the Mahiŋsāsakas and the Sammitiyas) hold that acts of body and voice being, as they are, just material qualities, reckoned as bodily and vocal intimation[2] are morally good if proceeding from what is good, and morally bad if proceeding from what is bad. But if, runs the counter-argument, they are to be considered as positively moral, and not *un*moral—as we are taught[3]—then all the characteristics of the morally good or bad must apply to them, as well as material characteristics.

[1] *Th.*—If that be so—if *rūpa* involved in bodily action be of morally good import—then it must have a mental object, and the mental attributes of 'adverting,' ideating,[4] co-ordinated application, attending, willing, anticipating,

[1] I.e., the Ariyan Way or Order (niyāma), with its Paths and Fruits (*Bud. Psy. Eth.*, pp. 254, 335).

[2] See *Compendium*, p. 264; *Bud. Psy. Eth.*, 192 f.; and below, X. 10, 11.

[3] *Bud. Psy. Eth.*, p 169, especially *n.* 5.

[4] Ābhogo, from bhuj, to bend, turn (cf. our 'bow,' 'bough,' from the common Aryan root bhugh), is synonymous with āvajjana (or āvaṭṭana), the preceding term. Popularly equivalent to manakkāra (mind-doing, mentation), it is technically defined, with the former term, as the adverting of consciousness, when attention is arrested or roused. It is tantamount to 'what is in the mind'; hence the rendering 'ideating.' Cf. *Milinda* (translation), i. 147 : 'Would a wind that had died away acquiesce in being produced again? No, it can have no idea (ābhogaŋ), or will (cetanaŋ) to be reproduced . . . it is an unconscious thing.'

aiming,[1] which you deny. But otherwise it is not good.

[2] All these things you can predicate about the good contact proceeding from good consciousness, as well as about the good feeling, perception, volition, faith, energy, mindfulness, concentration, understanding, that proceed from good consciousness, and have an object of thought, but you cannot do so about *rūpa* involved in bodily action.

[3] Or again, you would admit that, if *rūpa* of the kind you name has no mental object, it will have no mental adverting, ideating, and so on; but you would deny that contact, feeling, perception, and the rest, similarly proceeding from good thought—good, but without mental object—lacked mental adverting, ideating, and so on.

[4] Now take the matter involved in the bodily action, resulting from good thought: Is all of it morally good? You deny. But then you cannot maintain your proposition as generally true. For instance, would you call visible object which was the consequence of good thought, 'good' matter? Are audible, odorous, sapid, or tangible object, or the four elements: extended, cohesive, hot, and mobile, [if they 'happened' as] the result of good thought, 'good' matter? You deny. [5] Then would you call any of them, under the circumstances, indeterminate matter (neither good nor bad)? 'Yes' you say; yet you deny that the matter or material quality appearing, under the circumstances, as bodily action is indeterminate. That, you say, would be 'good.' . . .

[6] Let us then take your 'good' bodily action which, as matter, has no mental object: must you not equally allow that visible or other sense-object, or those four elements which, as matter, have no mental object, are also, under the circumstances, 'good'? But you deny. . . . [7] Similarly you refuse to see that, if you allow

[1] The last two are equivalents of cetanā, volition. The former is volition under the aspect of preparation, or exertion; the latter is the same, regarded as persistent.—*Comy.* The former—patthanā—in its popular meaning, is 'praying,' and is used as equivalent to āsiṃsā, hope.

any sense-object, or any element brought about by good thought, and having no mental object, to be indeterminate, you must equally allow the 'matter' of bodily intimation resulting from good thought and with no mental object, to be indeterminate. . . .

[8] You call this bodily intimation, which is consequent on good thought, 'good' matter [even though it is so unmental as] not to be conjoined with any [mental reaction or] 'contact.' Yet you would deny the possibility of this if, for 'bodily intimation,' you substitute any sense-object, or one of the elements.

[9] Taken conversely, you allow that any object of sense or an element consequent on good thought, but not conjoined with any mental reaction, is indeterminate (neither good nor bad). Yet you would deny the indeterminateness if, for sense-object or element, you substitute matter of bodily action born of good thought.

[10, 11] And if to 'not conjoined with mental reaction or contact' I add 'not having a mental object,' your attitude is the same, in both alternatives [8, 9].

[12-15] *The whole argument to be repeated for* 'vocal' *instead of* 'bodily intimation.'

[16] Next with respect to bodily intimation proceeding from bad thought. You affirm similarly that this is 'morally bad' matter. Then it too must have a mental object, and those mental attributes named above,[1] which you deny. But otherwise it is not morally bad. [17] All these things you can predicate about the bad reaction, or 'contact,' proceeding from bad consciousness, as well as about the bad feeling, perception, volition, lust, hate and dulness, pride, erroneous opinion, doubt, sloth, distraction, immodesty, and indiscretion, that proceed from bad consciousness, having a mental object, but you cannot do so about that bodily intimation, which is rūpa, or of material quality

[18][2] Or again, you will admit that, if bad rūpa of the kind you name has no mental object, it will have no mental adverting and other mental attributes named above; but

[1] See § [1].

[2] Cf. §§ 3, 4.

you will deny that contact, feeling, perception, volition, lust, hate, and so on, proceeding from bad thought, bad and having no mental object, lack mental adverting and those other attributes. . . .

[19] Now this that you call 'morally bad' matter proceeding from bad consciousness:—is all of it bad? Yes? Whether it be 'bodily intimation,' or other material quality? This you deny, so your proposition amounts to this: that some material qualities resulting from bad consciousness are bad, some not.

[20-23] And all that we have argued as to 'bodily intimation' as 'bad' matter applies to 'vocal intimation.'

[24][1] For instance, would you call visible object which was the consequence of bad consciousness 'bad' matter? Or audible, odorous, sapid, or tangible matter? Or any of the four elements? Or impure matter, tears, blood, sweat (if any of them happened as the result of bad consciousness) —would you call them 'bad' matter? You deny. [25] Then would you call any of them, under the circumstances, indeterminate matter? 'Yes,' you say. Yet you deny that the matter or material quality appearing, under the circumstances, as bodily or vocal action, is indeterminate. That, you say, would be 'bad.' . . .

[26][2] Let us then take your 'bad' vocal action, which, as material, has no mental object: must you not equally allow that any sense-object, or any of the four elements, or impure matter, tears, blood, sweat, which have no mental object, are also, under the circumstances, 'bad'? But you deny. . . . [27] Similarly you refuse to see that, if you allow any of these things, when brought about by thought, and having no mental object, to be indeterminate, you must equally allow the 'matter,' bodily or vocal, of action resulting from bad thought, and with no mental object, to be indeterminate.

[28-31] *are simply repetitions of* [8-11], *substituting* 'bad' *for* 'good,' 'vocal' *for* 'bodily,' *and adding* 'impure matter, tears, blood, sweat' *to the sense-objects and four elements.*

[1] Cf. [4], [5]. [2] Cf. [6], [7].

[32] *M. S.*—But if we may not say that matter is good or bad, is not deed or word as an act good or bad? [This being quite orthodox,] our proposition must be right.

[33] *Th.*—But if you maintain that matter is good or bad, you must not hesitate to say that all five organs and objects of sense, the four elements and impure matter, etc., are (intrinsically) good or bad—which you deny. [34] If body and bodily action be material, would you affirm that mind and mental action are so? If these, on the contrary, are both immaterial, would you affirm that both body and bodily action are immaterial? Or if body is material and bodily action immaterial, would you speak similarly of mind and mental action?[1] [35] To say that bodily action as well as body is material, involves such statements as 'sense-consciousness is material because the sense-organs are material.'

[36] You must not say that rūpa, or matter, is action (or karma). For was it not said by the Exalted One: '*I say, bhikkhus, that volition is karma; when we have willed, then we make action (or karma) by deed, word, and thought?*'[2]

[37] And again: '*When, Ānanda, there is action, subjective pleasure or pain arises because it is well determined by the deed. So also when there is speech or thought, subjective pleasure or pain arises because it is well determined by the action of speech or of thought.*'[3]

[38] And again: '*There are, bhikkhus, three modes of volitional acts of body, four modes of volitional acts of speech, and three modes of volitional acts of mind, all of which amount to immoral deeds, bringing forth*[4] *ill and entailing it as result. And there are a like number of modes of volitional acts of body,*

[1] The PTS adds a repetition of the first question in this section. Br. omits both the repetition and also the third question. They are all only so many parallel instances to show the unreasonableness of implicating the whole of matter in statements about bodily and vocal action.

[2] *Anguttara-Nik.*, iii. 415.

[3] *Ib.*, ii. 157 f.; *Saṃyutta-Nik.*, ii. 39 f.

[4] Read dukkhudrayaṃ. So the Br. translation.

speech, and mind amounting to moral [karma], bringing forth and entailing happiness as result.'[1]

[39] Once more: '*If, Ananda, this foolish man, Samiddhi, when asked by the Wanderer Pātaliputta, were to answer: "Brother Pātaliputta, it is when anyone has acted intentionally in deed, word, and thought that he comes to feel pleasant, or painful, or neutral feeling, felt as pleasure, as pain, or as neither:" so answering he would make right answer*'?[2]

Is the Suttanta thus? Then it is not right to say: Matter, or material quality, is karma (action).

---

10. *Of Vital Power.*

Controverted Point.—That there is no such thing as a material vital power.

From the Commentary.—Some, as, for instance, the Pubbaseliyas and Sammitiyas, hold that, because vital power is an immaterial fact distinct from consciousness, therefore there is nothing material in it.

[1] *Th.*—If there is not, you imply also that, in material (organic) phenomena, there is no such thing as 'a term of life, or a subsisting, no going on, being kept going on, no progress, procedure or preservation of them'[3]—but you

[1] We cannot trace this passage (cf. *Compendium*, pp. 145, 146). The Burmese translator adds a note: 'The Theravādin takes kāya, vacī, mano, when compounded with kamma, to denote merely a means (nimitta), and kamma by itself to denote volition (cetanā). But the opponent takes each compound to mean a moral act (of deed, word, or thought).' Hereby we see how certain purely *un*moral actions involved in gestures and speech, proceeding from moral thoughts, came to be regarded as also moral.

[2] *Majjhima-Nik.*, iii. 209. All four passages are quoted in Buddhaghosa's *Atthasālinī* (PTS), p. 88.

[3] This is the canonical formula for jīvitindriya, or vital power (see *Bud. Psy. Eth.*, § 9). The Burmese translator also reads ṭhiti as a *separate* synonym of āyu and the rest, and understanding each in the *instrumental* sense, he renders the passage thus: 'Is there no such thing as a means of living, subsisting, maintaining, moving, or preserving?'

deny that; in fact, you maintain the opposite. Hence your proposition falls through.

[2] With regard to the immaterial, you affirm both the existence of immaterial vital power and also its continuity, going on, etc. Why do you affirm the latter only, and deny the former?

[3] You admit that the life-term of immaterial organic phenomena is immaterial vital power: why not admit the corresponding counterpart in the case of material organic power? Why is it wrong to deny the latter when you admit the former?

[4] You say that, for you, the life-term of material organic phenomena is an immaterial vital power? Would you then maintain the contrary? No? Why not? [5] *Both* vital powers, you say, are immaterial. It seems to me you could with equal plausibility say that both were material.

[6, 7] You will admit that vital power is still present in one who has fallen into a cataleptic trance.[1] Yet you could not call his vital power (he being unconscious) immaterial. In which aggregates is the vital power included? In that of mental coefficients,[2] you say? But is that aggregate existent in one who has attained trance? 'No,' you say? I repeat my question. 'Yes,' you now say. But if anyone in trance has mental coefficients, he will also have the other mental aggregates—feeling, perception, cognitive consciousness. 'No,' you say? I repeat my question. 'Yes,' you now say.[3] Then that person cannot be in a cataleptic trance.

[1] Nirôdha, literally cessation (viz., of consciousness): the utmost result of Jhāna abstraction. Everything mental (immaterial) is suspended for a time.

[2] Sankhārā. These, in the Suttas, are defined as activity in deed, word, and thought; in Abhidhamma as fifty phases, more or less of them present in states of consciousness. 'The opponent thinks of the fifty, and denies; then of the three activities, and assents.'—*Comy.* Cf. XIX. 2.

[3] He denies with respect to mid-trance, but assents with respect to entrance into and emergence from trance.—*Comy.*

[8, 9] If there be no material vital power, no vital power can exist for the inmates of the unconscious sphere,[1] for how can they have an immaterial (or mental) vital power? The argument above as to mental coefficients, which you say they have, applies to them also. They cannot be as they are and yet possess all five aggregates, as in a five-mode existence.

[10] [If vital power be wholly psychical, it must be affected by mental conditions; for instance,] you will admit that vital power, springing from a consciousness that seeks rebirth, must, when that consciousness breaks off, be itself broken off in part. Now, would you say the same of a purely mental phase such as 'contact' (or mental reaction to stimulus)? Why not? You mean that contact would be broken off, not in part, but entirely? Now, would you say the same of vital power [it being, as you say, not material]? You deny. . . .

[11] *P. S.*—Are there then two vital powers (material and immaterial)?

Th.—Yes.

P. S.—Then you are committed to this—that we live with two lives, die with two deaths?[2]

Th.—Nay, that cannot truly be said. . . .

---

11. *Of a Result of Karma.*

Controverted Point.—That because of karma an Arahant may fall away from Arahantship.

[1] See above, I. 8; III. 11.

[2] 'At the moment of decease the two break off together.'—*Comy.* The *Compendium*, when treating of mind, takes note only of the psychic vital power. Cf. Introduction, p. 17: 'The activities of will and the other concomitant properties [or coefficients] are due to the psychic life (j ī v i t i n d r i y a), which infuses mental life into one and all, constituting the whole a psychosis or psychical state.' But when treating of matter, the author notices physical vital power (*Compendium*, p. 156). The doctrine as to the two is clearly stated in *Vibhanga*, 123: 'Vital power is twofold: material and immaterial.'

From the Commentary.—Such is an opinion held, for instance, by the Pubbaseliyas and Sammitiyas, the Arahant so falling being one who, in a former birth, calumniated one who was then Arahant. For any other comment, see the argument on the falling away from Arahantship (I. 2, p. 64 f.).

[1, 2] *Th.*—How can you affirm this without also affirming—which you will not—that those in the three lower stages of fruition may fall away from their fruit?

[3] And your claim is that he may fall away, not because of such karma, or prior action, as murder, theft, fornication, evil speech, matricide, parricide, Arahanticide, wounding a Buddha, or schism-making, but because of having calumniated Arahants. You affirm he may fall away because of having calumniated Arahants, but you deny that everyone who calumniates Arahants realizes Arahantship.[1] Therefore your proposition that falling is due to calumniation is absurd.

[1] 'The opponent, not discerning the constancy (niyāma) in the attaining (*leg.* sampāpuṇane) of Arahantship with such a karma, denies.'—*Comy.* The denial amounts to the admission that *some* who calumniated Arahants realize Arahantship. The converse of this is that all Arahants are not those who so calumniated. If those who did not so calumniate fall at all, their fall cannot possibly be due to calumniation, because they had not calumniated. Therefore the opponent's proposition is not universally valid on his own showing. The orthodox view, however, is that there can never be a true falling, because, among other reasons, all the previous karmas had been exhausted. It is not necessary here to work out this obvious argument, all that is necessary being to disprove the opponent's statement by refuting him on his own grounds.

BOOK IX

1. *Of Release through seeing the Good.*[1]

Controverted Point.—That the Fetters are put off for one who discerns a blessing (in store).

From the Commentary.—In our doctrine we are convinced that when anyone discerns (*a*) the 'world' (literally, 'the conditioned') as full of peril, and (*b*) Nibbāna as a blessing, the 'Fetters' are put off. But some—for instance, the Andhakas—take one of these two alternative statements, and say it is only[2] by the latter discernment that the Fetters are put off. It is to rebuke this partial view that the Theravādin speaks.

[1] *Th.*—But are not the Fetters also put off when the world[3] is considered as impermanent? You admit this, of course. But [then you should not confine yourself to the optimistic side].

[2] You admit, too, they are put off when the world is considered as full of Ill, as disease, as a canker, a piercing dart, as woe, as unbearable,[4] as an enemy,[5] as crumbling away, as a calamity, as oppression, as peril, as trouble, as fluctuating, as dissolving, as transient, as shelterless, as no retreat, as no refuge, as without protection, as empty, bare and void, as without soul, as full of danger, and mutable. [But your statement hereby becomes one-sided.]

[1] Ānisaŋsa (literally, 'praise,' with two intensive prefixes; commendable, because good; profit, advantage). The argument is that the realization of present actual evils is as strong a stimulus, as *vis a tergo*, to betterment, as the faith in the happiness of that betterment attained—the *vis a fronte*.

[2] In the PTS edition read va or eva for evaŋ.

[3] Sankhārā.

[4] Or 'an affliction' (ābādhato).

[5] Literally, 'as other.'

[3] You admit then that (at the same moment) a man can both consider the impermanence and so on of the world, and see the blessings in Nibbāna? No? But you have admitted that he loses the Fetters when he does both. You admit then that he can? But does this not involve us in two simultaneous mental reactions, two consciousnesses, and so on?

[4] *A.*—You reject my proposition. But did not the Exalted One say: '*Take, bhikkhus, the case of a bhikkhu who lives contemplating the happiness in Nibbāna, perceiving and feeling that happiness continually, constantly, and undiluted, convinced of it in his mind and permeated with it by insight?*[1] . . .

Surely then it is for one who discerns the happy prospect that the Fetters are put off.

---

2. *Of the Ambrosial*[2] *as an Object by which we are bound.*

Controverted Point.—That the Ambrosial as an object of thought is a 'fetter.'

From the Commentary.—This is an opinion held, for instance, by the Pubbaseliyas, and due to careless inference from such passages as 'He fancies things about Nibbāna.'[3]

---

[1] *Anguttara-Nik.*, iv. 14. Cf. the *Commentary* (Manorathapūraṇī) on this passage. The *K. V. Commentary* concludes that whereas the work of insight into the actual, the perilous present, occupies the entrant at the threshold of the Ariyan Way, the Fetters get removed, as, during his progress, he discerns the blessings of Nibbāna. The sense seems to require abbocchinnaŋ, 'without a break,' or 'uninterruptedly,' for abbokiṇṇaŋ, 'undiluted.' One is tempted to render cetasā adhimuccamāno by 'of his own freewill.'

[2] Amata, or 'not-dead.' As this term does not for Buddhists, as it might for Europeans, suggest immortal *life*, we have not rendered it by 'the Immortal,' but by a term which, though it literally *does* mean that, has a vague suggestion of bliss.

[3] See *Majjhima-Nik.*, i. 4.

[1] *Th.*—If you say that, are you prepared to admit that the Ambrosial is the object of consciousness accompanied by 'Fetters,' 'Ties,' 'Floods,' 'Bonds,' 'Hindrances,' 'Infections,' 'Graspings,' 'Corruptions'?[1] Is it not rather an object accompanied by the very opposite?

[2-4] You affirm that, on account of the Ambrosial occupying the mind, lust, hate, ignorance may spring up. But are you prepared to admit that the Ambrosial itself conduces to occasions for lusting, to lusting after, wishing for, being inebriated, and captivated by, languishing for? That it conduces to occasions for hatred, anger, and resentment? That it conduces to occasions for delusion, for depriving of knowledge, for blinding vision, for suspending insight, for siding with trouble,[2] for failing to win Nibbāna? Is it not rather the opposite of all these? How then can you say that, on account of the Ambrosial occupying the mind, lust, hate, and ignorance spring up? [5] All these things you may truly predicate as springing up because of the occupation of the mind with material qualities (*rūpa*). But material qualities are not the Ambrosial.

[6] You would not say that, whereas the Fetters spring up because of material qualities, the latter do *not* conduce to Fetters, Ties, Floods, and all such spiritual defects and dangers. How then can you affirm just the same of the Ambrosial: that, whereas the Fetters spring up because of it, it does not conduce to Fetters, and so forth? Or that, whereas lust, hate, and ignorance spring up because of the Ambrosial, nevertheless the Ambrosial is not an occasion for lusting and all the rest?

[7] *P.*—But was it not said by the Exalted One: '*He perceives Nibbāna as such, and having perceived it he imagines things about Nibbāna, with respect to Nibbāna,*

[1] On these spiritual categories cf. p. 115, § 1; and see *Bud. Psy. Eth.*, iii., chaps. v., x., xii., xiii.

[2] Br. reads vighātapakkhiyaŋ.

things as Nibbāna, that "Nibbāna is mine," dallying with the idea'?[1]

Therefore the Ambrosial is an object of thought not yet freed from bondage.

---

3. *Of Matter as Subjective.*

Controverted Point.—Whether matter should be termed subjective or objective.

From the Commentary.—It is an opinion of some—for instance, the Uttarāpathakas—that matter should be termed sārammaṇa (i.e., co-object), not because it is so in the sense of *making* a mental object [for itself], but inasmuch as it causes mental presentation. The argument seeks to point out the distinction beween the two meanings of ārammaṇa.[2]

[1] *Th.*—If that is so, you must also affirm of matter or body, that it has the mental features of 'adverting,' ideating, reflecting, co-ordinated application, attending, willing, anticipating, aiming[3]—things which you would, on the contrary, deny of matter.

[2] All, or any of them you can rightly affirm of mental properties, such as contact (mental reaction), feeling, perception, volition, cognition, faith, energy, mindfulness, concentration, understanding, lust, hate, illusion, conceit,

[1] *Majjhima-Nik.*, i. 4: a Sutta, says the *Commentary*, which is here inconclusive, because the Nibbāna spoken of is simply temporal well-being, so called. 'Falsely mistaken by the worldling for the real thing; a matter connected with the satisfaction of natural desires only,' wrote Buddhaghosa in the *Papañca Sūdanī* (*Commentary on the Majjhima-Nik.*).

[2] So Br. edition: ārammaṇa-dvayassa vibhāga-dassan'atthaŋ. The PTS reading is not intelligible. Sārammaṇa, in the orthodox view, means 'subjective,' because mind has mental object. The opponent takes sārammaṇa to mean 'objective,' because matter is presented as object. This confusion of the terms applicable to mind arises from the fact that he substitutes ārammaṇa for paccaya in the compound sappaccaya, and misreads sārammaṇaṭṭhena sārammaṇaŋ. Thus the word ārammaṇaŋ has two meanings—'object' and paccaya. See § 4.

[3] See VIII. 9, § 1.

erroneous opinion, doubt, mental inertia, distraction, immodesty, indiscretion—all of which you admit as subjective. But matter is not one of these, and therefore such things may not be affirmed of it.

[3] You deny in the case of matter all those mental features—adverting, etc.—but claim for it the term 'subjective,' which is really applicable to 'contact,' sensation, etc. These, as you admit, do not lack those mental features named.

[4] *U.*—But is not matter correlated (as an object)?[1] Of course you assent. Then as correlated it is surely right to apply the term 'subjective' to matter, etc. [since 'object' is one of the twenty-four (causal) relations].

---

4. *Of Bias as without Mental Object.*

Controverted Point.—That latent (immoral) bias[2] is without mental object.

From the Commentary.—Some—for instance, the Andhakas and certain of the Uttarāpathakas—hold that what are called the (seven) latent biases, being something distinct from mind, unconditioned, indeterminate, are thereby without concomitant mental object. The Theravādin's questions are to show what sort of phenomenon it is that 'has no mental object.'

[1] *Th.*—Then the forms of latent bias must be either material quality, or Nibbāna, or one of the five organs or five objects of sense,[3] which you deny.

[1] *Dhammasangaṇi*, § 595: rūpaŋ sappaccayaŋ (translated as 'conditioned' in *Bud. Psy. Eth.*); *Compendium*, 194.

[2] Anusaya. On this sevenfold 'Category of Evil,' see *Compendium*, p. 172, *n.* 2. In the *Yamaka* it bulks very large. The *Commentary* on that work attributes the metaphor to the relatively ineradicable nature of the seven modes lying latent throughout the life-term of the individual, and quotes the present argument as showing a rejection of all the qualities claimed for anusaya (*JPTS*, 1910-12, p. 86). This deep-rootedness is brought out in *Pss. of the Brethren*, verses 768, 839. Herbert Spencer's use of 'bias' first suggested to us the suitability for it. See *JRAS*, 1894, p. 324.

[3] Only sense-co-ordinating and sensations as co-ordinated have 'mental objects' (*Vibhanga*, 428).

But let us take the first form, the bias of sense-desire. If this is without mental object, must you not also affirm the same of all manifestations and notions of sense-desire —to wit, sense-desire as lust, as an outburst of lustful desire, as a Fetter, as a Flood, as a Bond, as an Obstacle? Would you not rather affirm just the opposite of these, that they are concomitant with mental object?

[2] Or again, in what aggregate is latent bias included? The aggregate of mental coefficients,[1] you say. But these are concomitant with object not less than the other mental aggregates: this you of course admit. How then can you maintain your proposition? [3] If you affirm that (*a*) the bias of sense-lust has the aggregate of mental coefficients involved with it, and yet is without mental object, you must say no less of (*b*) sense-lust in general. But you refuse (making of sense-lust as bias a thing apart). [4] Thus you get: (*a*) aggregate of mental coefficients without mental object; (*b*) aggregate of mental coefficients with mental object.

Then is that aggregate partly with, partly without, mental object? Then must you affirm the same of all the mental aggregates[2] . . . which you may not. . . .

[5] Or, passing over the next five latent biases—resentment, conceit, mere opinion, doubt, lust of rebirth—as disposed of by this same argument, take similarly the seventh—nescience—if this as latent bias is without object, it must be no less without mental object when figured as Flood, Bond, Outburst, Fetter, Obstacle—which you deny [keeping the latent bias a thing apart].

[6, 8] The argument about the aggregates applies no less to this form of bias.

[9] *A. U.*—But is it not right to say that, when an average man of the world is thinking of something that is morally good or indeterminate, he may be described as

[1] Sankhāra's. Cf. p. 229, *n*. 2.

[2] These were taught as being all 'with mental object.' See *Vibhanga*, p. 428.

'having latent bias'? And are not [at that moment] those forms of bias [latent in him] without mental object?

[10] *Th.*—But you could equally well say of him at such a moment that he had lust in his heart,[1] and you deny that lust is without mental object.[2] . . .

---

5. *Of Insight as without Mental Object.*

Controverted Point.—That insight[3] is without mental object.

From the Commentary.—Inasmuch as an Arahant cannot be said to lack insight, that insight must, at least at times, be practically without object, namely, when his visual consciousness is active, for then he is occupied with the visible object engaging his sense of sight. So think some, for instance, the Andhakas.

[1] *Th.*—Then insight must be either material quality, or Nibbāna, or one of the five organs of sense, or their five external objects (since these are the things that are without *mental* object). But this you deny. . . .

You deny also that understanding, as controlling power or force, as right views, as the search for truth by intuition,[4] is without mental object, affirming the contrary. Then why exclude insight?

[2-4] Here, too, you judge that the aggregate of mental coefficients is involved. But as in the preceding discourse, so here: you cannot say, a mental aggregate is without object, or partly so. And you cannot affirm that understanding, which is involved in that aggregate, is with mental object, while insight, also involved in it, is without.

[1] I.e., potentially, as something not extirpated.

[2] 'Hence the objectlessness of 'latent bias' is not properly substantiated.'—*Comy.*

[3] Ñāṇaŋ—i.e., Arahatta-magga-ñāṇaŋ—insight belonging to the highest Path, that of Arahantship.

[4] Dhammavicayo. Cf. *Bud. Psy. Eth.*, p. 18, *n.* 1 (reading E.g. for I.e.), with *Compendium*, p. 180, *n.* 3.

[5] *A.*—You deny that insight is objectless. Is it right to say that the Arahant is 'full of insight,'[1] while he is visually cognitive?

Th.—Yes.

A.—Has his insight at that moment an object?

Th.—Nay, that cannot truly be said. . . . [6] But if you substitute 'full of understanding' for 'full of insight,' you yourself admit that he is full of understanding while visually cognitive, and at the same time you deny that his understanding, during that process, has an object.[2]

---

6. *Of Past Ideas.*

Controverted Point.—That consciousness of a past object is without object.

From the Commentary.—Some—for instance, the Uttarāpathakas—hold that, since past and future mental objects are not actually existing, therefore mind recalling a past object is mind without object.

[1] *Th.*—But you admit that there is such a thing as a mental object that is past? Then how can you make such a self-contradictory statement? [2] Again, is there not adverting of mind, ideation, co-ordinated application, attention, volition, anticipation, aim, concerning that which is past? . . .

---

7. *Of Future Ideas.*

Controverted Point.—That a consciousness, having an idea that is future, is without object.

The *Commentary* makes no separate comment.

[1, 2] *are verbatim as in* 6, 'future' *substituted for* 'past.

[1] Ñāṇī. It is used as a synonym of paññavā in § 6. Cf. *Anguttara-Nik.*, iv. 340.

[2] The insight is potential, not always actualized, i.e., exercised about an object. There cannot be two mental objects at the same instant of time.

[3] *Th. continues.*—You admit of course concerning what is present, that there can be adverting of mind, ideation, and so on (6, § 2), so that consciousness of a present idea has its mental object. And you admit that there can be adverting of mind and the rest about the past and also about the future. Yet in both these cases mind, you say, is without mental object. [4] Why not also say then that, while there can be adverting of mind, etc., about the present, mind occupied about a present object is mind without object?

[5] *A.*—But you admit that a 'past object' does not exist [at the present moment]? Surely then a mind occupied with past object is occupied with no (that is, with a non-existent) object. . . .

---

8. *Of Initial Application of Mind and its Field of Operation.*[1]

Controverted Point.—That initial mental application 'falls' on all consciousness.

From the Commentary.—This may happen in two ways: by way of falling on consciousness as object, and by way of association,[2] as a concomitant of the consciousness in which it operates. In the absence of any rule[3] by which we can say, that such and such a consciousness

---

[1] Vitakka is the distinguishable sense, or *nuance*, in a given state of mental activity, of a 'directing-on-to an object.' In Buddhist psychology it is an occasional or particular, not a constant, factor of consciousness. See *Compendium*, 94 f., 238 f., 282. On the rather unusual term anupatita, cf. *Dhammapada*, verse 302. Burmese translators adopt two alternative renderings of vitakkānupatita: (*a*) Those things which *constantly accompany* the initial application or direction of the mind; (*b*) those things on which this vitakka *constantly falls.* The first alternative suggests the question: Does vitakka operate *in* all consciousness? The second suggests: Does it operate *on* all consciousness? While it may operate *on* all consciousness as its object, it does not operate *in* all consciousness, since it is absent in some, as in avitakka-citta.

[2] Sampayogato.

[3] Niyama.

cannot become an object of initial application, we might say that the thesis is true. But since some consciousness is brought to pass independently of any initial application, this does not fall on (i.e., operate in) all consciousness. [Hence the contradictory of the thesis is true.] Those who maintain the thesis—for instance, the Uttarāpathakas—fail to draw this distinction.

[1] *Th.*—If that is true, you must also be prepared to admit in detail that [other mental properties[1]] sustained application, zest, pleasure, pain, gladness, melancholy, indifference, faith, energy, mindfulness, concentration, understanding, lust, hate . . . indiscretion fall on (or operate in) all consciousness. But you are not so prepared. . . .

[2-4] Contrariwise, is there not concentration with sustained application only, not initial application; also concentration wherein there is neither kind of application? Were not, in fact, three kinds of concentrative exercise distinguished by the Exalted One: (1) With both modes of application; (2) with the sustained mode only; (3) with neither?[2]

Hence your proposition is wrong.

---

9. *Of Sound as purely Mental.*

Controverted Point.—That sound is nothing more than a diffusion of initial and sustained mental application.[3]

From the Commentary.—Because it was said, '*Applied and discursive thinking is productive of speech,*'[4] therefore some—for instance, the Pubbaseliyas—hold that sounds may occur even when cognition is proceeding without work of sense, because they consist merely in 'thrillings' [or irradiation] of initial and sustained applica-

---

[1] Cetasikā. Cf. vii. 3.

[2] *Dīgha-Nik.*, iii. 219; *Majjhima-Nik.*, iii. 162; *Saṃyutta-Nik.*, iv. 363; *Anguttara-Nik.*, iv. 300.

[3] In other words, that sounds are psychical 'thrillings' (vipphāra, or reverberations, or vibrations).

[4] *Majjhima-Nik.*, i. 301, where it is said that speech is an activity or co-efficient of mind, because there is first thought, then speech.

tion of mind.[1] The Theravādin submits that if sound can be so specialized, each mental property would send forth its own peculiar sounds. If not, then we cannot speak of auditory cognition of a sound that is merely a matter of intellect, and not an object of sense. But the Word: '*Hearing a sound, an irradiation of initial application of mind, he reveals*'[2] . . . shows there is auditory consciousness also.

[1] *Th.*—If this be true, you must affirm no less that sounds from mental contact are solely an irradiation of mental contact; that such as are from feeling are solely an irradiation of feeling. So also for such as are from perception, volition, thought in general, mindfulness, understanding. This you will not do.

[2] Must you not also affirm of a sound that is an irradiation of mental application, that it is [none the less] to be cognized by hearing, impinges on the ear, comes into the auditory avenue? This you deny; you affirm that such a sound is not cognizable by hearing, etc. How then can you speak of it *as sound?*

---

10. *Of Speech conforming to Thought.*

Controverted Point.—That speech does not accord with thought.

From the Commentary.—Inasmuch as anyone can decide [to think about one thing and] talk about another, therefore there is no accord, no sequence, no conformity between thought and speech. Speech can proceed even without thought. Such is the view of some—for instance, the Pubbaseliyas.

[1] *Th.*—If this be so, then *a fortiori* neither does speech accord with mental contact, feeling, perception, volition, nor with any property of consciousness. But surely, as you agree, the opposite is the case.[3]

[1] A phrase from *Dīgha-Nik.*, iii. 104, and *Anguttara-Nik.*, i. 170. *Dīgha-Nik.*, i. 213, in the same context, omits -vippharasaddaŋ sutvā and uses slightly different inflexions.

[2] See preceding references.

[3] I.e., speech occurs to, or proceeds from, one who has 'mental contact,' etc.

[2] You must, again, deny that speech accords with adverting, ideating, co-ordinated application, willing, intending, aiming—which you will not, the opposite being true.

[3] You admit that speech which is provoked by thought is co-existent, and one in its origin, with the thought. Yet this is in contradiction to your proposition.

[4] Again, you commit yourself to this, that one speaks of what one does not wish to speak, discourses, addresses [others], converses about what one does not wish. Surely the opposite is the case.

[5] *P.*—You say I am wrong, but you must admit that people can speak, discourse, address [others], converse about something different [from that which is occupying their minds].[1] Hence my proposition is tenable.

---

11. *Of Action conforming to Thought.*

Controverted Point.—That action does not accord with thought.

From the Commentary.—Inasmuch as anyone, when proposing to go in one direction, can go elsewhere, some—for instance, the Pubbaseliyas—hold that action is not in accord or conformity with, or consequent upon, thought.

[1-3] *Th.*—(*The argument is exactly similar to that in* IX. 10, §§ 1-3.)

[4] Again, you commit yourself to this, that one moves forward and backward, or looks ahead and back, or bends or extends, when not wishing to perform these respective acts. Surely the opposite is the case.

[5] *P.*—You say, I am wrong, but does it not happen that some one, thinking 'I shall go in one direction,' goes in another, or . . . thinking 'I shall hold forth something,' holds forth another? Hence my proposition is tenable.

[1] The illustration given in the *Comy.* is that of one intending to say cīvaraŋ (robe) and saying cīraŋ (fibre), as if *we* were to say 'coming' for 'comforting.' Speech not conforming to mental action, 'no blame attaches to the speaker.'

12. *Of Past, Future, and Present.*

Controverted Point.—That a past or future experience is actually possessed.

From the Commentary.—In this connection we must distinguish between actual and potential possession.[1] The former is of the present moment. But for a man who has acquired the Eight Attainments in Jhāna, the possession of them is potentially persistent, though not of all at once. But some, not discerning this distinction—for instance, the Andhakas—speak of past and future Jhānas as something actually and presently possessed.

[1] *Th.*—But is not the past extinct, departed, changed, come to an end, finished? [2] And is not the future unborn, not yet become, not come into being, not produced, not brought to pass, not manifested? How then can you call either something that is actually possessed?

[3] Is one who possesses a present material or bodily aggregate also in possession of a past and a future bodily aggregate? Then must you admit three bodily aggregates. Similarly, if he is actually in possession of five past and five future, as well as five present [bodily and mental] aggregates, you must admit fifteen aggregates. . . .

[4-6] A similar argument applies to the organs and objects of sense, to the eighteen elements, to the twenty-two controlling powers.

[7] *A.*—But are there not those who, meditating on the eight stages of emancipation, can induce the four Jhānas at their pleasure, can acquire the four serial grades?[2] Surely then it is right to say that one can have actual present possession of past and future things?

[1] More literally, 'the notion of being in possession of (samannāgata), and that of having acquired (paṭilābha).'—*Comy.*

[2] *Anguttara-Nik.*, iv. 410, 448. *Buddhist Suttas* (SBE XI.), 212, §§ 9, 10; *Pss. of the Brethren*, ver. 916, 917, 1172.

BOOK X

1. *Of Cessation.*

Controverted Point.—That before five aggregates seeking rebirth have ceased, five operative[1] aggregates arise.

From the Commentary.—Some—for instance, the Andhakas—hold that if, before a unit of sub-consciousness lapses, another unit of consciousness, with its [operative] fourfold aggregate and the material aggregate sprung from it, has not arisen, the living continuum must be cut off.[2]

[1] *Th.*—Is there then a congeries of ten aggregates? Do ten aggregates arrive at actuality? If you deny, where is your proposition? If you assent, you must answer for two copies of each aggregate [which is unorthodox].

[2] The same argument holds if you maintain that only four operative aggregates[3] may arise, substituting 'nine' for 'ten' [i.e., five *plus* four].

[3] And the same argument holds if you maintain that only operative insight[4] arises, substituting 'six' for 'nine' [i.e., five *plus* one].

[4] *A.*—When the five aggregates seeking rebirth cease, does the Path then arise?

[1] Kiriyā, here meaning that which induces action, such as bodily movement, etc. It is not specialized, as in *Compendium*, pp. 19, 235 f.; and may therefore be consciousness entailing merit or demerit. The aggregates (khandha's) must be conceived as series of life-moments.

[2] Cf. *op. cit.*, 126.

[3] Excluding the material aggregate.

[4] I.e., insight understood as in IX. 5.—*Comy.*

Th.—Yes.

A.—What! do the dead, does one who has ended his days, develop the Path?[1]

---

2. *Of the Path and Bodily Form.*

Controverted Point.—That the physical frame of one who is practising the Eightfold Path is included in that Path.

From the Commentary.—Those who, like the Mahiŋsâsakas, Sammitiyas and Mahâsanghikas, hold that the three factors of the Path: —supremely right speech, action, and livelihood—are material, are confronted with the contradiction that, since the factors of the Path are subjective, they imply mental attributes lacking in matter.

[1] *Th.*—You must then be prepared to affirm also that bodily form is [like the Path-factors] subjective, having the mental attributes of adverting, ideating, co-ordinated application, attending, volition, anticipating, aiming. You deny this and rightly, for surely the opposite is true.

[2, 3] The three factors of the Path [in which you deem things corporeal to be included]—supremely right speech, action, livelihood—these, you affirm, are not subjective, not having the mental attributes above-named. [4-5] But the other five factors of the Path—supremely right views, aspiration, endeavour, mindfulness, concentration—these, you admit, are subjective, and have the mental attributes above-named.

[6, 7] If you affirm the absence of these mental characteristics from those three factors of the Path, you must also affirm their absence from all these five factors of the Path.

[8] *M. S. M.*—But you admit that supremely right

[1] 'By sophistry' (chalavâda, *Comy.*), he has shifted from psychological to religious ground, then skips back again, drawing a false analogy between the final death of any one life and momentary death. The aggregates *typify* the life of worldly desires, which for the convert is superseded by the higher life of the Path. Psychologically and physically, the cessation of their continuity means death. Cf. below, X. 3.

speech, action, and livelihood are factors of the Path, [and these are manifestations of corporeality]. Surely then the practiser's physical frame is included in the Path.[1]

---

3. *Of Path-Culture and the Senses.*

Controverted Point.—That one may develop the Path while enjoying the fivefold cognitions of sense.

From the Commentary.—Some, like the Mahāsanghikas, with reference to the Sutta: '*When he sees an object with the eye, he does not grasp at it in idea*,'[3] hold to the view stated above. The Theravādin's argument is that, if this be so, either the Path developed is of a worldly nature, or the developer's sense-experience must be of the nature of the Path. But neither is possible, because sense-cognition is worldly, and has not Nibbāna as its object.[2]

[1] *Th.*—But you will admit—(i.) that the five kinds of sense-consciousness have a seat and an object that have already sprung up; (ii.) that their seat and object are antecedent; (iii.) that their seat is of the subject while their object is external, that seat and object are not yet broken up while operative; (iv.) that seat and object are of different varieties; (v.) that they do not enjoy mutually their respective ranges and fields; (vi.) that they come to pass not without co-ordinated application or attention[3]; (vii.) that they are not unmixed; (viii.) are not without order in time; (ix.) are without order of contiguity; and (x.) without any ideation?[4] Now if all this be true, your proposition cannot be true.

[1] I.e., in part of it. The opponents regard those three factors as physical, the Theravādin as psychical. For instance, according to the latter's doctrine, sammāvācā is not so much the right utterance itself as that factor in the religious character by which right speech is engendered.

[2] The Path is a concern of *mano*, not of the five senses; again, i.—x. are not predictable of the Path.—*Comy.*

[3] By the mind adverting to external object.—*Comy.*

[4] Quoted from *Vibhanga*, 307. 'Leaving aside the automatic fall (incidence in a presented object), there is not even the semblance of *minding* about it [in sense].'—*Comy.*

[2] Consider visual consciousness and one of the Path-subjects — Emptiness[1] — does the former come to pass concerning the latter? If you deny,[2] you are opposing your thesis. If you assent, I ask whether it is right doctrine to say not only:

'*Because of the eye and the visible object visual consciousness arises,*'

but also:

Because of the eye and Emptiness visual consciousness arises?

Is the Suttanta thus? [Of course not.]

[3] Again, if your proposition be true, you must also affirm that visual consciousness arises concerning the past and the future. Also that it arises [not solely because of visible object, but also] concerning mental contact, feeling, perception, volition, thought, the organs of sight, hearing, smell, taste, touch, and the objects of hearing, smell, taste, touch—impossible affirmations.

Now you can admit that representative (ideational) consciousness does arise concerning Emptiness, concerning the past and the future, concerning phases of mind, factors of experience, as stated just now.

And one may develop a Path while enjoying representative cognition concerning any one of those matters, but not during the enjoyment of sense-consciousness, which as such is not concerned with them.

[4] *M.*—Well, but was it not said by the Exalted One: '*Here, bhikkhus, when a bhikkhu sees an object with the eye, he does not grasp at the general characters nor at the details of it, . . . or hears a sound, . . . or smells, . . . tastes, . . . touches a tangible . . .*'?[3]

Surely here there is Path-practice by one who is enjoying the five sorts of sense-consciousness? . . .

[1] *Compendium*, 67, 216, and above, iii. 2.

[2] Because of the orthodox formula below. See *Majjhima-Nik.*, i. 259; *Saŋyutta-Nik.*, iv. 87.

[3] *Anguttara-Nik.*, i. 113; cf. *Dialogues* i. 80, *n.* on the terms rendered by 'characters,' 'details,' and their being generally taken to refer to sex-attraction. See also Appendix: Nimitta.

4. *Of Sensations as Moral and Immoral.*

Controverted Point.—That the five kinds of sense-consciousness are good and bad (have positive moral quality).

The *Commentary* contributes no discussion.

[1-3][1] *Th.*—(*Verbatim* similar to X, 3, §§ 1-3.) *The argument being here, too, that the senses are limited to sense-objects, ethical and intellectual matters being the concerns of intellect, will, etc.*

[4] *M.*—Well, but was it not said by the Exalted One: '*Here, bhikkhus, when a bhikkhu sees an object with the eye, he grasps, . . . or again, does not grasp, at the general characters, or the details of it, . . . or hears a sound, etc. . . .*'? Surely then the five sorts of sense-consciousness are good and bad.

---

5. *Of Sensations and Ideation.*

Controverted Point.—That the five kinds of sense-consciousness as such are co-ideational.[2]

From the Commentary.—Here again the Mahāsanghikas, for instance, carelessly interpret the Teacher's words, quoted in the foregoing. They hold them to mean that the five kinds of sensations as such are accompanied by ideation, because sexual ideas are generated by immoral *thoughts.*

(*The argument is verbatim similar to the preceding, the authority appealed to being that in* X. 2.)

[1] The *Commentary* refers also to the preceding discourse.

[2] Sābhogā. See VIII. 9, § 1, note.

6. *Of Two Codes of Morals.*

Controverted Point.—That one who is engaged in the Path is practising a double morality.

From the Commentary.—From such passages in the Word as '*When a man is established in virtue he is gifted with wisdom,*'[1] some, like the Mahāsanghikas, hold that, inasmuch as the virtuous person is developing the Path which is not of the world, with a morality that is of the world, he must, at the moment of realization, be possessed simultaneously of both a worldly and an unworldly morality. The argument begins by showing that each morality would involve two separate sets of mental processes.

[1] *Th.*—You must then be prepared to affirm that he is possessed of his dual morality with a dual mental contact, dual feeling, dual perception, dual volition, dual thought, dual faith, dual energy, dual mindfulness, dual concentration, dual understanding. . . . [2] If his moral code be worldly, those processes will be worldly. [3] If his moral code be both, they will be double. The mental contact, the feeling, etc., that he experiences, will be both worldly as well as unworldly [or supramundane]—which you of course deny. . . .

And if you say that one actually engaged on the Path is possessed of a worldly code of morals, you are calling such an one in effect an average person or worldling—which you of course refuse to do. . . .

[4-6] Your position, you say, is this: (1) one actually engaged on the Path practises a worldly morality in the three factors relating to conduct—right speech, right action, right livelihood—but not in the five factors relating to mental life.[2] (2) In those three factors his morals are both worldly and supramundane, but they are only the latter in the other five factors. My position is that you must affirm one and the same higher morality for all the eight.[3]

[1] *Saṃyutta-Nik.*, i. 13, 165; quoted in *Milindapañha*, 34.

[2] See X. 2.

[3] Implied, not stated in so many words.

[7] *M.*—Well, but does the Path come to be[1] when worldly morality has ceased?

Th.—Yes.

M.—What! can anyone without morals—his virtue defective, imperfect, cut off—develop the Path?

Th.—Nay, that cannot truly be said. . . .

---

7. *Of Virtue or Morality as Automatic.*[2]

Controverted Point.—That virtuous conduct is automatic (and not a property of consciousness).

From the Commentary.—It is held by some, like the Mahāsanghikas, that when there has been moral conduct, even though it has ceased, there is an accretion of virtue, and hence the doer becomes virtuous. The argument is analogous to that on giving as not mental (VII. 4).

[1] *Th.*—But is virtue either material qualities, or Nibbāna, or an organ or object of sense [since these are the opposites of properties of mind]? . . . [2] You would not call mental contact, feeling, perception, volition, faith, energy, mindfulness, concentration, understanding, *unmental.* But if virtue cannot be identified with anything that is not mental, it must be a property of mind. . . .

[3-5] If virtue be no property of consciousness, you must affirm that it has not a result consciously sought after. Is not the opposite true? But if it has a result to be desired, it is also something mental. . . . The mental properties just enumerated—they have both consciously desired results and are mental. In admitting this, you must also admit that virtue is of the same dual character. But you contend that virtue, on the contrary, is so anomalous as to *have* a consciously desired result, yet to *be* not mental. . . .

[6-8] Again, if virtue be not a thing of the mind, you must admit that it has not a result, not an effect [in

[1] Literally, 'arise.'

[2] A-cetasikaŋ.

future consciousness][1]; yet is it not precisely something having such a result and effect? You would surely not say that it is non-mental and not productive of effect, as you would admit in the case of an organ or object of sense? Again, you would not consider that these non-mentals have such a result; yet this is what you say of virtue:—that it is both non-mental and yet fruitful of results in consciousness.

[9-10] With reference to the Path-factors, you would call the three factors relating to virtuous conduct non-mental, while calling the other five mental [which you are not justified in doing].

[11] *M.*—But if I am wrong, you must then admit that when virtuous acts have ceased, the doer becomes *im*moral. You deny this? Then I am right to say that virtue is [i.e., goes on] without mind, mechanically.

---

8. *Of Virtue as conforming to Thought.*

Controverted Point.—That virtue does not proceed in adaptation to[2] thought.

From the Commentary.—This is merely a pendant to the previous discourse.

[1-5] *The argument is exactly similar to* X. 7, 'does not proceed in adaptation to thought' *being substituted for* 'is automatic (or a property of consciousness),' *and the middle sections* [3-8] *on* 'result' *and* 'effect' *being omitted.*

---

9. *Of Growth through Observance.*

Controverted Point.—That virtue grows through [the mere fact of] being undertaken.

From the Commentary.—Here, from a careless interpretation of the verse in the Word, beginning—

'By planting pleasant parks and woods,'

---

[1] See pp. 205, *n.* 3, 207, *n.* 2.

[2] Literally, roll along after, in accordance with (anu-parivattati). Cf. *Bud. Psy. Eth.*, §§ 671, 772.

wherein it is said—

'Merit doth grow continually,'

some, like the Mahāsanghikas, hold that virtue grows naturally when once the virtuous life has been undertaken, accumulating independently of the mind's action. The argument is similar to a previous discourse.

[1-4] *The argument is exactly similar to* VII. 5 (p. 200), 'virtue grows through being undertaken' *replacing* 'merit derived from a gift . . . enjoyed keeps growing,' § 2 *being omitted, and in* § 3, 'the giver of a gift' *being replaced by* 'one who has undertaken a life of virtue.'

---

10. *Are Acts of Intimation Virtue?*

Controverted Point.—That acts of intimation are moral acts.

From the Commentary.—Some, like the Mahāsanghikas and Sammitiyas, thinking that 'bodily intimation is karma of deed, vocal intimation is karma of speech,' believe that such acts have a moral quality. But intimation (as gesture or speech) is a material matter, while morality or virtuous conduct is not so, but is a deliberate (i.e., mental) act of abstinence.

[1] *Th.*—But the conduct called moral—abstaining from taking life, from stealing, from fornication, lying, and strong drink—do you affirm that these are so many modes of intimation? You do not. . . .

[Acts intimating minor courtesies such as] salutation, rising to welcome, presenting clasped hands, acts of propriety, offering a seat, a couch, water for the feet, a towel[1] for the feet, rubbing the back in the bath[2]—are these morality? Yes, you say. But you would not affirm they

[1] Pādakathaliya. See *Vin. Texts*, i. 92 *n*. Of Buddhaghosa's alternative renderings, there given, the Burmese translator of the *Kathā Vatthu* uses the latter. The 'footstool (pādapīṭha) for the washed feet' included in the Vinaya is here omitted.

[2] The same translator renders this word, nhāne, by 'with powder.'

are the five abstinences just named. Those are moral—are these?

[2] *M. S.*—But if acts of intimation are not moral, are they immoral? If not, then they are moral.

---

11. *Of Non-Intimation as Immoral.*

Controverted Point.—That acts not intimating [a moral purpose] are immoral.

From the Commentary.—Some, like the Mahīsanghikas, hold this view, based on the idea of a possible accumulation of demerit [in the past], and on the fact that moral precepts may be broken at the dictates of another.

[1] *Th.*—But the conduct that is immoral—taking life, theft, fornication, lying, intemperance—do you affirm that these are so many modes of *non*-intimation? You deny. (Then they are intimative, and some immoral acts are therefore intimative [of moral purpose].)

[2] If anyone giving in charity has resolved on some evil deed, do his merit and his demerit both grow thereby? If you assent, you are involved in two sets of mental procedure.[1] And if you assent to this anomaly, you have good and bad, low and excellent, sinister and radiant states of mind simultaneously present, when, in fact, as the Exalted One said, they are as far apart as earth and sky, etc.[2] [3] Similarly for all courtesies shown by one who has resolved on some evil deed.

[4] *M.*—But an evil deed, you admit, had been resolved upon, hence it is right to say that acts non-intimative of a *moral* thought behind them are *im*moral.

[1] As in X. 1.

[2] As in VII. 5.

BOOK XI

1. *Of Three Facts about Latent Bias.*

Controverted Points.—(i.) That latent bias[1] is unmoral (indeterminate).

From the Commentary.—That latent bias in its seven forms is (i.) unmoral, (ii.) without moral or immoral motive, (iii.) independent of mind, is an opinion held, for instance, by the Mahāsanghikas and the Sammitiyas. They allege that it is not right to say that the average man, while moral, or unmoral consciousness is going on, has latent bias, since the motive or condition of such consciousness cannot cause latent bias [to manifest itself], nor is such consciousness conjoined with any form of bias.

[1] *Th.*—But are you prepared to identify latent bias with any of the morally indeterminate ultimates—with resultant or with inoperative indeterminates, with matter or body, with Nibbāna, or with the organs and objects of sense? Of course you deny this. . . .

[2-8] Again, take each form of bias—unless you can prove that each form is something different in kind or degree from the corresponding kind of 'fetter,' or 'outburst,' or 'flood,' or 'yoke,' or 'hindrance,' which are indisputably immoral states, you cannot call the corresponding form of bias unmoral, whether it be sensual desires, or enmity, or conceit, or mere opinion, or doubt, or lust of life, or nescience.[2]

[9] *M. S.*—Well, but would you say that an average man, while thinking moral or *un*moral thoughts, had latent bias?

Th.—Yes.

[1] On this term see III. 2 f.; IX. 4.

[2] The 'seven forms.'

M. S.—Do you tell me then that good and bad ideas can come together side by side in consciousness?

Th.—Nay, that cannot truly be said. . . .

M. S.—Then latent bias must be unmoral.

Th.—Then you must go further and admit that lust is unmoral, because you will agree that the average man, when thinking good or unmoral thoughts, has not got rid the while of the root-condition of lust or greed. . . .

(ii.) That latent bias is without moral motive (or root-condition).[1]

[10] *Th.*—Since you cannot identify latent bias with any ultimate [cf. § 1], these being admittedly independent of the root-conditions or *hetu's*, it only remains for you to show that each form of latent bias is something different in kind or degree from the corresponding kind of 'fetter,' or 'outburst,' or 'flood,' or 'yoke,' or 'hindrance,' which are indisputably motived by the root-conditions of lust, or enmity, or dulness. . . .

[11] *M. S.*—You urge that latent biases are not unconditioned by these root-conditions, and you still maintain that an average person, while thinking moral or unmoral thoughts, is possessed the while by forms of latent bias. But you deny that these forms are conditioned by any of the root-conditions accompanying those thoughts. Surely then latent bias is unconditioned.[2]

Th.—You admit that such an average person is still possessed of lust, even while thinking moral or unmoral thoughts. But you deny that that lust is conditioned by the '*hetu*' accompanying those thoughts. According to you, therefore, lust is unconditioned—which is absurd.

[1] On hetu, see *Compendium*, 279 f.; cf. *Duka-paṭṭhāna* (PTS), xii., xiii.

[2] The argument is complicated by rāga being classed as both (i.) 'root-condition,' or hetu (as such it is sometimes called lobha), and (ii.) the first in the list of seven forms of latent bias: kāma-rāga.

(iii.) That latent bias is independent of consciousness.

[12-19] *Argued* verbatim *as in* IX. 4, §§ 1-8, *substituting* 'independent of' *or* 'conjoined with' 'consciousness' *for* 'without' *or* 'with' 'mental object' *respectively.*

[20] *M. S.*—You affirm that an average person is still possessed of latent bias, even while thinking moral or unmoral thoughts. But you deny that the latent bias is conjoined with such thoughts. Surely then latent bias is independent of mind.

Th.—If, as you admit, such a person is still possessed of lust while thinking moral or immoral thoughts, your denial that lust is conjoined with those thoughts does not necessarily lead to the false conclusion that lust is independent of mind.

---

2. *Of Insight.*

Controverted Point.—That it is wrong to say 'he has insight' of one who, though he has banished nescience, has thoughts not conjoined with insight.

From the Commentary.—Some, like the Mahāsanghikas, hold that one who, having banished spiritual ignorance by Path-insight, is experiencing ordinary cognitions by way of sense, cannot at the time be said to 'have insight,' since Path-consciousness is then not active. The criticism reveals their ineptitude in the notion of what an [Ariyan] person is, and also the propriety of ascribing insight to one who, having acquired insight [has it always potentially, if not actually].[1]

[1] *Th.*—Then you must also admit it is not right to say that, when lust has departed, a man has 'done with lust.' Similarly for hate, and for dulness, and for worldly corruptions generally. [2] If, on the contrary, you maintain that it *is* right to affirm these latter propositions, then it is no less right to say, of one for whom nescience is departed, but for whom cognition not conjoined with insight is active, that he has insight.

[1] Cf. this borrowing of a modern turn (anticipated by Aristotle) in X. 12, p. 243.

[3] *M.*—But if it be right to say thus of that person, is it in virtue of *past* insight? Can he be said 'to have insight' by an insight that has ceased, that is past, that has subsided? You deny this . . .

---

3. *Of Insight and Ordinary Consciousness.*

Controverted Point.—That insight (ñ ā ṇ a) is not conjoined with consciousness.

From the Commentary.—Some, like the Pubbaseliyas, hold that, inasmuch as an Arahant, who is said to have insight on account of that which he has won by the Path, may experience sense-cognitions which are not conjoined with that insight, therefore insight is independent of ordinary consciousness. The criticism shows that, if insight be detached from consciousness, it must be identifiable with one of the categories of things that are other than consciousness.

[1] *Th.*—But are you prepared to identify insight with all that is admittedly detached from consciousness: —with matter, Nibbāna, or the organs and objects of sense? Scarcely! . . .

Or are you prepared to declare 'insight' as having nothing in common with understanding?[1] For you will admit that understanding, as controlling power or force, as supremely right view, as intuitive search for truth,[2] is not detached from, but is bound up with, consciousness?

[2] Insight, again, as we agree, includes, involves the activity of the aggregate of the coefficients of consciousness, [3] as also does understanding. Both of these are conjoined with consciousness. How then can insight be detached from it? [4] Hence, if you maintain that insight and understanding, both involving conscious coefficients, are respectively detached from and conjoined with con-

[1] P a ñ ñ ā. It is possible to translate both terms by the same English term, none fitting exactly. Both are aspects of 'knowledge.' Cf. Ledi Sadaw, *JPTS*, 1914, 142; Mrs. Rh. D.: *Buddhism*, 1914, pp. 94, 130, 201; also on the *Paṭisambhidāmagga*, *JRAS*, 1906, 239 f.

[2] Cf. *Dhamma-saṅgaṇi*, § 292.

sciousness, you are committed to this: that the aggregate of coefficients is in part conjoined with, in part detached from, consciousness—which you of course deny. . . .

[5] *P.*—You contend then that an Arahant who is enjoying cognitions by way of sight, etc., may be said to 'have insight'?

Th.—Yes.

P.—But is his insight conjoined with *that* consciousness (sight, etc.)?

Th.—Nay, that cannot truly be said. . . .

P.—Then my proposition holds.

Th.—But such an argument holds equally for 'understanding,' if you substitute that for 'insight.' And you have admitted the connection between understanding and consciousness.

---

4. *Of the Utterance, 'This is Pain and Sorrow!'*

Controverted Point.—That from utterance of the word, 'This is Ill!' insight into the nature of Ill is set working.

From the Commentary.—Some, like the Andhakas, hold that this befalls the devotee at the moment when he enters on the Path.[1] The opponent's reply admits both utterance and insight. In the last question, to which the opponent replies in the negative, he is asked whether, by the procedure he upholds, he is not committed to allow an insight issuing from each syllable: I-daŋ du-kkhaŋ?

[1] *Th.*—But you deny that a similar result ensues on the utterance of the other three Truths: This is the Cause, this the Cessation, this the Path leading to the Cessation of Ill. Why is this? [2] Why deny for these what you affirm for the first Truth?

[3] Or why deny, as you do, that insight into the impermanence of each of the five aggregates (body-mind) follows from statement of the fact? [4] Or, once more,

[1] When he is fleeing from Ill rather than envisaging positive happiness. See above, IX. 1; cf. II. 5, 6.

that insight into the soullessness of each aggregate follows from a statement of the fact? [5-6] On what grounds can you defend the sequence in one case only out of the three sets of five propositions?

[7] Now do you mean to tell me that insight issues from every syllable of this formula:—This—is—pain—and—sor—row?[1]

A.—Nay, that cannot truly be said.[2] . . .

---

5. *Of the Force of the Magic Gift* (*Iddhi*).

Controverted Point.—That one who has the gift of magic potency might live on for a *kappa* [on earth].

From the Commentary.—The interval, **kappa**, here means a 'great' cycle (**mahākappa**[3]), not its fourth part, the 'incalculable cycle' (**asankheyyakappa**[4]), nor the mere 'life-term' (**āyukappa**). Now some, like the Mahāsanghikas, hold this view, because they have not thoroughly grasped the real advantage lying in the development of the steps to magic potency. The opponent, knowing that his vital principle or functioning is but the result of karma, has to deny that his vital functions are determined by **iddhi**. All that magic potency can effect is to avert things that would bring about an untimely death.

[1] *Th.*—But is his life-span, is his destiny, is his acquisition of individuality a thing of magic potency [that he should be able to prolong one interval of it]? For this is what you are herein affirming.

And do you reckon the *kappa* as past or as future?

[And why restrict yourself to one *kappa*?] Why not say 'might live on for two, three, four *kappas*'?

[2] Again, do you mean that, given life, he could live on for the remainder of his life, or that he could live on

[1] **Dukkha** includes both. In PTS text read **duti** for **ruci**.

[2] *Ibid.*, read, for **Āmantā**, **Na h'evaŋ vattabbe—pe—**

[3] See *Compendium*, 142, *n.* 1 (in which page, for [*n.*] 3 read 1, and 2nd *fn.* as 2). Cf. *Anguttara-Nik.*, ii. 126, 142. On **iddhi** see *Bud. Psychology*, 127, 161.

[4] Cf. Childers' *Pali Dictionary*, *sub voce* **kappa**.

for the remainder of his life if there were no [organic] life left?

M.—He could live on for the remainder of his life, given life.

Th.—Then he could certainly not live on for a *kappa.*[1]

M.—[Well then] if there were no [organic] life left.

Th.—What! he could live on though dead, though deceased? . . .

[3] [Again, what could he effect by the magic gift in the duration of consciousness?] Could he by it succeed in preventing any phase of consciousness that had arisen from ceasing, contact, for instance, or feeling, or perception, or volition, and so on?

[4] Or could he by it make any one of the five aggregates (body-mind) permanent?

[5] Or could he by it prevent (*a*) beings liable to re-birth[2] from being born? Or (*b*) beings liable to grow old, from old age?[3] Or (*c*) beings liable to disease, from disease,[4] or (*d*) liable to die, from death? . . .

[6] *M.*—But was it not said by the Exalted One: '*Ānanda, whosoever has cultivated, developed, established, built up, and persistently practised the four Steps to Iddhi, so as to be able to use them as a vehicle and as a basis, he, should he desire it, could remain in the same birth for a* kappa, *or for that portion of the* kappa *which had yet to run*'?[5]

Does not this support my proposition?

[1] The normal duration of human life being at the most 100 years (*Saṃyutta-Nik.*, ii. 94 f.).—*Comy.*

[2] Literally, having the quality or nature of birth.

[3] In the *Netti* (p. 23) it is said that by iddhi old age may be deferred, and youthfulness prolonged till death.

[4] From this it may be inferred that Buddhists did not attach much importance to the therapeutic value of magic potency, or iddhi.

[5] *Dialogues*, ii. 110 f. The four Steps are will, effort, thought, investigation, each united to earnest thought and the struggle against evil. 'Iddhi' *means* accomplishment. Cf. *Milinda*, i. 198 f. (translation), where the question is again argued without reference to the *Kathāvatthu.* Whether *kappa* here meant *āyukappa* only or not, the Mahāsanghika takes it to mean *mahākappa.*

[7] *Th.*—But was it not also said by the Exalted One: '*O bhikkhus! against four things there is none that can be surety, be he recluse or brahmin, be he deva, or Māra, or Brahmā, or anyone whatever in the world. Against which four? Against the old age of those subject to decay. Against the infirmities of those liable to infirmities. Against the dying of those whose nature it is to die. Against the coming to pass of the consequences of the evil deeds done in the past—deeds that were corrupt, tending to re-becoming, vain, of evil effect, making for birth, decay, and death*'?[1]

Is the Suttanta thus?

Hence it is not right to say that one who has the gift of magic potency might live on for an æon.

---

6. *Of Concentration.*

Controverted Point.—That the continuity of consciousness[2] is concentration of mind (s a m ā d h i).[3]

From the Commentary.—Some, like the Sabbatthivādins and Uttarāpathakas, hold that, because of the Word—'*to spend seven days and nights motionless, speechless, in the experience of absolute bliss*'—the flow of consciousness itself may constitute concentration. They do not take the latter term as meaning collectedness of thought, even when the coefficient of individualizing intentness (e k a g g a t ā) has arisen in a momentary unit of consciousness.

[1] *Th.*—Your statement must include of course past and future states of consciousness in the series. You forgot that, and you must agree that the past having ceased and the future being unborn, it is not right to say that they form a [present] concentrated state of mind.[4]

[1] *Anguttara-Nik.*, ii. 172.

[2] C i t t a - s a n t a t i. See *Compendium*, 6, 153, *n.* 1; 157, *n.* 4; 252 f.

[3] S a m ā d h i means the placing, establishing of consciousness exclusively and voluntarily on any single object. E k a g g a t ā is the essential factor in consciousness, the cultivation of which may bring about the state called S a m ā d h i.

[4] There is no use in speaking of a 'state' without a 'function' of mind. And only the present state can be functioning (p a c c u p - p a n n a m e v a c i t t a ŋ k i c c a k a r a ŋ h o t i).—*Comy.*

[2] *S. U.*—Then is concentration confined to a momentary conscious unit?

Th.—Yes.

S. U.—But if you could affirm that concentration is involved in each momentary unit of consciousness, you should say no less that one had won the ecstasy[1] of Jhāna on the actual occasion of any sense-cognition, or at the very moment of thinking immoral thoughts, accompanied by lust, hate, dulness, or any of the ten corruptions.[2] . . .

[3] *Th.*—If your proposition is true, it must also be true [*a fortiori*] that a series of *bad* conscious units is concentration, whether it is accompanied by lust, hate, or any of the ten corruptions. This you deny. . . .

[4] *S. U.*—But if we are wrong, did not the Exalted One say: '*I, friend Jainas,*[3] *am able, without moving the body or using the voice, to spend seven nights and days in the experience of absolute bliss*'?[4]

Surely then the flow of consciousness constitutes concentration of mind.

---

7. *Of the Causality of Things.*[5]

Controverted Point.—That a cause of things is predetermined.[6]

From the Commentary.—Some, like the Andhakas, hold that, because of the Word—'*There is a cause, and that is elemental*'[7]—

---

[1] Here appanā-samādhi is meant (*Compendium*, p. 56).

[2] See above, pp. 65, 66, *nn.* 4; *Compendium*, p. 173.

[3] Nigaṇṭha Jains.

[4] *Majjhima-Nik.*, i. 94.

[5] Dhammaṭṭhitatā—i.e., the state of being a cause by which resulting things are established. See above, VI. 2, and Appendix.

[6] Parinipphanna. On nipphanna (here intensified by the prefix) see *Compendium*, pp. 156 (*c*), 157, *n.* 6.

[7] *Saṃyutta-Nik.*, ii. 25; *Anguttara-Nik.*, i. 286. In these passages it is stated that, whether Tathāgatas arise to point it out or not, always the natural order holds good that (1) causation in the physical and psychical world goes on; (2) all things are impermanent, pregnant with ill, soulless.

each term in the chain of Causal Origination is, as a cause, elemental, and is therefore predetermined. The Theravādin shows that, if it were predetermined by another cause, this cause would in turn be predetermined by yet another, and so on *ad infinitum*.

[1] *Th.*—Is then the cause of causes predetermined [by something else]? You deny. For if you assent,[1] you commit yourself to this: that, because of the continued eventuating due to endless causation, there can never be an end made to Ill, nor any cutting off the round of rebirth, nor any Nibbāna free from the residual stuff of rebirth.

[2] Again, is the cause of any one of the five aggregates (body, mind) predetermined? If you assent, you commit yourself to the admission that the cause itself is predetermined by something else. And if you deny—and I insist, and take no denial—you, assenting, commit yourself to this—that there is, for this endless causation,[2] no making an end of Ill, no cutting off of the round of rebirth, no Nibbāna without stuff of rebirth. . . .

---

8. *Of Impermanence.*

Controverted Point.—That impermanence is predetermined.

From the Commentary.—Some, like the Andhakas, hold that impermanence itself is no less predetermined than impermanent things, such as the body, etc. By this they are involved either in a plural order of impermanence, or in an interminable series of temporal features, each predetermined in its own way, with no prospect of coming to the end of predetermination.[3]

[1-3] *Th.*—Then is impermanence predetermined by impermanence already predetermined. And if you admit this,

[1] He judges that the correlation may hold by way of contiguity and reciprocity (two of the twenty-four Paccayas or conditioning relations). —*Comy.*

[2] Literally, predetermination of one by the other.

[3] The idea is that things possess impermanence as a characteristic feature. If this characteristic were predetermined, it should possess another feature of impermanence equally predetermined.

you imply that there is no making an end of ill, no cutting off the round of rebirth, no Nibbāna without residual stuff of rebirth. This holds good for both decay and death, the two manifestations of impermanence.

[4-5] [Take now these manifestations of impermanence in the five aggregates, body-mind:] body is undoubtedly predetermined and characterized by impermanence in the form of decay, dissolution, disappearance. But you cannot equally affirm all this of impermanence, decay, or death itself. So for the mental aggregates. . . .

BOOK XII

1. *Of Self-Restraint.*[1]

Controverted Point.—That self-restraint is [positive] action (karma).

From the Commentary.—This is a view held, for instance, by the Mahāsanghikas, and based on the Sutta: '*When he sees an object, hears a sound, etc., he grasps, etc., at the general characters thereof,*'[2] etc. They hold that both self-restraint and want of self-restraint amount to overt action, or karma. In our doctrine it is volition that constitutes karma. And it is argued that just as volition, proceeding by way of deed, word, and thought, gets the name of action of body, speech, and mind, so, if self-restraint be action, that self-restraint, proceeding by way of sense-control, would get the name of visual karmas, auditory karmas, etc. This, as not warranted by the Suttanta, the opponent rejects till the fifth sense is mentioned. Here he stumbles at the ambiguity of kāya: 'sentient skin-surface' and 'intimating body.'

The Sutta quoted is concerned with the presence and absence of self-restraint, not of karma, hence it is inconclusive.

[1] *Th.*—If this be so, you imply that ocular self-restraint is moral action of the eye; so for the other senses—you cannot admit this. . . . But as to self-restraint, involved in sense-control of body and in control of mind, you at first deny it[3] to be moral action, and then

[1] Cf. above, III. 10.

[2] *Anguttara-Nik.*, ii. 16; also *Dialogues*, i. 80, and elsewhere. The 'general characters' (nimitta), according to the Commentators, are usually taken, in this connection, as referring to sex-features and sex-attraction. Self-restraint is the carrying out of the volition (cetanā), which alone ranks as morally effective action—i.e., karma.

[3] He rejects for kāya as organ of touch; accepts for it as the vehicle of intimation. As to 'mind,' he rejects it as organ of sense, accepts it as an avenue of karma.

assent to the proposition that it is moral action. Why then do you not concede this for the remaining four senses? That which you admit as true for mind, the co-ordinator of sense, you must admit as true no less for the five senses.

[2] Want of self-restraint you admit of course is [immoral] action (karma): is it eye-karma when self-restraint is not practised by the controlling power of sight? . . . (*proceed as in* § 1).

[3] *M.*—But if I am wrong, was it not said by the Exalted One: '*Here, bhikkhus, a bhikkhu, when he sees an object with the eye, grasps at the general characters thereof,*' . . . [again] '*does not grasp at the external appearance, . . . when he hears a sound, . . . cognizes a thing with the mind, . . . does not grasp, etc*'?[1]

Surely both self-restraint and want of it are herein shown to be morally effective action?

---

2. *Of Action.*

Controverted Point.—That all action (karma) entails moral result (vipāka).

From the Commentary.—Some, like the Mahāsanghikas again, hold this view, basing their opinion on the Sutta quoted below. Now whereas the Master, without any qualification, spoke of volition as moral action (karma), the argument here shows that only good or bad volition as entailing moral result was meant, and that volition which is morally indeterminate is without moral result. The Sutta quoted is inconclusive, since it refers to the experience of results in actual life or lives, given the necessary conditions.

[1] *Th.*—Do you imply that all volition entails result [volition being moral action]? If you deny, then your proposition is not universally valid. If you do imply that volition entails result, then you are committed to this—that volition which is indeterminate as to moral result entails moral result; that volition which is inoperative and

[1] See preceding note.[2]

therefore indeterminate as to moral result entails such result, whether such volition be exercised in any one of the three spheres of life, or in that which is not included in them.[1] . . . All of this you must deny. . . . [2] For do you not hold that resultant or inoperative volition, which is indeterminate as to moral result, cannot be said to entail result? Where then is your universal proposition?

[3] *M.*—But if I am wrong, was it not said by the Exalted One: '*I declare, bhikkhus, that there can be no annulment of voluntary deeds done and accumulated, without experience of the results thereof, be it in this life or in the after-life*'?[2]

Wherefore all action surely entails result.

---

3. *Of Sound as Result [of Karma].*

Controverted Point.—That sound is a result of karma.

From the Commentary.—Here again some, like the Mahāsanghikas, from carelessly interpreting such passages as, '*He by the doing, the accumulating, the augmenting, the abundance of that karma, is gifted with the voice of a Brahmā god,*' have adopted this view. The argument shows that 'result of karma' is a term applying to mental states only, which have been transmitted by karma, but does not apply to material things. The retinue, for instance, attending a Superman is not a vipāka, or specific result of karma.[3]

[1] *Th.*—[Now what can rightly be predicated of a 'result of karma'?] Such a result is a matter of feeling, pleasant, painful, or neutral; it is conjoined with feeling

[1] *Dhammasangaṇi*, § 583.

[2] *Anguttara-Nik.*, v. 292 ff.

[3] But the pleasure derived from well-being of this kind is vipāka. Vipāka is essentially a subjective phenomenon, subjective experience, emotional and intellectual. Sound, as object, is something 'other,' or external. The importance of speech-sounds for thought doubtless provoked the exceptional position claimed by the heterodox for sound. Sadda means both sound and word; hence, without a qualifying context, sadda means as much vocal sound as sound in general.

of these three kinds; it is conjoined with mental contact, feeling, perception, volition, thought; it goes with a mental object; with it go adverting, ideating, co-ordinated application, attention, volition, anticipation, aiming. Is sound anything of this kind?[1] Is it not rather the opposite?

[2] Now mental contact is result of karma, and of mental contact it is right to predicate any of the foregoing characteristics, and wrong not to. But the opposite holds with regard to sound.

[3] *M.*—But if I am wrong, was it not said by the Exalted One: '*He through having wrought, having accumulated, having piled up, having increased such karma, becomes reborn with the voice of a Brahmā god, like that of the karavīka bird*'?[2] Hence surely sound[3] is a specific result of karma.

---

4. *Of the Sense-Organs.*

Controverted Point.—That the sense-organs are results of karma.

From the Commentary.—Here again it is a Mahāsanghika belief that, because the sense-organs have arisen through the doing of past actions, therefore they are results (understood as subjective or mental). Of them the sixth, or co-ordinating, sense *may* at times be such a result, but not the others.

[1-4] *The argument follows that of the previous dialogue* verbatim, the 'sixth sense' (*man'āyatana*) being omitted.

[1] In the PTS edition the reply should here be, Na h'evaŋ vattabbe.

[2] *Dīgha Nikāya*, iii. 178.

[3] Though the sense-organs are well produced through karma, they are not designated as vipāka's.—*Comy.*

5. *Of the Seven-Rebirths'-Limit.*[1]

Controverted Point.—That he who is said to be liable to seven more rebirths at most is assured of final salvation[2] only at the end of the seven-rebirths' interval.[3]

From the Commentary.—This is a belief held, for instance, by the Uttarāpathakas. The Theravādin's object is to show that there is no such immutably fixed order. There is only (1) the 'true order' of the Ariyan Path, and (2) the 'false order,'[4] to which belong the five heinous crimes entailing inevitable retribution in the very next existence.

[1] *Th.*—Is such an one capable of murdering mother, father, or Arahant, of shedding with malign heart a Tathāgata's blood, of creating schism? You deny. . . .

[2] And is he incapable of penetrating Truth during the interval? You deny. Then he cannot possibly become guilty of those heinous crimes, which admit of no intervening rebirth without retribution. You now assent, admitting that he is incapable of that penetration. Then you imply that he may commit those crimes, which of such a man you deny.

[3] Is there a fixed order of things[5] (among the Paths) by which the seven-rebirths'-limit man is bound to go through all the seven? You deny. Then your proposition cannot hold. Do you in other words hold that there are applications of mindfulness, supreme efforts, steps to potency, controlling powers, forces, factors of enlightenment, by [culture in] which the seven-births'-limit person is destined to go through all seven?

[1] That is, seven at the outside, possibly fewer. See I. 4.

[2] I.e., in the Ariyan fourfold Path and its climax. On niyato see V. 4; cf. VI. 1.

[3] According to the Burmese translation of the text, the question turns on whether such a person is subjectively assured of his own state, or whether he must go through his last seven lives before he becomes so assured? The Commentary paraphrases -paramatā by -paramatāya, and the Br. translator takes this as either instrumental or locative. The sense is the same.

[4] Cf. I. 3.

[5] On *niyama* and *niyāma*, see Appendix: Assurance.

[4] Is not the opposite the case? And how then can you maintain your proposition?

[5] You maintain that such a person is not so destined except by the fixed order of the First, or Stream-winner's Path. But are all who enter on that Path destined to go through all the seven rebirths?

[6] *U.*—You say I am wrong; nevertheless you must admit that the person in question *is* a seven-births'-limit person? Surely then my proposition stands? . . .

---

6. *Sequel to the Foregoing.*

[1] *U.*—Again, if you maintain it is wrong to say that the kolankola,[1] or one ranking in the First Path next above him of the seven rebirths' limit, is assured of salvation by his rank,[2] I ask, Does not his rank itself [guarantee that he shall attain]?

[2] And does not the next higher rank in the First Path, that of eka-bījin, or 'one-seeder,' also guarantee final salvation?

---

7. *Of Murder.*

Controverted Point.—That a person who has attained to sound views[3] may yet designedly commit murder.

From the Commentary.—Some, like the Pubbaseliyas, hold that, since a person who has attained to sound views has not entirely put

---

[1] Explained by Buddhaghosa, commenting on *Anguttara-Nik.*, i. 233, as meaning 'a goer from family (kula) to family,' 'kula here standing for bhava' (rebirth). See above, p. 77, *n.* 3.

[2] Burmese translators give alternative renderings—*in* or *by* his rank—for kolankolatā.

[3] Diṭṭhisampanno puggalo, a technical term of religious life, wherein the word diṭṭhi no longer means erroneous opinion, but the opposite. Such an one is still a learner (sekha), but has put away all but the last fetters and residual lust, hate, and nescience, and is incapable, so the Buddha taught, of any of the misdeeds or of the irreverence mentioned above.—*Saṃyutta-Nik.*, ii. 43 f.; vi. *s.v.* Diṭṭhi; *Anguttara-Nik.*, iii. 438 f.

away enmity, and since he who takes life has enmity in his heart, therefore one who thinks rightly may yet commit wilful murder.

[1] *Th.*—Then you imply that he may designedly commit [any murder, even the worst, to wit] matricide, parricide, Arahanticide, or with enmity at heart may wound a Tathāgata, or create schism in the Order. . . .

[2] You imply, moreover, that [since he may commit such a deed] he can have no reverence for Master, Doctrine, Order, or Training, [3] while you know, on the other hand, that such a person feels just the opposite.

[4] You imply, moreover, that such a person may defile[1] Buddha shrines, desecrate them, spit on them, behave as an infidel in presence of them ?[2]

[5] But was it not said by the Exalted One : '*Just as the ocean, bhikkhus, remains of the same nature, and passes not beyond the shore, just so is the body of precepts which I have established for those who are hearers of my word, and which they their lives long do not pass beyond*' ?[3]

Hence it is not right to say that a person who has attained to sound views may designedly deprive a living creature of life.

---

8. *Of Evil Tendency.*[4]

Controverted Point.—That for a person holding sound views evil tendencies are eliminated.

From the Commentary.—This view is due to the lack of making proper distinction, by such as the Uttarāpathakas, between an evil

---

[1] See *Vin. Texts*, iii. 277, *n.* 3.

Apabyāmato, Br. asabyākato, Br. translation: abyāsakato. The Burmese scholar, U. Pandi, suggests we should read apabyākato, by which he understands 'blasphemously.' The Commentary on *Saṃyutta-Nik.*, i. 226, only remarks: apabyāmato karitvā abyāmato katvā.

[3] *Vin. Texts*, iii. 303.

[4] Duggati denotes evil destiny, and connotes the sense-desires of beings involved therein. The orthodox position is, that one who holds sound views may still possess sense-desires which may involve such a destiny.

destiny and the natural desires concerning objects of sense felt by those who are involved in such a destiny.

[1-4] *Th.*—But you concede that such a person [though safe as to his destiny] may still get infatuated with any purgatorial objects of sense,[1] may commit fornication with females that are not human, whether demons, animals, or fairies; may keep worldly possessions, such as goats and sheep, poultry and swine, elephants, cattle, horses and mules, partridges, quails, peacocks and pheasants.[2] If you assent to all this, your proposition cannot stand. Moreover, you cannot possibly admit all this in the case of an Arahant. Contrariwise, you repudiate it for him, while you admit (as you must) that it may prove true for one who has [merely] sound views.

[5] *U.*—Then if I am wrong, *you* imply that the person holding sound views may yet be reborn in purgatory, in the animal kingdom, in the realm of the Petas? If you deny, you must also retract your contradiction.[3]

---

9. *Of Him who has reached the Seventh Rebirth.*[4]

Controverted Point.—That for a person in the seventh rebirth evil tendencies are eliminated.

The text gives only the opponent's rejoinder, similar to § 5 *in the foregoing.*

[1] In PTS edition [1] the reply to the second question should also be Amantā.

[2] See above, IV. 1. [5].

[3] The Commentary finds the rejoinder inconclusive, because the question refers to the taṇhā which may entail purgatorial retribution, but not to the taṇhā for purgatorial objects of desire.

[4] Sattamabhavika, or Sattamaka, terms which we have not met elsewhere. See XII. 5.

BOOK XIII

1. *Of Age-Long Penalty.*

Controverted Point.—That one doomed to age-long retribution must endure it for a whole kappa.

From the Commentary.—This concerns those who, like the Rājagirikas, hold the notion that the phrase, '*one who breaks up the concord of the Order is tormented in purgatory for a* kappa,'[1] means that a schismatic is so 'tormented for an entire kappa.'[2]

[1] *Th.*—But this implies that the cycle may start when a Buddha is born into the world, or when the Order is dissolved, or when the condemned person is committing the act incurring the penalty, or when he is dying. . . .

[2] It also implies that if he live for a past kappa, he may live for a future one—nay, for two, three, or four. . . . And if during his kappa there be a cosmic conflagration,[3] whither will he go?

R.—To another plane of the universe.[4]

Th.—Do the dead go thither? Do they go to the sky?

R.—The dead go.

Th.—Can the act involving the penalty take effect in a subsequent life? You must deny.[5]. . . . Hence he must go to the sky. This implies that he has the gift of iddhi[3]—

[1] *Itivuttaka*, § 18.

[2] On the loose significance of the time-term kappa, see above, XI. 5. The orthodox view was that the purgatorial retribution lasted for the *remainder* of the cycle or cosmic era.

[3] Literally, 'should the kappa burn.' . . .

[4] Loka-dhātu.

[5] See above, p. 260.

else he could not. Now can one doomed to age-long retribution practise the four steps to Iddhi—will, effort, thought, investigation? . . .

[3] *R.*—But if I am wrong, was it not said by the Exalted One:

> '*Doomed to the Waste, to purgatorial woe*
> *For age-long penalties, provoking schism,*
> *Of discord fain, fixed in unrighteousness,*
> *From the sure haven doth he fall away,*
> *Breaking the concord of the Brotherhood,*
> *Age-long in purgat'ry he waxeth ripe*'?[1]

Hence my proposition is true.

---

2. *Of a Doomed Man's Morality.*

Controverted Point.—That a person doomed for a kappa may not acquire moral consciousness.

From the Commentary.—So, for instance, the Uttarāpathakas, making no distinction between that lower goodness of the world of sense-desire, which such a person may alone acquire, and the sublimer, or the highest goodness, by which he would be able to avert his doom.

[1] *Th.*—Yet you admit that he may make gifts [to the Order]—how then can your proposition hold? And not only gifts—namely, of raiment, alms, food, lodging, medicaments against illness, various kinds of food, drink—but also that he may render homage at a shrine of older faiths,[2] decorate it with a wreath, with incense, with ointment, salute it by marching round.[3] . . .

[1] *Itivuttaka*, § 18. The Commentary adds that these stanzas 'were uttered by the Buddha with reference to the normal life-cycle (āyukappa) in purgatory. This is one-eightieth part of a great kappa.' As thus included it is also called an antarakappa.

[2] Cetiya, a pre-Buddhist term for anything worthy of being revered as a memorial. Buddhism has applied it to the four classes of recognized memorials—paribhoga-, dhātu-, Dhamma-, and udissa-cetiya's. The last includes images.

[3] In Br. abhidakkhiṇaŋ, or consummate offering.

[2] *U.*—You contradict my proposition. Now you admit that he may acquire good consciousness arising out of that [purgatorial discipline]. Yet this implies that he may also acquire good consciousness belonging to the Rūpa- and Arūpa-spheres,[1] and belonging even to the supramundane mind. . . .

---

3. *Of Abettors of Cardinal Crimes.*

Controverted Point.—That a person who, as abettor, is involved in 'immediate retribution' may enter on the True Path of Assurance.

From the Commentary.—Such a person, who at death inherits the immediate effect of karma, may have abetted any of the cardinal crimes (matricide, etc.) in one of two ways—by a permanent or standing injunction to commit the crime, or by an occasional injunction. An abettor of the former class is already assured of his doom along the Wrong Path, because of the will to accomplish such a course having arisen. He is incapable of entering the True Path. But the other class of abettor is not incapable. So do we conclude in our doctrine. But some, like the Uttarāpathakas, judge of the latter class as we do of the former only.

[1] *U.*—Do you mean that such a culpable abettor can enter on both the False and the True Path of Assurance? If you deny, neither can you affirm your proposition.

Again, if he become worried and uneasy after his connection with the deed, how can he ever enter on the True Path of Assurance?[2]

[2] *Th.*—You say he is incapable of entering on that Path. But are you assuming that one or other of the five cardinal crimes has actually been committed [through his abetment]? Your proposition implies this.[3]

[1] In Jhāna-ecstasy.

[2] Stress is laid by the opponent on the evil character of worry (kukkucca-pattimattaŋ gahetvā).—*Comy.* It is one of the Five Hindrances, taken together with uddhacca (distraction, or flurry). See *Dialogues*, i., p. 82, § 68.

[3] 'Actual commission of any one of the five is to be proved incapable of entering on the True Path of Assurance.'—*Comy.* This, we judge, refers to the principal offender. If there be no actual commission, the abettor is *a fortiori* not liable to severe retribution.

Again, you affirm that an abettor of such crimes, when he has withdrawn his instigation, and has dispelled his worry and remorse, is still incapable of entering upon the True Path of Assurance. Hereby you imply that some one of the grave misdeeds just named has been actually committed [at his instigation]. But can you maintain your position in the face of his reforming before the commission of the act?

[3] *U.*—But has he not previously instigated someone to commit it? How then can you judge him capable of entering on the True Path of Assurance?

---

4. *Of One whose Salvation is Morally Certain* (niyata).

Controverted Point.—That one who is morally certain of salvation has entered the Path of Assurance.[1]

From the Commentary.—Niyāma (Assurance) is of two kinds, according as it is in the wrong or the right direction. The former is conduct that finds retribution without delay,[2] the latter is the Ariyan Path. And there is no other. All other mental phenomena happening in the three planes of being are not of the invariably fixed order, and one who enjoys them is himself 'not assured.' Buddhas, by the force of their foresight, used to prophesy: 'Such an one will in future attain to Bōdhi' (Buddhahood). This person is a Bodhisat, who may be called Assured (Niyata), by reason of the cumulative growth of merit.[3] Now the Pubbaseliyas and Aparaseliyas, taking the term 'Assured' without distinction as to direction, assumed that a Bodhisat was becoming fitted to penetrate the Truths in his last birth, and therefore held that he was already 'Assured.'

---

[1] Here the text (both PTS and Br.) has niyāma, while the Commentary has niyama. The former is technically more correct. See V. 4, and Appendix: Assurance.

[2] Ānantariyakamma. See above, VIII. 9-11.

[3] Read for puññassa datvā, puññ' ussadattā. The title of Niyata is extended to a Bodhisat by courtesy, so to speak, because his final salvation, through accumulating merit, amounts almost to a certainty, is highly probable. Cf. IV. 8.

[1] *Th.*—Do you imply that the so-called 'Assured' enters upon the True Path of Assurance when assured of immediate retribution, and upon the False Path of Assurance when assured of final salvation? That having first practised the Path, he afterwards enters upon the Assurance; that having first practised the Stream-Winner's Path, he afterwards enters upon the Assurance of the Stream-Winner, and so on . . . That finally, entrance upon Assurance comes after practise of the applications in mindfulness and the rest of the Factors of Enlightenment?

[2] *P.A.*—But in contradicting us, you imply that the Bodhisat was not fitted by that last birth to penetrate the Truths.

Th.—Nay, I say not so.

P.A.—Then he was [already] assured of entering upon the Path of Assurance.

---

5. *Of One in the Toils.*

Controverted Point.—That a Hindrance is cast off by one who is entangled in it.

From the Commentary.—The Uttarapāthakas are among those who hold that, just as there is no purifying work left for the purified, so it must be one entangled, obstructed, cloaked by the Hindrances, who abandons them.

[1] *Th.*—Equally then he who is infatuated abandons lust; he who is malign, stupid, corrupt, abandons hate, dulness, corruptions, respectively. Now, does he cast off lust by lust, hate by hate, and so on?

U.—[If this is not so, you are suggesting that the Hindrances are cast out by the Path.] Now you allow that lust, for instance, and the Path are both conscious experiences. But do you not hereby imply a combination of two rival mental procedures? Lust is immoral, the Path is moral—does not your position imply that good and bad, moral and immoral, radiant and sinister mental states confront each other in the mind? And was it not said by the Exalted One: '*These four things are very far apart: the sky and the earth, the hither and the yonder shore of the ocean, whence the sun rises and where he sinks. . . . Hence far is norm of good from that of evil*'?[1]

Hence it is also wrong to say good and bad states confront each other in the mind at the same moment.

[2] *Th.*—But was it not said by the Exalted One: '*With consciousness thus concentrated, made pure, translucent, cleared, void of defilement, made supple, wieldy, firm, imperturbable, he applies and bends over the mind to insight into the destruction of Intoxicants*'?[2]

[3] *U.*—But was it not also said by the Exalted One: '*He thus knowing, thus seeing, his heart is set free from the Intoxicants — sense-desires, lust of becoming, error and nescience*'?[3]

Hence surely it is one who is entangled by the Hindrances who casts them off.

---

6. *Of Captivity and Release.*

Controverted Point.—That a Fetter is cast off by one who is in thrall to it.[4]

From the Commentary.—This follows the preceding argument. To be 'in thrall to' means to be up against the Fetters, to have reached the state of being possessed of them.

The discourse is similar to XIII. 5.

---

7. *Of Jhāna as Enjoyment.*

Controverted Point.—That the expert enjoys Jhāna, and the desire for Jhāna has Jhāna as its object.[5]

[1] Quoted in full on p. 201 f. [2] *Dialogues*, i. 92.

[3] *Ibid.*, 93. 'This is inconclusive, not being spoken concerning one still in the toils.'—*Comy.* With this discourse cf. III. 8.

[4] Literally, is face to face with it.

[5] Jhāna-exercises, rightly valued, are solely a means, not an end, the end, for the Ariyan, being adhicitta, or the consciousness called,

From the Commentary.—This opinion, held, for instance, by the Andhakas, is based upon the Word : '*He attaining to and abiding in First Jhāna finds enjoyment in it.*'

[1] *Th.*—Do you mean that a given Jhāna is the mental object to that same Jhāna? If you deny,[1] your proposition falls. If you assent, you must equally admit that he touches a given mental contact with the same contact, feels a given feeling with that feeling, and so on for perception, volition, thought, applied and sustained intellection, zest, mindfulness, understanding. . . .

[2] You admit that desire for Jhāna and Jhāna itself are forms of conscious experience? But are you prepared to admit further that they constitute two conscious processes going on at once? You deny; then your former admission is invalid. And if you admit further that desire for Jhāna is wrong while Jhāna itself is good, you bring the good and the bad up against each other in the same consciousness—things as 'far apart as earth and sky,' etc.[2]

[3] *A.*—But, if I am wrong, was it not said by the Exalted One: '*Take the case, bhikkhus, of a bhikkhu who, aloof from sensuous ideas, aloof from evil ideas, entering into, abides in First Jhāna : he enjoys it, he yearns over it, and by it he is delighted*'?[3]

Hence surely the expert enjoys Jhāna, and the desire for Jhāna has Jhāna as a mental object.

---

especially in later books, supramundane. For the more worldly aspirant the end was rebirth in the Rūpa, or Arūpa heavens.

[1] For fear of not conforming to the Suttas.—*Comy.*

[2] See VII. 5; XIII. 5.

[3] *Anguttara-Nik.*, ii. 126. Here such an expert is aspiring to the Brahma-heavens (Rūpa-loka) only, and is contrasted with the 'disciple of the Exalted One.' 'The passage is inconclusive, inasmuch as it refers to pleasure in and desire for Jhāna after, and not during the exercise of it.'—*Comy.*

8. *Of Lust for the Unpleasant.*

Controverted Point.—That there is such a thing as lusting for what is disagreeable.

From the Commentary.—In the Sutta-passage:—'*Whatsoever feeling he feels, pleasant, painful, or neutral, he delights in and commends that feeling*'—the reference is to *erroneous* enjoyment.[1] But some, like the Uttarāpathakas, emphasizing the 'delights in,' hold that one can delight in painful feeling as enjoyment of passionlessness.

[1] *Th.*—Do you go so far as to maintain that of the beings who delight in the painful, some wish for it, long for it, seek, search, hunt for it, and persist in cleaving to it? Is not rather the opposite your genuine belief? You assent. Then how do you maintain your proposition?

[2] Can anyone have at once a latent bias of lust for painful feeling and a latent bias of aversion from pleasant feeling?[1] Will not these two forms of bias be [really] directed inversely, the former craving pleasure, the latter hating pain?

[3] *U.*—But if I am wrong, was it not said by the Exalted One: '*He, thus, expert in complacency and antipathy, delights in and commends whatsoever feeling he feels, pleasant, painful, or neutral, and persists in cleaving to it*'?[2]

Hence surely there is such a thing as lusting for the unpleasant?

---

9. *Of the Unmorality of a Natural Desire for Objects of the Mind.*

Controverted Point.—That to crave for objects of the mind is unmoral.

[1] *I.e.* to being subjugated to feeling.

[2] *Majjhima-Nik.*, i, 266. 'Delight,' the Sutta goes on, 'is grasping after the things of sense, which cause the feelings.'

From the Commentary.—Some, like the Pubbaseliyas, hold that the sixth kind of objects of sense-experience,[1] coming after any of the five forms of sensations, is neither moral nor immoral.

[1] *Th.*—If that be so, this craving must belong to one of the moral indeterminates—to wit, resultant or inoperative indeterminates—matter, Nibbāna, or the organs and objects of the five senses. But you must deny this [as not doctrinal].

Or what reason have you for dissociating this sixth form of taṇhā [natural desire or craving] from the rest? If you admit that a craving for objects of sight, sound, and so on is immoral, you must admit as much concerning the co-ordination of these.

[2] Did not the Exalted One call craving immoral? Does not this condemn your proposition? Did he not call appetite (or greed) immoral? and is not craving for objects of the mind a kind of greed?

[3] Your contention is that a craving for objects of the mind is an unmoral appetite, but you are not justified in using lôbha with this qualification, when in the other five modes of sense it is called immoral.

[4] Again, was it not said by the Exalted One: '*This natural desire is concerned with rebirth, is accompanied by delight and lust, dallying here and there—to wit, desires of sense, desire for rebirth, desire not to live again*'?[2] . . .

[5] *P.*—But if I am wrong, is not this [threefold] craving a craving for certain ideas or mental objects?[3]

Hence surely such a craving is as such immoral.

[1] The co-ordination of different successive sensations as a concrete single percept and image—*e.g.*, of orange colour, smell, roundness, and certain other touches into an orange—was conceived by Buddhists as a sort of sixth sense.

[2] *Saṃyutta-Nik.*, iii. 26; *Vin. Texts*, i. 95, *reading* 'non-existence' *for* 'prosperity.' (Vibhava may conceivably mean either; but the traditional reading is, as the Commentary to the *Kathāvatthu* says, the goal of the Annihilationists.)

[3] 'This is inconclusive, because the citation shows nothing as to a non-ethical nature, but refers to the process of natural desire concerning a mental object.'—*Comy.*

10. *Of Desire for Ideas and the Cause of Ill.*

Controverted Point.—That the natural desire for objects of mind is not the Cause of Ill.

From the Commentary.—This, too, is an opinion of the Pubbaseliyas and others. The argument follows the preceding.

[1] *Th.*—What reason have you for dissociating this form of craving from the other five? If you admit that a craving for objects of sight, sound, and so on, is immoral, you must admit as much concerning the co-ordination of these as ideas (percepts or images).

[2-5] *Continue to imitate the preceding argument*, XIII. 9.

BOOK XIV

1. *Of the Mutual Consecutiveness of Good and Bad.*

Controverted Point.—That a basis[1] of bad thought is consecutive to a basis that is good, and conversely.

From the Commentary.—That which is good cannot directly and immediately follow after what is bad, nor conversely. Such reciprocal consecutiveness is anomalous. Some, however, like the Mahāsanghikas, hold that, inasmuch as one can both like and then dislike the same thing, therefore there has been, in such a case, reciprocal consecutiveness. Good and bad thoughts cannot occur consecutively during the stages of javana (apperception) in one and the same process of cognition, inasmuch as each course of good or of bad thought entails a distinct preliminary 'adverting' of consciousness.

[1] *Th.*—You are implying that the adverting,[2] the adjusting of the mind arising for ethically bad consciousness is precisely the adverting and adjusting of the mind arising for ethically good consciousness. You say 'No,' while insisting on your proposition. Then you must mean that the good consciousness can arise without our adverting or adjusting the mind? You maintain the opposite to this? Then, if the good consciousness in question arise for a mind already adverted and adjusted, it must be

[1] Literally, root, or conditioning state.

[2] The seven terms characteristic of this work should here be supplied. See, e.g., VII. 5, 2. The Commentary here for the first time explains that 'adverting' (āvaṭṭanā=āvajjana) is the turning of the mind from the subconscious life-flux to full consciousness, and that 'adjusting' (or 'aiming,' paṇidhi) is the further move on to a definite mental object, and persistence thereon.

wrong to say that a basis of what is bad is consecutive to what is good.

[2] Does what is bad arise for wrongly directed attention? You assent. Do you say as much of the good which, according to you, is consecutive thereto? Is it not truer to say that the good consciousness was preceded by rightly directed attention? You agree. Then that bad thought cannot be immediately consecutive to this good thought.

[3] Again, are you prepared to admit that the idea of resignation follows immediately on that of sense-desires? That the idea of benevolence follows immediately on that of malignity? That the idea of kindness follows immediately on that of cruelty, the idea of love on that of malevolence, pity on unkindness, sympathetic joy on spleen, equanimity on resentment? . . .

[4-6] *The same argument is now applied to refute the second half of the proposition, to wit,* 'that a basis of what is good is consecutive to a basis of what is bad'?

[7] *M.*—But if I am wrong, you will admit that one can fall in and out of love with one and the same object? Surely then my proposition is right, that a bad thing is consecutive to a good thing and conversely.[1]

---

2. *Of the Development of Sense-Organs.*

Controverted Point.—That the sense-mechanism starts all at once to life in the womb.

From the Commentary.—Our doctrine teaches that at a [human] rebirth the development of the embryo's sense-mechanism or mind is not congenital, as in the case of angelic[2] rebirth. In the human embryo, at the moment of conception, the co-ordinating organ (m a n ā y a t a n a) and the organ of touch alone among the sense-organs,

---

[1] The parallel drawn is inconclusive, inasmuch as it refers to passion and its opposite arising about the same object, not to the consecution of the moral and the immoral.—*Comy.*

[2] O p a p ā t i k a.

are congênital. The remaining four organs (eye and ear mechanism, smell and taste mechanism) take seventy-seven days to come to birth, and this is partly through that karma which brought about conception, partly through some other karma.[1] But some, like the Pubbaseliyas and the Aparaseliyas, believe that the sixfold sense-organism takes birth at the moment of conception, by the taking effect of one karma only, as though a complete tree were already potentially contained in the bud.

[1] *Th.*—Do you imply that the sense-mechanism enters the womb with all its main and minor parts complete, not deficient in any organ? You deny . . . [Then let us speak more in detail:] You admit that the organ of sight starts by consciousness seeking rebirth?[2] Now, you would not claim, for that questing consciousness that [at its taking effect] hands, feet, head, ears, nostrils, mouth and teeth take their start? Why claim an exception in the case of the visual, or other sense-organs?

[2] *P.A.*—Then you claim that four of the sense-organs—eye, ear, smell, taste — come later into being. Are you implying that, to bring this about, one makes karma in the mother's womb? You deny, but your position implies it.

Th.—But you say, do you not, that in the embryo hair, down, nails, teeth, bones, appear at a subsequent stage. Do *you* imply a special embryonic karma done to bring these to birth? You deny. Then why assail my position? [3] Or it may be you do not admit the subsequent appearance of hair, etc.? But was it not said by the Exalted One:

> '*At first the* "kalala" *takes birth, and thence*
> *The* "abbuda." *Therefrom the* "pesī" *grows,*
> *Developing as* "ghana" *in its turn.*
> *Now in the* "ghana" *doth appear the hair,*
> *The down, the nails. And whatsoever food*

[1] These are technically called janaka-karma and upatthambaka-karma (reproductive and maintaining karmas). — *Compendium*, p. 143 f. (A. 1, 2).

[2] I.e., the potential resultant of some dying man's last conscious act.

And drink the mother of him takes, thereby
The man in mother's womb doth live and grow'?[1]

Hence it is right to assign a later appearance to hair, and so forth.

---

3. *Of Immediate Contiguity in Sense.*

Controverted Point.—That one sensation follows another as an unbroken fused sequence.

From the Commentary.—In view of the swift alternations of seeing and hearing at performances of dancing and singing, some, like the Uttarāpathakas, hold that the sense-cognitions arise in a mutually unbroken succession.

[1] *Th.*—Do you imply that the mental adverting, adjusting, etc.,[2] conjured up by visual consciousness is the *same* as that conjured up by auditory consciousness? Would you not affirm that this was wrong? And if wrong, do you mean that the auditory consciousness brings about no adverting or adjustment of mind?[3] Is not the opposite true? But if it be true, then your proposition falls.

[2] Again, you agree that 'visual consciousness' occurs to the person attending to a visible object. But you cannot urge that auditory consciousness also occurs to such an one attending to a visible object. . . . In other words, if visual consciousness have only visible object as its object, and nothing else, the unbrokenly succeeding auditory consciousness must have the same kind of object only and nothing else. . . .

Our doctrine says: '*Because of eye and visible objects visual consciousness arises.*'[4] Can you substitute the words

[1] *Saṃyutta-Nik.*, i. 206; *Jātaka*, iv. 496; cf. *Milinda*, i. 63. The Pali terms denote four stages in fœtal growth.

[2] I.e., can auditory consciousness possibly occur to one who has not adverted or adjusted the mind? The argument is similar to that in XIV. 1. However swiftly one sense-operation follows another, it is judged that 'adverting' is an essential preliminary in each.

[3] See above, VIII. 9.

[4] *Saṃyutta-Nik.*, ii. 72 f.; cf. *Majjhima Nik.*, i. 259.

'auditory consciousness'? You deny this.[1] But I repeat the question, and ask, Is the Suttanta thus? Nay, you say, the former quotation was alone right. But if your proposition be right, you are implying that the given visual consciousness is none other than the given auditory consciousness.

[3-4] The same argument holds whichever two of the five kinds of sense we take.

[5] *U.*—But if I am wrong [consider any kind of dramatic performance], when there is dancing, singing, reciting, does not the spectator see objects, hear sounds, smell odours, taste tastes, and touch tangibles? Surely then it is right to say that the five kinds of sense-cognition arise in unbroken unitary sequence.[2]

---

4. *Of the Outward Life of an Ariyan.*

Controverted Point.—That the Ariyan 'forms' [of speech and action] are derived from the four primary qualities of matter.[3]

From the Commentary.—The Uttarāpathakas and others hold that Ariyan speech and action are material qualities derived, as such, from the four primary elements of matter, the Doctrine teaching that *all material qualities are the four primary qualities of matter, or are derived from them.*'[4]

---

[1] As heterodox.

[2] 'The illustration is inconclusive, because it only alludes to a mixed state of rapidly alternating grouped objects of mind, not to the succession in a unity.'—*Comy.* It is tantalizing that our historical materials concerning a drama, which was apparently ultra-Wagnerian in providing stimuli for all the senses, are so slender.

[3] Extended, cohesive, hot, and mobile elements, popularly called earth, water, fire, air.

[4] *Majjhima-Nik.*, i. 53; cf. 185.

[1] *Th.*—You admit that the qualities[1] of the Ariyan are moral, and not unmoral. But the primary qualities of matter are not moral; they are unmoral. . . .

[2] Again, there is in these primary qualities nothing akin to the absence of intoxicant, fetter, tie, flood, bond, hindrance, infection, grasping, corruption, characteristic of the Ariyan's qualities. On the contrary, the former are concomitant with these [ethically undesirable things].

[3] *U.*—But if I am wrong, was it not said by the Exalted One: '*Whatever matter there is, bhikkhus, is the four primary qualities and their derivatives*'?[2] Hence it is surely right to say that the material qualities of the Ariyan are derived from the primary qualities.

---

5. *Of Latent Bias as Something Apart.*[3]

Controverted Point.—That latent bias, in any of the seven forms, is different in kind from a patent outbreak of the vice.

From the Commentary.—Some, like the Andhakas, hold this view, inasmuch as an average worldly person, while his thoughts are ethically good or neutral, may be said to have latent bias for the seven vices, but not to be openly manifesting them.

[1] *Th.*—Do you equally maintain that the lusts of sense are different in kind from the lusts of sense openly manifested? You deny, but you cannot then maintain your proposition. You cannot maintain that the lusts of sense are the same as those lusts manifested, and yet deny

[1] Evidently rūpa is here taken in the limited sense of 'forms' of speech and action—in fact, conduct. Cf. the *Yamaka* (i., p. xi), in which book rūpa is used in the sense of 'forms' of consciousness. It should also be recollected that the Path-factors—supremely right speech and action—are mental properties through which corresponding conduct is effected. See above, X. 2.

[2] *Anguttara-Nik.*, v. 348.

[3] This theory was discussed in IX. 4; XI. 1.

the identity in the case of the manifesting of them and the latent bias.

[2-7] This argument holds good for the other six forms —enmity, conceit, erroneous opinion, doubt, lust of life, ignorance.

[8] *A.*—But if I am wrong, may not an average worldly man, while thinking what is good or unmoral, be said to have latent bias, but not to be openly manifesting any of its forms?

Th.—If you conclude from this that your proposition is right, you must equally admit that, whereas such a person may also be said to have lust, though he be not openly manifesting it, lust is different in kind from open manifestation of it.

---

6. *Of Unconscious Outbursts of Corruption.*

Controverted Point.—That outbursts of corruption take place unconsciously.

From the Commentary.—The Andhakas, for instance, hold that lust and other wrong states may arise even in one who is attending to Impermanence, etc., and besides, it has been said: '*Sometimes, Master Bhāradvāja, when he is thinking: "I will attend to the unbeautiful," he attends to it as beautiful.*'[1] Hence we are liable to involuntary outbursts of corruption.

[1] *Th.*—You imply that such outbursts come under the non-mental categories—matter, Nibbāna, organ or object of sense. . . . Are they not rather to be classed as lust-ridden, hate-ridden, dulness-ridden mind, as immoral, corrupted consciousness, the existence of which you of course admit?

[1] *Saŋyutta-Nik.*, iv. 111. The PTS text of the *Saŋyutta* reads, for subhato manasikarotīti, subhato āgacchati. The speaker is King Udena conversing with Piṇḍola-Bhāradvāja. Cf. *Vin. Texts*, i. 302 f.; iii. 79 f.; 382 f.

---

7. *Of Desire as inherent in Heavenly Things.*

Controverted Point.—That lust for the things of the Rūpa heavens is inherent to and included therein.

From the Commentary.—Just as sensuous lusts are inherent in the world of sense-experience, and are said to be included in it, the lust for life in the Rūpa heavens and the Arūpa heavens was held, by the Andhakas and the Sammitiyas, to be as stated.

[1] *Th.*—You imply that the desire which seeks attainment in Jhāna, the desire which seeks rebirth in the heavens, and the delighting, under present conditions, in celestial bliss,[1] are all three concomitant, coexistent, associated and conjoined with their respective kinds of consciousness, are one in genesis and cessation, one in seat and object with those kinds. If you deny, your proposition falls.

[2] Is a desire for sound inherent and included in the sphere of sound, or is a desire for the other objects of sense inherent and included in their respective spheres? Why not affirm here instead of denying? If the desires are to be denied here, neither can you affirm them in the case of the heavens.[2]

[3-4] The same arguments apply to the desire for the things of the Arūpa heavens.

[5] *A.S.*—But if you admit that we may speak of sensuous lusts as inherent and included in the world of sense-experience, it is surely right to affirm analogous desires in the case of the Rūpa and Arūpa heavens.[3]

[1] According to the Commentary these three terms refer respectively to moral (k u s a l a) consciousness, resultant (v i p ā k a) consciousness, and inoperative (k r i y ā) consciousness—five modes in each of the three—on the Rūpa plane. Cf. *Compendium*, Part I., 2, §§ 8, 9.

[2] For the point in this argument see XVI. 10, § 2.

[3] The orthodox position is that such desires are inherent in and confined to the world (earth, purgatory, lower heavens) of sense-experience (K ā m a l o k a).

8. *Of the Unmoral and the Unrevealed.*

Controverted Point.—That error is unmoral.

From the Commentary.—As to the term a-vy-ā-kata, literally 'undeclared,' applied to the four categories: result-in-consciousness[1] (vipāka), inoperative consciousness[1] (kiriyā), matter and Nibbāna, it means 'cannot be declared to be either moral or unmoral, because of the absence of moral [or karmic] result-in-consciousness' (avipākatta). Applied to speculative opinion on unproveable matters, it means undeclared (akathitatta).[2] Now some, like the Andhakas and Uttarāpathakas, making no such distinction, speak of erroneous views as unmoral in their result [itself a very erroneous view].

[1] *Th.*—Then you must be prepared to class it as one of the unmoral categories—result, inoperative consciousness, matter, Nibbāna, organ and object of sense[3]—which you may not do. You must also be prepared to admit that other mental factors, the conscious processes or acts accompanying erroneous opinion, are unmoral. Else you have this anomaly: that all these together constitute a state of immoral consciousness, while the erroneous opinion alone is unmoral.[4]

[2] Again, the unmoral has no moral fruit or result, while erroneous opinion is of the opposite nature. Nay, were not evil views ranked as paramount offences by the Exalted One?[5] [3] Did he not say: '*Wrong views, Vaccha, are immoral, right views are moral*'?[6] And did he not say also: '*For the holder of wrong views, Puṇṇa, I declare one of two destinies, either purgatory or the animal world*'?[7]

[1] See above, XII. 2, 3. [2] A Christian would say 'unrevealed.'

[3] See above, XI. 1, XIII. 9.

[4] Diṭṭhi-gata, or wrong views, is a factor in akusala-cittaŋ, bad consciousness (*Bud. Psy. Eth.*, pp. 98-101). The idea here seems to be: How can a part be *un*moral, while the whole is *im*moral?

[5] We cannot trace this phrase *verbatim*. The Br. translator reads, for paramāni (paramount), pamāṇāni, 'as their measure.'

[6] *Majjhima-Nik.*, i. 490.

[7] Cf. *ibid.*, i. 388; *Saŋyutta-Nik.*, iv. 307.

[4] *A.U.*—But did not the Exalted One say: '*This, Vaccha, is unsolved* (a v y ā k a t a)*:—that the world is eternal, or that it is not eternal. This, too, is unsolved* (*avyākata*)*—that the world is finite, or that it is infinite. And so, too, are these: that the soul and the body are the same, or are different things; that a Tathāgata comes to be after death, or not, or both comes to be and does not come to be, or that neither happens*'?[1]

Surely then erroneous opinions are unmoral.

[5] *Th.*—But was it not said by the Exalted One: '*Of a person holding wrong views, bhikkhus, whatever karma of deed, word and thought he completes and carries out in accordance with those views, be it volition, aspiration, adjustment of mind, or other activities, all those things conduce to the undesirable, to the unpleasant, to the disagreeable, to trouble, to ill*'?[2]

Hence it is surely wrong to say that 'erroneous opinions are unmoral.'

---

9. *Of the Unincluded.*

Controverted Point.—That erroneous opinions [may enter into] 'the Unincluded.'[3]

From the Commentary.—Inasmuch as when a man of the world has attained to Jhāna, he may be called passionless as to sense-desires, but not free from erroneous opinions, some, like the Pubbaseliyas, hold that erroneous views beset also that other consciousness which is 'Unincluded.'

---

[1] *Saṃyutta-Nik.*, iv. 393, 401 (neither is quite *verbatim* as the text).

[2] *Anguttara-Nik.*, v. 212.

[3] The opponent would break down the exclusive content of the term a-p a r i y ā p a n n a—the Unincluded—which, according to the Abhidhamma Piṭaka, is reserved for the consciousness and conscious experiences of those qualifying in the Path, and for Nibbāna (*Dhamma-sangaṇi* [*Bud. Psy. Eth.*], §§ 992, 1287). Such consciousness would not be shared by a 'man of the world' or 'average person' (p u t h u j j a n a, literally, one of the many-folk, or *hoi polloi*). It is 'not included' in the mental range of one whose interests are confined to any sphere of *life* in earth or in heaven.

[1] *Th.*—Then you must be prepared to class them among the category of the 'Unincluded,' to wit, as Path, Fruit, Nibbāna, as one of the Four Paths, or Four Fruits, as one of the Factors of Enlightenment—which you may not do.

[2] *P.*—But if I am wrong, why do you admit that a worldly person [in Jhāna] may be called passionless as to sense-desires, but deny that he has lost all erroneous opinion?

Surely then it is right to say that erroneous opinion may enter into 'the Unincluded.'

BOOK XV

1. *Of Correlation as specifically fixed.*

Controverted Point.—That one phenomenon can be related to another in one way only.

From the Commentary.—Some, like the Mahāsanghikas, hold that if anything be correlated to another as its moral condition or motive (hetu),[1] it is not correlated to that other by way of [subject-]object, or of contiguity, or of immediate succession.[2] Or again, if anything be correlated to another as its object, it is not correlated to that other by way of contiguity, or immediate succession.

[1] *Th.*—But take the attitude of investigation,[3] is not that correlated both as moral condition and as dominance? You assent. Then your proposition falls through.

Again, is not predominant desire-to-do the dominant factor in coexistent mental states? If so, we ought to admit a dual correlation by way of [i.] dominance, [ii.] coexistence. [2] The same holds when energy is the dominant factor. Or if dominant energy be considered as 'controlling power' or faculty (indriya), we ought to admit a dual correlation by way of dominance and controlling power. Or if we consider dominant energy as a factor of the Path,[4] we ought to admit a dual correlation by way of dominance and path or means (magga). [3] The same holds when apperception[4] is the dominant factor. Or if dominant consciousness be considered as nutriment (or cause, āhāra),

[1] See *Compendium*, p. 279 f. [2] *Ibid.*, 191, § 7.

[3] Vīmaṃsā. *Ibid.*, 177, *n.* 3. This in terms of hetu is amoha=paññā=intelligence, understanding, insight.

[4] Citta in this connection is an abbreviation for javana-citta, apperceptional consciousness.

we ought to admit a dual correlation by way of dominance and nutriment. [4] The argument holds when we consider conscious dominance as controlling power, or investigation as a dominant factor, or, again, as part of the Path, or means.

Once more, if, on adequately revering an Ariyan phenomenon,[1] reflection arises having that phenomenon as its dominant object, we ought here to admit the dual relation—dominance and object.

[5] Or again, if this or that previous moral consciousness be related to this or that subsequent moral consciousness as consecutive, and is also repeated, have we not to admit here the dual correlation of contiguity and repetition?[2] [6] The same being valid for immoral states? [7] The same correlation being valid if, for moral, or immoral, we substitute 'inoperative' or 'unmoral' states?

[8] *M.*—Nevertheless, you admit the definitely distinct modes of correlation, such as 'moral condition, or hetu,' contiguity, immediate succession? Then surely my proposition is right.

---

2. *Of Reciprocal*[3] *Correlation.*

Controverted Point.—That whereas actions are conditioned by ignorance, we may not say that ignorance is conditioned by actions.

[1] Dhamma; i.e., a Path, a Fruit, Nibbāna, corruptions extirpated, or not yet extirpated. On this specific culture see *Compendium*, pp. 58, 69.

[2] Āsevanā, from āsevati, to serve over and over again (ā + si, or sī, to bind, hence to be a pendant, or dependent), is a difficult term to translate. In the *Compendium* (p. 192, § 12) we used 'succession,' but repetition, or even retention, is in some respects better. The Burmese translators render by 'repetition so as to form a habit'; hence, habitual repetition.

[3] Añña-m-añña, or one-another. The discourse shows that a classification of relations in recent philosophy has been anticipated. See Hon. Bertrand Russell's *Our Knowledge of the External World*, etc., London, 1914, p. 47. See Appendix: Paccaya.

From the Commentary.—This view, held, for instance, by the Mahāsanghikas, is met by the opposite doctrine that there is a reciprocal conditioning obtaining between ignorance and actions, and so on.[1]

[1] *Th.*—But is not ignorance coexistent with action?[2] If so, here is a reciprocal correlation [namely, of coexistence].

[2] Again, 'grasping is conditioned by craving.' Now, is it wrong to say that craving is conditioned by grasping?[3] Yes, you say. But the argument above is valid here also.

[3] *M.*—'Birth, bhikkhus, is conditioned by decay and death, the tendency to become is conditioned by birth'—is the Suttanta thus?

Th.—No.

M.—Neither is the reciprocal conditioning correlation between ignorance and activities reciprocal, nor that between craving and grasping.

[4] *Th.*—'*Mind and body, bhikkhus, are conditioned by rebirth-consciousness, and this by mind and body*'—is the Suttanta thus?[4]

M.—Yes.

Th.—Then the conditioning relation may be reciprocal.

---

3. *Of Duration.*[5]

Controverted Point.—That duration is predetermined.

From the Commentary.—Taking the word duration (a d d h ā) in the sense of period of time, they[6] who hold this opinion base it on the

---

[1] Namely, in the P a ṭ i c c a - s a m u p p ā d a formula; see VI. 2.

[2] S a n k h ā r e n a. 'Here only non-meritorious activity is meant. The correlation between this and ignorance may be analyzed into "related by way of co-existence, reciprocity, presence, continuance, association."'—*Comy.*

[3] Here 'grasping' excludes k ā m a-grasping (which=t a ṇ h ā).—*Comy.* On the four 'graspings' see *Bud. Psy. Eth.*, pp. 323 f.

[4] *Saṃyutta-Nik.*, iii. 114.

[5] The opponent evidently uses a d d h ā in this sense, suggestive of M. Bergson's concept of time.

[6] No adherents are named. Possibly the Andhakas. See above, XI. 8.

Sutta quoted below. The argument seeks to show that no interval whatever is predetermined, except as mere time-notion. But matter, etc., when meaning the five aggregates (bodily and mental) is predetermined.

[1] *Th.*—Then must duration be one of the five aggregates, which of course it is not. This holds good whether you take past,[1] [2] future, or present duration. [3] Now, you say that any past aggregate, bodily or mental, constitutes past duration; any future, any present aggregate, future or present duration respectively. Then are there five past durations, five future, five present durations? . . . [4] fifteen durations in all? Or, if they are regarded as twelve past, future, present organs-and-objects-of-sense, are there thirty-six durations in all? . . .

[5] Or if we consider them as eighteen elements, are there fifty-four durations? or as controlling powers,[2] are there sixty-six durations?

[6] *Opp.*—But was it not said by the Exalted One: '*There are these three subjects of discourse,*[3] *bhikkhus—which are the three? One may talk about past time: "Thus was it in times past." Or about future time: "Thus will it be in future times." Or about the present: "Thus is it now at present"*'?[4]

Hence surely duration is predetermined?

---

4. *Of Instants, Moments,*[5] *Seconds of Time.*

Controverted Point.—That any stroke of time is predetermined.

From the Commentary.—The same argument is followed as in the foregoing.

---

[1] Insert Amantā in PTS edition.

[2] See above, p. 15 f.

[3] Kathāvatthūni.

[4] *Anguttara-Nik.*, i. 197. Cf. p. 95, § 60.

[5] Khaṇa, laya, muhutta: 10 'instants' = 1 'moment,' 10 'moments' = 1 'second.' There is no *measured* coincidence between second and muhutta.

5. *Of the Intoxicants (Āsava's).*

Controverted Point.—That the four āsava's are themselves non-āsava.[1]

From the Commentary.—The Hetuvādins held that, inasmuch as over and above the four Intoxicants there is no other Intoxicant with which they can be said to be 'co-intoxicants,' therefore they must themselves be non-intoxicant.'

[1] *Th.*—Then you must be prepared to classify them with one of the [approved] non-āsava's—the Path, Fruit, Nibbāna, one of the four Paths or Fruits, one of the Factors of Enlightenment—which you, of course, may not do.

[2] *H.*—If I am wrong, I ask you to show me any other āsava, concomitant with which those four may be pronounced co-āsava. . . .

---

6. *Of Decay and Death.*

Controverted Point.—That the decay and death of spiritual[2] things is itself spiritual.[3]

From the Commentary.—Decay and death are not predetermined, and therefore do not come under the categories 'mundane,' 'supramundane.' The Mahāsanghikas and others do not grasp this salient feature.

[1] *Th.*—Then you must be prepared to classify it with one of the [approved] spiritual things—Path, Fruit, Nibbāna, etc.[4] . . . For instance, is the decay and death of the Stream-Winner's Path the Path itself? If you deny, your proposition falls through. If you assent, you

[1] The four are sensuous desires [lust of] life renewed, erroneous opinion, ignorance. See *Compendium*, 227; *Bud. Psy. Eth.*, iii., ch. iv.

[2] Or supramundane, or transcendental (l o k u t t a r a).

[3] Cf. above, XI. 8, on the falsely including the notion 'impermanence' among things impermanent.

[4] See XV. 5.

must also apply your proposition to all the other stages, and say, finally, that the decay and death of the fruit of arahantship is itself fruit of arahantship—which you may not. Nor will you be prepared to admit decay and death as identical with any one of the Factors of Enlightenment.

[2] *M.*—Then, is the decay and death of supramundane things a mundane thing? You deny.[1] Then it must be supramundane.

---

7. *Of Trance.*

Controverted Point.—That to attain cessation of consciousness is supramundane.

From the Commentary.—Inasmuch as what is called [trance or] attaining cessation of feeling and perception is not a positive mental state, but is the suspension of the mental aggregates, it is neither a mundane nor a supramundane state. Some, however, like the Hetuvādins, hold that since it is certainly not mundane, it must be supramundane.

The argument is similar to that in XV. 5 [1], *and* 6 [2].

---

8. *The Same (continued).*

Controverted Point.—That to attain cessation of consciousness is mundane.

[1] *Th.*—You must, then, be prepared to classify it as one of the things admittedly mundane—the five aggregates, or as belonging to one of the three spheres of life, that of sense, or the Rūpa or Arūpa worlds—which you refuse to do.

[2] *Similar to* 6 [2].

[1] The Buddha himself did not class it as of either category.—*Comy.*

9. *Of Trance* (iii.).

Controverted Point.—That a person may die while in a state of trance.

From the Commentary.—The Rājagirikas and others hold that since life is so uncertain, even one who has attained in Jhāna to trance may die, no less than anyone else. The argument shows that there is[1] a time for dying and for not dying.

[1] *Th.*—You must, then, admit that, while in that state, he has all the *mental* symptoms[2] betokening death—to wit, in mental contact, feeling, perception, volition, consciousness. But you agree that all moribund mental symptoms are absent. Hence your proposition falls through.

[2] You will further agree with this: not only that for one in a state of trance is all mental life in abeyance, but also that death is accompanied by contactual, emotional, volitional, and cognitive symptoms.[2]

[3] Moreover, can poison, weapons, or fire affect the body of one in trance? You deny.[3] You assert, on the contrary, that those causes of death cannot affect him. Then, can you maintain your proposition?

[4] Or do you now maintain that poison, weapons, or fire can affect his body?[4] Then, is his attainment not genuine? . . .

R.[5]—But in opposing my proposition you imply that there must be some principle of certainty (or uniformity) by which one is assured of not dying while in trance. If you say that such an assurance does not exist, your proposition cannot stand.

[5] *Th.*—But one who is enjoying visual consciousness is not dying, even though there be no uniform principle of certainty by which he is assured of being kept from death. Hence I assert as much of one who is in trance.

[1] *Read, for* samāpannāya, samānāya.

[2] This word is not in the Pali text.

[3] Because of the abnormal power of his attainment.—*Comy.*

[4] 'He assents because of the body's natural liabilities. Hence there is no abnormal power in the attainment.'—*Comy.*

[5] In *Commentary*, PTS edition, read, for sakavādissa, paravādissa.

10. *Of Trance as a Means of reaching the Unconscious Sphere.*

Controverted Point.—That trance conduces to rebirth in the unconscious sphere.

From the Commentary.—Some, like the Hetuvādins, make no distinction between the two kinds of trance-attainment: the merely mundane, practised by worldly folks, and the supramundane, or spiritual. The former does conduce to rebirth in the sphere of unconscious life, the latter does not.

[1] *Th.*—Can you say of anyone who has attained to trance that [in his character] are the three moral conditions—absence of greed, of hate, of dulness, also faith, energy, mindfulness, concentration, and understanding? Is not the contrary [usually] the case? . . .

[2] You admit of course that one in trance is without mental reaction, feeling, perception, volition, cognition? But you cannot maintain that a Path[1] can be practised in the absence of these.

[3] Finally, your proposition implies that *all* who attain to trance are tending to rebirth in the Unconscious Sphere—which you must deny. . . .

[4] *H.*—But you admit, anyway, that in trance one is unconscious, and in that sphere one is unconscious. Hence I maintain that this tendency is a fact.

---

11. *Of Karma and its Accumulation.*

Controverted Point.—That karma is one thing, its accumulation[2] is another.

From the Commentary.—They who hold this view, for instance the Andhakas and Sammitiyas, judge that the accumulating of karma goes on automatically, independently of moral action, of mental action.

---

[1] Magga, 'path,' is used, more generally, to denote a systematic 'means,' or method conducing to celestial rebirth. It is only the Ariyan Path or Paths that are means leading away from rebirth.—*Bud. Psy. Eth.*, pp. 43 f.; 71 f.; 82 f.

[2] Upacaya may be rendered by 'conservation.'

[1] *Th.*—Are you then prepared to admit that each mental phase—mental reaction, feeling, perception, volition, cognition, also faith, energy, mindfulness, concentration, understanding, also the ten corruptions (kilesa's) —is a different thing from its accumulation? Of course not. Then neither can you affirm your proposition.

[2] Again, do you imply that karmic accumulation is coexistent with karma? You deny? But think! You assent.[1] Then [*a fortiori*] meritorious (or good) karma is coexistent with good karmic accumulation? No? Nay, you must admit it is. Then [it follows that] karma, [being inseparably] conjoined with feeling, is both coexistent with its accumulation, and also inseparably conjoined with corresponding feeling.

[3] Similarly for demeritorious (or bad) karma.

[4] Again, you admit of course that karma is coexistent with consciousness and has a mental object, but you do not admit as much of its accumulation. That is to say, you agree that karma, being coexistent with consciousness, is broken off [as mental process] when consciousness is broken off. But, by your view of the different nature of karmic accumulation, you hold that when consciousness stops, karmic accumulation does not [necessarily] stop. So that we may get a cessation of karma as conscious process, and a continuation of karmic accumulation as product!

[5] You admit, further, that karmic accumulation is where karma is.[2] Surely this implies that an act (kamma) and its (accumulation or) conservation is one and the same thing. . . . And that, the conservation of karmic energy being where karma is, result is produced from that conservation; and that you must conclude that there is no differ-

[1] 'Karma is "conjoined with consciousness"; its accumulation, by the thesis, is automatic, hence the vacillation.'—*Comy.*

[2] Kammamhi=kamme sati, or patiṭṭhite. 'Where there is karma, or where it is established, the "accumulating" begins, but the latter lasts till results mature. Just as the seed retains all the plant-energy till it sprouts.'—*Comy.*

ence in kind between karma, its conservation and its result.[1] Yet this you deny.

Now you have admitted that karma has a mental object,[2] and you also admit [of course] that result, which is produced from the conservation of karma, has a mental object. But you deny that the conservation is of this nature, even while you admit that where karma is, there, too, is its conservation, producing the result! . . .

[6] Finally, was it not said by the Exalted One: *Here, Puṇṇa, is one who plans activities in deed, word and thought, either malevolent or benevolent. In consequence hereof he is reborn in a world either of malevolence or of benevolence; and when his mental reaction to good and bad shall set in, his sensations are in accordance herewith, and his feelings are a mixture of pleasure and pain, as is the case with human beings, with certain of the devas, and with some of the fallen angels.*[3] *Now thus, Puṇṇa, is the rebirth of creatures conspicuous and obscure:*[4]*—by that which he does is he reborn, and being reborn mental reactions affect him. And so I say, Puṇṇa, that beings are the heirs of their own actions (karma)?*[5]

Hence it is not right to say that conservation of karma is a thing apart from karma itself.

[1] He asks concerning the oneness of these three.—*Comy.*

[2] See above, § 4.

[3] Vinipātikā, asuras.

[4] Bhūtābhūtassa. Cf. the term bhavābhavesu, *Pss. of the Brethren,* 305, *n.* 4.

[5] *Majjhima-Nik.*, i. 390.

BOOK XVI

1. *Of Control.*

Controverted Point.—That one can control the mind of another.[1]

From the Commentary.—Some, like the Mahāsanghikas, hold that the attainment of power and authority in the world is only genuine if it include power to control the *consciousness* of others.

[1] *Th.*—Do you mean that one can bid the consciousness of another not to lust, not to hate, not to be bewildered, not to be corrupted? Of course you deny. But how then can you maintain your view? Or do you mean that one can bid any mental phase uprisen in another's consciousness—reaction, feeling, perception, volition . . . understanding—to cease? Equally you deny. . . . [2] Or do you mean that anyone puts away lust, hate, or any evil mental coefficient[2] on account of another? Or practises the [Ariyan] Path, or applications in mindfulness, or any other set of the factors of enlightenment[3] because of another? Or masters the Four Truths—understanding Ill, putting away its Cause, realizing its Cessation, practising the Path thereto—because of another? Or finally, do you mean that anyone makes another the doer of his actions, that anyone's happiness and ill are wrought by another, that one acts while another experiences? If you deny, you must deny your own view.

[1] To *know* (or, as we say, 'read') the thoughts of another was one of the supernormal knowledges (see above, V. 7; *Compendium*, p. 209), but control or influence over another so as to prevent corruption was not assumed for it.

[2] See above, p. 226, *n*. 2.

[3] See *Compendium*, p. 179.

[3] And was it not said by the Exalted One :—

''Tis thou alone dost work thine evil deeds ;
'Tis thou alone dost make thyself corrupt ;
'Tis thou alone dost leave the wrong undone ;
'Tis thou alone dost purify thyself.
Self-wrought is cleanness and impurity.
None may his brother's heart[1] make undefiled' ?[2]

Hence it is surely wrong to say that one can control the mind of another.

[4] *M.*—But have not some admittedly won power and authority ? Surely this includes control over others' minds.

---

2. *Of Assisting Another's Mind.*

Controverted Point.—That one can help the mind of another.

The Commentary merely ranges this under the preceding discourse.

[1] *Th.*—Do you mean that one can so help another as to bid his consciousness not to lust or to hate, or to be bewildered, or to be corrupted ? . . . Or that one may bring forth in the heart of another any of the moral conditions, to wit, disinterestedness, love, understanding, or any of the five 'controlling powers [of enlightenment], to wit, faith, energy, mindfulness, concentration, understanding, etc. . . . (*the remainder agrees* verbatim *with* XVI. 1).

---

3. *Of making Another Happy according to his Deserts.*

Controverted Point.—That one can bestow happiness on others.[3]

[1] Literally, 'another.'

[2] *Dhammapada*, verse 164.

[3] One can bestow the *conditions* of happiness to some extent, but not the actual state of mind.

From the Commentary.—This view is derived by its adherents, notably the Hetuvādins, from the Sutta quoted below. But the words of the Exalted One were spoken to show how the arising of happiness in others is conditioned. Producing happiness in others is not like bestowing food upon them; hence the citation is inconclusive.

[1] *Th.*—Your proposition implies that one can also cause misery in others. But you deny this, while you maintain the opposite with respect to happiness.

[2] You imply further that you can hand over your own happiness to another; or others' happiness, or his own happiness, to another. You deny. To whom then?

You imply, finally, that anyone causes another to act for him, that one's own welfare and ill are wrought by another, that one acts while another experiences.

[3] *H.*—But did not the venerable Udāyin say: '*Verily of many unhappinesses doth the Exalted One rid us, many happinesses doth he bestow upon us, of many bad things doth he rid us, many good things doth he bestow upon us*'?[1]

Hence one may hand on happiness to another.

---

4. *Of Attending to All at Once.*

Controverted Point.—That one can attend to everything simultaneously.

From the Commentary.—Attention has two aspects, according as we consider the method or the object of attention. To infer from the observed transience of one or more phenomena that 'all things are impermanent' is attention as [inductive] method. But in attending to past things, we cannot attend to future things. We attend to a certain thing in one of the time-relations. This is attention by way of object of consciousness. Moreover, when we attend to present things, we are not able at the present moment to attend to the consciousness by which they arise. Nevertheless some, like the Pubbaseliyas and Aparaseliyas, because of the Word, '*All things are impermanent*,' hold that in generalizing we can attend to all things at once.[2] And because they hold that in so doing we must also attend to the consciousness by which we attend, the argument takes the line as stated.

---

[1] *Majjhima-Nik.*, i. 447.

[2] Sabbe sankhāre ekato manasikaroti.—*Comy.*

[1] *Th.*—Do you imply that we know the consciousness by which we so attend? You deny.[1] But I ask you again—now you assent.[2] Then do we know as consciousness the consciousness by which we so attend? You deny. But I ask you again—now you assent. Then is the subject of consciousness its own object? You deny. But I ask you again—now you assent. Then do we experience mental reaction by the same mental reaction? Do we feel a feeling by that feeling? And so on for perception, volition, cognition, applied thought, sustained thought, zest, mindfulness, understanding? If you deny, you undo your previous affirmations. . . .

[2] When we attend to the past as past, do we then attend to the future as future? You deny. But I ask you again—now you assent. But this commits you to a collocation of two parallel mental processes. . . . And this holds if I substitute 'present' for 'future.' . . . And if you claim that we can, while attending to the past as past, attend also to the future as such, and to the present as such, we get a collocation of three parallel mental processes. . . . And—[3-4] [we may ring the changes with] the same argument on other permutations of the time relations. . . .

[5] *P.A.*—But was it not said by the Exalted One:

'When he by wisdom doth discern and see:
"Impermanent is everything in life!"
Then he at all this suffering feels disgust.
Lo! herein lies the way to purity.
When he by wisdom doth discern and see,
That "Everything in life is bound to Ill! . . ."
That "Everything in life is Void of Soul!"
Then he at all this suffering feels disgust.
Lo! herein lies the way to purity'?[3]

Hence we can attend to all at once.

[1] Because it cannot be subject and object at once.—*Comy.*

[2] Because we are already aware of the nature of our thought in general, or because of the thesis advanced.—*Comy.*

[3] *Pss. of the Brethren*, verses 676-678; ascribed to Aññā-Kondañña, the first among the first five disciples to grasp the new gospel.

5. *Of Matter as a Moral Condition (hetu).*[1]

Controverted Point.—That material qualities are moral conditions.

From the Commentary.—'Condition' [hetu] may signify more specially one of the moral conditions or motives and their opposites: appetite—disinterestedness, hate—love, dulness—intelligence; or, more generally, any condition or causal relation whatever. Now, the Uttarāpathakas make no such distinction, but relying on the letter of the Word—'*the four primary qualities*[2] *are conditions [of secondary qualities*']—claim that bodily or material qualities may be [moral] conditions.

[1] *Th.*—Your view implies that (i.) material qualities must act as one or other of the six motives of moral or immoral conduct; (ii.) they have a mental object or idea, having the properties of mental adverting, adjustment, etc.[3] From both of these implications you dissent, hence you cannot maintain your position.

[2-3] Indeed, you are ready to maintain the contrary of (ii.), that proposition being quite true when applied to the six moral conditions, but untrue of material qualities.

[4] *U.*—But are not the four primary qualities conditions of the secondary material qualities that are derived from them?[3] Of course you assent. Hence, the four being material, material qualities *are* conditions [however you understand 'conditions'].

---

6. *Matter and Concomitant Moral Conditions.*

Controverted Point.—That material qualities are accompanied by moral conditions.

[1] On Buddhaghosa's analysis of hetu, see *Bud. Psy. Eth.*, p. 274, *n.* 1. The alternative meanings above are known as hetu-hetu, or mūla (root), and paccaya-hetu. On hetu, see *Compendium*, p. 279.

[2] Extended, cohesive, calorific, and mobile elements (*Compendium*, p. 268, and above.

[3] See VIII. 9.

From the Commentary —The foregoing dissertation applies here also.

[1] *Th.*—That is (i.) they must be accompanied by one or more of the six motives or moral conditions, either good or bad; (ii.) they have a mental object or idea, having the properties of mental adverting, adjustment, etc. . . . (see XVI. 5 [1–2]).

[2] If you admit that disinterestedness, love, and the other four,[1] as moral conditions, have a mental object and involve mental adverting, adjustment, etc., then you must describe material qualities in the same terms. [3] And if that be so, you cannot deny either attribute to material qualities without equally denying it to the moral conditions.

[4] *U.*—But is not matter in causal relations? You agree. Then it is surely right to say material qualities are accompanied by [moral conditions or] motives.

---

7. *Of Matter as Morally Good or Bad.*

Controverted Point.—That material qualities are (i.) good or moral, (ii.) bad or immoral.

From the Commentary.—Some, like the Mahiṃsāsakas and Sammitiyas, relying on the Word—'*acts of body and speech are good or bad*'—and that among such acts we reckon intimations of our thought by gesture and language,[2] hold that the physical motions engaged therein are [morally] good or bad.

[1] *Th.*—Do you mean to imply that material qualities have a mental object, and the properties of mental adverting, of adjustment, etc.? Surely you agree that the opposite is true? [2] And that, whereas you can predicate those things of the three moral motives or conditions, and of the five moral controlling powers, [3] they do not fit the case of material qualities. . . .

(ii.) [4-6] The same argument holds good for material qualities as immoral.

[1] See XVI. 5, '*From the Commentary.*'

[2] *Bud. Psy. Eth.*, p. 217; *Vibhanga*, p. 13.

[7] *M.S.*—But is not karma (moral action) of body and of speech either good or bad? Surely then material qualities [engaged therein] are also either good or bad?

---

8. *Of Matter as Result.*

Controverted Point.—That material qualities are results [of karma].

From the Commentary.—Some, like the Andhakas and Sammitiyas, hold that, just as consciousness and its concomitant attributes arise because of karma that has been wrought, so also do material [i.e., corporeal] qualities arise as results [of karma].[1]

[1] *Th.*—Do you mean to imply that matter is of the nature of feeling, pleasurable, painful, or neutral, that it is conjoined with feeling, with mental reaction, and other phases of consciousness, that it has the properties of mental adverting, adjustment, etc.? Is not the contrary the case? If you assent, you cannot maintain your proposition.

[2] All those things are mental characteristics, not material. But you wish to see in matter a 'result' of karma, without the mental characters which are the properties of 'result.' . . .

[3] *A.S.*—But is not consciousness and its concomitant attributes, which arise through actions done, 'result'? Surely then material qualities, which arise through actions done, are equally 'result'?

---

9. *Of Matter as belonging to the Material and the Immaterial Heavens.*

Controverted Point.—That matter belongs to (i.) the material heavens, (ii.) the immaterial heavens.

[1] On 'result,' vipāka, as technically a conscious or mental phenomenon, see above, VII. 7, 8.

From the Commentary.—Some, like the Andhakas, hold that since matter, which is the product of actions done in the world [and heavens] of sense-desire, belongs therefore to that world, so if it be the product of actions done in the material or immaterial heavens, it belongs equally to those heavens.

[1] *Th.*—Then you must describe matter [in terms descriptive of (i.) that is to say] as seeking attainment in Jhāna, as seeking rebirth on those planes, as living happily under present conditions, as accompanied by a mind that seeks that attainment and that rebirth, and that lives in that happiness; as coexistent with such a mind, associated, conjoined with it, one with it in genesis, in cessation, in physical basis, as having the same objects before it . . . [2] and you must describe matter [in terms descriptive of (ii.) that is to say] in the same terms as we apply to (i.). But is not the contrary true as to both (i.) and (ii.)? . . .

[3] *A.*—But is not matter which is due to actions done in the world of sense-desires called 'belonging to'[1] that world? If that is so, then matter due to actions done in either of the other worlds of existence should surely be called 'belonging to' either the Material Heavens or the Immaterial Heavens.

---

10. *Of Desire for Life in the Higher Heavens.*

Controverted Point.—That lust for life in Rūpa or Arūpa spheres is included among the data thereof.

From the Commentary.—So think the Andhakas, and by the same analogy as they hold the previously stated opinion (XIV. 7) with regard to celestial lustings in general. That is a view they share with the Sammitiyas, but this is theirs alone.

[1] *Th.*—*Similar to* [1] *in* XVI. 9.

[2] And you cannot maintain your view without admitting that a corresponding lust for the objects of hearing, smell-

[1] 'Belonging to' is in Pali simply the name of the world in question with adjectival import. On the extension of the term 'world of sense-desire' (kāmāvacărā), see *Compendium*, p. 81, *n.* 2.

ing, taste and touch is one of the data in the sphere of each of these respectively.[1]

[3] If you cannot affirm the latter, you cannot make an exception of the former.

[4] Next with regard to (ii.) lust for life on the Arūpa [immaterial] plane as a datum thereof—my first argument used above (XVI. 9) holds good. [5, 6]. So does my second used above (XVI. 10, 2). If your proposition is to stand, then a desire for each sense-object must be among the elemental data of the sphere of that particular object. You cannot make an exception of the desire for life in the immaterial sphere.

[7] *A.*—But is not desire for life in the plane of sense [kāmadhātu] among the elemental data of that plane?[2] Then surely you cannot make an exception as to desire for life in the Rūpa and Arūpa spheres?

[1] Rūpa may refer to (i.) matter, (ii.) *visible* object, (iii.) a sphere or heaven of 'celestial' matter, where sight supersedes the more animal senses. Lust for the objects of the other senses is introduced in the argument not so much to oppose rūpa as (ii.), to other sense-objects, as to oppose conceivable if unfamiliar parallels — 'datum included in the sphere (or heaven) of sound,' smell, etc.—to the familiar more ambiguous: 'datum included in the sphere (or heaven) of Rūpa.'

[2] Desire, 'lower' or higher, is always an element in the Kāma loka or world of matter, terrestrial, infernal, sub-celestial, but never, in orthodox doctrine, in the Rūpa or Arūpa worlds.

BOOK XVII

1. *Of an Arahant having Accumulating Merit.*

Controverted Point.—That there is accumulation of merit in the case of an Arahant.

From the Commentary.—This is an opinion carelessly formed by such as the Andhakas: that because an Arahant may be seen distributing gifts to the Order, saluting shrines, and so on, he is accumulating merit. For him who has put away both merit and demerit, if he were to work merit, he would be liable to work evil as well.

[1] *Th.*—If the Arahant have accumulation of merit, you must allow he may also have accumulation of demerit. . . . And [2] you must equally allow that he achieves meritorious karma, and karma leading to the imperturbable,[1] that he does actions conducing to this or that destiny, or plane of rebirth, actions conducing to authority, influence, riches, adherents and retainers, celestial or human prosperity. . . . [3] You must further admit that, in his karma, he is heaping up or unloading, putting away or grasping, scattering or binding, dispersing or collecting.[2] If he does none of these things, but having unloaded, put away, scattered, dispersed, so abides, your proposition is untenable.

[4] *A.*—But may not an Arahant give gifts—clothing, alms, food, lodging, medicaments for sickness, food, drink? May he not salute shrines, hang garlands on them, and perfumes and unguents? May he not make consummate oblations before them? You admit this. But these are all merit-accumulating acts. . . .

[1] See p. 190, *n.* 2. [2] See I. 2, § 63.

2. *Of Arahants and Untimely Death.*

Controverted Point.—That an Arahant cannot have an untimely death.

From the Commentary.—From carelessly grasping the Sutta cited below, some—to wit, the Rājagirikas and Siddhatthikas—hold that since an Arahant is to experience the results of all his karma before he can complete existence, therefore he cannot die out of due time.

[1] *Th.*—Then are there no murderers of Arahants? You admit there are. [2] Now when anyone takes the life of an Arahant, does he take away the remainder of life from a living man, or from one who is not living? If the former, then you cannot maintain your proposition. If the latter, there is no murder, and your admission is wrong.

[3] Again, you admit that poison, weapons, or fire may get access to the body of an Arahant. It is therefore clear that an Arahant may suffer sudden death. [4] But if you deny, then there can be no murderer.

[5] *R.S.*—But was it not said by the Exalted One: '*I declare, bhikkhus, that there cannot be destruction [of karmic energy] ere the outcome of deeds that have been deliberately wrought and conserved has been experienced, whether that destruction be under present conditions, or in the next or in a subsequent series of conditions*'?[1]

Hence there is no untimely dying for an Arahant.

[1] *Anguttara-Nik.*, v. 292 f., and above, p. 266. The *Commentary* paraphrases this passage in detail. The following is an approximate rendering. The commentator follows the negative form of statement in the Pali of the Sutta, which is rendered above in positive form: '*I do not declare* (n a v a d ā m i) *the annulment*—that is, the complete cutting off of the recoil (p a r i v a ṭ u m a - p a r i c c h i n n a b h ā v a ŋ) —*of deeds done by free will without* their result *having been experienced*—i.e., obtained, partaken of. Nor do I declare that such destruction may be realized *under present conditions*, but not hereafter. Nor do I declare that such destruction may be effected *in the very next rebirth*, or the rebirth next to that; nor that it may be effected *in subsequent rebirths;* nor that it may be effected in one rebirth where opportunity of maturing results arises, and not in another where no such opportunity arises. Thus in all manner of conditions,

3. *Of Everything as due to Karma.*

Controverted Point.—That all this is from karma.

From the Commentary.—Because of the Sutta cited below, the Rājagirikas and Siddhatthikas hold that all this cycle of karma, corruptions and results is from karma.

[1] *Th.*—Do you then include karma itself as due to karma?[1] And do you imply that all this is simply the result of bygone causes?[2] You are committed here to what you must deny.

[2] Again, you imply, by your proposition, that all this is [not so much from karma as] from the result of [still earlier] karma. If you deny,[3] you deny your first proposition. If you assent,[4] you imply that one may commit murder through [not karma, but] the result of karma. You assent?[5] Then murder, [though a result], is itself

---

given renewed existence and eventuation of karmic result, there is no place on earth wherein a living being may be freed from the consequences of his own evil deeds. All this the Buddha implied in the Sutta quoted. Hence the opponents' premises for establishing his view —that any act which has not obtained its turn of eventuation should invariably be experienced by an Arahant as result—have not been well established.'

For the opponents akāla (untimely) meant one thing, for the Theravādin another. To judge by the Theragāthā Commentary (*Pss. of the Brethren*, pp. 232, 266), the orthodox opinion was that no one, in his last span of life, could die before attaining Arahantship.

[1] This is rejected as fusing karma with its result.—*Comy.*

[2] That the present is merely a series of effects and without initiative. See on this erroneous opinion (stated in *Anguttara-Nik.*, i. 173 ff.; *Vibhanga*, 367) Ledi Sadaw, *JPTS*, 1913-14, p. 118.

[3] If all is from karma, then that causal karma effected in a past life must have been the result of karma effected in a still earlier life.—*Comy.*

[4] A shoot cannot produce a shoot, but in the continuity of life a seed is the product of another seed, and by this analogy karma is the result of previous karma. So at first rejecting, he then assents.—*Comy.* (freely rendered).

[5] He assents, because the murderous intent is, by his theory, the result of previous karma.—*Comy.* The PTS edition ought here to have Āmantā instead of the negation.

productive of [karmic] result? You assent? Then the result of karma is productive of result? You deny? Then it is barren of result, and murder must *a fortiori* be barren of [karmic] result. . . .

[3] This argument applies equally to other immoral acts —to theft, to wicked speech—lying, abuse, slander, and idle talk—to burglary, raiding, looting, highway robbery, adultery, destroying houses in village or town. It applies equally to moral acts: to giving gifts—e.g., giving the four necessaries [to the religious]. If any of these is done as the result of karma, and themselves produce karmic result, then [you are on the horns of this dilemma: that] either result-of-karma can itself produce effects [which is heterodox], or any good or bad deed has no karmic result [which is heterodox]. . . .

[4] *R.S.*—But was it not said by the Exalted One:

''Tis karma makes the world go round,
Karma rolls on the lives of men.
All beings are to karma bound
As linch-pin is to chariot-wheel.'[1]

'By karma praise and fame are won.
By karma too, birth, death and bonds.
Who that this karma's divers modes discerns,
Can say "there is no karma in the world"'?[2]

Hence surely all this is due to karma?

---

4. *Of Ill (Dukkha) and Sentient Organisms.*

Controverted Point.—That Ill is wholly bound up with sentience.

From the Commentary.—'Ill' [dukkha] must be understood in two ways: as bound up with and as not bound up with life [indriya's]. According to the former, Ill is referred to the seat of

---

[1] *Sutta-Nipāta*, verse 654.

[2] We cannot trace these four lines.

suffering; according to the latter, Ill covers liability to trouble through the law of impermanence with its 'coming to be and passing away.' But the Hetuvādins, for instance, do not draw this distinction. They hold that painful sentience alone constitutes that dukkha, to understand which the holy life, according to the teachings of the Exalted One, is led.

[1] *Th.*—But you commit yourself to saying this: that only that which is bound up with sentience is impermanent, and conditioned, has arisen through a cause, is liable to perish, to pass away, to lose desire, to cease, to change.[1] But are not all these terms suitable to insentient things?[2] You assent; but you refute your proposition in so doing.

[2] You mean, do you not, that what is *not* bound up with sentience is impermanent, etc., and yet is not Ill.[3] But if you call 'what *is* bound up with sentience' equally impermanent, etc., must you not also say that 'this is not ill'? If you deny, [and by your proposition you must deny], then must you not contrariwise include 'that which is *not* bound up with sentient life' under the notion of what '*is* ill'?

[3] Did not the Exalted One call whatever is impermanent Ill? And is not the insentient also impermanent?

[4] *H.*—You deny the accuracy of my proposition.[4]

[1] These all making up the content of the idea of Ill or sorrow or suffering. Cf. Ledi Sadaw, *JPTS*, 1914, p. 133.

[2] E.g., the earth, a hill, a rock, are insentient, and also impermanent. —*Comy.*

[3] Br. omits 'not.'

[4] 'Insentient objects cause both physical pain (dukkha) and grief (domanassa) to a sentient subject; for instance, fire in hot weather, or air in cold weather. Again, the destruction of property, etc., is always a source of mental pain. Hence the insentient may be called "Ill" even without a reference to the idea of impermanence; but as they are not produced by karma and corruption, they cannot be said to constitute the Ariyan fact of "Ill." Moreover, the destruction of grass, wood, etc., and of such physical things as seed, etc., does not constitute the Ariyan fact of the "cessation of Ill." It is the sentient that is both Ill and also an Ariyan fact. But the insentient is the former *only*, and not the latter. The Theravādin in denying the Hetuvādin's proposition shows this difference.'—*Comy.*

But you are thereby committed to this: that just as the higher life is lived under the Exalted One for understanding Ill as bound up with sentient life, it is also lived for the purpose of understanding Ill that is not bound up with sentient life.

Th.—Nay, that cannot truly be said.

H.—And you are further committed to this: that just as Ill that is bound up with sentient life, once it is thoroughly understood, does not again arise, neither does it again arise when it is not bound up with sentient life and is thoroughly understood.

You deny[1] . . . but I hold my proposition stands.

5. *Of 'save only the Ariyan Path.'*

Controverted Point.—That save only the Ariyan Path, all other conditioned things may be called 'Ill.'

From the Commentary.—This is held by such as the Hetuvādins, because the Ariyan Path was stated by the Exalted One in the Four Truths as 'a course going to the cessation of Ill.'[2]

[1] *Th.*—Then you call the Cause of Ill[3] also Ill? If you deny, you cannot maintain your proposition. If you assent, do you mean that there are but three Truths?[4] If you deny, your proposition falls. If you assent, do you not contradict the words of the Exalted One, that the Truths are four—Ill, Cause of Ill, Cessation of Ill, Way going to the Cessation of Ill?

[2] If now you admit that the Cause of Ill is also Ill, in what sense do you judge it to be so?

[1] Albeit the Theravādin makes these two denials, it is nevertheless orthodox to include impermanent insentient things in the category of Ill. Hence his denials must not be taken as proving the opponent's proposition.—*Comy.*

[2] In his first sermon, *Buddhist Suttas* (SBE, XI.), 148 f.; *Vinaya Texts*, i. 95; also in the Nikāyas, *passim*.

[3] The Second Truth.

[4] I.e., are the First and Second equal to each other?

H.—In the sense of impermanence.

Th.—But the Ariyan Path, is that impermanent?

H.—Yes.

Th.—Then is not that also Ill? . . .

You say then that the Path is impermanent but not Ill, while the Cause of Ill is both impermanent and Ill. [It is impossible for you to maintain such a position]. . . .

[3] *H.*—But if the Path be 'a way going to the cessation of Ill,' I maintain that, when we speak of all other conditioned things as Ill, this Ariyan Path is excepted.

---

6. *Of the Order and the Accepting of Gifts.*

Controverted Point.—That it ought not to be said 'The Order accepts gifts.'

From the Commentary.—This view is now held by those of the Vetulya[ka]s, who are known as the Mahāsuññatāvādins.[2] They believe that the Order, in the metaphysical sense [paramatthato] of the word, *is* the Paths and the Fruits. These cannot be said to accept anything.

[1] *Th.*—But is not the Order worthy of offerings of hospitality, of gifts, of salutations, as the world's supreme field of merit? How then can it be wrong to say it accepts gifts? [2] Were not its four pairs of men, its eight classes of individuals[3] declared by the Exalted One to be worthy of gifts? [3] And are there not they who give to it?

[4] Finally, was it not said by the Exalted One:—

> '*As doth the holy flame its offering,*
> *As doth the bounteous earth the summer rain,*
> *So doth the Order, in rapt thought expert,*
> *The Gift accept*'?[4]

Hence surely the Order accepts gifts.

[5] *M.*—But can a Path accept? Can Fruition accept? . . .

[1] See XXIII. 1.

[2] So PTS ed. Br. has 'Mahāpuññavādins.'

[3] *Dīgha-Nik.*, iii. 255.

[4] We cannot trace this passage.

7. *Of the Order and the Purifying of Gifts.*

Controverted Point.—That it ought not to be said that 'The Order purifies[1] gifts.'

From the Commentary.—Those who hold the view just discussed, hold as a corollary that Paths and Fruits are not able to purify gifts.

[1, 2] *Similar to* XVII., 6, §§ 1, 2.

[3] And are there not those who, having made a gift to the Order, make their offering effective? [2]

[4] *M.*—But does a Path, does Fruition 'purify'? . . .

---

8. *Of the Order and Daily Life.*

Controverted Point.—That it should not be said that 'The Order "enjoys," "eats," "drinks."'

The reason and the adherents as above.

[1] *Th.*—But you must admit that there are those who partake of the meals of the Order, both daily and on special occasions, both of rice-gruel and of drink.

[2] Moreover, did not the Exalted One speak of 'meals taken in company,' 'in turn,' 'of food left over,' and 'not left over'? [3] [3] And did He not speak of eight kinds of drinks:—'mango-syrup, jambu-syrup, plantain-syrup, môcha-syrup, honey-syrup, grape-juice, lilyroot-syrup, and phārusaka-syrup'? [4] How then can you maintain your view?

[4] *M.*—But does a Path, does Fruition 'enjoy,' 'eat,' 'drink'? . . .

[1] Visodheti—i.e., causes to fructify, makes more fruitful (in merit).—*Comy.*

[2] Dakkhiṇaŋ ārādheti, a less obvious phrasing than the instrumental phrase of the *Sutta-Nipāta*, verse 488, ārādhaye dakkhiṇeyyehi. 'They gain, they win great fruit even by a trifling offering. . . . Little (when so offered) becomes much, much becomes more.'—*Comy.* In the text the usual gifts to the Order are then detailed. See above, p. 199, § 3.

[3] *Vinaya Texts*, i. 38 f.

[4] *Ibid.*, ii. 132. The *Commentary* does not enrich our scanty knowledge about the less obvious kinds.

9. *Of the Order and the Fruit of Giving.*

Controverted Point.—That it should not be said that 'a thing given to the Order brings great reward.'

The reason and the adherents as above.

[1, 2] *Similar to* XVII. 6, §§ 1, 2.

[3] And was it not said by the Exalted One: '*Give, lady of the Gotamas, to the Order. In that giving thou shalt also render honour to me and to the Order*'?[1]

[4] Again, was it not said to the Exalted One by Sakka, ruler of the gods:

'*Of men who bring their offerings,*
Of creatures who for merit seek,
Makers of merit for fair doom:—
Where must they give to reap reward?

The four who practise in the Paths,
The four established in the Fruits:—
Such is the Order upright, true,
By wisdom and by virtue stayed.
Of men who bring their offerings,
Of creatures who for merit seek.
Makers of merit for fair doom,
Who to the Order make their gift:—
Theirs is't to reap a rich reward.'[2]

This Order sooth abounds and is grown great,
In measure as the waters of the sea,
These be the valiant students, best of men,
Light-bringers they who do the Norm proclaim.
They who because of them do give their gifts,
Oblations fair, and seemly sacrifice,
They to the Order loyal, firm in faith,
Commended by the wise, win great reward.
And mindful thenceforth of the offerings made,
Joy is their heritage[3] *while in this world.*

[1] *Majjhima-Nik.*, iii. 258. [2] *Saṃyutta-Nik.*, i. 233.

[3] The *V. V. Commentary* explains vedajātā by jātasomanassā.

Thereafter, conquerors of selfishness[1]
And of the root thereof, free from all blame,
Lo! to a brighter world they win their way!'[2]

Hence surely a thing given to the Order brings great reward.

---

10. *Of the Buddha and the Fruit of Giving.*

Controverted Point.—That it should not be said that 'Anything given to the Buddha brings great reward.'

From the Commentary.—From the same source comes the theory that because the Exalted Buddha did not really enjoy anything, but only seemed to be doing so out of conformity to life here below, nothing given him was really helpful to him.

[1] *Th.*—Now was not the Exalted One of all two-footed creatures the highest and best and foremost and uttermost, supreme, unequalled, unrivalled, peerless, incomparable, unique? How then could a gift to Him fail to bring great reward? [2] Are there any equal to Him in virtue, in will, in intellect?

[3] And was it not said by the Exalted One: '*Neither in this world nor in any other is any to be found better than, or equal to the Buddha who has reached the summit of them who are worthy of offerings, who are desirous of merit, who seek abundant fruit*'?[3]

Hence surely anything given to the Buddha brings great reward.

11. *Of the Sanctification of the Gift.*

Controverted Point.—That a gift is sanctified by the giver only, not by the recipient.

From the Commentary.—Some, like the Uttarāpathakas, hold this view for this reason: If a gift were sanctified by the recipient, it would become a great blessing. Now if the donor gives and the donee

---

[1] In the PTS edition read maccheramalaŋ samūlaŋ.

[2] *Vimāna-Vatthu*, 34, 25-27.

[3] Not traced.

produces the result, this would mean that the former causing the latter to act for him, his own happiness or misery would be wrought by another. In other words, one would sow, another reap. [This is heresy.][1]

[1] *Th.*—Now are not some who receive gifts 'worthy of offerings, attentions, gifts, salutations, the world's supreme field of merit'? [2] And did not the Exalted One pronounce the four pairs of men, the eight kinds of individuals to be worthy of gifts? [3] And are there not those who, having offered a gift to a Stream-Winner, Once-Returner, Never-Returner or Arahant, make the gift effective? How then can you maintain your proposition?

[4] *U.*—But if a gift may be sanctified by the recipient, does not he become the agent for quite a different person?[2] Does not one person work the happiness or the misery of another? Does not one sow, another reap?

Th.—Now was it not said by the Exalted One: '*There are four ways, Ānanda, of sanctifying a gift. Which are the four? A gift may be sanctified by the giver, not by the recipient; a gift may be sanctified by the recipient, not by the giver; or it may be sanctified by both; or, again, by neither*'?[3] Hence it is surely wrong to say: 'A gift is sanctified only by the giver, not by the recipient.'

[1] See above, I. 1 (p. 48 f.); XVI. 1-5; a perverse application of the doctrine of individual becoming and individual karma to two distinct contemporaneous individuals. Cf. *Buddhism*, London, 1912, p. 134.

[2] Añño aññassa kārako. This question would be reasonable if the opponent had meant that the donor's will is moved to act (literally, be done) by the donee. But he meant that the donor's will is sanctified, purified, in the sense of great fructification depending upon the person of the donee. Hence the question is to no purpose.—*Comy.*

[3] *Majjhima-Nik.*, iii. 256; cf. *Dīgha-Nik.*, iii. 231; *Anguttara-Nik.*, ii. 80 f. (order of third and fourth alternatives reversed in all three).

BOOK XVIII

1. *Of the Buddha and this World.*

Controverted Point.—That it is not right to say 'The Exalted Buddha lived in the world of mankind.'

From the Commentary.—Some, like the Vetulyakas,[1] carelessly interpreting the Sutta, 'born in the world, grew up in the world, dwelt, having overcome the world, undefiled by the world,' hold that the Exalted One, when born in the heaven of Delight,[2] dwelt there while visiting this world only in a shape specially created. Their citation of the Sutta proves nothing, since the Master was undefiled, not by being out of the world, but by the corruptions of heart with respect to the things in the world.

[1] *Th.*—But are there not shrines, parks, settlements, villages, towns, kingdoms, countries mentioned by the Buddha?[3] [2] And was he not born at Lumbinī, super-enlightened under the Bôdhi tree? Was not the Norm-wheel set rolling by him at Benares? Did he not renounce the will to live at the Chāpāla shrine?[4] Did he not complete existence at Kusinārā?

[3] Moreover, was it not said by the Exalted One: '*Bhikkhus, I was once staying at Ukkaṭṭhā in the Subhaga*

[1] See above, XVII. 6.

[2] Tusita-bhavana. This was traditionally the Buddha's last celestial life (*Pss. of the Sisters*, 8).

[3] Reading Buddha-vuttāni with Br. and the PTS edition. The Siamese printed edition reads -vutthāni, 'dwelt in by the Buddha.' Either compound is very uncommon in older Pali.

[4] *Dialogues*, ii. 113. 'Sankhāra' may be used for cetanā, the foremost of the sankhāra's.

Wood by the King's-Sāl Tree.'[1] . . . '*I was once staying at Uruvelā by the Goatherds' Banyan before I was super-enlightened.*[2] . . . *I was once staying at Rājagaha in the Bamboo Wood at the Squirrels' Feeding-ground. . . . I was once staying at Sāvatthī in Jeta's Wood, Anāthapiṇḍika's Park. . . . I was once staying at Vesālī in the Great Wood at the Gable House Hall*'?

Surely then the Exalted Buddha lived among men.

[4] *V.*—But did not the Exalted One, '*born in the world, enlightened in the world, live, having overcome the world, undefiled by the world*'?[3]

Hence it is surely not right to say 'The Exalted Buddha lived in the world of mankind.'[4]

---

2. *Of how the Norm was taught.*

Controverted Point.—That it is not right to say 'The Exalted Buddha himself taught the Norm.'

From the Commentary.—This is another point in the foregoing heresy. The created shape taught the Norm on earth to the Venerable Ānanda, while the Exalted One lived in the city of Delight and sent forth that shape.

[1] *Th.*—By whom then was it taught?

V.—By the special creation.

Th.—Then must this created thing have been the Conqueror, the Master, the Buddha Supreme, the Omni-

[1] *Majjhima-Nik.*, i. 326.

[2] *Saṃyutta-Nik.*, v. 185. The Buddha is in many Suttas related to have been staying at each of these places, and as telling 'bhikkhus that he had done so on this or that occasion.

[3] *Saṃyutta-Nik.*, iii. 140, where the first two words quoted—l o k e j ā t o—seem to have been omitted.

[4] On this 'Docetic' heresy, which throve later among Mahāyānist Buddhists, Prof. Anesaki's article, *s.v.* 'Docetism,' *Ency. Religion and Ethics*, should be consulted.

scient, All-seeing, Lord of all things, Judge of Appeal of all things! . . .[1]

[2] I ask again: By whom was the Norm taught?

V.—By the venerable Ānanda.

Th.—Then must he too have been the Conqueror, the Master, etc. [3] But was it not said by the Exalted One: *Sāriputta, I may teach the Norm concisely and I may teach it in detail, and I may teach it both ways. It is only they who understand that are hard to find'* ?[2]

Hence surely the Buddha himself taught the Norm.

[4] And again, was it not said by the Exalted One: '*By the higher knowledge, bhikkhus, do I teach the Norm, not without the higher knowledge; a Norm with [reference to] cause do I teach, not one without; a wonder-working Norm do I teach, and none not wonder-working. And that I, bhikkhus, thus teach the Norm, a homily should be made, instruction should be given, to wit, let this, bhikkhus, suffice for your content, let this suffice for your satisfaction and for your gladness:—the Exalted One is Buddha Supreme! the Norm is well revealed! the Order is well trained! Now when this declaration was uttered, ten thousand world-systems trembled'* ?[3]

Hence surely the Exalted Buddha himself taught the Norm.

---

3. *Of the Buddha and Pity.*

Controverted Point.—That the Exalted Buddha felt no pity.

From the Commentary.—The procedure of those who have not conquered their passions, on the occasion of misfortune, to the objects of their affection, inclines the beholder to say that compassion is only

---

[1] Of these eight titles, the first three are frequent in the Nikāyas; the last four are found usually in later books; but *Anguttara-Nik.*, i. 199, has the last one: dhammā Bhagavaŋ-paṭisaraṇā.

[2] *Anguttara-Nik.*, i. 133.

[3] This passage is found *verbatim* to "well trained" at *Anguttara-Nik.*, i. 276. The burden of it does not constitute one of the Eight Causes of Earthquake enumerated in *Dialogues*, ii. 114 f. But cf. *ibid.* 112; i. 55.

passion. Hence some, like the Uttarāpathakas, judge that the passionless Buddha felt no compassion.

[1] *Th.*—But this implies that neither did he feel love or sympathetic joy or equanimity. You deny. [2] But could he have these and yet lack pity?[1]

[3] Your proposition implies also that he was ruthless. Yet you agree that the Exalted One was pitiful, kindly to the world, compassionate towards the world, and went about to do it good.[2] [4] Nay, did not the Exalted One win to the attainment of universal pity?[3]

[5] *U.*—But if there was no passion (rāga) in the Exalted One, surely there was in him no compassion (karuṇā)?

---

4. *Of the Buddha and Fragrant Things.*

Controverted Point.—That [even] the excreta of the Exalted Buddha excelled all other odorous things.

From the Commentary.—Out of an indiscriminate affection for the Buddha, certain of the Andhakas and Uttarāpathakas hold this view.

[1] *Th.*—This would imply that the Exalted One fed on perfumes. But you admit only that he fed on rice gruel. Hence your proposition is untenable.

[2] Moreover, if your proposition were true, some would have used them for the toilet, gathering, saving them in basket and box, exposing them in the bazaar, making cosmetics with them. But nothing of the sort was done. . . .

---

5. *Of a One and Only Path.*

Controverted Point.—That the fourfold fruition of the religious life is realized by one path only.

[1] Referring to the Four Sublime Moods or Infinitudes, exercises in the development of these emotions. See above, p. 76, *n.* 2. It is noteworthy that the opponent does not reserve the last of them, 'equanimity,' as alone predicable, from *his* point of view, of the Buddha.

[2] Except the third, these phrases are hard to trace in the Nikāyas, albeit the ascription in other terms is frequent enough.

[3] See *Paṭisambhidā-Magga*, i. 126 f., 'The Tathāgata's Insight by Great Pity.'

From the Commentary.—The same sectaries, on the same grounds, hold that the Exalted One, in becoming Stream-Winner, Once-Returner, Never-Returner, Arahant, realized all these four Fruits by one single Ariyan Path [and not in the four distinct stages each called a path].

[1] *Th.*—This implies a fusion of the four distinct conscious procedures [experienced in each stage of progress], which you deny.

Moreover, if there be one path only, which of the four is it?

A. U.—The path of Arahantship.

Th.—But do we teach that by that path the three first of the ten Fetters are removed—to wit, theory of soul, doubt, and infection of mere rule and ritual? Did not the Exalted One say that these are removed by the Stream-Winning Path?

[2] And are gross passions and malevolence removed by the path of Arahantship? Did not the Exalted One say that the fruit of the Once-Returner was the state of having reduced these to a minimum? [3] And is it by the path of Arahantship that that minimum is removed? You know it is not. If you assent, I can refer you to the words of the Exalted One, who said that the fruit of the Never-Returner was the state of having removed that minimum without remainder.

[4] *A.U.*—But if we are wrong, and the Exalted One developed each Path in succession, can he be called Stream-Winner and so on? You deny, but you have implied it.[1]

[5] *Th.*—But if the Exalted One realized these four fruits of the religious life by one Ariyan Path only, and the disciples by four Paths, they have seen what he did not see, they arrive at where he did not arrive, they realize that which he did not realize. You cannot admit this . . .

---

6. *Of the Transition from One Jhāna to Another.*

Controverted Point.—That we pass from one Jhāna to another [immediately].

[1] On the theory, combated above, IV. 4, 9, that past acquisitions remain permanent possessions instead of being wrought up into higher powers. See also p. 66, and *Saṃyutta-Nik.*, v. 356 f.

From the Commentary.—Some, like the Mahiŋsāsakas and certain of the Andhakas, hold that the formula of the Four Jhānas [in the Suttas] warrants us in concluding that progress from one Jhāna-stage to another is immediate without any accessory procedure.

[1] *Th.*—Does this imply that one can pass over from First to Third, from Second to Fourth Jhāna? You deny [setting an arbitrary limit]. . . .

[2] Or take only a passing over from First Jhāna attainment to that of Second—which you affirm to be possible—you are implying that the mental process—adverting, reflecting, co-ordinating, attending, willing, wishing, aiming[1] —called up for First Jhāna is the same as that required for Second Jhāna. But you dissent. Do you mean that no [preliminary] mental process of adverting, etc., is required for Second Jhāna? On the contrary, you agree that Second Jhāna arises after a certain mental process—adverting, etc. Therefore one does *not* pass over directly from First Jhāna to the next.

[3] [Again, take the objects and characteristics of First Jhāna.] The First Stage, you admit, may come to pass while one is considering the harmfulness of sense-desires;[2] moreover, it is accompanied by application and sustentation of thought. But neither that object nor these characteristics, you must admit, belong to the Second Stage. Yet your proposition really commits you to asserting identity between First and Second Jhāna.

[4] The same argument [2] applies to transition from Second to Third Jhāna. [5] [Again, take the specific objects and characteristics of the Second Stage:] the Second Stage, you admit, may come to pass while one is considering the harmfulness of application and sustentation of thought; moreover, it is accompanied by zest. But neither that object nor these characteristics, you must admit, belong to the Third Stage. Yet your proposition really commits you

[1] Cf. VII. 5, § 2.

[2] Kāma; the object being to supersede earthly consciousness (that of the Kāma-lōka) by a heavenly or angelic consciousness (that of the Rūpa-lōka).

to an assertion of identity between Second and Third Jhāna.

[6] The same argument [2, 4] applies to transition from Third to Fourth Jhāna. [7] [Again, take the specific objects and characteristics of the Third Stage:] the Third Stage, you admit, may come to pass while one is considering the harmfulness of zest; moreover, it is accompanied by happiness. But neither that object nor these characteristics, you must admit, belong to the Fourth Stage. Yet your proposition really commits you to an assertion of identity between Third and Fourth Jhāna.

[8] *M. A.*—But was it not said by the Exalted One: '*Here, bhikkhus, when a bhikkhu, aloof from sense-desires, etc. . . attains to and abides in First . . . Fourth Jhāna*'?[1]

According to that [formula] one does pass over immediately from Jhāna to Jhāna.

---

7. *Of Jhāna and its Intervals.*

Controverted Point.—That there is an intermediate stage between the First and Second Stages.[2]

From the Commentary.—The Sammitiyas and certain other of the Andhakas hold the view that, in the Fivefold Jhāna series,[3] the Exalted One did not intend to classify, but only to indicate, three forms[4] of concentration. But not knowing that form of concentration to be possible which is accompanied by sustained thought (s a v i c ā r a), and counting only initial application (v i t a k k a), they hold that the former intervenes between First and Second Jhāna, thus making up a later fivefold series.

---

[1] E.g., *Dialogues*, i. 84 f.; *passim* in Nikāyas.

[2] The words 'First,' etc., to 'Fourth,' in this discourse must be understood solely with reference to the fourfold classification.

[3] I.e., when First Jhāna is divided into two, according as it is accompanied or unaccompanied by initial application of thought. See *Bud. Psy. Eth.*, cf. p. 43 with p. 52. The Four Nikāyas recognize only four stages.

[4] Namely, as specified above, IX. 8, §§ 3, 4. The first and second divide First Jhāna into two aspects, the third refers to the other three Jhānas.

[1] *Th.*—But this is to imply intervening stages between contact or feeling, or perception. . . .

Again, why deny intermediate stages between Second and Third, or Third and Fourth Jhāna? If you deny them here, you must deny them between First and Second Jhāna. [3] You cannot maintain the intermediate stages between First and Second Jhāna only, [4] denying the existence of such stages between the others.

[5] You say that concentration of mind accompanied by sustained thought only, without its initial application, constitutes the intermediate stage. But why make an exception in this way? Or why not include the other two forms, accompanied by both or by neither? [6] If you deny that concentration with or without initial and sustained application of thought is a Jhānic interval, why not deny it in the case of concentration without initial application, but with sustentation of thought?

[7] You maintain that in the interval between the manifestation of two stages of Jhāna there is concentration in sustained thought only, without initial application of thought. But while such concentration is proceeding, is not the first Jhāna at an end and the second Jhāna manifested? You assent, but you contradict thus your proposition.

[8] *S. A.*—If we are wrong, does concentration in sustained thought only, without initial application of thought, constitute any one of the Four Jhānas? You say, no. Then it must constitute an interim state—which is what we affirm.

[9] *Th.*—But did not the Exalted One declare three forms of concentration, namely, in both applied and sustained thought, in the latter only, and where there is neither?[1] If so, you cannot single out the second form of concentration as a state intermediate between Jhānas.

[1] *Saṃyutta-Nik.*, iv. 363, etc. See above, IX. 8, § 4. For those unacquainted with the classic procedure in Jhāna, it may be explained that whereas, in the first stage of attained ecstasy, consciousness includes (*a*) initial and sustained application of thought, (*b*) zest,

8. *Of Hearing in Jhāna.*

Controverted Point.—That one who has attained Jhāna hears sound.

From the Commentary.—The opinion is held by some—the Pubbaseliyans, for instance—that because the Exalted One called sound a thorn to First Jhāna, and since sound, if not heard, cannot be a thorn in the flesh of one who had attained that state, it was inferable that such an one was able to hear.

[1] *Th.*—If so, it must be equally allowed that he can also see, smell, taste and touch objects.[1] This you deny . . . You must also allow that he enters Jhāna enjoying auditory consciousness. You deny, for you agree that concentration arises in one who is enjoying *mental* objects as such? [2] But if you admit that anyone who is actually enjoying sounds hears sounds, and that concentration is the property of one who is actually enjoying mental objects as such, you should not affirm that one in the concentration of Jhāna hears sounds. If you insist that he does, you have here two parallel mental procedures going on at the same time. . . .

[3] *P.*—But was it not said by the Exalted One that *sound is a thorn for First Jhāna?*[2] Hence one in Jhāna can surely hear sound.

Th.—You say that one in Jhāna can hear sound, and quote the Word as to it being for First Jhāna a 'thorn.' Now it was further said that thought applied and sustained is a thorn for Second Jhāna—does one in Second Jhāna have applied and sustained thought? . . . Again, it was further said that the mental factor last eliminated is a thorn

---

(c) pleasure, in the *second* stage (*a*) is eliminated, in the *third* (*b*), and in the fourth (*c*) are eliminated. Now, in 'fivefold Jhāna,' (*a*) was resolved into two stages. (*Theragāthā*, 916, gives a different pañcangiko samādhi.)

[1] 'But there is no five-door procedure (of sense) in Jhāna.'—*Comy.*

[2] *Anguttara-Nik.*, v. 133-135. 'This was said because sound induces distraction. When a loud noise strikes the ear, one is aroused from First Jhāna.'—*Comy.* See above, p. 123.

for the stage newly attained—zest for Third, respiration for Fourth Jhāna,[1] perception of visible objects for consciousness of space-infinity, this perception for that of consciousness as infinite, this perception for that of nothingness, perception and feeling for cessation of these in trance. Now is 'the thorn' actually present on the winning of the stage whence it is pronounced to be a thorn? If not, then how can you say that the 'thorn' of hearing sound is present to one in First Jhāna?

---

9. *Of the Eye and Seeing.*

Controverted Point.—That we see visible objects with the eye.

From the Commentary.—Here, judging by the Word—'*When he sees an object with the eye*'—some, like the Mahāsanghikas, hold that the sentient surface in the eye is that which 'sees.'

In the quoted passage the method of naming a necessary instrument is followed,[2] as when we say 'wounded by a bow,' when the wound was inflicted by an arrow. So the words 'sees with the eye' are spoken of a seeing by visual consciousness.

[1] *Th.*—Then you hold that we see matter by matter. . . . You deny. But think! And if you now assent,[3] you imply that matter is able to distinguish matter. You deny. But think! And if you now assent, you imply that matter is mind. . . .[4]

[2] Again, you are implying that the eye can 'advert' or reflect, co-ordinate, will, etc.,[5] albeit you agree that the contrary is true.

[1] So the Sutta. We should have expected sukha (pleasure or happiness). See Jhāna formula.

[2] Sambhāra-kathā. Cf. *Atthasālinī*, 399 f. in *Bud. Psy. Eth.*, p. 351, *n.* 2.

[3] 'First he rejects, because of the [separate] category, "object of vision"; then assents, with respect only to the eye.'—*Comy.*

[4] Rūpaŋ manoviññāṇaŋ.

[5] As in VII. 5, § 2. If the 'eye' sees, it should be immediately preceded by 'adverting' in the same way as the sense of sight (cakkhu-viññāṇa).—*Comy.*

[3, 4] These arguments hold good for similar claims put forward by you for the other four senses.

[5] *M.*—But was it not said by the Exalted One: '*Here, bhikkhus, a bhikkhu sees objects with the eye, hears sounds, and so on*'?[1] Hence surely we see visible objects with the eye and so on.

[1] *Dhammasangaṇi*, § 597, gives the passage *verbatim* as to the process—cakkhunā . . . rūpaŋ . . . passati; but though allusions to the visual process abound in the Nikāyas, we have not traced the exact passage as in an exhortation to bhikkhus, except in the 'Guarded Doors' formula, e.g., *Saŋyutta-Nik.*, iv. 104, where the formula has disvā, 'having seen,' for passati, 'sees.'

BOOK XIX

1. *Of getting rid of Corruption.*

Controverted Point.—That we may extirpate corruptions past, future, and present.[1]

From the Commentary.—Inasmuch as there is such a thing as putting away corruptions, and for one in whom this is completed both past and future, as well as present, corruptions are put away, therefore some—certain of the Uttarāpathakas, for instance—hold that we can now put away the corruptions of our past, etc.

[1] *Th.*—In other words, we may stop that which has ceased, dismiss that which has departed, destroy that which is destroyed, finish that which is finished efface that which has vanished. For has not the past ceased? Is it not non-existent? . . .

[2] And as to the future, you imply that we can produce the unborn, bring forth the non-nascent, bring to pass the unhappened, make patent that which is latent. . . . For is not the future unborn? Is it not non-existent? . . .

[3] And as to the present: does the lustful put away lust, the inimical put away hate, the confused put away dulness, the corrupt put away corruption? Or can we put away lust by lust, and so on? You deny all this. But did you not affirm that we can put away present corruptions? . . .

Is lust and is 'Path' a factor in conscious experience?[2] You assent, of course. But can there be a parallel con-

[1] For the 'ten corruptions,' see above, pp. 65, *n.* 4, 66, *n.* 4. On [1] f. cf. p. 85, § 2 f.

[2] Literally, 'conjoined with consciousness.' We cannot at the same time give play to immoral thought and be developing the Ariyan mind.

scious procedure [of both] at the same time? . . . If lust be immoral, and 'Path' moral consciousness, can moral and immoral, faulty and innocent, base and noble, sinister and clear mental states co-exist side by side [at the same moment]? You deny. Think again. Yes, you now reply. But was it not said by the Exalted One: '*There are four things, bhikkhus, very far away one from the other: what are the four? The sky and the earth, the hither and the yonder shore of the ocean, whence the sun rises and where he sets, the norm of the good and that of the wicked. Far is the sky, etc. . . .*'?[1]

Hence those mental opposites cannot co-exist side by side.

[4] *U.*—But if it be wrong to say 'we can put away past, future, and present corruptions,' is there no such thing as the extirpation of corruptions? You admit there is. Then my proposition stands.[2]

---

2. *Of the Void.*

Controverted Point.—That 'the Void' is included in the aggregate of mental co-efficients (sankhārakkhandha).

From the Commentary.—'The Void [or Emptiness] has two implications: (*a*) Absence of soul, which is the salient feature of the five aggregates [mind and body]; and (*b*) Nibbāna itself. As to (*a*), some marks of 'no-soul' may be included under mental coefficients (the fourth aggregate) by a figure of speech.[3] Nibbāna is not included thereunder. But some, like the Andhakas, drawing no such distinction, hold the view stated above.

[1] *Th.*—Do you then imply that the 'Signless,' that the 'Not-hankered-after' is also so included? If not, 'the

[1] See VII. 5, § 3, for the full quotation.

[2] The putting away of corruptions, past, future, or present, is not a work comparable to the exertions of a person clearing away rubbish-heaps. With the following of the Ariyan Path having Nibbāna as its object, the corruptions are 'put away' simply because they don't get born. In other words, the past has ceased; the cure as to present and future is preventive.—*Comy.*

[3] Ekena pariyāyena. Marks of other aggregates cannot be so included, even by way of figurative speech.

Void' cannot be,[1] [2] for you cannot predicate of the last that which you deny of the former two.

[3] Again, if the fourth aggregate be made to include 'the Void,' it must be not impermanent, not arisen through a cause, not liable to perish, nor to lose lust, nor to cease, nor to change!

[4] Moreover, is the 'emptiness' of the material aggregate included under the fourth aggregate? Or the 'emptiness' of the second, third, and fifth aggregates thereunder? Or is the 'emptiness' of the fourth aggregate itself included under any of the other four? [5] If the one inclusion is wrong, so are all the other inclusions.

[5] *A.*—But was it not said by the Exalted One: '*Empty is this,*[2] *bhikkhus—the* s a n k h ā r a'*s—either of soul or of what belongs to soul'?*

---

3. *Of the Fruits of Life in Religion.*

Controverted Point.—That the fruit of recluseship is unconditioned.

From the Commentary.—Our doctrine has judged that the term 'fruits of life in religion' means the mind in general which results from the processes of thought in the Ariyan Path, and occurs in the mental process attending the attainment of its Fruits. But there are some, like the Pubbaseliyas, who, taking it otherwise, mean by it just the putting away of corruptions and success therein.[3]

---

[1] All three being names for Nibbāna, they are adduced to expose the flaw in a theory which does not discriminate.—*Comy.* Cf. *Compendium*, p. 216.

[2] See I. 1, §§ 241, 242. The nearest *verbatim* reference that we can trace is *Saŋyutta-Nik.*, iv. 296; but even there the word s a n k h ā r ā, which here seems dragged in by the opponent, is omitted. 'The *Theravādin* suffers it to stand, because it is not inconsistent with the orthodox "s a b b e s a n k h ā r ā a n i c c ā," where s a n k h ā r ā stands for all five aggregates [exhausting all conditioned things].'—*Comy.*

[3] Hence unconditioned, i.e., unprepared, uncaused, unproduced by the four conditions—karma, mind, food, or physical environment (u t u). Cf. *Compendium*, p. 161.

[1] *Th.*—Do you then identify that 'fruit' with Nibbāna:—the Shelter, the Cave, the Refuge, the Goal, the Past-Decease, the Ambrosial?[1] Or are there two 'unconditioned's'? You deny both alternatives [but you must assent to one or the other]. If to the latter, I ask are they both . . . Nibbānas, and is there one higher than the other, . . . or is there a boundary . . . an interstice between them?[2]

[2] Again, do you imply that recluseship itself is unconditioned? 'No, conditioned,' you say. Then is its fruit or reward conditioned? . . .

[3, 4] You admit, again, that the four stages in the recluse's Ariyan Path—the Four Paths—are conditioned. Yet you would deny that the Four Fruits are conditioned!

[5] In fact, you would have in these four and Nibbāna five 'unconditioned's.' Or if you identify the four with Nibbāna, you then get five sorts of Nibbāna, five Shelters, and so on. . . .

---

4. *Of Attainment* (*patti*).

Controverted Point.—That attainment is unconditioned.

From the Commentary.—Some, like the Pubbaseliyas again, hold that the winning of any acquisition is itself unconditioned.

[1] *Is similar to* § 1 *in the foregoing.*

[2-4] *Th.*—Again, do you imply that the winning [through gifts] of raiment, almsfood, lodging, medicine, is unconditioned? But if so, the same difficulty arises as in the case of attainment in general (§ 1). In fact, you would have in these four and Nibbāna five 'unconditioned's.'

[5, 6] A similar argument is used for the winning of any of the Rūpa Jhānas (4), or of the Arūpa Jhānas (4), or of the Four Paths and Four Fruits, concluding with:—In fact, you would have in these eight and Nibbāna nine 'unconditioned's,' etc.

[1] Cf. VI. 1, § 1.

[2] *Ibid.* The text abbreviates even more than we do.

[7] *P.*—But if I am wrong, can you identify winning with any one of the five aggregates, bodily or mental?

If not, then it is unconditioned.

---

5. *Of 'Thusness.'*

Controverted Point.—That the fundamental characteristics of all things (*sabba-dhammā*) are unconditioned.

From the Commentary.—Some, like the Uttarāpathakas, hold that there is an immutable something called thusness (or suchness)[1] in the very nature of all things, material or otherwise [taken as a whole]. And because this 'thusness' is not included in the [particular] conditioned matter, etc., itself, therefore it is unconditioned.

[1] *Th.*—Do you then identify those fundamental characteristics or 'thusness' with Nibbāna, the Shelter . . . the Goal, the Past-deceased, the Ambrosial? Or are there two 'unconditioned's'? You deny both alternatives [but you must assent to one or the other]. If to the latter, I ask, are there two kinds of Shelters and so on? And is there a boundary or . . . interstice between them?

[2] Again, assuming a materiality (rūpatā) of matter or body, is not materiality unconditioned? You assent. Then I raise the same difficulties as before.

[3] I raise them, too, if you admit a 'hedonality' of feeling,[2] a 'perceivability' of perception,[2] a saṅkhāratā or

[1] Tathatā. The Br. translation renders this by 'immutable reality.' Cf. VI. 6, above. Br. reads here, differently from PTS edition: sabbadhammānaŋ rūpādibhāvasankhatā tathatā nāma atthi. On the metaphysical expansion of the notion, rendered by those who have translated Aśvaghoṣa from the Chinese as tathāta see T. Suzuki's *Awakening of Faith*, p. 58, etc. Tathatā does not occur again throughout the Piṭakas. The *Commentary* attaches no increased interest or importance to the term, and the argument in the text is exactly like that in the foregoing discourse. But because of the importance ascribed to 'thusness' or 'suchness' by certain of the Mahāyānists, and because of the unique abstract forms coined for the argument, we do not condense this exposition.

[2] Vedanatā, saññatā.

co-efficiency of mental co-efficients, a consciousness of being conscious.[1] If all these be unconditioned, are there then six categories of 'unconditioned's'?

[4] *U.*—But if I am wrong, is the 'thusness' of all things the five aggregates [taken together]?

Th.—Yes.

U.—Then that 'thusness' of all things is unconditioned.

---

6. *Of Nibbāna as Morally Good.*

Controverted Point.—That the element (or sphere)[2] of Nibbāna is good.

From the Commentary.—All 'good' mental states are so called, either because they can, as faultless, insure a desirable result-in-sentience (vipāka), or because they as faultless are free from the corruptions. The idea of faultlessness is applied to all except immoral states. The desirable result takes effect in a future rebirth, either at conception or later. The first term in the triad:—good, bad, indifferent—applies to the moral cause producing such a result. But the Andhakas makes no such distinction, and call Nibbāna 'good' just because it is a faultless state.

[1] *Th.*—Do you imply that it has a mental object, involving a mental process of adverting, reflecting, co-ordinating, attending, willing, desiring, aiming? Is not rather the opposite true?

[2] These things we can predicate of all morally good mental states—of disinterestedness, love, intelligence, faith, energy, mindfulness, concentration, understanding. But if we cannot predicate them of Nibbāna, then is the element of Nibbāna not rightly called morally good.

[3] *A.*—But is not the element of Nibbāna faultless? If so—and you do assent—then it, not being *im*moral, is moral.

[1] Viññāṇassa viññāṇatā.

[2] Nibbāna-dhātu, Nibbāna considered in itself, independently coming to pass, ultimate, irreducible.

7. *Of Assurance which is not Final.*

Controverted Point.—That the average man may possess final assurance.[1]

From the Commentary.—Certain of the Uttarāpathakas, judging by the Sutta—'*once immersed is so once for all,*' etc.[2]—hold the view above stated.

[1] *Th.*—Do you mean that he has that assurance even if he commit the worst crimes—matricide, parricide, Arahanticide, wounding a Buddha, breaking up the Order? 'Nay,' you say.[3]

Again, could an average man holding that assurance feel doubt about it? 'Yes,' you say. Then he cannot feel assured.

[2] Surely you agree that, if he feel assured, he cannot feel doubt.[4] Now has he put away doubt? 'No,' you say.[5] But think! You now assent.[6] Then has he put away doubt by the First Path? or the Second, Third, or Fourth Path? How, then?

U.—By a bad path.

Th.—[Do you tell me that] a bad path leads aright, goes to the destruction [of lust, hate, etc.], goes to enlightenment, is immune from intoxicants, is undefiled? Is it not the opposite of all this? . . .

[3] Could the Annihilationist view be adopted by a person assured and convinced of the truth of the Eternalist

[1] Accanta, i.e., ati + anta, very final. The Br. translator renders this by 'true,' because all assurance for a finite period is not a true assurance. Thus our conviction that the sun will rise to-morrow, though it is exceedingly likely to be justified, is based only on a *belief* that no cosmic dislocation will intervene, and is therefore no 'true' assurance either.

[2] See next page.

[3] 'The heretic, incorrigible as a tree-stump, is more or less assured of cherishing his fixed opinions in other future existences. But the matricide, etc., is assured of retribution in the next existence only. Hence he must reject.'—*Comy.*

[4] 'He assents, because a man cannot doubt his own opinion if it be repeatedly cherished.'—*Comy.*

[5] 'Because it has not been put away by the Ariyan Path.'—*Comy.*

[6] Doubt not overriding the cherished opinion.—*Comy.*

view?[1] 'Yes,' you say. Surely then the assurance of the average man in his Annihilationist convictions is no 'infinite assurance.'

[4] If you now deny in reply to my question, I ask again, has he put away [the Annihilationist view]? If so, by which of the Four Paths? You reply, as before, 'By a bad path.' That is to say, by a bad path he puts away a bad view. . . .

[5, 6] A similar argument may be put forward for an Annhilationist who adopts the Eternalist view.

[7] *U.*—If I am wrong,[2] was it not said by the Exalted One: '*Take the case, bhikkhus, of a person whose mental states are entirely black-hearted*[3] *and immoral—he it is who, once immersed, is so once for all*'?[4]

Surely then any average man can attain infinite assurance.

[8] *Th.*—Is that which you have quoted your reason for maintaining your proposition? You admit it is. Now the Exalted One said further: '*Take the case, bhikkhus, of a person who, having come to the surface, is immersed.*' Now is this [supposed to be] happening all the time?[5] Of course not. . . . [9] But again he said: '*Take the case, bhikkhus, of a person who, having emerged, so [remains]; of one who, having emerged, discerns, glances around; of one who, having emerged, swims across; of one who, having emerged, wins a footing on the shore.*'

Now is each of these persons doing so all the time?

And does any of these cases furnish you with a reason for saying that any average person can have final assurance [in his convictions]?

[1] In the eternal duration of soul and universe. The former view holds that the soul ends at death. *Dialogues*, i. 50, § 32.

[2] In the *Commentary*, PTS edition, p. 181, line 14, read **pucchā paravādissa. Suttassa.** . . .

[3] **Ekanta-kāḷakā . . . dhammā.**

[4] *Anguttara-Nik.*, iv. 11, the 'water-parable' of seven classes of persons. Discussed in *Puggala-Paññatti*, 71.

[5] The Theravādin asks this question in order to show the necessity of a critical study, by research, of the spirit of Texts, without relying too much on the letter.—*Comy.*

8. *Of the Moral Controlling Powers.*[1]

Controverted Point.—That the five moral controlling powers—faith, effort, mindfulness, concentration. understanding—are not valid as 'controlling powers' in worldly matters.

From the Commentary.—This is an opinion held by some, like the Hetuvādins and Mahiŋsāsakas.

[1] *Th.*—Do you imply that there can be no faith, or effort, or mindfulness, or concentration, or understanding in worldly concerns? You deny. [2] On the other hand, you maintain that there is faith, etc., in such a connection, but that none of them avail for moral control.

[3] You admit that both mind and mind as a controlling power are valid in worldly matters. And you admit a similar validity in both joy and joy as a controlling power, in both psychic life and psychic life as a controlling power.

[4] Why then exempt those five?

[5] Again, you admit that there is both a spiritual[2] faith and a controlling power of that faith—why not both a worldly faith and a worldly controlling power of faith? And so for the rest. [6] Why accept in the one case, deny in the other?

[7] Moreover, was it not said by the Exalted One: '*And I, bhikkhus, with the eyes of a Buddha surveying the world, saw beings living whose vision was dim with dust, in some but slightly, greatly in others, beings whose faculties were here keen, there blunt, of good disposition . . . apt to learn . . . some among them discerning the danger and defect of [rebirth in] other worlds*'?[3]

Surely then the five moral controlling powers are valid in worldly matters.

[1] Or five faculties or factors of 'moral sense' (**indriya**). See above, pp. 16; 65 f.; 194, *n.* 1. These five are pre-eminent in doctrine as ranking among the 'thirty-seven factors of Enlightenment.'

[2] Or supra-mundane and mundane.

[3] *Dialogues*, ii. 31 f. The two lacunæ (of one word each) occur in both Br. and PTS editions.

BOOK XX

1. *Of Unintentional Crime.*

Controverted Point.—That the five cardinal crimes, even when unintentionally committed, involve retribution immediately after death.

From the Commentary. – Inasmuch as the grounds for immediate retribution after death are very weighty and grave, some—for instance, the Uttarāpathakas—hold that even the unintentional infliction of such injuries calls for it.

[1] *Th.*—But you imply that if I accidentally take away life, I am a murderer, [2] and [similarly as to two of the other four wicked deeds forbidden by morality] that if I accidentally take what is not given, I am a thief . . . if I utter untruths unintentionally, I am a liar. You deny. Yet you wish to make exceptions [to the relative innocence of such acts] in just those five serious cases. . . .

[3] Can you cite me a Sutta judging *un*intentional crime like that which says: '*He that intentionally takes his mother's life incurs immediate retribution*'?[1] You cannot. Neither can you maintain your proposition.

[4] *U.*—But does not the fact remain that the mother's life is taken?[2] Surely then the unintentional slayer also incurs immediate retribution. [5-7] Similarly, too, does

[1] We cannot trace this passage. So far as his own future is concerned, the individual's mental acts rather than his deeds create it. Cf. *Majjhima-Nik.*, i. 372 f ; cf. iii. 207. See above, 80, *n.* 5; cf. 274.

[2] This question is answered in the affirmative with reference to accidental loss of life under medical treatment.—*Comy.*

one who unintentionally kills father or Arahant, or sheds a Buddha's blood, incur a like doom.

[8] *Th.*—[Now as to the fifth of such crimes]: do you imply that all schismatics incur such a doom? You deny. But think again! You now assent.[1] But does a schismatic who is conscious of right incur it? You deny. But think again! You now assent. But was it not said by the Exalted One: '*There is a kind of schismatic, Upāli, who incurs disaster, purgatory, misery for an æon, who is incurable; there is a kind of schismatic, Upāli, who does not incur such a doom, who is not incurable*'?[2]

Hence it is not right to say that a schismatic who is conscious of [stating what is] right incurs such a doom.

[9] *U.*—But was it not said by the Exalted One: '*He who breaks up the Order is doomed to remain for an æon in states of suffering and woe*'?

'*He who delights in party strife, and adheres not to the Dhamma, is cut off from Arahantship.*[3] *Having broken up the Order when it was at peace, he must be cooked for an æon in purgatory*'?[4]

Hence surely a schismatic incurs retribution immediately after death.

---

2. *Of Insight.*

Controverted Point.—That 'insight' is not for the average man.

From the Commentary.—'Insight' (ñ ā ṇ a) is of two kinds—worldly and spiritual. The former is intellection concerned with various

---

[1] He denies, because he is judging such an one to be convinced that his side is in the right; he assents, in the case of one who knows that right is on the other side.—*Comy.* Cf. *Anguttara-Nik.*, i. 85 f. Similarly in the following change of reply.—*Comy.*

[2] *Vinaya*, ii. 205, v. 202, 203; *Vinaya Texts*, iii. 268. The latter mistakes bad doctrine or discipline for good, good doctrine or discipline for bad, and records his opinion by his acts. His intentions are good. In the *Vinaya* passage a t t h i, 'there is,' is rendered as s i y ā, 'there may be.'

[3] Literally, from the y o g a k k h e m a, or safety, salvation. Cut off that is, while this world-cycle lasts.

[4] *Ibid.*

attainments, and in noting the course of karma by way of righteous acts of giving, etc.; the latter is intuition concerned with the Paths and their Fruits, Path-intuition being learned by analysis of truth.[1] Now some, like the Hetuvādins, failing to distinguish this, accept only Path-intuition as insight.[2] Hence they deny it in the average man.

[1] *Th.*—But you imply that a worldly man has no analytic discernment, no analytic understanding, no ability to investigate or examine, no faculty of research, no ability to mark well, observe closely, mark repeatedly.[3] Is not the opposite true?

[2] Again, you admit, do you not? that there is not one of the four Rūpa-jhānas or of the four Arūpajhānas to which a man of the world may not attain, and that he is capable of liberality towards the Brethren as to the four requisites: raiment and so forth. Surely then it is not right to say a worldly man can have no insight.

[3] *H.*—If he can have insight, does he by that insight recognize the truth about Ill, eliminate its cause, realize its cessation, develop the Path going thereto? You admit that he does not. Therefore, etc. . . .

---

3. *Of the Guards of Purgatory.*

Controverted Point.—That in the purgatories there are no guards.

From the Commentary.—Some—for instance, the Andhakas—hold that there are no such beings, but that the hell-doomed karmas *in the shape* of hell-keepers purge the sufferers.

[1] *Th.*—Do you imply that there are no punishments inflicted[4] in the purgatories? You maintain the contrary? But you cannot maintain both propositions.

[1] The instantaneous penetration (ekābhisamaya) of truth by one who has reached the Path is intuitive, but he is also able to analyze truth. See Appendix: article 4.

[2] On the ambiguity of this term, see also II. 2.

[3] Cf. *Dhamma-sangaṇi*, § 16. All these are synonyms of ñāṇa.—*Comy.* We have brought out the force of the prefix '.pa' in the first two (paññā, pajānanā).

[4] Kamma-kāraṇāni. On this term, see *JPTS*, 1884, 76, and references given.

[2] You admit that on earth there are both punishments and executioners? Yet you deny that the latter exist in purgatory. . . .

[3] Moreover, was it not said by the Exalted One:

> '*Not Vessabhu nor yet the Petas King,*
> *Soma, Yama, or King Vessarana—*
> *The deeds that were his own do punish him*
> *Who ending here attains to other worlds*'?[1]

Hence there are guards in purgatory.

[4] Again, was it not said by the Exalted One: '*Him, bhikkhus, hell's guards torture*[2] *with the fivefold punishment; they thrust a hot iron stake through one hand, then another through the other hand, then one through the foot, then another through the other foot; they thrust a hot iron stake through the middle of the chest. And he thereupon feels painful, piercing, intolerable suffering, nor does he die till that evil deed of his is cancelled*'?[3]

[5] Again, was it not said [further] by the Exalted One: '*Him, bhikkhus, hell's guards make to lie down and flay him with hatchets . . . they place him head downwards and flay him with knives . . . they bind him to a chariot and drive him to and fro over burning, blazing, glowing ground . . . they lift him up on to a great hill of burning, blazing, white-hot coals and roll him down the fiery slope . . . they double him up and cast him into a hot brazen jar, burning, blazing, glowing, where he boils, coming up like a bubble of foam, then sinking, going now to this side, now to that.*[4] *There he suffers fierce and bitter pain, nor does he die till that evil karma is cancelled. Him, bhikkhus, they cast into the Great Purgatory. Now this:*

[1] We cannot trace these verses, hence cannot indicate the context.

[2] Our text has kammaŋ kārenti; the *Nikāya* (PTS edition) has . . . karonti.

[3] *Majjhima-Nik.*, iii. 182 f.; *Anguttara-Nik.*, i. 141. The Br. translation here and below reads: 'and he dies till that evil deed,' etc.

[4] *Milinda*, ii. 261 (translation); *Jātaka*, iii. 46 (text).

In districts measured out four-square four-doored,
Iron the ramparts bounding it, with iron roofed,
Iron its soil welded by fiery[1] *heat,*
Spreading a hundred leagues it stands for aye'?[2]

Hence there surely are guards in purgatory.

4. *Of Animals in Heaven.*

Controverted Point.—That animals may be reborn among the devas.

From the Commentary.—Among devas many—for instance, Erāvaṇa—assume animal shapes, such as those of elephants or horses, but no animals are reborn as such among them. Some, however, like the Andhakas, assume that because such celestial shapes have been seen, therefore these were celestially reborn animals.

[1] *Th.*—Do you then imply that conversely devas are reborn as animals? Or that the deva-world is an animal kingdom? That there may there be found moths, beetles, gnats, flies, snakes, scorpions, centipedes, earthworms? You deny all this. Then you cannot maintain your proposition. . . .

[2] *A.*—But is not the wondrous elephant Erāvaṇa there, the thousand-wise yoked celestial mount?[3]

[3] *Th.*—But are there also elephant and horse stables there, and fodder and trainers and grooms? . . .

5. *Of the Ariyan Path.*

Controverted Point.—That the Path is fivefold [only].

From the Commentary.—Some, such as the Mahiṃsāsakas, hold that in general terms the [Ariyan] Path is only fivefold. They infer

---

[1] The Br. and the *Nikāya* have j a l i t ā; the PTS a l i t ā may be a misprint.

[2] *Majjhima-Nik.*, *ibid.*; *Anguttara Nik.*, *ibid.*

[3] Y ā n a, literally vehicle. See above, p. 127, *n.* 4.

this both from the Sutta, 'One who has previously been quite pure,' etc., and also because the three eliminated factors– speech, action, and livelihood—are not states of consciousness like the other five.[1]

[1] *Th.*—But was not the Path pronounced by the Exalted One to be eightfold—namely, right views, right purpose, right speech, action, and livelihood, right effort, mindfulness, and concentration? [2] And did he not also say:

> '*Of all the means the Eightfold Path is best,*
> *And best of all true things the Stages Four;*
> *Best state of mind disinterestedness,*[2]
> *And of all bipeds best the man-who-sees*'?[3]

Surely, then, the Path is eightfold.

[3] But you tell me that though these three—right speech, right action, right livelihood—are factors of the Path, nevertheless they are not path, [4] while the other five are both factors of the Path and Path. Why this distinction?

[5] *M.*—But was it not said by the Exalted One: '*For him who has hitherto been quite pure in karma of deed and of word and of livelihood, this Ariyan Eightfold Path will go to perfection of development*'?[4]

Hence surely the Path is fivefold.

[6] *Th.*—But was it not said by the Exalted One: '*In whatsoever doctrine and discipline, Subhadda, the Ariyan Eightfold Path is not found, neither in it is there found a saintly man*[5] *of the first, or of the second, or of the third, or of the fourth degree. And in whatsoever doctrine and discipline, Subhadda, the Ariyan Eightfold Path is found, in it is such a saintly man found. Now in* this *doctrine and discipline, Subhadda,*

[1] As discussed above, X. 2.

[2] Virāgo, absence of greed or passion.

[3] *Dhammapada*, ver. 278.

[4] We have not traced this passage. Purity of act, word, and life, is essential as a preliminary qualification for the Path; much more are these three factors of the Path.

[5] Samaṇo.

is found the Ariyan Eightfold Path, and in it, too, are found men of saintliness of all four degrees. Void are the systems of other teachers, void of saintly men'?[1]

Hence surely the Path is eightfold.

---

6. *Of Insight.*

Controverted Point.—That insight into the twelve-fold base is spiritual.[2]

From the Commentary.—There is an opinion—held by the Pubbaseliyas, for instance—concerning the 'twelve constituent parts' in the First Sermon, 'The Turning of the Norm Wheel'—namely, that knowledge based on those twelve belongs to the Four Paths and Fruits.

[1] *Th.*—Do you mean that there are twelve kinds of insight? You deny. I ask again. You admit.[3] Then are there twelve [First or] Stream-winning Paths? or Fruits thereof? Or twelve of any of the other Paths or Fruits? . . .

[2] *P.*—But was it not said by the Exalted One: '(A, i.) *That this Ariyan Truth concerning Ill,*[4] *O bhikkhus, was not among the doctrines handed down, but there arose in me the vision, there arose in me the insight* (**ñāṇaŋ**), *there arose in me the wisdom, there arose in me the understanding, there arose in me the light;* (ii.) *that this Ariyan fact of Ill must be comprehended;* (iii.) *that it was comprehended;* (B, i.) *that this was the Ariyan Truth concerning the Cause of Ill;* (ii.) *that the Cause of Ill was to be put away . . .;* (iii.) *was put away;* (C, i.) *that this was the Ariyan Truth concerning the Cessation of Ill;* (ii.) *that this Cessation was to be realized;* (iii.) *had been realized;* (D, i.) *that this was the Ariyan Truth concern-*

[1] *Dialogues*, ii. 166.

[2] Lokuttara. See above, p. 184, *n*. 4.

[3] He first denies because of the oneness of the Paths; he then assents because of the diverse knowledge—as to nature, the need to do and the being done—respecting each Truth.—*Comy*.

[4] The Br. translator renders 'That this Ill constitutes an Ariyan fact.'

ing the Path going to the Cessation of Ill; (ii.) *that that Path was to be developed;* (iii.) *that it had been developed'?*[1]

Hence surely the insight based on these twelve parts is spiritual.

[1] *Vinaya Texts*, i. 96 f.; *Buddhist Suttas* (SBE, XI.), 150-152. 'The citation is inconclusive, as it does not show the twelve kinds of Insight of the Ariyan Path, but merely a distinction between prior and later knowledge.—*Comy.*

BOOK XXI.

1. *Of our Religion.*

Controverted Point.—That our religion is (has been and may again be) reformed.[1]

From the Commentary.—Because after the three Councils at which the differences in our Religion were settled, some—for instance, certain of the Uttarāpathakas—hold that it has been reformed, that there was such a person as a Reformer of the Religion, and that it is possible yet to reform it.

[1] *Th.*—What, then, has been reformed—the Applications in Mindfulness? the Supreme Efforts? the Steps to Iddhi? the Moral Controls? the Moral Forces? the Seven Branches of Enlightenment? Or was that made good which had been bad? Or was that which was allied with vicious things—Intoxicants, Fetters, Ties, Floods, Yokes, Hindrances, Infections, Graspings, Corruptions—made free herefrom? You deny all this, but your proposition [as stated] implies one or the other.

[2] Or do you mean that anyone has reformed the religion founded by the Tathāgata? If so, in which of the doctrines enumerated has he effected a reform? Again you deny. . . .

[3] Or if you hold that the religion may again be reformed, what in it is there that admits of reformation?

[1] Literally, 'made new.'

2 *Of Experience as Inseparable from Personality.*

Controverted Point.—That an ordinary person is not exempt[1] from experiencing the phenomena[2] of all the three spheres of life.

From the Commentary.—That is to say, at one and the same moment, since his understanding does not suffice to distinguish the three kinds. Our doctrine only entitles us to say that the individual is inseparable from such [mental] phenomena as arise at present in him.

[1] *Th.*—You imply that an ordinary person is inseparable from the contacts, the feelings, perceptions, volitions, cognitions, faiths, efforts, mindfulnesses, concentrations, understandings, belonging to all three spheres? You deny; but what else can you mean?

[2] Again, you imply that when he makes a gift, say, of raiment, etc , at that moment he is enjoying not only the giver's consciousness, but also the Rūpa-consciousness of the Four Jhānas, the Arūpa-consciousness of the four Arūpa-Jhānas.

[3] *Opponent.*—But is an ordinary person capable of distinguishing whether his actions leading to a Rūpa-world or Arūpa-world? If not, then surely he cannot be separated from actions leading to all three spheres.

3. *Of Certain Fetters.*

Controverted Point.—That Arahantship is won without a certain 'Fetter'-quantity being cast off.

From the Commentary.—Some—for instance, the Mahāsanghikas—hold this view with respect to the Fetters of ignorance and doubt, for the reason that even an Arahant does not know the whole range of Buddha-knowledge.

---

1 Avivitto, rendered below 'inseparable.'

2 Dhammehi. The Br. translator of the text (unlike the Br. translator of the *Commentary*) reads here kammehi (actions), as in the final sentence of this discourse.

[1] *Th.*—Do you imply that Arahantship is won without the extirpation of theory of soul, or doubt, or contagion of mere rule and ritual, or lust, or hate, or dulness, or indiscretion?[1] You deny that you do, but your proposition cannot then be maintained.

[2] Or do you imply that the Arahant is prone to lust, hate, dulness, conceit, pride, despair, corruption? Is not the opposite true of him? How then can you say there are certain Fetters he has not cast off?

[3] *M.*—[If I am wrong, tell me]: does an Arahant know with the complete purview of a Buddha? You agree he does not. Hence I am right.

---

4. *Of Supernormal Potency* (*iddhi*).

Controverted Point.—That either a Buddha or his disciples have the power of supernormally performing what they intend.

From the Commentary.—'Iddhi' is only possible in certain directions. It is absolutely impossible by it to contravene such laws as that of Impermanence, etc.[2] But it is possible by iddhi to effect the transformation of one character into another in the continuity of anything,[3] or to prolong it in its own character. This may be accomplished through merit or other causes, as when, to feed bhikkhus, water was turned into butter, milk, etc., and as when illuminations were prolonged at the depositing of sacred relics. This is our orthodox doctrine. But some, like the Andhakas, hold that iddhi may always be wrought by will, judging by the venerable Pilindavaccha willing that the palace of the king be all of gold.[4]

[1] *Th.*—Do you imply that the one or the other could effect such wishes as 'Let trees be ever green! ever blos-

[1] It is curious that the Theravādin does not confine himself to one or other of the Fetter-categories. However, there *was* more than one category, and the list given may have formed another of them. Cf. *Bud. Psy. Eth.*, p. 308.

[2] I.e., of Ill (as inseparable from life), and of No-soul, and other natural laws, as in the text.

[3] Santati. See *Compendium*, p. 252

[4] *Vinaya Texts*, ii. 65.

soming! ever in fruit! Let there be perpetual moonlight![1] Let there be constant safety! Let there be constant abundance of alms! Let there be always abundance of grain'? [2] Or such wishes as 'Let this factor of consciousness that has arisen [contact, feeling], etc., not cease!' [3] Or such wishes as 'Let this body, this mind, become permanent!' [4] Or such wishes as 'Let beings subject to birth, old age, disaster, death, not be born, grow old, be unfortunate, die!' All this you deny. Where then is your proposition?

[5] *A.*—But if I am wrong, how was it that when the venerable Pilindavaccha resolved: 'Let the palace of Seniya Bimbisāra, King of Magadha, be only of gold!' it was even so? . . .

---

5. *Of Buddhas.*

Controverted Point.—That Buddhas differ one from another in grades.

From the Commentary.—We hold that, with the exception of differences in body, age, and radiance,[2] at any given time, Buddhas differ mutually in no other respect. Some, however, like the Andhakas, hold that they differ in other qualities in general.

[1] *Th.*—Wherein then do they differ—in any of the matters pertaining to Enlightenment?[3] in self-mastery?[4] in omniscient insight and vision? . . .

---

6. *Of All-Pervading Power.*

Controverted Point.—That the Buddhas persist in all directions.

[1] Junhaŋ. The Br. translator renders this by 'growth.'

[2] Some manuscripts read pabhāva-mattaŋ, measure of power, which is scarcely plausible for a Buddhist. Pacceka Buddhas are presumably not taken into account.

[3] See p. 65.

[4] Vasībhāva, literally, the state of one who has practice.

From the Commentary.—Some, like the Mahāsanghikas, hold that a Buddha[1] exists in the four quarters of the firmament, above, below, and around, causing his change of habitat to come to pass in any sphere of being.

[1] *Th.*—Do you mean that they persist[2] in the eastern quarter? You deny. Then you contradict yourself. You assent.[3] Then I ask, How is [this Eastern] Buddha named? What is his family? his clan? what the names of his parents? or of his pair of elect disciples? or of his body-servant? What sort of raiment or bowl does he bear? and in what village, town, city, kingdom, or country?

[2] Or does a Buddha persist in the southern . . . western . . . northern quarter? or in the nadir? or in the zenith? Of any such an one I ask you the same questions. . . . Or does he persist in the realm of the four great Kings?[4] or in the heaven of the Three-and-Thirty? or in that of the Yāmā or the Tusita devas? or in that of the devas who rejoice in creating, or of those who exploit the creations of others?[5] or in the Brahma-world? If you assent, I ask you further as before. . . .

---

7. *Of Phenomena.*

Controverted Point.—That all things are by nature immutable.[6]

From the Commentary.—Some, like the Andhakas and certain of the Uttarāpathakas, hold this, judging from the fact that nothing

---

[1] In the PTS edition for buddhā read buddho atthīti.

[2] Tiṭṭhanti, lit. 'stand'; the word used in XIII. 1 for 'endure.'

[3] He denies with respect to [the locus of] the historical Sakyamuni [*sic*]; he assents, since by his view the persisting is in different places.—*Comy.*

[4] On the possible birthplace of these deities, see Moulton, *Zoroastrianism*, 22-27, 242.

[5] Cf. *Compendium*, p. 140 f.

[6] Niyatā. On this term, see above, V. 4; VI. 1. 'Not fixed' below is a-niyato. On the three alternatives in § 1, see Childers's Dictionary, *s.v.* rāsi. The three are affirmed in *Dīgha-Nik.*, iii. 217.

[however it may change] gives up its fundamental nature, matter, e.g., being fixed *as* matter, and so on.

[1] *Th.*—Do you mean that they all belong to that Order of things, by which the wrong-doer is assured of immediate retribution on rebirth, or to that other Order by which the Path-winner is assured of final salvation? Is there not a third congeries that is not fixed as one or the other? You deny. But think. Surely there is? You assent. Then you contradict your proposition. And you must do so, for did not the Exalted One speak of three congeries?

[3] You affirm [as your reason] that matter is fixed as matter, and that mind (or each mental aggregate) is fixed as mind. Well, then, under which of those three congeries do you find them fixed?[1]

[4] *A. U.*—But if I may not say that matter, or mind is fixed as matter, or mind respectively, tell me, can body become mind, can become one of the four mental aggregates, or conversely? Of course not. Surely then I am right.

---

8. *Of Karma.*

Controverted Point.—That all karmas are inflexible.[2]

From the Commentary.—The same parties hold also this opinion, judging by the fact that karmas which work out their own effects under present conditions in this or the next life, or in a posterior series of lives, are fixed with respect one to the other.

[1, 2] *Similar to* §§ 1, 2 *in the foregoing.*

[3] *Th.*—Do you mean that karma which eventuates in

[1] They are not immutable in badness, nor in goodness, wrongness, nor rightness. Therefore, since these are the only two categories admitted as immutable, they must come under the third or mutable 'non-fixed' category or congeries (r ā s i).

[2] There are two uniformities in Nature, by one of which the worst offenders are assured of immediate retribution after death, and by the other of which the Path-winner is assured of final salvation. And there is a third alternative group which is neither.

this life is a fixed fact as such? You assent.[1] Then does it belong to either of the fixed orders? You deny. [Then it belongs to no fixed order.] The same holds good with respect to karma, results of which will be experienced at the next rebirth, or in a succession of rebirths.

[4] *A. U.*—But you admit, do you not, that none of these three kinds of karma is mutually convertible with the other two? How then am I wrong?

[1] This kind of karma, if capable of eventuating at all, [invariably] works out its effects in this very life; if not, it becomes inoperative [ahosi-kamma]. So the Theravādin assents.—*Comy.* That is, each of these three kinds of karma retains its own characteristics.

BOOK XXII

1. *Of the Completion of Life.*

Controverted Point.—That life may be completed without a certain Fetter-quantity having been cast off.

From the Commentary. — Inasmuch as the Arahant completes existence without casting off every Fetter with respect to the range of omniscience, some, like the Andhakas, hold the aforesaid view, similar to what has been noticed above (theory of the Mahāsanghikas, XXI. 3).

The dialogue resembles XXI. 3, verbatim.

---

2. *Of Moral Consciousness.*

Controverted Point.—That the Arahant is ethically conscious when completing existence at final death.

From the Commentary.—Some, like the Andhakas, hold this view on the ground that the Arahant is ever lucidly conscious, even at the hour of utterly passing away. The criticism points out that moral (ethical or good) consciousness inevitably involves meritorious karma [taking effect hereafter]. The doctrine quoted by the opponent is inconclusive. It merely points to the Arahant's lucidity and awareness while dying, to his ethically neutral and therefore inoperative presence of mind and reflection at the last moments of his cognitive process [javana]. But it was not intended to show the arising of morally good thoughts.

[1] *Th.*—You are implying that an Arahant is achieving karma of merit, or karma of imperturbable character;[1] that

[1] Or 'for remaining static,' āneñjābhisankhāraŋ. See the same line of argument in XVII. 1. The alternatives refer to the sensuous and to the immaterial planes of existence.

he is working karma affecting destiny, and rebirth, conducive to worldly authority and influence, to wealth and reputation,[1] to beauty celestial or human. . . .

[2] You are implying that the Arahant, when he is passing away, is accumulating or pulling down, is eliminating or grasping, is scattering or binding, is dispersing or collecting.[2] Is it not true of him that he stands, as Arahant, neither heaping up nor pulling down, as one who has pulled down? That he stands, as Arahant, neither putting off nor grasping at, as one who has put off? As neither scattering nor binding, as one who has scattered? As neither dispersing nor collecting, as one who has dispersed?

[3] *A.*—But does not an Arahant pass utterly away with lucid presence of mind, mindful and aware? You agree. Then is this not 'good' consciousness?[3]

---

3. *Of Imperturbable (Fourth Jhāna) Consciousness.*

Controverted Point.—That the Arahant completes existence in imperturbable absorption (ā n e ñ j e).

From the Commentary.—Certain of the Uttarāpathakas hold that the Arahant, no less than a Buddha, when passing utterly away, is in a sustained Fourth Jhāna[4] [of the Immaterial plane].

[1] *Th.*—But does he not complete existence with ordinary (or normal) consciousness?[5] You agree. How then do you reconcile this with your proposition?

[1] Literally, great following or retinue.

[2] Cf. I. 2, § 63.

[3] On the technical meaning of 'k u s a l a, a - k u s a l a' (good, bad), see above, p. 339, 'From the Commentary.' 'Good' meant 'producing happy result.' Now the Arahant had done with all that.

[4] Wherein all thinking and feeling have been superseded by clearness of mind and indifference. See p. 190, *n.* 2; *Dialogues*, i. 86 f.

[5] P a k a t i - c i t t e—i.e., sub-consciousness (unimpressed consciousness, b h a v a n g a c i t t a). All sentient beings are normally in this mental state. When that ends, they expire with the (so-called act of) 'decease-consciousness [c u t i - c i t t a, which takes effect, in itself ceasing, as reborn consciousness in a new embryo]. The Arahant's

[2] You are implying that he passes away with an ethically inoperative consciousness.[1] Is it not rather with a consciousness that is pure 'result'? [3] Whereas according to you he passes away with a consciousness that is unmoral and purely inoperative, I suggest that it is with a consciousness that is unmoral and purely resultant.

[4] And did not the Exalted One emerge from Fourth Jhāna before he passed utterly away immediately after?[2]

---

4. *Of Penetrating the Truth.*

Controverted Point.—That an embryo is capable of penetrating the truth.

From the Commentary.—Some—that is, certain of the Uttarāpathakas—hold that one who in his previous birth was a Stream-winner, and remains so, must have [as a newly resultant consciousness] grasped the Truth while an embryo.[3]

[1] *Th.*—You are implying that an embryo can be instructed in, hear, and become familiar with the Doctrine, can be catechized, can take on himself the precepts, be

---

normal mind when on the Arūpa plane would be imperturbable. But the question is asked with reference to the life-plane of all five aggregates' (not of four immaterial ones only).—*Comy.*

[1] Kiriyāmaye citte. Buddhism regards consciousness, under the specific aspect of causality, as either (1) karmic—i.e., able to function causally as karma; (2) resultant (vipāka), or due to karma; (3) non-causal (kiriyā), called here 'inoperative.' Cf. *Compendium*, p. 19 f. I.e., certain resultant kinds of consciousness, effects of karma in a previous birth, can never be causal again so as to effect another result in any *moral* order in the sense in which effects may become causes in the physical order. Again, there are certain ethically neutral states of consciousness consisting in mere action of mind without entailing moral consequences. The Buddhist idea is that the normal flux of consciousness from birth to death, in each span of life, is purely resultant, save where it is interrupted by causal, or by 'inoperative' thought.

[2] *Dialogues*, ii. 175.

[3] The Uttarāpathakas were perhaps 'feeling out' for a theory of heredity.

guarded as to the gates of sense, abstemious in diet, devoted to vigils early and late. Is not the opposite true?

[2] Are there not two conditions for the genesis of right views—'another's voice and intelligent attention?'[1]

[3] And can there be penetration of the Truth by one who is asleep, or languid, or blurred in intelligence, or unreflective?

---

5. *Three Other Arguments: (a) On Attainment of Arahantship by the Embryo; (b) on Penetration of Truth by a Dreamer; (c) on Attainment of Arahantship by a Dreamer.*

From the Commentary.—The attainment of Arahantship by very young Stream-winners, [notably the story of] the [phenomenal] seven-year-old son of the lay-believer Suppavāsā,[2] led the same sectaries to believe in even ante-natal attainment of Arahantship.[3] They hold further, seeing the wonderful feats, such as levitation, etc., that are experienced in dreams, that the dreamer may not only penetrate the Truth, but also attain Arahantship.

In all three cases the argument is simply a restatement of XXII. 4, § 3.

---

6. *Of the Unmoral.*

Controverted Point.—That all dream-consciousness is ethically neutral.

From the Commentary.—From the Word, '*There is volition, and that volition is negligible,*'[4] some—that is, certain of the Uttarāpathakas—hold the aforesaid view. But this was spoken with refer-

---

[1] *Anguttara-Nik.*, i. 87.

[2] This was a favourite legend. See *Pss. of the Brethren*, lxx. 'Sīvali,' the child-saint in question; *Jātaka*, No. 100; *Udāna*, ii. 8; *Dhammapada Commentary*, iv. 192 f. Also on the mother, *Anguttara-Nik.*, ii. 62.

[3] The embryonic consciousness carrying the force of previous, culminating karma into effect. See previous page, *n.* 1.

[4] *Vinaya*, iii. 112, commenting on *Vinaya Texts*, ii. 226. Abbohārika (or -ya), i.e., a-vohārika, not of legal or conventional status.

ence to ecclesiastical offences.[1] Although a dreamer may entertain evil thoughts of murder, etc., no injury to life or property is wrought. Hence they cannot be classed as offences. Hence dream-thoughts are a negligible quantity, and for this reason, and not because they are ethically neutral, they may be ignored.[2]

[1] *Th.*—You admit, do you not, that a dreamer may (in dreams) commit murder, theft, etc.? How then can you call such consciousness ethically neutral?

[2] *U.*—If I am wrong, was it not said by the Exalted One that dream-consciousness was negligible? If so, my proposition holds good.

---

7. *Of Correlation by Repetition.*[3]

Controverted Point.—That there is no correlation by way of repetition.

From the Commentary.—Inasmuch as all phenomena are momentary, nothing persisting more than an instant, nothing can be so correlated as to effect repetition; hence there never is repetition. This is also an opinion of the Uttarāpathakas.

[1] *Th.*—But was it not said by the Exalted One: '*The taking of life, bhikkhus, when habitually practised and multiplied, is conducive to rebirth in purgatory, or among animals, or Petas. In its slightest form it results in, and is conducive to, a brief life among men*'? [2] And again: '*Theft, bhikkhus, adultery, lying, slander, uttering harsh words, idle talk, intoxication, habitually practised and multiplied, are each and all conducive to rebirth in purgatory, among animals, or Petas. The slightest theft results in, conduces to destruction of property; the mildest offence against chastity gives rise to retaliatory measures among men; the lightest form of lying exposes the liar to false accusation among men; the mildest offence in slander leads to a rupture of friendship*

[1] Āpatti, explained (after an exegetic fashion) as attaŋ pīlanaŋ pajjatīti, 'is come to infliction of punishments.'

[2] Cf. *Compendium*, pp. 47, 52.

[3] Asevanā. See p. 294, *n.* 2.

among men; the lightest result of harsh words creates sounds jarring on the human ear; the slightest result of idle talk is speech commanding no respect[1] *among men; the mildest inebriety conduces to want of sanity among men*'?[2] [3, 4] And again: '*Wrong views, bhikkhus, wrong aspiration, effort, speech, activity, livelihood, mindfulness, concentration—each and all, if habitually practised, developed, and multiplied, conduce to rebirth in purgatory, among animals, among Petas*'? And again: '*Right views, right purpose, etc., habitually practised, developed, and multiplied, have their base and their goal and their end in the Ambrosial*'?[3]

---

8. *Of Momentary Duration.*

Controverted Point.—That all things are momentary conscious units.

From the Commentary.—Some—for instance, the Pubbaseliyas and the Aparaseliyas—hold that, since all conditioned things are impermanent, therefore they endure but one conscious moment. Given universal impermanence—one thing ceases quickly, another after an interval—what, they ask, is here the law? The Theravādin shows it is but arbitrary to say that because things are not immutable, therefore they all last but one mental moment.

[1] *Th.*—Do you imply that a mountain, the ocean, Sineru chief of mountains, the cohesive, fiery, and mobile elements, grass, twigs, trees, all last [only so long] in consciousness? You deny. . . .

[2] Or do you imply that the organ of sight coincides[4] for the same moment of time with the visual cognition? If you assent, I would remind you of what the venerable Sāriputta said: '*If, brother, the eye within be intact, but the object without does not come into focus, and there is no co-ordinated application of mind resulting therefrom, then a corresponding state of cognition is not manifested. And if the*

[1] Cf. the positive form of this term in *Vinaya Texts*, iii. 186, § 8.

[2] *Anguttara-Nik.*, iv. 247.

[3] *Saŋyutta-Nik.*, v. 54, but the word āsevito is wanting.

[4] Sahajātaŋ, 'come into being and cease together.'—*Comy.*

organ of sight within be intact, and the object without come into focus, but no co-ordinated application of mind result therefrom, a corresponding state of cognition is not manifested. But if all these conditions be satisfied, then a corresponding state of cognition is manifested'?[1]

Where now is your assertion about coincidence in time?

[3] The same Suttanta reference may be cited to refute you with respect to time-coincidence in the other four senses.

[4] *P. A.*—But are all things permanent, enduring, perduring, immutable?

Th.—Nay that cannot truly be said. . . .

[1] *Majjhima-Nik.*, i. 190.

BOOK XXIII

1. *Of United Resolve.*

Controverted Point.—That sexual relations may be entered upon with a united resolve.[1]

From the Commentary.—Such a vow may be undertaken, some think—for instance, the Andhakas and the Vetulyakas[2]—by a human pair who feel mutual sympathy or *com*passion[3] [not passion merely], and who are worshipping, it may be, at some Buddha-shrine, and aspire to be united throughout their future lives.

[1] *Th.*—Do you imply that a united resolve may be undertaken which does not befit a recluse, does not become a bhikkhu, or that it may be undertaken by one who has cut off the root [of rebirth], or when it is a resolve that would lead to a Pārājika offence?[4]

Or when it is a resolve by which life may be slain, theft committed, lies, slander, harsh words, idle talk uttered, burglary committed, dacoity, robbery, highway robbery, adultery, sack and loot of village or town be committed?. . .[5]

[You must be more discriminating in your use of the term 'with a united resolve'!]

[1] Ekādhippāyo. There is nothing objectionable in the relation so entered upon, except, of course, for the recluse or a member of the Order.

[2] See XVII. 6.

[3] Kāruññā, 'pity,' not the term anukampanā, which does much duty in Buddhism to express affection in social and conjugal relations. See *Ency. Religions*, 'Love, Buddhist.' On the belief in such repeated unions, see Mahā Kassapa's legend, *Pss. of the Brethren*, p. 359 f., and Bhaddā's (his wife's) verses, *Pss. of the Sisters*, p. 49.

[4] Meriting expulsion from the Order.

[5] *Dialogues*, i. 69.

2. *Of Bogus Arahants.*

Controverted Point.—That infra-human beings, taking the shape of Arahants,[1] follow sexual desires.

From the Commentary.—This belief arose in consequence of the dress and deportment of evil-minded bhikkhus, and is held by some—for instance, certain of the Uttarāpathakas.

[1] *Th.*—Would you also say that such beings, resembling Arahants, commit any or all such crimes as are stated above (XXIII. 1)? You deny; but why limit them to one only of those crimes?

---

3. *Of Self-governed Destiny.*

Controverted Point.—That a Bodhisat (or future Buddha) (*a*) goes to an evil doom, (*b*) enters a womb, (*c*) performs hard tasks, (*d*) works penance under alien teachers of his own accord and free will.

From the Commentary.—Some—for instance, the Andhakas—judge that the Bodhisatta, in the case of the Six-toothed Elephant Jātaka[2] and others, was freely so reborn as an animal or in purgatory, that he freely performed difficult tasks, and worked penance under alien teachers.

[1] (*a*) *Th.*—Do you mean that he so went and endured purgatory, the Sañjīva, Kālasutta, Tāpana, Patāpana, Sanghātaka, Roruva, and Avīchi hells? If you deny, how can you maintain your proposition? Can you quote me a Sutta to support this?

[2] (*b*).—You maintain that he entered the womb of his own free will.[3] Do you also imply that he chose to be reborn in purgatory, or as an animal? That he possessed

[1] It should be remembered that in a wider, popular sense, any religieux were—at least, in the commentarial narratives—called Arahants—i.e., 'worthy ones,' 'holy men.' Cf. *Pss. of the Sisters*, p. 180; *Dhammapada Commentary*, i. 400.

[2] No. 514.

[3] The PTS edition omits Ā m a n t ā here.

magic potency? You deny.[1] I ask it again. You assent.[2] Then did he practise the Four Steps to that potency—will, effort, thought, investigation? Neither can you quote me here a Sutta in justification.

[3] (*c*).—You maintain further that the Bodhisat of his own free will performed that which was painful and hard to do. Do you thereby mean that he fell back on wrong views such as 'the world is eternal,' etc., or 'the world is finite,' etc., or 'infinite,' etc., 'soul and body are the same,' . . . 'are different,' 'the Tathāgata exists after death,' 'does not exist,' 'both so exists and does not,' 'neither so exists nor does not'? Can you quote me a Sutta in justification?

[4] (*d*).—You maintain further that the Bodhisat of his own free will made a series of penances following alien teachers. Does this imply that he then held their views? Can you quote me a Sutta in justification? . . .

---

4. *Of Counterfeit States of Consciousness.*

Controverted Point.—That there is that which is not (*a*) lust, (*b*) hate, (*c*) dulness, (*d*) the corruptions, but which counterfeits each of them.

From the Commentary.—Such are with regard to (*a*) amity, pity, approbation; with regard to (*b*) envy, selfishness, worry; with regard to (*c*) the sense of the ludicrous; with regard to (*d*) the suppressing of the discontented, the helping of kindly bhikkhus, the blaming of the bad, the praising of the good, the declaration of the venerable Pilinda Vaccha about outcasts,[3] the declarations of the Exalted Ones about the incompetent or irredeemable.[4] Such is the opinion held, for instance, by the Andhakas.

---

[1] Free will, as liberty to do what one pleases through a specific power or gift, is practically a denial of karma. Hence this question.—*Comy.*

[2] He denies with reference to iddhi as accomplished by practice, then assents with reference to iddhi as accomplished by merit. *Comy.*

[3] Vasalā. *Udāna*, iii. 6.

[4] Mogha-purisā—e.g., Sunakkhatta, the Licchavi (*Dīgha-Nik.*, iii. 27 f.). The term is preceded by kheḷāsika-vādaṃ. 'declaration about spittle-eaters,' presumably a term of opprobrium, but the context of which we cannot trace

[1] *Th.*—Do you imply that there is that which is not contact, not feeling, not perceiving, not volition, not cognition, not faith, not energy, not mindfulness, not concentration, not understanding, but which simulates each of these?

[2] *Similarly for* (*b*), (*c*), (*d*).

5. *Of the Undetermined*

Controverted Point.—That the aggregates, elements, controlling powers—all save Ill, is undetermined.[1]

From the Commentary.—Such is the opinion held by some—for instance, certain of the Uttarāpathakas and the Hetuvādins. Their authority they find in the lines:

'Tis simply Ill that riseth, simply Ill
That doth persist, and then fadeth away.
Nought beside Ill it is that doth become;
Nought else but Ill it is doth pass away.[2]

[1] *Th.*—Do you then maintain that [the marks of the conditioned are lacking in, say, the material aggregate—that] matter is not impermanent, not conditioned, has not arisen because of something, is not liable to decay, to perish, to be devoid of passion, to cessation, to change? Is not the opposite true?

[2] Do you imply that only Ill is caused? Yes? But did not the Exalted One say that whatever was impermanent was Ill? Hence, if this be so, and since matter is impermanent, you cannot maintain that only Ill is determined.

[3] The same argument holds good for the other four aggregates (mental), for all the mechanism of sense,[3] for all controlling powers.[4]

END OF THE TRANSLATED TEXT

[1] Aparinipphanna. See p. 261, *n.* 6.

[2] Verses of Vajirā, Bhikkhunī. *Saṃyutta-Nik.*, i. 135; *Pss. of the Sisters*, p. 191. Cf. above, p. 61.

[3] This includes the categories 22-51, enumerated on p. 15 f.

[4] This includes those enumerated (52-73) on p. 16.

APPENDIX

NOTES ON—

1. PARAMATTHA, SACCIKA: THE REAL.

(I. 1., p. 9.)

IN the phrase paramaṭṭhena, saccikaṭṭhena, rendered 'in the sense of a real and ultimate fact,' these two terms are used synonymously. Saccika is also stated to be something existent (atthi); and this 'existent, as being not a past, or future, but a present existent, is explained to be vijjamāna, saṃvijjamāna:—something verifiably or actually existing (p. 22). Vijjamāna, a very important synonym of paramattha, means literally 'something which is being known,' present participle of the passive stem vid-ya, 'to be known.' It is rendered into Burmese by the phrase 'evidently existing.' Upalabbhati (p. 8, n. 3), 'to be known as closely as possible,' is the subjective counterpart of the existing real. Parama- is, by the Comy., defined as 'ultimate,' uttama, a word traditionally defined, in the *Abhidhānappadīpikā-sūcī*, as that which has reached [its] highest—ubbhūto atayattham uttamo.

According to Dhammapāla, in the *Kathāvatthu-anuṭīkā*, parama means paṭṭhāna, 'pre-eminent,' 'principal,' because of irreversibility (a-viparītabhāvato) or, incapacity of being transformed. And he further thought that the reality of that which is parama depends upon its being a sense-datum of infallible knowledge (aviparītassa ñānassa visayabhāvaṭṭhena saccikaṭṭho.

In his *Abhidhammattha-vibhāvanī*,[1] Summangalasāmi follows the K.V. Comy., but annexes Dhammapāla's 'irreversibility.'

[1] Comy. on the *Compendium of Philosophy*; see *ibid.*, p. ix.

Ariyavaŋsa[1] judged that uttama, applied to parama, excludes the other meaning of pamāna-atireka, 'surpassing in measure.' And he, too, agrees with Dhammapāla, that a thing is 'ultimate' because it is incapable of further transformations, or of analysis, and because it is the sense-datum of infallible knowledge.

Attha, in the term paramattha, Europeans usually render by 'meaning.' It refers rather to all that is meant (meaning in extension, not intension) by any given word. In its present connection it has nothing to do with the verbal meaning, import, sense or significance of a word. According to Ariyavaŋsa, it means either a thing *per se* (*sabhāva*), or a sense-datum (*visaya*). In the former sense, paramattha becomes an appositional compound of two terms, both applying to one and the same thing. In the latter sense, the compound is resolvable into paramassa attho. If, with Sumangalasāmi, we read uttamaŋ ñānaŋ into parama, we get, for paramattha in this latter sense, sense-field of highest knowledge.

Now, there are Buddhists in Burma who hold that if the 'real' can only be fitly described in terms of highest knowledge, only a Buddha can know it, and average folk can therefore only know the shadow of it (paramattha-chāyā). We, i.e., know the phenomenon but not the noumenon. This transcendentalism, however, is not orthodox doctrine.

Turning finally to the term saccika, or the more familiar sacca,[2] this may mean abstract truth (lakkhana-saccaŋ), as of a judgment, or concrete fact (vatthu-saccaŋ), as of a reality.[3] 'Truth' by no means always fits sacca. See, e.g., our translation of the Four Ariyan 'Truths,' p. 215 of the *Compendium*. The Second Sacca is reckoned to be a thing to be got rid of like

[1] In the *Maṇisāra-mañjūsa*, *Ṭīkā* on that Comy.; fifteenth century, A.D.

[2] Saccam eva saccikaŋ, *Maṇisāra-mañjūsa*. For English readers it may be stated that the doubled *c* (pron. *cch*) results from sat-ya.

[3] P. 188, *n*. 4.

poison. But we do not wish to discard a Truth. Hence we have substituted 'fact,' following Sumangalasāmi, who comments on the term 'Ariyan Truths' in the passage referred to as meaning 'realities' or 'facts' which 'Ariyanize those who penetrate them,' making them members of one stage or another of the Ariyan Path. Or, again, 'realities so-called because Ariyans penetrate them as their own property, or because they were taught by the greatest of Ariyans.'[1]

Ariyāvaṃsa, sub-commenting, holds that sacca imports actual existence, not liable to reversion; for instance, the reality of the characteristics of fire or other natural forces.[2]

Finally, in this connection, Ledi Sadaw's disquisition on conventional or nominal truth and real, ultimate, or philosophical truth in 'Some Points of Buddhist Doctrine' (*JPTS*, 1913-14, p. 129) and in his 'Expositions' (*Buddhist Review*, October, 1915), expanding the section in the K.V. Comy., (p. 63, *n.* 2), of this volume should be considered. In his own Comy. on the *Compendium of Philosophy—Paramattha-dīpanī*—he examines more closely the terms we are discussing. 'Attha,' he says, 'may mean: (*a*) things *per se* (sabhāva-siddha); or (*b*) things merely conceived (parikappa-siddha). The former (*a*) include mind, etc., verifiable existents, *severally*, by their own intrinsic characteristics, and, *simply*, without reference to any other thing. The latter (*b*) are not such verifiable existents. They exist by the mind . . . 'being,' 'person,' etc., are 'things' created by mental synthesis.[3]

Of these two classes, only things *per se* are termed paramattha, real. Attha may therefore be defined as that thing which is intelligible to mind and representable by signs, terms or concepts. Paramattha is that reality which, by its truly verifiable existence, transcends

[1] See III., p. 81, of Saya Pye's *Tīkagyaw and Maṇisāramañjūsā.*

[2] *Op. et loc. cit.* . . . aggalakkhaṇaṃ viya lokapakati viya.

[3] Or 'logical construction,' as Mr. Bertrand Russell would say (Lowell Lectures, 1914, p. 59).

concepts. . . . Ultimate facts never fail those who seek for genuine insight. Hence they are real. Concepts, on the other hand, not verifiably existing, fail them' (pp. 14-16).

---

2. ṬHITI: THE STATIC.

(I. 1., p. 55.)

IN the passage here quoted from the Suttas:—'of conditioned things the genesis is apparent, the passing away is apparent, the duration (as a third distinct state amidst change) is apparent'—the three stages of 'becoming' in all phenomena, always logically distinguishable, if not always patent to sense, are enunciated. That the midway stage is a constant like the others: that between genesis and decay there was also a static stage (perhaps only a zero point of change), designated as ṭhiti (from tiṭṭhati [STHĀ], to stand), was disputed by some—e.g., Ānanda, the author of the *Ṭīkā* on the three Abidhamma Commentaries by Buddhaghosa. But the *Compendium* itself states the traditional and orthodox tenet in the case of units of mental phenomena: 'one thought-moment consists of three time-phases, to wit, nascent, static, and arresting phases' (*Comp.*, pp. 25, 26, 125).

In the Sutta the word rendered by 'duration' is not ṭhiti, but ṭhitānaŋ, gen. plur. of ṭhitaŋ, or static [thing]. Commentarial philosophy tended to use the abstract form. It also distinguished (or commented upon as already distinguished) two kinds of duration (or enduring things): khaṇika-ṭhiti, 'momentary duration,' and pabandha-ṭhiti, or combined duration. The latter constitutes the more popularly conceived notion of jarā: decay, old age, degeneration in any phenomenon. The Puggalavādin was thinking of *this* notion when he answered the first question.

Now if, in the Sutta, duration was to be understood as a static stage between genesis and decay, it would almost certainly have been named in such an order. But it was named last. And it may well be that the more cultured intellect of the propounder of the Sutta did not accept the popular notion of any real stationariness (ṭhiti) in a cosmos of incessant change, but only took it into account as a commonly accepted view, expressing it, not as one positive phase in three positive phases of becoming, but negatively, as this 'otherness' of duration (i.e., a state of duration other than genesis and passing away) appears to ordinary intelligence.

---

3. Sabbam atthi: 'Everything Exists.'

(I. 6, p. 84 f.)

At first sight it would appear that the emphasis is on the first word: 'everything,' 'all.' This would be the case if the thesis were here opposed to ekaccam atthi: 'some things exist, some do not,' which is discussed in the next discourse but one. But the context shows clearly that, in both these theses, the emphasis is really on the word 'atthi': 'is,' in the sense of 'exists.'

Now the Burmese translator supplies after sabbaŋ, a term which, in Pali, is dhamma-jātaŋ. This, disconnected, is dhammassa jātaŋ: the arising or happening of dhamma; anything, that is, which exists as a fact, as opposed to a chimæra, or in the Pali idiom, a hare's horn. (We use the term 'thing' not in the sense of substance, or having a substrate, but as anything which is exhausted, as to its being, by some or all of the known twenty-eight qualities of body or matter, and by the facts of mind.

Should sabbaŋ be understood collectively—'all,' or distributively—'everything'? Taken by itself, one of the questions in § 1, p. 85: "Does 'all' exist in all [things]?" would incline us at first sight to the former alternative, at least in the case of the locative term. Yet even here we do not read the question as: Is there in the whole a whole? but as: Does the whole exist in everything, or every part? taking the nominative, sabbaŋ, collectively, the locative, sabbesu, distributively. And the context in general leads us to the latter alternative. The Sabbatthivādin believes in the continued existence of any particular [thing] past, present, and future. The Commentator accounted for this belief by that school's interpretation of this postulate: No past, present, or future dhamma's (facts-as-cognized) abandon the khandha-nature (sabbe pi atītādi-bhedā dhammā khandha-sabhāvaṃ na vijahanti). Once a dhamma, always a dhamma. The five aggregates (khandha's), in other words matter-mind, however they may vary at different times, bear the same general characteristics all the time.

Perhaps the following quotation from John Locke's critics, taken from Green and Grose's *Hume*, vol. i., p. 87, may help to show the Commentator's meaning with reference to the rūpakkhandha, or material aggregate: 'But of this (that is, of another thing which has taken the place of a previous thing, making an impact on the sensitive tablet at one moment, but perishing with it the next moment), the real essence is just the same as the previous thing, namely, that it may be touched, or is solid, or a body, or a parcel of matter; nor can this essence be really lost. . . . It follows that real change is impossible. A parcel of matter at one time is a parcel of matter at all times.'

Thus, the Sabbatthivādin might say, because a parcel of matter to which we assign the name 'gold' was yellow, fusible, etc., in the past, is so now, and will be so in future, therefore gold 'exists.' Again, because fire burned yesterday, burns to-day, and will burn to-morrow, therefore fire exists.

In some such way this school had come to believe in the immutable existence, the real essence of all or everything, taken in the distributive sense of everything without exception; but not always excluding the collective sense. Rūpā—e.g., in § 3: 'Do past material qualities exist?'—refers to the rūpakkhandha, i.e., in a collective sense. That, however, does not preclude any one of the twenty-eight qualities of body (*Compendium*, pp. 157-160) from being taken distributively, or prevent any material object composed of eight or more of these qualities from being discussed separately.

In the heckling dialectic of the paragraph numbered 22 (p. 89, f.), we have found it necessary to supply certain terms chosen according to the context, and from the Commentary. The Pali reader should consult the Burmese edition of the latter, since there are errors of printing and punctuation in that compiled by Minayeff (PTS edition p. 45). It may prove helpful if we give in English the Burmese translation of the Commentary from p. 45, l. 18, PTS edition: 'Atha naŋ Sakavādī: yadi te.' . . .

Theravādin: 'Let that thing of yours, which, on becoming present after having been future, be taken into account as "having been, is." And let it equally be spoken of as "*again* having been, is." Then a chimæra which, *not* having been future can*not* become present, should be spoken of as "not having been, is not." But does your chimæra repeat the negative process of not having been, is not? If so, it should be spoken of as "again not having been, is not." '

The Opponent thinks: 'An *imaginary* thing cannot, having been future, become present, because of its very non-existence. Let it then be spoken of as "not having been, is not" ("na hutvā na hoti nāma tāva hotu.") But how can such a thing repeat the negative process (literally 'state': bhāvo)? If not, it cannot be spoken of as "*again* not having been, is not."

The Sabbatthivādin is here and throughout represented as dealing with mere abstract ideas of time—i.e., with abstract names for divisions of time—and not with things or facts. The object of the Theravādin, in introducing imaginary things, is to refute arguments so based. His opponent is not prepared to push his abstractions further by allowing a repetition of a process which actually never once takes place.

---

4. Paṭisambhidā: Analysis.

(See p. 179, V. 5.)

In this, the earliest Buddhist doctrine of logical analysis, the four branches (or 'Four Paṭisambhidā's), frequently referred to are (1) Attha-paṭisambhidā: analysis of meanings 'in extension.' (2) Dhamma-paṭisambhidā: analysis of reasons, conditions, or causal relations. (3) Nirutti-paṭisambhidā: analysis of [meanings 'in intension' as given in] definitions. (4) Paṭibhāna-paṭisambhidā: analysis of intellect to which things knowable by the foregoing processes are presented.

1. 'Attha' does not refer to verbal meanings. Ledi Sadaw and U. Pandi agree with us that it means the 'thing' signified by the term. Hence it is equivalent to the European notion of denotation, or meaning in extension.

2. The latter authority holds that dhamma refers to *terms*. [He has, by the way, a scheme of correspondence between the branches of the literary concept *kavi*, and the above-named branches :—

Attha-kavi ...	...	Attha-paṭisambhidā.
Suta-kavi ...	...	Dhamma- ,,
Cintā-kavi ...	...	Nirutti- ,,
Paṭibhāna-kavi	...	Paṭibhāna ,,

suggested by the mutually coinciding features.] But in the *Abhidhānappadīpikā-sūcī*, art. dhamma, this term, in the present connection, is taken to mean *hetu*, or *paccaya* (condition, or causal relation): hetumhi ñāṇaṇ dhamma-paṭisambhidāti ādīsu hetumhi paccaye.

3. Nirutti (ni[r]: '*de*'; utti: 'expression') means, popularly, 'grammar'; technically it is 'word-definition' (viggaha, vacanattha). E.g., Bujjhatīti Buddho —'Buddha is one who knows'—is a definition of the word 'Buddha.' Such a definition is nirutti, the meaning being now expressed or uttered. Hence nirutti may stand for the European connotation, or meaning in intension.

4. Paṭibhāna (paṭi: '*re*'; bhā: 'to become apparent') is defined in the *Abhidhānappadīpikā-sūcī* : paṭimukhā bhavanti, upaṭṭhahanti ñeyyā etenāti paṭibhānaṇ: 'Paṭibhāna' means that by which things knowable (1, 2, 3) become represented, are present. The representative or ideating processes are

not themselves paṭisambhidā, but are themselves (as knowables) analyzed in 'analytic insight' (paṭisambhida-ñāṇaŋ).[1]

Thus the scope of this classic doctrine is entirely logical. And while it is regarded as superior to popular knowledge, it is distinct from intuition. Men of the world may develop it, but not intuition. Ariyans, who attain to intuition, might not have developed it to any great extent.

Paṭisambhidā in the *Vibhanga*.
(PTS edition, chap. xv., p. 293 f.)

The definition quoted above, § 2, cites this work: hetumhi ñāṇaŋ dhammapaṭisambhidā, p. 293. In the list of exegetical definitions of the four branches, entitled 'Suttanta-bhājaniyaŋ,' we find (1) Attha-paṭisambhidā defined as analysis of phenomena, dhammā, or things that 'have happened, become, . . . that are manifest'; (2) dhamma-paṭisambhidā, defined as knowledge of conditions (*hetū*), of cause and effect (*hetuphala*), 'of phenomena *by which* phenomena have happened, become,' etc. Thus (1) may be knowledge of decay and death; (2) is then knowledge of the causes (*samudaya*) of decay and death. Similarly for the third and fourth Truths (Cessation and the Path). But (2) may also refer to the Doctrine, or Dhamma:—'knowledge of the Suttas, the Verses,' and the rest.

[1] Paṭibhāna is here defined as a technical term of Buddhist philosophy. Its popular meaning of fluency in literary expression is well illustrated in the *Vangīsa Saŋyutta* (i. 187 of the *Nikāya*). Vangīsa, the irrepressibly fluent ex-occultist, is smitten with remorse for having, because of his rhetorical gifts (paṭibhāna), despised friendly brethren, and breaks forth once more to express his repentance, admonishing himself—as Gotama, i.e., as the Buddha's disciple (*Comy.*)—to put away conceit. When the *afflatus* was upon him in the Buddha's presence, he would ask leave to improvise with the words: 'It is manifest [is revealed] to me, Exalted One!' The response is: 'Let it be manifest to thee, Vangīsa!' And he would forthwith improvise verses. Cf. *Pss. of the Brethren*, p. 395, especially pp. 399, 404.

Of the third and fourth branches, nirutti-paṭis° is always, in this chapter, defined as abhilāpa, or verbal expression, or statement. And paṭibhāna-paṭis° is always defined as 'knowledge in the knowledges,' as if it referred to psychological analysis.

In the following section or Abhidhammabhājaniyaṃ, we find an inverted order in branches 1, 2. The dhamma's considered are all states of consciousness. If they are moral or immoral—i.e., if they have karmic efficacy (as causes)—knowledge of them is called dhamma-analysis. Knowledge of their *result*, and of all *un*moral or inoperative states, which as such *are* results, is called attha-analysis. As to 3, 4: knowledge of the connotation and expression of dhamma's as paññatti's (term-concepts) is nirutti-analysis. And 'the knowledge by which one knows those knowledges' (1-3) is paṭibhāna-analysis.

We are greatly indebted to the kindness of Ledi Sadaw Mahāthera for a further analysis of Paṭisambhidā: 'In this word, paṭi means visuṃ visuṃ (separately, one after another); sam means 'well,' 'thoroughly' bhidā means to 'break up.' Thus we get: Paṭisambhidā is that by which Ariyan folk well separate, analyze [things] into parts.

This, as stated above, is fourfold:

1. Attha-paṭisambhidā includes—(*a*) Bhāsit'attha, meaning in extension, things signified by words; (*b*) Paccayuppann'attha, things to which certain other things stand in causal relation; (*c*) Vipāk'attha, resultant mental groups and matter born of karma; (*d*) Kiriy'-attha; inoperative mental properties—e.g., 'advertings' of the mind, etc.; (*e*) Nibbāna, the unconditioned.

2. Dhamma-paṭisambhidā includes—(*a*) Bhāsita-dhamma, or words spoken by the Buddha; (*b*) Paccaya-dhamma, things relating themselves to other objects by way of a cause; (*c*) Kusala-dhamma; (*d*) Akusala-dhamma, thoughts moral and immoral; (*e*) Ariya-magga-dhamma, the Ariyan Path.

3. Nirutti-paṭisambhidā is grammatical analysis of sentences.

4. Paṭibhāna-paṭisambhidā is analytic insight into the three preceding (1-3).

Further details may be found in the Commentaries on the *Paṭisambhidāmagga*[1] and the *Vibhanga.*

---

5. Paṭisambhidā, Abhisamaya : Analysis and Penetration. (II., 9, 10.)

The latter term means literally 'beyond-well-making-go,' and, in this physical sense, is used once or twice in the Vedas and the Upaniṣads. Mental activity, however, borrowed the term now and then in the older Upaniṣads, so that the double usage obtained contemporaneously, just as we speak of 'getting at,' or 'grasping' either a book, or a meaning in it. In Buddhist literature the secondary psychological, and *meta*physical meaning would seem alone to have survived. Buddhaghosa, commenting on the *Dīgha-Nik.* (i. p. 32: 'samaya'), distinguishes three uses of the compound term, one of which is that which is used in the discourse in question, namely, paṭivedha, or penetration, piercing, that is, by, as it were, an inthrust of mind. In the opening of the 'Abhisamaya-vagga,' *Saŋyutta-Nik.*, ii., 133, it is applied to one who comprehends, and is used synonymously with 'acquiring a vision (eye) for things'; in the 'Vacchagotta-Saŋyutta' (*ibid.*, iii. 260) it is used synonymously with insight, vision, enlightenment, penetration. In the Milinda questions, again, we find it associated with paṭivedha: 'Who have penetrated to a comprehension of the Four Truths (or Facts)' (transl. ii. 237). Similarly in the Dhammapada Comy.: 'Aggasāvaka-vatthu' (i. 109 f.).

The analytic aspect of intellectual activity being, as we

[1] This work itself describes the four branches with some fulness. See PTS edition, ii. 147 f.

have seen, so emphatically developed in the doctrine of Paṭisambhidā, we are brought up against a dual view of cognition in Buddhist philosophy, suggestive of the sharper and more systematically worked out distinction in Henri Bergson's philosophy between *l'intelligence*—the mind as analytic—and intuition, or that immediacy of insight which 'by a sort of intellectual sympathy' *lives*, or recreates that which it is coming-to-know.

In the Ariyan—to resume Dr. Ledi's note on Paṭisambhidā—intuition or insight (ariya-magga-ñāṇa) is accompanied by analysis. In the case of puthujjana's ('average sensual folk,' or it may be clever or learned, but not truly religious folk), much analytic insight may be developed after adequate studies. But that which they may thus acquire by sutamaya-ñāṇa (cf. XX., 3), i.e., intellect developed by information, is not so much a genuine intuitive insight as erudite insight. Thus in the Commentaries it is said:—"But the worldling wins no intuitive insight even after he has acquired much learning." But there is no Ariyan who has not attained intuitive insight. And it is peculiarly his to practise that ekābhisamaya, or penetration into the unity of the real and the true, which is arrested and dismembered in analysis. His endeavour is, in the metaphor of the *Kathā-vatthu* (II. 10), not to be content with the wand, wooden or gold, of language, pointing only at, but never revealing that which it tries to express, but to enter into the 'heap of paddy or of gold.' That power of penetration, according to Ledi Sadaw (*JPTS.*, 1914, p. 154 f.), he can attain by persistent cultivation transforming his analytic, inferential knowledge. When won, its distinctive quality is the power of cognizing the purely phenomenal, the purely elemental stripped of the crust of the pseudo-permanencies:—'person,' 'being,' 'self,' 'soul,' 'persistent thing.' The wand of language points to all these crust-names. By abhisamaya, paṭivedha, intuition, he gets beneath them.

6. (A). NIYAMA, NIYĀMA : 'ASSURANCE.'

(V., 4, p. 177 ; VI., 1, p. 185 ; XIII., 4, p. 275.)

N i y a m a means 'fixity,' but n i y ā m a is 'that which fixes.' The former is derived from n i - y a m - a t i, to fix; the latter from the causative : n i y ā m e t i, to cause to be fixed. When the Path—i.e., a certain direction, course, tendency, profession, progressive system of a person's life —is called s a m m a t t a, or, contrariwise, m i c c h a t t a-n i y ā m a, both forms are understood in the causal sense. Thus the former 'path' inevitably establishes the state of exemption from a p ā y a's (rebirth in misery), and the latter inevitably establishes purgatorial retribution after the next death. N i y ā m a, then, is that by which the N i y a m a (the fixed, or inevitable order of things) is established, or that by which fixity is brought about, or marked out in the order of things.[1] (With reference to the apparently indiscriminate use of n i y a m a, n i y ā m a—see p. 275, *n.* 1—the Burmese are wont carelessly to write the former for the latter, because they *always* pronounce the *a* short and quick.[2])

Our choice of Assurance may seem to give an undue subjectivity to the pair of terms. It is true that it lends itself here to criticism. And we confess that the wish to get a term with the religious expressiveness that Assurance bears with it for readers nurtured in Christian tradition overbore our first thought of choosing certainty, fixity, fixed order. We may, however, add to our apology (1) that in XIX. 7, § 1, 'assurance' is opposed to 'doubt,' which is unquestionably subjective ; (2) that both 'assurance' and the Greek *plērophoria*[3] have both an objective and a subjective import. 'Assurance' may mean a means or orderly arrangement through which we attain assured feeling, say,

[1] Cf. *Buddhism*, London, 1912, p. 119 f.

[2] Cf. English 'drummer,' which gives the sound of the short Indian *a*.

[3] See Rom. xiv. 5; Col. ii. 2 ; 1 Thess. i. 5 ; Heb. vi. 11—'to the full assurance of hope to the end.'

about our property. The Greek word is simply a 'full conveyance,' to wit, of news or evidence.

We should not therefore be far from the truth in considering our twin terms rendered by Assurance as the more *subjective aspect* of the Buddhist notion of course or destiny popularly and objectively expressed as Path (m a g g a)—path good or bad:—the Way, narrow or broad, the Path, *hodos, via,* of Christian doctrine, 'the way of his saints,' 'the way of the evil man' of the Jewish doctrine (*Prov.* ii. 8, 12).

---

6. (B). Niyama and Karma.
(XXI. 7, 8.)

The two discourses so numbered deal with the belief or disbelief in a rigid, inexorable uniformity of cause and effect in the cosmos, as obtaining not only as a general law, but also in all particular successions of cause-effect. In other words, can we *predict* for every phenomenon (d h a m m a), for every act (k a m m a), a corresponding, assignable result? Is *this* result the immutable invariable result of *that* cause?

The term for such an immutable fixed result, for the Buddhist, is n i y a t a, an adjectival past participle corresponding to n i y ā m a, on which see note A. The idea of predictability is also taken into account—see the interesting little discourse, V. 8:—*Of Insight into the Future*—but the more prevailing notion qualifying the belief in cosmic order is that of fixity and of flexibility.

The orthodox view is that, in the whole causal flux of 'happenings'—and these comprise all d h a m m a's, all k a m m a's—there are only two rigid successions, or orders of specifically fixed kinds of cause-and-effect. These are—(1) The s a m m a t t a-n i y ā m a; (2) the m i c c h a t t a-n i y ā m a. By or in the latter, certain deeds, such as matricide, result in purgatorial retribution immediately after the doer's next death. By or in the former, the Path-graduate will win eventually the highest 'fruit' and

Nibbāna. Neither result is meted out by any Celestial Power. Both results are inherent to that cosmodicy or natural order which *includes a moral order* (kamma-niyāma), and which any judge, terrestrial or celestial, does or would only *assist in carrying out*. To that a Buddhist might adapt and apply the Christian *logion* :—'Before Abraham was, I am'—and say :—'Before the Judge was, IT IS.' That some happenings are moral, some immoral, is not so because of any pronouncements human or divine. The history of human ideas reveals mankind as not *creating* the moral code, but as evolving morally in efforts to *interpret* the moral order.[1]

But these two fixed orders do not exhaust the universe of 'happenings.' There is a third category belonging to neither. Hence the objection of the Theravādin to the word 'all.' Dhamma's is a wider category than kamma's or karma. What is true of dhamma's is true of kamma's, for the former category includes the latter. But the line of reasoning in the discourse on dhamma's refers to mind and matter as exhausting the universe of existence.

As regards matter, we may illustrate by a modern instance. The opponent would maintain that both radium and helium are substances immutably fixed, each in its own nature, because of the, as yet, mysterious radio-active properties of the former, and because of the—so to speak —'heliocity' of the latter. Now the Theravādin would not know that radium may change into helium. But from his general point of view he would reply that anyway neither radium nor helium is immutably fixed, because they do not belong to either of the fixed orders recognized in his doctrine. Thus would he conclude respecting all dhamma's that are not kamma's.

Concerning these, that is, moral and immoral acts, the opponent submits that the universal law of causation is uniform to this extent, that every kind of action must invariably, inevitably have its specific reaction, that the

[1] Cf. *Buddhism*, London, 1912, chap. v.

same kamma must have the same effect. This is accepted as true in tendency, and as a general theory only. But whereas Buddhist philosophy did not anticipate the Bergsonian insight into the *effects* of vital causes amounting to new and unpredictable *creations*, it did and does recognize the immense complexity in the eventuation of moral results. Kamma's, it teaches, are liable to be counteracted and deflected, compounded and annulled in what might be called the 'composition of moral forces.'[1] Hence there is nothing rigid, or, as we should say, definitely predictable, about their results in so far as they come under the Third or residual category mentioned above, and not under either of the two 'fixed' niyata orders.

7. Ṭhitatā, Niyāmatā.

(VI. 1, p. 187; XI. 7, p. 261.)

Ṭhiti may be used to mean *cause*. And the yet more abstract form ṭhitatā, although, in the latter reference, we have called it 'state of being a cause,' is used concretely as in the former reference (see *n.* 2), meaning 'causes' by which resulting things are established. For in Abhidhamma only bhāva-sādhana definitions—i.e., definitions in terms of 'state,' are recognized (see *Compendium*, p. 7). Hence dhātu-dhamma-ṭhitatā becomes that which, as cause, establishes elements as effects. Thus it is applied to each term in the chain of causation (paṭicca-samuppāda): to ignorance as the cause of karma (sankhāra's), to these as the cause of consciousness, and so on.

Synonymous with this is the term dhamma-niyāmatā, meaning that which as cause *invariably fixes* things, in our minds, as effects.

Bearing these implications in mind, we may render the commentarial discussion of the Sutta-passage (p. 187, § 4, as follows: 'What I have described above as dhātu-dhamma-ṭhitatā, or -niyāmatā, is no other than

[1] See, e.g., on classes of karma, *Compendium*, p. 148 f.

the terms "ignorance," etc. Whether the Tathāgatā has arisen or not, volitional actions of mind (karma) come into being because of ignorance, and rebirth-consciousness comes into being because of volitional actions of mind, etc. Hence in the phrase "because of ignorance the actions of the mind," ignorance is termed dhammaṭhitatā, because, as a cause or means, it establishes the dhamma's which are actions of mind. Or again, "ignorance" is termed dhamma-niyāmatā because, as cause or means, it invariably fixes or marks them.'

The difference between the two synonyms would seem to be that -ṭhitatā is objective, -niyāmatā is subjective. In other words, the basic principle 'ignorance,' or any other anga in the chain, is there as a cause *per se*, whether Tathāgatas arise or not. But because of the stability of the law of causality, or uniformity in the order of phenomena (dhamma-niyāmatā), or orderly progression of the Norm, we are enabled by the principle of induction to infer the effect from the cause.

It is clear, from our Commentary, that dhamma in this connection means 'effects' [in the Chain of Causation]. Moreover, the *Abhidhānappadīpikā-sūcī* refers both synonyms to effect:— *ṭhitā va sā dhātu dhammaṭhitatā dhamma-niyāmatā ādīsu* '*paccayuppanne*'—i.e., 'in the effect.' This last term=*paṭicca-samuppanna*, and is opposed to paccaya: cause, condition, and paṭicca-samuppāda: any concrete cause (in the causal formula). See 'Paccaya.'

---

8. Nimitta.

(X. 3, § 4, p. 246.)

Nimitta is derived by some from ni+mā, to limit; and is defined as 'that which limits its own fruit (effect)': attano phalaŋ nimināṭēti (*Abhidhānappadīpikā-sūcī*). According to this definition it denotes a causal factor, limiting, determining, conditioning, characterizing, etc., its own effect.[1] Hence anything entering into a causal

[1] Cf. p. 226, *n*. 1.

relation, by which its effect is signified, marked, or characterized, is a nimitta. An object, image, or concept which, on being meditated upon, induces samādhi (Jhāna) is a nimitta (see the stages specified in *Compendium*, p. 54). False opinion (diṭṭhi) engendered by hallucination concerning impermanence—in other words, a perverted view of things as permanent—is a nimitta (*ibid.*, p. 217). This functions either as a *cause* of 'will-to-live,' or as a *sign* of worldliness. Emancipation from this nimitta is termed animittavimokkha (*ibid.*, p. 216). Again, sexual characters are comprised under four heads: linga, nimitta, ākappa, kutta, nimitta, standing for outward characteristics, male or female (*Bud. Psy. Eth.*, §§ 633, 634).

Later exegeses, deriving the word from the root *mih*, to pour out, are probably derivations *d'occasion*.

Now in this argument (X. 3) the opponent confuses the na nimitta[-gāhī]—'does not grasp at the general [or sex] characters of the object seen, heard, etc.'—of the quotation with animitta, a synonym, like 'emptiness' (suññatā) of Nibbāna. He judges that the Path-graduate, when he is not -nimitta-grasping, is grasping the a-nimitta or signless (Nibbāna), instead of exercising self-control in presence of alluring features in external objects, whether these be attractive human beings or what not.

According to the Commentary the expression cited, 'does not grasp at, etc.,' refers 'not to the moment of visual or other sense-consciousness, but to the javanakkhaṇa, or moment of apperception; hence even in the worldly course of things it is inconclusive.' This is made clearer in the following discourse (X. 4), where ethical matters are stated to lie outside the range of sense-consciousness as such.

---

9. Sangaha: Classification.

(VII. 1, p. 195.)

This little discourse is interesting for its bearing on the historic European controversy between Universals and

Particulars, dating from Herakleitus and Parmenides, two and a half centuries before the date of our work, with the problems: How can the Many be One? How can the One be in the Many? Both the Kathāvatthu and its Commentary oppose the limiting of groupable things to mental facts. If certain things be counted one by one, they reach a totality (gaṇanaŋ gacchanti), say, a totality of five. This total needs a generic concept to express itself. If the five units happen to possess common, say, bovine, attributes, we apply the concept 'bullocks,' 'cows.' So with the concept 'dog,' which holds together all individuals possessing canine attributes. Again, if we were to count by groups, say, three bullocks and three dogs, the units would reach the same total. But we should require a more general, a 'higher' concept—'animal,' or the like—to include both species. Now whether we have relatively homogeneous units under a general notion, or relatively heterogeneous groups under a wider notion, they reach hereby an abridged statement (uddesaŋ gacchanti) in the economy of thought.[1]

The Theravādin, as we have recorded, does not approve of the crude rope simile, because the material bond is necessarily different from the mental concept, and the term, physical and mental, binding units together. Neither does he altogether disapprove of the simile, since language, rooted in sense-experience, compels us to illustrate mental processes by material phenomena.

---

10. Paribhoga: Utility.

(VII. 5.)

Paribhoga is enjoyment. Utility, as ethicists and economists use the term, is enjoyability, positive benefit.

[1] It is interesting to compare the gaṇana (number), sangaha (class), uddesa (abridged statement), of Tissa's *Kathā-vatthu* with such disquisitions on number, class, general term, as that by Mr. Bertrand Russell in his examination of Frege's *Grundlagen der Arithmetik* in '*Our Knowledge of the External World*,' p. 201 f.

And the opponents claim that 'there is merit consisting in the fact, not that the good deed was done with benevolent intention, but that the deed done is bestowing enjoyment or utility.' The orthodox argument seeks only to prove the unsoundness of this way of reckoning merit (for the doer), either on grounds of psychological process [1] or of ethics [2, 3]. His own position, stated positively, is that the donor's will (cetanā) or intention is the only standard, criterion, ultimate court of appeal, by which to judge of the merit (to himself) of his act. Posterity may bless him for utility accruing to it. But if he gave as a benefactor *malgré lui*, he will in future be, not better, but worse off.

---

11. Paccaya: Correlation.

(XV. 1, 2.)

The word paccăya,[1] used in popular diction, together with hetu, for 'cause' or 'reason why,' is closely akin to our 'relation.' *Re* and *paṭi* (paccaya is contracted from paṭi-aya) are coincident in meaning. *Aya* is a causative form of *i*, 'to go,' giving 'go back' for the Latin [*re*]*latus*, 'carry back.' Now 'relation,' as theory of 'things as having to do with each other,' put into the most general terms possible, includes the class called causal relation, viz., things as related by way of cause-effect. But paccaya, as relation, implies that, for Buddhist philosophy, all modes of relation have causal *significance*, though the causal *efficacy*, as power to produce the effect, may be absent. To understand this we must consider everything, not as statically existing, but as 'happening,' or 'event.' We may then go on to define paccaya as an event which *helps* to account for the happening of the paccayuppanna, i.e., the effect, or 'what-has-happened-through-the-paccaya.' These two terms are thus 'related.' Dropping our notion of efficient cause (A as having power to produce B), and holding to the 'helping to happen' notion,

[1] Pronounce *păch-chăyă* with the same cadence as 'bachelor.'

we see this recognized in the definition of paccaya as 'that which was the essential mark of helping, of working up to (upakāraka),' namely, to a given happening.[1] It may not produce, or alone bring to pass, that happening; but it is concerned therewith.

Calling it the paccaya, A, and the other term, the other happening, B, the paccayuppanna, and referring to the twenty-four classes of relations distinguished in Abhidhamma, A may 'help' as being 'contiguous,' 'repeated,' a 'dominant' circumstance, or by 'leading towards,' as 'path' (magga-paccaya) or means. But only such a paccaya as 'will' (cetanā) related, as 'karma,'[2] to a result (vipāka), is adequate to produce, or to cause that result B.

In the expression idappaccayatā—'conditionedness of *this*—'this' (ida) refers to B, but the compound refers to A: A is the 'paccaya-of-*this*.' The abstract form is only the philosophic way of expressing paccaya. The terms discussed above—dhamma-ṭhitatā, dhamma-niyāmatā—are synonymous with idappaccayatā, and mean B is established through A, is fixed through A. This does not mean 'is produced (solely) by A,' but only 'happens whenever A happens,' and 'happens because, *inter alia*, A happens.' In other words, by a constant relation between A and B, we are enabled to infer the happening of B from the happening of A.

The classification of relations by the Hon. B. Russell, referred to on p. 294, *n*. 3, is as follows:—'A relation is symmetrical if, whenever it holds between A and B, it also holds between B and A;' asymmetrical, 'if it does *not* hold between B and A.' But of yet greater interest is it to see this learned author, ignorant to all appearances of perhaps one subject only—Buddhist philosophy—generalizing the whole concept of causality in terms of relations, namely, 'that what is constant in a causal law is not' A or B,

[1] *Buddhist Psychology*, London, 1914, p. 194 f.

[2] In the mode called janaka-kamma (reproductive karma). See *Compendium*, *loc cit.*

'but the *relation* between A and B . . . that a causal law involves not one datum, but many, and that the general scheme of a causal law will be 'Whenever things occur in certain relations to each other, another thing, B, having a fixed relation to those A's, will occur in a certain time-relation to them' (*op. cit.*, 215 f.). Or again, 'The law of causation . . . may be enunciated as follows:—There are certain invariable relations between different events,' etc. (p. 221). These 'invariable relations' are, for Buddhists, the twenty-four kinds of paccayas, including the time-relation, which are conceived, not as efficient causes, but as 'events' which in happening 'help' to bring about the correlated event called paccayuppanna.

---

12. Time and Space.

In the *Abhidhānappadīpika-sūcī*[1] time is defined under three aspects :—

1. 'Time is a concept by which the terms of life, etc., are counted or reckoned.

2. 'Time is that "passing by" reckoned as "so much has passed," etc.

3. 'Time is eventuation or happening, there being no such thing as time exempt from events.'

The second aspect refers to the fact of change or impermanence; the third brings up the fact of perpetual becoming. From perpetual becoming we get our idea of abstract time (mahā-kāla), which is eternal, and lacks the common distinction of past, present, future, but which, to adopt M. Bergson's phraseology, 'looked at from the point of view of multiplicity, . . disintegrates into a powder of moments, none of which endures.'[2] . . .

[1] For the general reader we may state that this valuable book, by the venerable scholar Subhūti Mahā-Thera, published at Colombo 1893, is an Index and Comy. on a work on Pali nouns, written by the rammarian Moggallāna in the twelfth century A.D.

[2] *Introd. to Metaphysics*, 51.

Now it is clear from the *Kathāvatthu*[1] that, for Buddhism, time-distinctions have no objective existence of their own, and that reality is confined to the present. The past reality has perished; the future reality is not yet become. And when Buddhist doctrine says that reality is present, both these terms refer to one and the same thing *per se*. When this gives up its reality, it gives up its presence; when it gives up being present, it ceases to be real.[2]

Things in time are not immutably fixed.[3] In Ledi Sadaw's words:—As in our present state there is, so in our past has there been, so in the future will there be, just a succession of purely phenomenal happenings, proceedings, consisting solely of arisings and ceasings, hard to discern . . . because the procedure is ever obscured by our notion of continuity.'[4] Thus they who have not penetrated reality 'see only a continuous and static condition in these phenomena.'[5]

Now each momentary state or uprising of mind[6] is logically complex and analyzable, but psychologically, actually, a simple indivisible process. There is a succession of these states, and their orderly procession is due to the natural uniformity of mental sequence—the Chitta-niyāma.[7] And they present a continuous spectrum of mind in which one state shades off into another, laterally and lineally, so that it is hard to say 'where,' or when one ends and the other begins.

The laws or principles discernible in these mental continua of the Chitta-niyāma are, according to Buddhist philosophy, five of the twenty-four casual relations (paccayā), to wit, 'contiguity,' immediate contiguity (in time), absence, abeyance, sufficing condition. Explained without such technicalities, the past state, albeit

[1] See I. 6-8. [2] See I. 6, § 5. [3] See I. 10.

[4] 'Some Points of Buddhist Doctrine,' *JPTS*, 1913-14, p. 121.

[5] *Ibid.*, 155.

[6] *Ekakkhaṇika-cittuppāda.*

[7] See Mrs. Rh. D., *Buddhism*, 1912, p. 119, and Ledi Sadaw's 'Expositions' (*Buddhist Review*, October, 1915).

it is absent, gone, has become wrought up into its immediate successor, the present state, as a new whole. These five are compared to the five strands of a thread on which are strung the pearls of a necklace.[1] But each indivisible whole was real only while it lasted.

Matter, no less than mind, is logically resolved into different qualities, which we group, classify, explain. But nature gives us simple, indivisible wholes, qualities mutually inseparable, even in a dual existence such as that of intelligent organisms. The whole is actually indivisible, body and mind being inseparable.

Now what time is to life, space is to matter. Space, like time, is a permanent concept or mental construction, which constitutes a sufficing condition for the movement of bodies. It is void, unperceivable, without objective reality.

---

13. Accanta : Finality.

(XIX. 7.)

A c c a n t a is a t i - a n t a :[2] beyond the end, or the very last. Like e k a n t a, it is rendered by Burmese translators 'true,' and for this reason: The only assurance we get from science that the sun will rise to-morrow, and at a given time, is our belief in the uniformity of Nature, a belief established by past observation yielding no exception to the rule. The belief amounts, as we say, to a moral certainty—i.e., we can act upon it. But since, for all we *know*, some unforeseen force may divert the relative positions of sun and earth, the uniformity of physical nature is not an order of things which has reached finality in certainty. In other words, it is not 'true' absolutely.

[1] Cf. *Compendium*, p. 42; Mrs. Rh. D., *Buddhist Psychology*, 1914, p. 194 f.

[2] This, when pronounced a t y a n t a, slips into the full cerebral double *c* (which is pronounced *cch*). Cf. p a c c a y a (see Note 11).

14. Nipphanna, Parinipphanna: determined, predetermined.

(XI. 7; XXIII. 5).

This word is, according to the *Abhidhānappadīpikāsūcī*, derived from the root 'pad,' 'to go,' through its causal verb 'pādeti,' 'to move or set agoing.' The prefix 'ni' alters the meaning of 'being set agoing' into 'being accomplished' (siddhiyaŋ). Ledi Sadaw qualifies this meaning by 'accomplished by causes, such as karma, etc.' (kammādīhi paccayehi nipphāditaŋ). Now karma is psychologically reduced to volition (cetanā). Hence anything accomplished by volition is 'accomplished by causes,' or 'determined.' And if karma happens to be past, the word under discussion implies 'predetermination.' This term is technically applied to the eighteen kinds of material qualities,[1] the remaining ten, in the dual classification of matter, being termed anipphannarūpa's, or 'un-predetermined.'

The following quotation from the Abhidhammāvatāra (p. 74 PTS. Ed.) is in point:—'(It may be urged that) if these (ten) be undetermined, they would be unconditioned. But how can they be unconditioned when they are changing their aspects (vikāratta)? These (un-) determined, too, are conditioned. Thus the conditionedness of the (un-) determined may be understood.' From the Buddhist point of view, Nibbāna alone is unconditioned. Therefore the Conditioned includes both the 'determined' and the 'undetermined.'

The Kathā XXIII. 5 indicates the general use of the term parinipphanna. The Burmese translators do not distinctively bring out the force of the prefix 'pari.'

A paṭiccasamuppannadhamma, *i.e.*, anything that springs into being through a cause, is necessarily conditioned (sankhata). And one of the characteristic marks of the conditioned is impermanence. The universal

[1] See *Abhidhammāvatāra*, loc. cit.; *Compendium*, p. 156.

proposition—'Whatever is impermanent is ill'—is a Buddhist thesis. Mind and matter are both impermanent and are, therefore, ill. In other words, our personality — or more analytically, personality *minus* craving—constitutes the First Ariyan Fact of Ill. Ill, thus distributed, is determined. But the opponent errs in regarding the content of the term parinipphanna as exhausted by Ill proper. By this unnecessary restriction he errs in his application of the contrary term aparinipphanna to other factors of life.

Since a Dhamma or phenomenon other than Nibbāna is conditioned, it follows that each link in the chain of causation is conditioned. Take mind-and-body (nāmarūpa):—this we have shown to be a paṭiccasamuppanna because it comes into being through causes. And though it may also act as a paṭiccasamuppāda or causal antecedent in turn, it is not determined *as such*, i.e., *quâ* cause. Dhammaṭhitatā is nothing more than a paṭiccasamuppāda stated in an abstract form. Now in XI. 7 the opponent regards 'the state of being a cause' as different from the causal element and, therefore, as determined separately from the thing itself. In other words, the opponent holds that causality or causation itself, connoted by the term dhammaṭhitatā, is determined.

Again, aniccatā and jaratā, as mere aspects of 'determined' matter, are two of the admittedly anipphannarūpa's. And by analogy, aniccatā of mind would be equally undetermined In fact, aniccatā, as a mere mark of the conditioned, is not specially determined, as the opponent, in XI. 8, would have it to be.

---

15. Willing, Anticipating, Aiming.

(VIII. 9, § 1, p. 221 f.)

Since sending this discourse to press, we have discovered that the triad:—'willing, anticipating, aiming' (*cetanā, patthanā, paṇidhi*), so often in the present work added to the four other mental activities: 'adverting, ideating, co-ordinated application, attending,' occurs in the *Anguttara-Nikāya*, v. 212 f. E.g. 'when a person has all the attributes of the Ariyan Eightfold Path, coupled with true insight and emancipation, whatever he does in accordance with the rightness of his views, what he wills, anticipates, aims at, whatever his activities:—all these will conduce to that which is desirable, lovely, pleasant, good and happy.'

INDEXES

I. PASSAGES IN THE *KATHĀ-VATTHU* QUOTED FROM THE PIṬAKAS.[1]

II. SUBJECTS.

III. PALI WORDS DEFINED OR DISCUSSED.

---

[1] The passages are quoted by volume and page of Oldenberg's Vinaya, volume and number of Fausböll's Jātaka, volume and page of the Four Nikāyas P.T.S. ed., section and page of *Khuddaka-pāṭha* and *Udāna*, P.T.S. ed., section of *Iti-vuttaka* and *Dhammasangaṇi*, P.T.S. ed., page of *Vibhanga*, and verse of the other works, all P.T.S. ed.

I

PASSAGES IN THE *KATHĀ-VATTHU* QUOTED FROM THE PIṬAKAS

(C. appended to the page number means that the passage is quoted in the Commentary only.)

VINAYA.

PAGE	
63	iv. 74
114	i. 295
118	i. 2 (in footnote, read *Vin. Texts*, i. 78)
128	i. 34
169	i. 8
270	ii. 238
280	i. 10
319	iv. 75 f.
319	i. 246
344	ii. 205; v. 202 f.
349 f.	i. 11
354	i. 209
361 C.	iii. 112

DĪGHA-NIKĀYA.

PAGE	
16 f.	iii. 232
55	iii. 274
59	iii. 175
63 C.	i. 202
119	ii. 275
146, 277	i. 84, 83
151	i. 82
155	iii. 33
158	iii. 132
167	iii. 145
182	ii 88
198	i. 213
218 C.	i. 34
220	ii. 56
239	iii. 219
240 C.	iii. 104
258	ii. 103
265	i. 70
267	iii. 173
329	i. 73 f., etc.
342	ii. 38
348	ii. 151

MAJJHIMA-NIKĀYA.

PAGE	
16 f.	i. 341
62	i. 138
64 C.	i. 271
67	i. 139
95	iii. 16 f.
122	i. 301
128	i. 85, 92
151	ii. 19
158	i. 483
169	i. 171
193	i. 259
211	i. 73
214 C.	i. 85

II

SUBJECTS

III

PALI WORDS DEFINED OR DISCUSSED